A MORTUARY OF BOOKS

THE GOLDSTEIN-GOREN SERIES IN AMERICAN JEWISH HISTORY

General editor: Hasia R. Diner

A Mortuary of Books

The Rescue of Jewish Culture after the Holocaust

Elisabeth Gallas

Translated from the German by Alex Skinner

NEW YORK UNIVERSITY PRESS

New York

NEW YORK UNIVERSITY PRESS
New York
www.nyupress.org

References to Internet websites (URLs) were accurate at the time of writing. Neither the author nor New York University Press is responsible for URLs that may have expired or changed since the manuscript was prepared.

Library of Congress Cataloging-in-Publication Data

Names: Gallas, Elisabeth, author.
Title: A mortuary of books : the rescue of Jewish culture after the Holocaust / Elisabeth Gallas.
Description: New York : New York University Press, [2019] | Series: The Goldstein-Goren series in American Jewish History | Includes bibliographical references and index.
Identifiers: LCCN 2018047263 | ISBN 9781479833955 (cl : alk. paper)
Subjects: LCSH: Holocaust, Jewish (1939–1945). | Jews—History—20th century. | Jews— Civilization. | Cultural property—Destruction and pillage—Europe. | Cultural property— Repatriation—Europe. | World War, 1939–1945—Destruction and pillage—Europe. | Jewish property—Europe—History—20th century.
Classification: LCC D804.3 .G3535 2019 | DDC 305.892/4009045—dc23

In memory of my mother, Olivia Gallas

CONTENTS

ABBREVIATIONS

AHC	Ardelia Hall Collection
AJC	American Jewish Committee
AJCON	American Jewish Congress
AJCONF	American Jewish Conference
ALLIANCE	Alliance Israélite Universelle
CJR	Conference on Jewish Relations
CLAIMS CONFERENCE	Conference on Jewish Material Claims against Germany
COMMISSION	Commission on European Jewish Cultural Reconstruction
COMMITTEE ON RESTORATION	Committee on the Restoration of Continental Jewish Museums, Restoration Libraries, and Archives
COUNCIL	Council of Jews from Germany
CRIF	Conseil Représentatif des Institutions Juives de France
DP	Displaced Person
ERR	Einsatzstab Reichsleiter Rosenberg (Reichsleiter Rosenberg Taskforce)
HU	Hebrew University of Jerusalem
HUC	Hebrew Union College
JA	Jewish Agency
JCR	Jewish Cultural Reconstruction, Inc.
JNUL	see NLI
JOINT	American Jewish Joint Distribution Committee
JRSO	Jewish Restitution Successor Organization
JTC	Jewish Trust Corporation
JTS	Jewish Theological Seminary New York
LBI	Leo Baeck Institute

MFA&A	Monuments, Fine Arts, and Archives Unit (US Forces)
NLI	National Library of Israel (until 2011, Jewish National and University Library)
OAD	Offenbach Archival Depot
OMGUS	Office of the Military Government in the US Zone of Germany
RSHA	Reichssicherheitshauptamt (Reich Security Main Office)
WJC	World Jewish Congress
YIVO	Institute for Jewish Research (New York), former Yidisher Visnshaftlekher Institut / Yiddish Scientific Institute (Vilnius)

Introduction

On the morning of February 27, 1946, the sixty-ninth day of the proceedings, Yiddish-speaking poet and partisan Abraham Sutzkever was called to the witness stand at the International Military Tribunal in Nuremberg. Lev Smirnov, deputy prosecutor for the Soviet Union, asked Sutzkever, one of only three Jewish witnesses to testify at the tribunal, to give an account of Jewish life in Vilna (Vilnius) under German occupation, the atrocious living conditions in the ghetto, and the Germans' persecution and murder of Vilna Jewry.[1] Sutzkever had endured the occupation "from the first to nearly the last day," having been interned in the ghetto there for more than two years. While standing in court—Sutzkever refused to sit, feeling that he "was saying kaddish for the dead"[2]—he frequently interspersed his testimony with personal reminiscences. Barred from using his native Yiddish, he recalled a first incident, which occurred in the summer of 1941, in short Russian sentences: German soldiers had compelled him, a rabbi, and a boy from his neighborhood to dance naked around a bonfire in front of the Old Synagogue while throwing its Torah scrolls into the flames. Forced to sing Russian songs at gunpoint as the sacred scrolls went up in smoke, the three came close to passing out.[3] The fact that Sutzkever chose to mention this brutal and traumatic "act in the circus,"[4] as the Germans had called it, in the short amount of time available for his testimony indicates the existential significance he attributed to it. He considered the Nazis' deliberate destruction of religious and cultural treasures a key element in their policy of annihilation, one that must be acknowledged during the court proceedings. The Jews of Vilna—one of the most prominent centers of Jewish cultural activity in Eastern Europe, home to precious collections and famous cultural and educational institutions—were exposed in the most drastic way to the cultural genocide that accompanied the Nazis' systematic acts of mass murder. The situation there represented in nuce what Polish-born Jewish jurist Raphael Lemkin—initiator of the UN

Genocide Convention of 1948—had in mind when he emphasized that the "systematic and organized destruction of the art and cultural heritage in which the unique genius and achievement of a collectivity are revealed in fields of science, arts and literature" must be understood and legally addressed as "an attack targeting" this collectivity.[5]

Sutzkever's diary from the time of occupation meticulously documents both sides of the Nazis' destructive frenzy: "The Germans were to wipe from the face of the earth five centuries of Jewish culture in Vilna."[6] During his internment, he had to watch, daily, as German special forces hunted down "the printed Jewish word with the same zeal and relentlessness that the Gestapo exhibited when tracking down every last hidden Jew."[7] From January 1942 on, the Reichsleiter Rosenberg Taskforce (Einsatzstab Reichsleiter Rosenberg; ERR) rampaged through Vilna, its staff confiscating every artifact and book of Jewish provenance they could lay their hands on. Much of this material was sold to paper mills and leather factories, incinerated, or used as heating fuel; selected parts were confiscated and transferred to Germany. Sutzkever was among the forty Jewish forced laborers working in the occupied premises of the renowned Yiddish Scientific Institute (Yidisher Visnshaftlekher Institut; YIVO), which served as the task force's depot. They were obliged to sort and prepare for transport the valuable items chosen for further use in German research institutes. Faced with the threat of total cultural destruction, they decided to form a clandestine group and smuggled documents, books, and works of art into the ghetto, where they were hidden away. It is thanks to the dedication of this group, known as the "Paper Brigade," that some of the most precious literary, artistic, and scientific materials from Jewish Eastern Europe, including manuscripts by Sholem Aleichem and drawings by Marc Chagall, have survived to this day.[8] Sutzkever was one of the few members of the brigade to survive. After fleeing to join the partisans in the forests surrounding Vilna in September 1943, he escaped to Moscow with the help of the Jewish Anti-Fascist Committee, specifically the famous writer, activist, and war correspondent Ilya Ehrenburg. Immediately after the liberation of Vilna by the Soviet Army in July 1944, Sutzkever returned there, devoting himself to cached cultural property—the only glimpse of hope still emanating from this city of death, as he noted at the time: "If not for the hidden cultural treasures, I don't know if I would have had enough strength to return to my home city. [. . .] I knew that everyone has been executed by the murderers. I knew that my eyes would be blinded with pain as soon as I saw the Wilia River. But the Hebrew letters that I had planted in Vilna's soil sparkled at me."[9] Yet his hopes soon faded again. Together with the few other survivors he encountered there, Sutzkever aimed to establish a museum of Jewish art and culture with the remaining material. This plan faltered due to Soviet resistance, and once again they had to prevent material from being dispersed and confiscated. They decided to send it west. Sutzkever and his comrade Shmerke Kaczerginski single-handedly transported partial collections in suitcases via Poland to Paris, where they were sent on to the YIVO in New York, their home ever since.

By other routes, the portion of the Vilna holdings stolen by Rosenberg's task force made it to the United States as well. After their incorporation into the Nazi Institute for Research on the Jewish Question (Institut zur Erforschung der Judenfrage) in Frankfurt am Main, the precious collections had been evacuated to the Hesse town of Hungen in 1944 due to increasingly severe bombing raids. American soldiers of the Monuments, Fine Arts, and Archives Unit (MFA&A), tasked with protecting the European cultural heritage, discovered these books and other objects while advancing into German territory. All of them were placed under the stewardship of the American military government, which initiated a large-scale cultural restitution campaign to return millions of books, archival documents, artworks, and ritual objects to their former owners, states of origin, or official trustee organizations representing the Nazis' victims. Among the restored collections were more than four hundred boxes of books and other objects from Vilna; after negotiations, which will be discussed in the following chapter, these were handed over to the YIVO in New York, the official successor to the destroyed institute in the Lithuanian capital. YIVO soon developed into the most important commemorative and research center for Eastern European Yiddish culture worldwide, the material fragments saved from Vilna playing an important part in its attempts to create a sense of continuity between past and present.

The miraculous story of Sutzkever's acts of cultural rescue and the salvage of YIVO property through the herculean American restitution program attests to both the tremendous attention Jews paid to the theft of cultural property and the importance they attached to its preservation and restoration. In the immediate postwar period, the historically un-precedented German confiscation, spoliation, and dispossession of books, documents, and artworks were followed by an equally unprec-edented history of restitution, one often endowed with a tremendous symbolic charge by the individuals and organizations involved. The present book aims to tell this story. It took place between 1944 and 1952 in Europe, the United States, and Israel, but its true center was the Of-fenbach Archival Depot. From this essentially American institution on German soil—established during the winter of 1945 by the American military government to house and eventually restore the books, archival materials, and ritual objects of mainly Jewish provenance found by the MFA&A—more than four million items were either returned to their former owners or distributed to the new sites of Jewish community life. Objects and documents from every corner of Europe were to be found in Offenbach. They rendered visible the wide geographical scope of the German war of extermination while also laying bare the magnitude, diversity, multilingualism, and centuries-old traditions of European-Jewish culture now reduced to material fragments.

*   *   *

One of the four main protagonists discussed in this book, later historian of the Holocaust Lucy S. Dawidowicz (1915–1990), who came to work at the Offenbach Archival Depot in 1947 as an employee of the Ameri-can Jewish Joint Distribution Committee (also known as the Joint), left one of the most impressive accounts of the place. Her recollections give us a sense of the feelings that overwhelmed contemporaries at the sight of the depot, which she called a "mortuary of books." Every single vol-ume stored there seemed to her a "testament of a murdered civilization," which it was absolutely imperative to save.[10] Dawidowicz devoted several months to finding, identifying, claiming, and sorting volumes originating in Vilna. A research assistant at the YIVO in New York and one of the last international fellows to have joined the YIVO in Vilna as late as 1939, she was closely familiar with its library holdings. Dawidowicz was one of the few individuals to experience the striking contrast between before and after—a rich, vibrant library reduced to piles of books and fragments. She was eventually to play the key role in organizing the transfer of the Vilna collections from Germany to the United States.

But far from all the books stored in Offenbach could be identified in the same way as these collections, let alone be restored to their owners. Hundreds of thousands of documents and volumes were heirless and unidentifiable. In accordance with the prevailing laws on restitution after armed conflict—agreed upon by the Allies at the Paris Conference on Reparations in November and December 1945 and at subsequent meetings of the Allied Control Council—they were most likely to be returned to their countries of origin. Most Jewish actors strongly opposed this. After the murder of two-thirds of Europe's Jewish population and the destruction of their institutions, few Jews would benefit from such returned objects. To the contrary, they mostly risked disappearing into state collections. The idea that even more of the Jews' cultural heritage might be lost to them or restituted to states without significant Jewish communities—perhaps even to the German state—was unbearable to Jewish campaigners. In order to bring about a change of policy, they had to challenge the basic assumptions of the Allies' postwar reconstruction program. The latter had to be convinced that in this case, traditional jurisprudence was invalid because the crime it was attempting to respond to had changed the conditions for restitution itself, leaving virtually no direct heirs to the confiscated and looted property—in fact leaving almost no Jews in Europe at all. Restoring cultural objects to their previous state of ownership had become impossible, so a new approach was imperative. Jewish organizations in the United States and Great Britain made impassioned pleas for a softening of the territorial principle and for regulations that would allow stolen property to be returned to Jewish ownership, even if this generally required its transfer to new places. They proposed the transformation of heirless goods into the collective property of the Jewish people, which could be claimed by an agency entrusted with representing that people. These impulses prompted the formation of a New York–based organization that was to be the leading protagonist of cultural restitution in the early postwar period: the Jewish Cultural Reconstruction, Inc. (JCR). Established in 1947, the American administration recognized this corporation—made up of leading international Jewish organizations in the United States, Palestine/Israel, and Europe—as the Jewish trustee for heirless cultural property in 1949. Its official recognition as a nonstate body that could act in the name of all Jews was a novelty in the history of Jewish politics. For the first time,

Jews could represent their interests as equal partners in an international agreement. Also novel was the potential to treat heirless property like individual property in private law; departing from the routes previously envisaged, this property instead followed the paths taken by the Jewish people, distributed to places where this collective claimant was now located. This extraordinary decision gave the Jewish collectivity a voice and a meaningful status in the realm of transitional justice—in contrast to Nuremberg, where Jewish representatives had fought in vain to gain official status as plaintiffs or amicus curiae.[11] Through the agreement reached at the military government's German headquarters in February 1949, the American administration acknowledged that in the wake of the Holocaust, the treatment of Jewish cultural property, especially books and ritual objects, was a sensitive issue, one that had to be resolved in full accordance with Jewish concerns. The overriding necessity of finding a just approach to the masses of objects in American hands must surely have played into this decision: those involved were overwhelmed by the sheer quantity of material. Eventually, JCR took charge of more than half a million books and several thousand ritual objects, distributing them to hundreds of Jewish communities and institutions around the world.

What makes the history of JCR even more significant is the fact that the negotiations on its status and recognition as a Jewish representative touched on the many questions fundamental to Jewish life in the first few years after Nazi rule. How could justice be done after such monstrous crimes? What could restitution, reconstruction, and compensation actually mean? Where and how could Jews live in safety after the Holocaust? Where might Jewish life flourish anew? And how should the memory of the disaster and the murdered be preserved?

By examining the specific nature of the objects the JCR took charge of, we can begin to grasp why these issues were addressed so comprehensively during the course of its work. The status of the books and Judaica in the Jewish self-perception spoke to the foundations of the collectivity itself and demanded extraordinary care and attention from those who dealt with them.[12] In much the same way as the Jewish groups and individuals who dedicated themselves to saving books, documents, and other treasures during the atrocities, the postwar actors too recognized these items' special role in ensuring the memory and continuity of Jewish history. In addition to the objects' distinctive character, the import of cultural salvage within the struggle to reestablish Jewish life after the Holocaust was also due to the unique composition of JCR's members. This was an initiative launched by Jewish intellectuals—it was not politicians, lawyers, or diplomats who had come up with, and realized, the idea of a comprehensive and legally binding cultural restitution program, but a group of scholars. The core of the JCR, and its broader milieu, consisted of renowned Jewish academics of the day. Its initiator and head was historian Salo Wittmayer Baron (1895–1989), first holder of a chair in Jewish history, literature, and institutions in the United States. His closest colleague there was political theorist Hannah Arendt (1906–1975), while the JCR board of directors also included such leading scholars as Gershom Scholem (1897–1982), Horace M. Kallen (1882–1974), Judah L. Magnes (1877–1948), Koppel S. Pinson (1904–1961), Cecil Roth (1899–1970), and Max Weinreich (1894–1969). It was above all Baron, Arendt, and Scholem who gave the JCR its remarkable character. Through their personalities, education, and outlook, they molded the form and implementation of early cultural restitution. Equally significant, their work for the JCR, which brought them very close to the postwar realities of annihilation and destruction in Europe, left traces in their historical consciousness and intellectual biographies. The present book emphasizes the crucial role of their involvement in the JCR's and, in the case of Lucy Dawidowicz, YIVO's salvage operations within their thinking and activities. This engagement—I argue—was a crucial element in their efforts to foster Jewish culture and scholarly life in the United States and Israel after 1945.

The (Re)Discovery of Nazi Cultural Genocide: On the State of Research

Surprisingly, despite its famous protagonists, JCR's history was long ignored. This has changed in the last five years, so in the following survey, I will also try to trace new directions in the research that were taken after this book's first German publication. As always, there are obvious and less obvious reasons for researchers' initial lack of interest. One of the most obvious reasons is that the protracted and complex postwar negotiations on restitution between Jewish representatives, the

Allies, and later West Germany rendered JCR's initiative peripheral. It was limited to cooperation with the US military government because by far the greatest portion of looted cultural property happened to be recovered in the American occupation zone, and the JCR had almost entirely finished its work when the German authorities began, step by step, to take over responsibility for restitution and compensation from the Allies in 1952. In addition, not much later, the functions of the JCR and its parent organization, the Jewish Restitution Successor Organization (JRSO)—which was the agency established to deal with the restitution of communal and institutional Jewish property and assets (other than cultural) in the American zone of Germany from 1948 on—were merged into the activities of the Conference on Jewish Material Claims against Germany (Claims Conference). The latter benefited from the efforts of its smaller predecessors, but due to its success at the negotiations on the Luxembourg Agreement with West Germany, signed on September 10, 1952, it was to largely overshadow this preceding history.[13] Another aspect that depressed knowledge of JCR's mission was the declining general interest in cultural robbery and restitution from the 1950s on. Instead of building on the findings and insights of the Jewish scholars who, in the early aftermath of World War II, farsightedly highlighted the significance of cultural destruction within the genocidal project, the topic was mostly neglected and mistakenly categorized as of minor importance. This found emblematic expression in the failure to integrate article III—"Cultural Genocide"—into the 1948 UN Genocide Convention. Apart from the many political reasons prompting the various parties to forego its inclusion, they lacked awareness of the formative role of cultural destruction within the genocidal act.[14] What undoubtedly added to the tendency to ignore these crimes was the fact that so many European—but especially German and Austrian—collections and private individuals were still benefiting from the Nazis' vast campaign of plunder: the majority of looted items remained in their possession. As a consequence, Nazi cultural robbery and restitution were barely addressed in public discourse during the Cold War. This in turn also tended to give the topic a peripheral status within later research on restitution, which increasingly became a field of contemporary history in its own right. After 1990, there was growing interest in processes of transitional justice, especially its retributive and restorative forms in response to World War II. This was bound up with the new accessibility of archives in Eastern Europe but no less with the vast number of claims for the return of nationalized property to its former owners in these regions, which became possible after the fall of the Soviet Union. The entire history of the loss, revocation, and reinstatement of ownership in Europe during and after World War II came to the fore once again.[15] This triggered new research initiatives. Initially, most scholars who examined this topic took an overarching approach to restitution after 1945 from a legal, institutional, and structural perspective.[16] Of this work, studies that examine the wider symbolic significance of restitution in light of war, injustice, and terror, and that highlight its consequences for the twentieth-century European history of memory, have been of particular interest to the present book.[17]

The turn of both public and scholarly attention to cultural theft and restitution came a little later, instigated by spectacular finds of looted art in German and European museums or private collections in the late 1990s and early 2000s. Research on the restitution of cultural goods has, therefore, chiefly been initiated by museum curators, librarians, and the staff of the Claims Conference and related institutions. Since the so-called Washington Declaration of 1998 on the recovery and return of cultural goods lost as a result of Nazi persecution, European cultural institutions have stepped up their efforts to inspect their holdings and establish provenance, work that has been flanked by studies on the history of cultural theft and restitution processes since 1945.[18] For some time, the study of the Nazi theft of art progressed more rapidly than that of art restitution, while research on art restitution and the often spectacular, valuable, and famous works involved attracted far more attention than the restoration of looted books or ritual objects.[19] This has changed in recent times. A growing number of researchers have emphasized the importance of the theft of books and archives for Jewish contemporaries, seeking to place it in the context of the debate on the reconstruction of Jewish culture after the catastrophe.[20] Nonetheless, most of the related discussions and findings have barely touched on the role of JCR in this story. Another reason scholars have been so slow to acknowledge this organization's importance is the dispersal of its material across many different archives, a significant portion of which has been lost or destroyed.

An initial but long-forgotten set of publications on the Offenbach Archival Depot and Jewish organizations at the time was written shortly after they had completed their work, mostly by persons involved.[21] The first comprehensive overview of American initiatives to salvage and restitute books after the Second World War, which dedicates a full chapter to the depot, was written by Leslie Poste, an MFA&A officer who worked there, but it was never published.[22] It was another forty years before further articles and chapters started to appear on the history of the depot.[23] Michael Kurtz was ultimately to furnish us with a rich, original, source-based, and informed overview of the efforts initiated by the American government to achieve cultural restitution in the European theater of war and the American occupation zone.[24] His study includes consideration of the specific features of Jewish restitution claims after 1945, providing an introductory account of the JCR's work.[25] The same goes for most of the attempts to reconstruct Jewish efforts to salvage cultural property: they are of an introductory character or are focused on specific locations and collections.[26] Significant here are the writings of Frits Hoogewoudt, Patricia Kennedy Grimsted, and Evelyn Adunka, which have laid the groundwork for the reconstruction of the history of the Offenbach Archival Depot and the fate of Jewish collections after the war.[27] When it comes to the role of Israeli actors and the National Library of Israel in the salvage operation, the work of Dov Schidorsky has played a pioneering role and is continued by a range of younger scholars from the Hebrew University.[28] Two as-yet-unpublished but comprehensive works have helped fill the research gap on JCR's history and its institutional milieu. The first is the study on the JRSO by Ayaka Takei, which is based on rich source material and is still the only work available on its operations. While this thesis is only marginally concerned with the JCR, it sheds light on its institutional background by touching on numerous legal problems of the kind the JCR was to face.[29] The second key contribution in this context is Dana Herman's dissertation "Hashavat Avedah: A History of Jewish Cultural Reconstruction, Inc.," which provides a detailed and systematic examination of the copious sources on the JCR's organizational history.[30] The present work builds on the valuable findings of these studies. It augments them with an account that depicts the debates on restitution as attempts to come to terms with historical injustice, allowing us to hear the voices of the actors involved. This perspective enables me not just to reconstruct the history of cultural restitution anew but also to place it within different, broader frameworks associated with postwar efforts to rebuild Jewish existence.[31]

The increasing awareness of efforts to achieve restitution in the late 1940s is also linked with a general trend over the last decade among scholars of contemporary history to scrutinize the aftermath of World War II as a specific period in its own right. Here Jewish postwar history, and above all the history of survivors in and from Europe, is a particularly prominent field of inquiry, one that has challenged entrenched periodizations and interpretive models relating to the postwar world, Jewish reconstruction endeavors, and the evolution of Holocaust awareness and commemoration.[32] The present study is located within this research context of transnational aftermath studies. I attempt to provide a comprehensive portrayal of those aspects of the rebuilding of Jewish life after 1945 inherent in the salvage and distribution of European Jewish cultural treasures while also exploring the debate on the legacies and function of this contested heritage in the new centers of Jewish life, especially the United States.

As mentioned earlier, part of the project of teasing out new semantic layers of restitution involves foregrounding the perspective of its key actors. As yet, the research on Hannah Arendt, Salo W. Baron, Lucy S. Dawidowicz, and Gershom Scholem has tended to ignore their tremendous engagement in the restitution of looted libraries and ritual objects from Europe. Against the background of their important roles and outstanding oeuvres within the Jewish (and non-Jewish) intellectual worlds of the twentieth century, this commitment has been treated as a footnote. I take the opposite approach, shedding light on this backstory to open up new perspectives on their intellectual and political positioning in times of turmoil and uncertainty. I uncover this unknown history by investigating these key figures' institutional engagement, writing, and thinking in the 1940s and 1950s. There are specific reasons scholars have mostly ignored this key experiential element in their intellectual development. In the cases of Baron and Dawidowicz, one explanation lies in the asymmetry between their position and standing within the American Jewish community during their lifetimes and the meager amount of research examining their biographies and oeuvres. Interest in Baron, as the last historian to produce a (eighteen-volume) master narrative of Jewish history (*A Social and Religious History of the Jews*), has increased palpably in recent times. This found expression in the academic celebration of the 120th anniversary of his birth in 2015, featuring a symposium and the publication of a volume containing both important new biographical insights and explorations of the relevance of his work and thought to various fields within and beyond Jewish studies.[33] Despite this, studies of Baron as an individual and of his oeuvre are still astonishingly rare. In addition to Festschrift contributions and essays by several of his students,[34] Robert Liberles's intellectual biography remains the only monograph on Baron's life and activities.[35] While the latter book casts light on his position within—and extensive work on behalf of—the JCR, it does not discuss this institution's significance in detail.[36] When it comes to his scholarly role and output, David Engel and Michael Brenner have highlighted important aspects of Salo Baron's vast legacy. Both underline his pioneering role in contemporary Jewish historiography, with Engel in particular locating Baron's writings in the context of postwar history.[37] Less research has been done on Dawidowicz as yet despite her role as the "doyenne of Holocaust literature." Most studies of the historiography of the Holocaust or in Jewish intellectual history have failed to fully acknowledge her work despite making repeated reference to her 1975 opus magnum, *The War against the Jews, 1933–1945*. To fill the lacunae, Nancy Sinkoff is working on a comprehensive biography of Dawidowicz, having previously produced a new edition of her memoirs and seminal essays on her activities.[38] Scattered references to Dawidowicz's contribution to the restitution of the YIVO library can be found in studies of YIVO's history and studies of cultural restitution in general. But the full postwar history of YIVO is another topic awaiting proper scholarly attention.[39]

In contrast to Baron and Dawidowicz, there is a vast literature on Arendt and Scholem, yet so far there has been little acknowledgment of their work for the JCR. Arendt, one of the most prominent and oft-cited female intellectuals of the twentieth century, has been studied across the broadest array of disciplines, extending far beyond the topics of relevance to the present study.[40] The pivotal biography by Elisabeth Young-Bruehl breaks with the tendency to neglect Arendt's postwar activities, devoting lengthy passages to her work for the JCR and relating it to the key political and historical issues with which she was concerned.[41] Also relevant in this context are the studies by Natan Sznaider, who highlights Arendt's experiences with the JCR and identifies links between this experiential realm and her historical and political consciousness.[42] Moreover, we can glean indications of the significance of Arendt's work for the JCR to her thinking and acting in the postwar period from a number of shorter essays, which point to her political commitment or locate her within specific post-1945 intellectual debates.[43] Of the numerous studies chiefly concerned with Scholem's scholarly activities, the first substantive indications of his role in post-1945 restitution have come from Dov Schidorsky and Noam Zadoff. The latter ascribes key significance in Scholem's biography to his 1946 trip to Europe, undertaken at the behest of the Hebrew University to take stock of stolen Jewish cultural goods.[44] Above all, new insights into Hannah Arendt and Gershom Scholem have come from their correspondence, published in German in 2010 and in English in 2017. This volume includes letters resulting from their collaborative work for the JCR and presents Arendt's reports on her trips to Germany on behalf of the JCR in 1949 and 1952. For the first time, the volume has enabled scholars to examine the alliance between Arendt and Scholem and bring out how their outstanding achievements in the realm of cultural restitution relate to their writing and thinking in the postwar period. Nonetheless, the numerous reviews of the German publication of these letters show that it is hard to assess the relevance of this experience to Arendt and Scholem and that this topic requires further historical deciphering. Few reviewers devoted more than a few lines to the activities in the 1940s that united these two very different scholars before their famous dispute following Arendt's 1963 report on the Eichmann Trial. And this despite the fact that at least a third of their letters is devoted to their shared commitment to Jewish culture after World War II.[45]

To help provide a more thorough exploration of these contexts, I have pursued an integrative perspective. I examine institutionalization, political and legal decision-making in early cultural restitution, and the prominent role of JCR within this context, combining these topics with an intellectual history approach that foregrounds the views and perceptions of the scholars involved. This is one of the reasons the present study is structured in such a way as to cast light on the historical context and genesis of the JCR while also contextualizing the leading protagonists. The goal here is to bring out the significance of this initiative as well as its powerful impact on those involved. The first part of this book is an introduction to the history of the Offenbach Archival Depot, a topic that throws into relief an array of crucial issues. These issues range from the cooperation between the American military government and the international Jewish organizations in the immediate postwar period, through the legal and political resistance that threatened to thwart the restitution of cultural property, to the significance of the salvage of books to the Jewish history of memory after the Holocaust. I work on the assumption that the depot served as both a symbolic and highly concrete vantage point within the actors' collision with Nazi crimes and their reverberations. The catastrophic wave of destruction and its preceding history, both of which were reflected in the amassed objects, were as much a part of the Offenbach experience as the as-yet-unwritten Jewish future in these objects' prospective homes. By seeking to reconstruct the history of the JCR, the second part of the book casts light on strategies intended to shape Jewish life after 1945. The JCR and its historical genesis, which extends over several years, including the last few years of the war, neatly encapsulate the legal, political, and cultural aspects of the debate on post-Holocaust Jewish survival and how best to organize Jewish life in response to catastrophe. This debate included crucial deliberations on, and visions of, the new Jewish cultural centers in the United States and Israel. The last part of the book, which again delves into the political activities pursued by Arendt, Baron, Dawidowicz, and Scholem in light of their experiential history, turns the perspective back toward the past. These scholars' efforts to salvage cultural goods caused them to directly confront the events and consequences of the Holocaust. This confrontation materialized and resonated in quite different forms in their thoughts and actions. Above all else, their deep commitment refutes the commonly held notion that in the immediate postwar period, Jewish and non-Jewish actors shied away from taking action in response to what had happened and had—if at all—a merely latent awareness of the scope and monstrosity of these events.

The history of the postwar restitution of Jewish cultural treasures and, in particular, stolen books that I seek to reconstruct here thus opens up a horizon far broader than it may appear at first sight. Inherent in this history are key moral and legal-political questions about the postwar European order centered on the relationship between the Allies, the

Germans, and Jewish survivors or international Jewish organizations, as this relationship relates to the dispensation of justice and reconstruction. This history also offers insights into the many-layered processes of negotiation on Jewish existence after the Holocaust as they unfolded during this period, especially in the United States. Traces of related experiences extend into the tropes and understandings that influenced or even formed Jewish intellectual history in the postwar era. Against this background, the field of cultural restitution, a seemingly peripheral phenomenon within the broader political context of the time, serves as a magnifying glass that highlights—and allows us to make connections between—the legal, political, cultural, and intellectual turning points engendered by the profound civilizational rupture that had occurred. The history of cultural restitution allows us to delve into multiple layers of the Jewish response to the atrocities while laying bare the Jews' complex struggle for survival and continuity in the second half of the twentieth century.

1

Confronting the Present

The Offenbach Archival Depot

The American Antithesis of Nazi Plunder

In April 1948, Severin Rochmann, a rabbi working in a camp for Jewish displaced persons in Zeilsheim near Frankfurt, entered the American military government's Offenbach Archival Depot for the first time. Towering before him, on four floors of what had been an I. G. Farben industrial complex on the banks of the River Main, were millions of books, manuscripts, incunabula, Torah scrolls, ritual objects, and documents. American soldiers and civilian assistants had brought these cultural assets—looted and confiscated between 1933 and 1945 by Nazi units such as the ERR—to Offenbach with the aim of identifying them and returning them to their owners. Most of the items assembled there came from major Jewish libraries, schools, and synagogues across Europe. The crates also held thousands of volumes seized from private Jewish collections throughout the former German-occupied areas. What the rabbi saw far exceeded his expectations. A few months later, Rochmann—together with a German staff member from the depot, Peter Leinekugel—went on to write a descriptive report about the activities in Offenbach in which he articulated his astonishment at the collection: "It is surely no exaggeration to state that there is no longer a city in Germany, perhaps in all of Europe, that accommodates within its walls such a large number of Hebrew books. [. . .] If one compiled a bibliography of all these books it would undoubtedly be a comprehensive work, a near-complete catalogue of all Hebrew and Jewish books." At the same time, Rochmann was struck by the tragic quality of the place: "All the books and other treasures housed in the Archival Depot amount to one of the saddest testaments to the Nazis' war on Judaism [. . .]. They await their previous owners. Many will never make it back into the hands of their former custodians. They were wiped from the book of life by the Nazi regime's campaign of annihilation. But these books and objects, these precious relics, will always enjoin us to remember those they once belonged to."[1]

The special character of this place is evident in these few lines written in 1948. Being in the depot, surrounded by a chaotic mass of items crammed into the available space, was like standing amid the preserved remnants of Jewish culture in Europe. But, much like Germany's displaced persons camps for Jewish survivors en route to emigration, this place was of a transitory character. For a short time, the depot served as a kind of warehouse of Jewish tradition and knowledge, its holdings reflecting the diversity and breadth of Europe's pre-1933 Jewish worlds. The history of the European Jews' persecution and annihilation was inscribed in this place and its collection. But it was to be no enduring memorial. In a historically unparalleled restitution process, its holdings were to be returned to their previous owners as quickly as possible. The groundwork for this process had already been laid during the war: as early as autumn 1943, the Civil Affairs Division of the US War Department had established the MFA&A, a unit operating in the European theater tasked with protecting cultural heritage at risk of looting, bombardment, and other war-related threats.[2] After the war, its main task was to seek out and recover the millions of cultural assets displaced and confiscated by the Nazis. Similar units existed in the British and French zones.[3] In cellars, mines, castles, collieries, country estates, and cultural institutions, they found endless quantities of books, documents, and artifacts hidden by the relevant German plunder units to protect them from Allied bombs and keep them out of Allied hands. The MFA&A officers found more than 1,400 such caches, transferring the works of art, library and archival holdings, and ritual objects stashed there to specially created collecting points. Seven such points were established in the American occupation zone to store items and organize restitution; the main ones were located in Munich, Offenbach, and Wiesbaden, with smaller counterparts in Bamberg, Celle, Marburg, and Nuremberg. The American zone was the central locus of cultural restitution because most looted cultural assets were found there. In response, the American authorities launched the earliest and most comprehensive initiatives to salvage and return them. Their pioneering role in restitution policy, however, was chiefly the result of the comprehensive preparatory work done by various political interest groups within the United States before Germany's surrender; another key factor was America's geographical distance from the European theater of war, which had spared it the kind of material damage, confiscations, and destruction suffered by the Soviet Union, France, and—to a more limited degree—the United Kingdom.

The American MFA&A officers sought to reverse the damage done by the Nazis' notorious looting raids and Rosenberg's confiscation policy. With respect to the Offenbach Depot, established in early 1946, which chiefly housed stolen Jewish books, documents, archival materials, and ritual objects, they expressed this aspiration explicitly: "The antithesis of the plundering Nazi Einsatzstab Reichsleiter Rosenberg, the Offenbach Archival Depot, without fanfare, has accomplished the biggest book-restitution operation in library history. [. . .] This restitution operation forever will remain as living proof of the ideals of democracy."[4]

The Americans saw the depot as the lynchpin of initiatives to salvage Jewish cultural assets and linked it with hopes of the reconstruction and continued existence of the Jewish cultural and intellectual world and the prospect of a new, democratic Europe. Many Jews, meanwhile, began to view it as a monument to the Nazis' violence and destruction.

Processes of Looting

The Nazi looting of art and cultural assets had had a particularly delete-rious effect on Jewish cultural property, which was a key target of the Germans' zealous destruction, desecration, and confiscation of "enemy" objects. After January 1933, Hitler's seizure of power sparked the devel-opment of a complex system of (sometimes competing) German institutions and units concerned with the expropriation and destruction of Jewish cultural assets. This system was far from peripheral within the new political apparatus. It involved "meticulously prepared campaigns" central to Nazi power politics that were "carried out with painstaking professionalism."[5] The looting of famous and valuable works of art from European museum and private collections, which was often personally sponsored and exploited by Nazi leaders, must be clearly distinguished from the multifaceted programs of spoliation and destruction targeted at Jewish books and ritual objects.[6] These initiatives were motivated less by illicit enrichment and avarice than the anti-Semitic conviction that taking Jewish books and other items was an important means of eliminating Jews' cultures of knowledge and intellectual traditions in Europe—and thus a key component in the ideological struggle against them.[7] Initially the focus was on the wanton destruction of Jewish libraries and book holdings categorized as "un-German," manifested most strikingly in the public book burnings of 1933. But the Nazis increasingly recognized the value of Jewish and other proscribed printed works for their own research and ideological warfare. They had modified their approach accordingly by the time of the Reichspogromnacht (or Kristallnacht), when the Security Service (Sicherheitsdienst) ordered the seizure of the archival material in every synagogue and Jewish business.[8]

The key protagonist in the Nazi program of cultural spoliation was Alfred Rosenberg. As commissioner for the education and training of NSDAP (Nationalsozialistische Deutsche Arbeiterpartei) members, he was entrusted with the creation of a National Socialist university, the so-called Hohe Schule on the shores of the Chiemsee, which was established in January 1940. To this end, he was authorized by Hitler to begin working in the "fields of research and the establishment of libraries."[9] Rosenberg was thus given free rein to order the plundering of libraries and other collections of cultural assets in all the occupied areas if their holdings seemed relevant to his research institute.[10] His task force, the ERR, was set up in July 1940, followed in March 1941 by the official opening of the first subdivision of the university, the Institute for Research on the Jewish Question in Frankfurt am Main. Over the next few years, the institute, headed by historian Wilhelm Grau, came to house one of the largest collections of stolen Judaica and Hebraica in the world in its building on the Bockenheimer Landstraße in Frankfurt's Westend.[11] As a result of the ERR raids that plagued France and Eastern Europe in particular, the institute library comprised more than 40,000 volumes of the Jewish education and welfare organization Alliance Israélite Universelle Paris; 20,000 volumes from the Lipschuetz Jewish bookstore in Paris; parts of the private Parisian libraries of Guy, Maurice, and Robert Rothschild; and 760 crates from the archive of the Rothschild Frères Bank in Paris. Rosenberg's library also contained all the important Jewish collections from the Netherlands, including 20,000 volumes from the Bibliotheca Rosenthaliana; more than 25,000 volumes taken from the Sephardic community of Amsterdam; and the collections of the Netherlands Israelite Seminary of Amsterdam (Nederlands Israelitisch Seminarium) and the Spinoza Society. Around 280,000 volumes in the library came from the task force's depots in Riga, Kaunas, Vilna, Minsk, and Kiev—including the lion's share of the YIVO collection. ERR operations extended from Scandinavia through the Soviet Union and France to Greece, and the library in Frankfurt had soon accumulated a collection of tremendous quantity and quality.[12] Even before its foundation, the mayor of Frankfurt, Friedrich Krebs, had ceded to Rosenberg responsibility for the venerable collection of Judaica and Hebraica held by the city and university library. The core of the institute's holdings thus constituted one of the largest and most important Jewish libraries in continental Europe.[13] Fears that it might be destroyed by Allied bombings of Frankfurt prompted the library's near-complete transfer to, and concealment in, various official buildings and the castle complex in the Hesse town of Hungen in mid-1943.

Before the institute's establishment in Frankfurt, a central library for the planned Hohe Schule had been founded in Berlin in early 1939 under the leadership of Walter Grothe, an institution that later engaged in extensive cooperation with the Frankfurt Institute. To protect it from bomb attacks, in October 1942, much of the central library was relocated to St. Andrä in Carinthia, and from September 1944 onward it was cached at the Tanzenberg monastic estate twenty miles away. The seven hundred thousand volumes of the central library included collections looted by the ERR in Paris, such as the private collection of Édouard de Rothschild; holdings from the library of the eminent rabbinical school established in 1829 by the consistoire (École Rabbinique); divisions of the Alliance; Hans Fürstenberg's famous private library in Berlin; and numerous collections from the Soviet Union, mostly plundered by the Künsberg Unit (Kommando Künsberg), which answered to the Ministry of Foreign Affairs.[14] Another prominent player in the Nazi program of cultural spoliation was the "Ancestral Heritage" (Ahnenerbe) organization, which functioned as a subunit of the *Schutzstaffel* (SS) under the leadership of Heinrich Himmler. Set up in 1935, by 1944 it consisted of forty research groups. Within the Nazi interpretive paradigm, these groups explored topics in archaeology, history, racial science (*Rassenkunde*), ethnology, biology, medicine, and genetics. Units of this organization also looted in the Soviet Union, chiefly in the wake of the SS's brutal campaigns.[15] The research institutions where anti-Jewish "science" (*Gegnerforschung*; "enemy science") was carried out during the Nazi period were key beneficiaries of the comprehensive looting of books and archival materials. Prominent among them were the Institute for the Study of the Jewish Question (Institut zum Studium der Judenfrage, founded in 1935 in Berlin as part of the Reich Propaganda Ministry [Reichspropagandaministerium]); Office VII Ideological Research and Evaluation of Worldviews (Amt VII Weltanschauliche Forschung und Auswertung) of the Reich Security Main Office (Reichssicherheitshauptamt; RSHA), founded in 1939; the Reich Institute for the History of the New Germany (Reichsinstitut für die Geschichte des neuen Deutschland) in Berlin, founded in 1935, led by Walter Frank; the Reich Institute's Research Department on the Jewish Question (Forschungsabteilung Judenfrage), founded in 1936, initially led by Wilhelm Grau in Munich; the aforementioned Institute for Research on the Jewish Question in Frankfurt am Main, to which Grau later moved following the transfer of all the Munich Research Department's responsibilities to Berlin; and the Department of Jewish Research (Referat Judenforschung) at the Institute for German Work in the East (Institut für deutsche Ostarbeit) in Kraków (founded in 1940), led by Josef Sommerfeldt. Research on the "Jewish question" was also being pursued and promoted at many universities. All National Socialist research contexts saw the appropriation and recoding of the questions and content central to scholarly studies on Jewish topics, the strengthening of anti-Semitic research traditions, and the ideological reconfiguration of both the materials and findings of predominately Jewish science and teaching. These processes were complementary to the expulsion and murder of the German and European Jewry.[16] They were directly linked with the Nazi regime's anti-Jewish policies, undergirding and "legitimizing" acts of violence against Jews and their advancing annihilation. Rivaling Rosenberg's collecting mania, Office VII of the RSHA, under the supervision of Himmler, Reinhard Heydrich, and Franz Alfred Six, built up the second-largest library of looted materials.[17] It systematically confiscated and collected all the files, archival materials, and books of those political parties, lodges, and political associations labeled as "enemies," along with major holdings of individual Jewish communities and institutions. Contemporary witnesses estimated the holdings of this library at between two and three million volumes. These were stored in the occupied Grand Landlodge of the Freemasons of Germany (Große Landesloge der Freimaurer von Deutschland) in Berlin-Schöneberg and in a nearby synagogue. A labor unit (Arbeitskommando), which the Reich Association of Jews in Germany (Reichsvereinigung der Juden in Deutschland) was compelled to set up in 1941 and that initially included eight Jewish scholars, dealt with books of Jewish provenance among these holdings.[18] Among other things, the Jewish collection included books taken from the Vienna Jewish Community (Israelitische Kultusgemeinde Wien); the holdings of the Jewish communities of Berlin, Warsaw, Munich, Hamburg, Gleiwitz (Gliwice), and Breslau (Wrocław); the Jewish Theological Seminary (Jüdisch-Theologisches Seminar Fraenkel'sche Stiftung) in Breslau; the library of the former Central Association of German Citizens of the Jewish Faith (Central Verein deutscher Staatsbürger jüdischen Glaubens); the holdings of the Hochschule für die Wissenschaft des Judentums in Berlin; and several hundred thousand volumes from the private libraries of Karl Adler, Ludwig Marcuse, André Maurois, Ernst Posener, Walther Rathenau (Rathenau Foundation), Arthur Rubinstein, Isac Leo Seeligmann, and Joseph Wirth.[19]

The classicist Ernst Grumach was appointed head of the Jewish labor unit. He and Berthold Breslauer, previously archivist of the Bleichröder banking house, were the only members of the first forced labor team to survive.[20] All its other members were deported to Auschwitz with their families in 1943. The group of twenty-five forced laborers who replaced them, who had escaped the great wave of deportations from Berlin because they were married to non-Jewish women, survived the war purely by chance. In August 1943, Himmler ordered the establishment of new repositories in Silesia, Bohemia, and Thuringia to protect the books and manuscripts from war damage, decimating the library holdings in Berlin. Most of the collections that remained there, such as major divisions of the Vienna Jewish Community Library and the Berlin Library of the Hochschule der Wissenschaft des Judentums, were consumed in fires resulting from aerial bombings. Following Germany's capitulation, the small number of books that survived these fires fell prey to the plunder carried out by both the general population and soldiers. What was left after the war Grumach handed over to the American military authorities, who in turn transferred them to Offenbach. He also helped the MFA&A units, local Jewish actors and private individuals in their search for holdings of the RSHA library. His "Report on the Confiscation and Treatment of Former Jewish Library Holdings by the State Police Authorities, 1933–1945" was the first detailed account of the library's component parts and their whereabouts after 1943 and was thus crucial to finding and salvaging its books and manuscripts.

It is impossible to state with certainty how many books and objects the Nazi units confiscated and displaced over the course of the war. But the situation in Western Europe differed significantly from that in Eastern Europe. The cultural landscape of the East—particularly in Poland and the western parts of the Soviet Union—was pillaged with the utmost brutality and almost entirely destroyed. This obviously applied first and foremost to the Jewish cultural infrastructure. Polish refugees tried to publicly raise awareness of this fact in the free world as early as 1943 by proclaiming that "the world center of Jewish literature lies in ruins."[21] But in these regions, the Nazi campaign of cultural robbery and destruction also severely damaged non-Jewish institutions and collections. Holdings vilified as socialist or communist or belonging to the Slavic cultural heritage in general, which the Nazis also classified as inferior, were subjected to equally untrammeled destruction. Western Europe was not subjected to the same mania. Highly valuable collections of paintings and other art objects were certainly carried off by the German occupiers. But when it came to books, files, documents, and ritual objects, it was almost exclusively Jewish cultural heritage that was stolen. From France alone more than two hundred collections of books and art of Jewish provenance ended up in the Reich, with state property being largely left untouched.[22]

In April 1946, Alfred Rosenberg was interrogated before the International Military Tribunal in Nuremberg and found guilty on four counts. He was condemned to death for his crimes and his significant role in the Nazi power system. Meanwhile, many of his accomplices and senior figures from other task forces escaped sentencing and continued to work in West German museums, archives, and libraries after 1949.

Restitution to Western Europe

This short outline of the processes of Nazi theft and destruction underscores the significance of the Offenbach Archival Depot, which officially opened in March 1946, as a collecting point for stolen books and ritual objects. Like few other postwar American institutions or activities, the depot embodied the imponderables and successes of the restitution procedures relating to stolen Jewish assets after the Second World War. Over the course of the depot's existence, more than 3.5 million books and manuscripts, along with several thousand Torah scrolls and other ritual objects, passed through its sorting and distribution process. In September 1945, under the leadership of two officers (Julius H. Buchman and Richard H. Kuhlke) and the civilian Glenn Goodman from the MFA&A, the Americans had initially established a library collecting point for books and archival materials of Jewish origin in Frankfurt am Main. It was housed in what had formerly been the Freiherrlich Carl von Rothschild Public Library, which had served as the Library for Modern Languages and Music (Bibliothek für Neuere Sprachen und Musik) during the Nazi era.[23] The first finds made by the MFA&A were brought here along with the roughly one hundred thousand remaining volumes from the cellar of the bombed-out building that formerly housed Rosenberg's institute. The Rothschild building on the banks of the Main, only slightly damaged by bombs and now usable after being cleared out and repaired, soon housed more than one million volumes found in the region.[24] Under American leadership, sixty German civilians (mostly former employees of the Frankfurt City Library) carried out the work of sorting and identification here. With very limited means, they first tried to restore the books, which had often been found in damp conditions, by placing newspapers between their pages to draw out the moisture and hanging them out to dry on washing lines. Some of the books, infested by mold and bookworms, were taken to the Sachsenhausen City Hospital for disinfection. Attempts were then made to bring an initial degree of order to the book holdings, which were stored on the building's accessible floors. The Jewish publicist Robert Weltsch, who had entered Germany in 1945 on a British permit and visited the Frankfurt collecting point, provides us with an impression of the place. In a 1946 newspaper article on his travel experiences, he describes his first encounter with the collection:

> The library in Frankfurt, collected under the aegis of Alfred Rosenberg, is probably the largest Jewish library in the world. [. . .] A provisional inspection reveals that the books have been arranged on large shelves,

with corresponding labels if the book contained the stamp of a particular library. A vast number of shelves bear the legend [. . .] "Hebrew books, place of origin unknown." In this system of classification, "Hebrew books" are all those printed in Hebrew type, from Tanakh and Talmud and Rambam [Maimonides] and She'elot ve-Teshuvot [Responsa] to [Abraham] Mapu and Sholem Aleichem and Yiddish *Volkskalender* [folkloristic almanacs]. The Nazis amassed their booty here indiscriminately with no idea of its content. [. . .] You never know if you're going to find a precious old Hebrew book alongside a Yiddish page-turner.[25]

The quantity of materials recovered from the holdings amassed by Rosenberg in Frankfurt, which made up just a fraction of those discovered by MFA&A officials in Hungen, prompted Weltsch to speculate that he might be looking at the largest Jewish library left at the time. This explains why the Offenbach Depot later attracted such particular attention from contemporaries. By April 1945, MFA&A officers Robert Posey and Lincoln Kirstein had discovered the cache containing Frankfurt's ERR library in nearby Hungen.[26] Over the summer, senior staff discussed the transfer of the more than one million books and objects to Frankfurt. According to the assessments of depot workers, however, this would have caused the Rothschild building to collapse. Following attempts to find an alternative, I. G. Farben's premises in Offenbach were chosen. The American army had taken over this former industrial complex after the war and moved the refugees it found there to specially created camps. A large collecting depot was now established in the newly available sections of the complex. Its infrastructure made it far better suited to storage than the Frankfurt palace: it featured plenty of space on several floors, heatable rooms, lifts, transportation devices, furnished offices, and direct access to water and railroad tracks. In December 1945, therefore, the order was given to vacate and shut down the Frankfurt site and transfer its holdings to Offenbach.

Glenn Goodman and a number of his colleagues from Frankfurt established a branch office in the Hungen castle complex, which carried out an initial inspection of the masses of crates, bundles, and documents and prepared them for transport.[27] The journalist Janet Flanner, a reporter for the *New Yorker* active across Europe at the end of the war, reported on the disturbing effect of the castle grounds:

In a brick kiln in the town of Hungen was the most insultingly housed cache of all. Here were hidden the most precious Jewish archives, tomes and synagogue vessels from all over Europe, including the Rosenthalian collection from Amsterdam and that of the Frankfurt Rothschilds. In the Kiln, the repository for the Jewish material Rosenberg planned to use in his projected post-war academy, where anti-Semitism was to be taught as an exact science, priceless illuminated parchment torahs were found cut into covers for Nazi stenographers' typewriters or made up into shoes. Here, too, were thousands of Jewish identity cards, marked with a yellow "J," all that remained of Jews who had perished in Nazi crematories. There was no blaze of aesthetic beauty here, no emblems of dynastic Teutonic history. There was nothing in the ugly rooms except the rubbish and mean utilities to which these remnants of Jewish lives, identities and God-loving faith had been finally reduced.[28]

Once it had become apparent that these haphazardly amassed objects, papers, and books included the precious Jewish collections from Paris and Amsterdam, the gruesome castle grounds were permanently guarded by soldiers. Other eyewitnesses described the disastrous situation in Hungen in much the same way as Flanner: "So many boxes had been piled on top of one another that those at the bottom had yielded to the pressure and burst open, creating a picture of disorder and destruction. This rampant chaos was no doubt exacerbated when the entire warehouse was plundered by locals, hoping to find objects of value during the final days of national collapse [at the end of the war]."[29]

With the help of German prisoners of war and civilian assistants, the castle and the adjacent buildings, all of which were filled with books, manuscripts, works of art, and silver objects, were cleared by mid-December 1945. The packing and transportation of these materials was completed under the most difficult of circumstances: there was a lack of vehicles and personnel, staff members' supply situation was poor, and the mass of stolen goods was immense. Finally, however, in cars, buses, and trains, the objects were moved via Frankfurt to Offenbach.[30]

Nazi memorabilia (busts, Hitlerian cultic objects, and insignia) were destroyed on site, while propaganda material and ERR records were collected separately and passed either to the American army's document centers in Fechenheim and Oberursel or to the Library of Congress in

Washington, DC, whose task force, the Library of Congress Mission to Europe, was active in Germany. This body was dedicated to the collection of historically valuable documentary material that was no longer needed on site (for the Nuremberg trials, for example). Its primary task, however, was to acquire any German publications that could be found from the 1933–45 period for use in American libraries while also fostering cooperation between the latter and German publishers and libraries. This sparked the development of a kind of exchange service for German and American libraries that was intended to promote the democratic reconstruction of the German library system. While pursuing these objectives, mission staff also worked alongside MFA&A officers at the various collecting points in the American occupation zone and later did much to help transfer various book holdings to the United States.[31]

In the Offenbach Depot, a lack of heating fuel and logistical difficulties meant that staff had to wait until March 2, 1946, to begin rehousing materials. The military government's internal announcement declared the Offenbach Archival Depot "a first priority Monuments, Fine Arts and Archives restitution project," a dedicated repository for all books and archival materials found in the American zone.[32] The depot's supervision differed from other collecting points: it was managed by the military government of Greater Hesse but at the same time answered directly to OMGUS. This appears to have been the result of the complex legal situation of (mostly heirless) Jewish property, which was to remain under the control of the military governor.[33] In cooperation with Goodman, the MFA&A officers Everett Lesley and Clyde K. Harris laid the groundwork for the Offenbach operation, roughly systematizing the incoming books and objects, establishing working procedures, appointing reliable staff, and taking the first steps toward returning identified objects. Finally, on March 5, 1946, the MFA&A reported to the American military government that "the Offenbach Archival Depot, the largest collection of Jewish material in the world, is now in operation. [. . .] The first restitution will be made within a few days."[34] Once again, we see a reference to the vast size of the collection, which the Americans would henceforth strive to salvage and restore as fairly as possible. They also began to transfer books and archival material from other collecting points and caches in the American zone and Berlin to Offenbach.[35] Within a few months, several million books and some thousand ritual objects had arrived at the depot, where they were distributed across the several floors of the building. There was a lack of shelving, so piles of books stacked in boxes were stored throughout the building. An impression of the situation there is conveyed in notes made by Seymour Pomrenze, a Jewish archivist at the US National Archives, US Army captain, and MFA&A officer, who served as the depot's initial director: "My first impressions of the Offenbach collecting point in February 1946 were overwhelming and amazing at once. As I stood before a seemingly endless sea of crates and books, I thought what a horrible mess! [. . .] Beyond the mess, however was an ever larger mission. Indeed, the only action possible was to return the items to their owners, as quickly as possible."[36]

The sorting and cataloging began immediately. Toward the end of March 1946, with the help of MFA&A units, staff of the military government, and 176 German civilians procured by the Employment Office (Arbeitsamt), Pomrenze had already initiated the first restitutions.[37] To this end, crates of books were examined, inventoried, and repacked. A number of branches were established to structure the work: an administrative branch dedicated to personnel, security, supplies, transportation, and maintenance; an operational branch responsible for storage and warehousing, care and restoration, sorting, boxing, crating, and shipment; and a liaison branch, tasked with forging links with official emissaries of the collections' home countries and institutions of origin. Pomrenze created specific rooms for particularly precious holdings: there was one for storing Torah scrolls, menorahs, silver ritual objects, and textiles; one for manuscripts and rare books; and another for the 350,000 volumes of the Prussian State Library (Preußische Staatsbibliothek) discovered in freight cars in Czechoslovakia and salt mines near Ransbach, which were sent back to East Berlin in April 1946.[38]

The Americans in the depot often described a problematic working relationship with the German staff. Given the significance of their task, they considered the Germans negligent and thoughtless.[39] Leslie Poste, head of the MFA&A archives and libraries division, provided the most drastic description of their attitude: "The German workers felt that all of this Nazi loot was their rightful booty; that the entire restitution operation was the undoing of work in which they still believed."[40] This negative impression was shared by Isaac Bencowitz, who succeeded Pomrenze as director and referred to the German staff as "definitely unreliable."[41] The few sources available from the German side seem to underscore this impression. An expressive example is the Festschrift compiled by the German staff to mark the depot's first anniversary. It is testimony to their casual and scarcely empathetic approach to the work and the objects they encountered in Offenbach. The ironically jolly songs and rhymes recorded in the publication revolve chiefly around working conditions, food supplies, and football. There are virtually no references to the significance of their task in the depot, which they appear to have perceived as little different from employment in any other public institution.[42] The later historian Lucy S. Dawidowicz, who took part in the festivities surrounding this first anniversary as an emissary of the Joint, was appalled by the glaring gap between the German employees' perception and her own, as she recalled in her later memoirs of the time:

> Early in march [. . .] the German staff had a party to celebrate the Depot's first anniversary. [. . .] I sat through the evening aloof and expressionless. The Depot, I wrote home, is the last place in the world where I can forget the crimes the Germans committed against the Jews. When I worked, holding the orphaned books in my hands, I often thought that it was easier to be with *amkho*, with living people, than with these inanimate remnants of the world the Germans had destroyed. [. . .] They were the relics of six million murdered Jews. Such thoughts continued to haunt me at the Depot and never more insistently than at that Depot party.[43]

Both public and internal statements by Germans concerning the Offenbach Archival Depot bear witness to this perceptual dichotomy. In contrast to the Jewish visitors and helpers, for whom this place laid bare the entire history of annihilation, the German staff and German journalists who visited the depot seemed unable to relate to the reality of the crimes rendered so visible there. An article on the depot's work entitled "Culture and Decency" ("Kultur und Anstand"), published in the *Frankfurter Rundschau* in October 1946, certainly underlined the successes of the restitution process and explicitly highlighted the need to find "a civilized way out of the wretchedness into which those in power [Alfred Rosenberg] have plunged the German people." But it ignored the responsibility of the general population, the specific features of the robbery of the Jews, and its magnitude.[44] Like the contributions to the Festschrift, German news reports are testimony to the speechlessness often engendered by these events. Above all, though, both demonstrate most Germans' inability and unwillingness to confront or try to come to terms with them.[45] People tended to pin the blame on others, leaving the process of accounting for and commemorating the past to the Allies and the victims of Nazi rule.

The latter worked frantically to get the restitution process up and running. Depot policy was based on the directives issued by the American military government's restitution program and thus the measures laid down in the Paris Conference on Reparations in December 1945, which was adopted by the Allied Control Council for Germany in 1946.[46] The affirmation of the principle of restitution by the Allied Control Council, which was to be operationalized within each zone of occupation, provided for the return of—and compensation for—property and assets confiscated as a result of the war to the relevant countries on the basis of the principle of territoriality. This implied that, irrespective of the character and ownership of the looted objects, they must be restored to the territory from which they were taken. Only states could make claims and appoint representatives for the identification of removed property.[47] These legal provisions considered neither the claims of individual institutions and nonstate collectives nor sovereign, belligerent states' dispossession of their own citizens, as had already befallen the German and Austrian Jews before the outbreak of war. The principle of territoriality made the practice of restitution highly problematic because neither Jewish representatives nor Jewish institutions worldwide were entitled to make claims on heirless material or unidentifiable items of Jewish provenance. According to the legislation applied, such objects were returned to their countries of origin regardless of the number of Jews still living there after the Holocaust. This also meant that all the material formerly owned by German and Austrian Jews who had been murdered or could not be identified would have had to be surrendered to the German and Austrian successor states. A logic opposed to the project of restitution threatened to hold sway, with the perpetrators legally profiting from their crimes.[48] This directly affected the work being done at the central collecting points. The American authorities soon recognized the flaws of these legal provisions and, on the basis of military government law no. 52 regulating the "blocking and control of property," ordered the depot staff to focus chiefly on collections of undisputed ownership from Western Europe. Pomrenze and his staff thus started calling on the various countries to file claims for restitution. To comply with this request, fifteen European states that had suffered German raids appointed so-called restitution officers. These officers reported to the American Military Government Land Greater Hesse and were permitted to help examine material at the collecting points, identify items from their country, and initiate their dispatch.[49]

One of the first such restitution officers at the Offenbach Depot was Dirk Petrus M. Graswinckel, director of the National Archive of the Netherlands. During the first few months, he supported the relevant work at the depot and found a large number of Dutch library holdings that were then earmarked for restitution. Some of the holdings identified with Graswinckel's help had already been shipped to Amsterdam by March 12, 1946. These included smaller collections, such as those of the famous Gottschalk and Herzberger Jewish antiquarian bookshops as well as entire libraries. Among them were the library of the Ets Haim Jewish-Portuguese Seminary in Amsterdam; the Bibliotheca Rosenthaliana; the holdings of the Spinoza Society in the Hague and those of the Spinoza House in Rijnsburg (Vereniging het Spinozahuis Den Haag/Rijnsburg); the collections of the Netherlands Israelite Seminary, which existed until 1943; and the holdings of the Netherlands Association for Jewish Sciences (Genootschap voor de Joodse Wetenschap in Nederland) in Amsterdam. Objets d'art, including a large number of medals, were found and sent back to the Jewish Historical Museum in Amsterdam (Joods Historisch Museum Amsterdam).[50] Before the Second World War, the Netherlands was home to one of the oldest and largest Jewish communities in Western Europe, and the goal now was to reconstruct its cultural and religious institutions. Only a fraction of Dutch Jewry had survived the German occupiers' war of annihilation, and many of them subsequently immigrated to the United States and, from 1948 onward, to Israel. Nonetheless, the Dutch government sought to reconstruct the Jewish infrastructure as rapidly as possible. And while anti-Semitic tendencies emerged among the non-Jewish population immediately after the war, the American and Dutch authorities, along with international Jewish actors and observers, nonetheless agreed on the need to get the restitution of stolen items under way and thus support the rebuilding of Jewish life in the Netherlands.[51]

Graswinckel supervised the shipment and distribution process on site but had already returned to Offenbach by the end of March to prepare a new shipment for April. He also did his best to expedite the return of stolen Dutch items found elsewhere. From the British-run depot in Tanzenberg Castle, Austria, he acquired ninety thousand Dutch books,[52] and in the Düsseldorf City Archive (Stadtarchiv Düsseldorf), he found stolen archival material from the city of Leiden and books from the Leeuwarden synagogue.[53] Holdings from other find sites administered by the MFA&A like castles in the vicinity of Bamberg—items that Glenn Goodman had examined and identified as Dutch—arrived in Offenbach in April 1946 and were passed to Graswinckel. The organization of Dutch restitution was considered a model for the work of the Offenbach Depot because complete and precious collections were restituted quickly and successfully in close cooperation with representatives from the target country.[54] This resulted in the reopening of the venerable Bibliotheca Rosenthaliana in Amsterdam as early as November 1946. Rabbi Isac Leo Seeligmann, who had survived internment in Theresienstadt and initially returned to Amsterdam, became the first postwar director of this famous library. Viewed as a symbol of a new dawn, its reopening was greeted with enthusiasm across the world. Max Weinreich, director of research at YIVO in New York, was one of those sending his good wishes to Amsterdam: "The Jewish people, including the Jewish community of your country, have suffered at the hands of the Germans beyond compare. But Germany had set out to annihilate the Jewish people and Jewish culture altogether. May your work grow from strength to strength and may the resurrection of the Rosenthaliana testify to the fact that, ultimately, the spirit is more powerful than the forces of evil."[55]

An equally positive picture emerges when it comes to other Western European countries. The restitution of French assets was particularly straightforward. Between April and July 1946, the French restitution officers Jean Prinet, Paul de la Boulaye, and Philippe Gagnat had already delivered 10 crates of archival documents from the Rothschild banking house in Paris and 734 crates of volumes looted from the Alliance, the École Rabbinique, and the Lipschuetz bookstore.[56] First and foremost, it was the art historian Rose Valland who made a significant contribution to the recovery and restitution of stolen items from France. During the German occupation, she had worked at the Musée du Jeu de Paume in Paris and was eyewitness to numerous confiscations by ERR soldiers, who used the museum as an intermediate storage site for stolen goods. Risking her life, she cataloged and documented this pillage and passed information to the French resistance. After the war, she was one of the key sources of information for the restitution officers and was herself appointed Officier des Beaux-Arts (the French equivalent of an MFA&A officer). This appointment brought her to the Offenbach Depot in May 1946, where she helped identify French property.[57] The French items made up a large portion of the depot's holdings. The rabbi Maurice Liber of the École Rabbinique also helped identify French-Jewish items in Offenbach and did much to ensure that, by July 1947, more than 320,000 objects had been returned to France. A request submitted by the French government to the American restitution branch in December 1946, to return to France all the holdings in the French language, was opposed. The American leadership argued that the respective texts clearly also originated from Belgian, German, Polish, and Russian collections and restitution to France was thus inappropriate.[58] This incident shows how the officials tried to rigorously uphold the transparency and legality of procedures. Other returns during the first few months of the depot's existence involved Belgian assets. The collections of Jewish libraries from Antwerp and Brussels, a conglomeration of more than 1,900 volumes, were identified and earmarked for return by the Belgian representative Raymond Le Marie.[59]

In mid-April 1946, Isaac Bencowitz, captain in the US Army, MFA&A officer, and a chemist of Russian-Jewish origin, took over the leadership of the depot. He was considered especially qualified because he knew several Slavic languages, and thanks to his profession, he had valuable knowledge of the conservation and restoration of paper. With the help of his assistant, Corporal Reuben Sami, who had been trained as a librarian in Jerusalem, Bencowitz's greatest achievement was to establish a novel sorting system. The Western European holdings had been relatively easy to restitute due to successful cooperation with the national authorities and institutions of origin and the depot staff's mastery of the languages necessary to identify them. The sorting and return of the extensive library holdings of the many private and institutional collections from Eastern and southeastern Europe, meanwhile, proved far more difficult. Often the German staff was unable to identify them. Bencowitz hoped to improve and simplify work routines through the classification of ex libris stamps, found in most books, which provided information on their origin. Within two months, lists were drawn up featuring photographs of these stamps. They were sorted according to country and could easily be checked against the books. This meant that even untrained assistants who were unable to decipher the titles could allocate individual volumes to specific institutions and names. In addition to their practical import, the catalogs produced in this way also had symbolic value. They contained the often ornate stamps and symbols of more than four thousand private individuals and institutions in thirty-five different languages. More than two-thirds of these stamps indicated Jewish provenance. They were a testament to the rich book culture of Jewish Europe before the Nazi annihilation and reflected the vast radius of Nazi raids.[60] In addition to Sami, Bencowitz managed to engage the few Jewish experts intermittently available to him at the depot in this work, including the aforementioned Maurice Liber and the American-Jewish historian Koppel S. Pinson, director of education and culture at the Joint. In this role, the latter did his best to supply the surviving Jews in the displaced persons camps (DP camps) with books for schooling and for cultural and religious purposes. He regularly visited the depot to obtain books for the camp libraries while concurrently supporting Bencowitz's work. The American military rabbi Isaiah Rackovsky contributed here too, working at the depot between March and June 1946. Bencowitz provided both Pinson and Rackovsky with their own offices to evaluate and sort through materials in Hebrew and Yiddish that were particularly hard to identify. Ernst Grumach was also involved in the identification of ex libris, particularly those of German book collectors. During his time as a forced laborer in the RSHA's looted collection, he had gathered information on those who had been stolen from, their books, and their fates, which he now made available to the MFA&A. His reports reveal both the vast scale of the raids and their role in the Nazis' anti-Jewish policies.[61] He helped match ex libris stamps with individuals and provided information on the person's status if possible. The lists of names of former owners he compiled bear witness to the European Jews' history of persecution, murder, flight, and emigration from 1933 onward, as outlined in a brief excerpt:

> F27 Albert Forbiger was a well-known classical philologist of the mid nineteenth century. The books with this ex-libris are from the Vienna Community Library (Wiener Gemeindebibliothek); F49 is the writer Salomon Friedlaender, usually known by his pseudonym of "Mynoma," recently died in Paris; [. . .] K2 Robert Kaelter, was a rabbi in Danzig, his son formerly head of the Jewish school in Königsberg, now lives in Palestine, address to be ascertained through the Jewish Agency; [. . .] L16 Emil Lask, professor of philosophy at the University of Heidelberg, fell in the First World War. Entitled to inherit was his sister Helene Lask, who lived in my home until her evacuation. The rest of the library is in my possession; L61 Arthur Lilienthal, was department head in the Reich Association of Jews in Germany (Reichsvereinigung der Juden in Deutschland), lost in the East. Relatives of his wife live in South Africa (?), address to be ascertained with the help of Mr. Ewalt Koch, Nuremberg; [. . .] P33 Joachim Prinz, formerly a rabbi in Berlin, now in America; [. . .] Sch 22 Reinhold Scholem, proprietor of a printing works in Berlin, related to Prof. Gershom Scholem in Jerusalem; [. . .] W 60 is the former Königsberg professor of Egyptology Walter Wreszinsky; his widow lives in São Paulo, Brazil.[62]

These instructions were of great practical significance to the American MFA&A officers and their German assistants since they usually lacked all knowledge of the individuals involved.[63] With the help of such information and the catalogs initiated by Bencowitz, which were copied and handed out to every member of the sorting division, holdings could be identified far more quickly. But organizing the restitution of these books, most of which originated from Jewish households, communities, or cultural institutions in Germany, Austria, and Eastern Europe, was a far greater challenge for the American authorities compared to organizing the looted Western European collections.

Jewish Organizations in Offenbach

Holdings whose legal status was unclear and whose owners or inheritors often proved impossible to ascertain remained at the depot at first.

The problem of identification was also pressing because the depot's staff struggled to establish former owners due to their lack of Hebrew and Yiddish. According to an MFA&A memorandum, in June 1946, more than one million books, manuscripts, and archival materials of Jewish origin were stored in Offenbach to which no formal claim had yet been made and that faced an uncertain future.[64] In an attempt to resolve these problems, Bencowitz frequently deliberated with relevant staff in the American military government, Jewish representatives, and members of the MFA&A. A number of ideas were developed on the best approach to this material. The key actors agreed that the holdings ought to be relocated in toto in order to keep them together outside of Germany to the benefit of Jews as a collectivity.[65] But it was to be two more years before the fate of these collections was fully resolved.

In the interim, Bencowitz and his successors focused on the restitution of uncontroversial items. By mid-1948, therefore, apart from the successful restoration of Western European collections, just two significant transfers of material had been made. Both were down to the initiative of Jewish organizations. The first involved the loan of less valuable unidentifiable books and ritual objects to DP camps in the American occupation zone, while the second centered on the salvage of YIVO holdings from Vilna that had made it to the depot. For the loan of books and Judaica, the American judge Simon Rifkind came into play. He worked as an adviser on Jewish affairs to the American forces and the military government from October 1945 to March 1946. In January 1946, Rifkind approached the deputy military governor Lucius D. Clay and asked him to help the Joint provide Jewish survivors in the transit camps with religious, pedagogical, and fiction books from the collections in Offenbach.[66] The military government had previously rejected identical requests by the Joint, prompting Rifkind to discuss the matter with Clay in person. He emphasized how poorly equipped the DP camps were beyond the physical and sanitary necessities, highlighting the camp residents' need to read. Therefore, he proposed the assembly of a team of experts under the auspices of the Joint to select books from Frankfurt and Offenbach. This team should be composed of Koppel Pinson; the rabbi Alexander Rosenberg, director of the Joint's religious division; and Samuel Sar, dean of Yeshiva College New York. After some hesitation, Clay approved the loaning of depot holdings on the proviso that material capable of restitution be excluded and clear lists of loans be compiled.[67]

As a senior member of staff at the Joint and member of the Commission on European Jewish Cultural Reconstruction (hereafter Commission) in New York—which championed the return of looted Jewish cultural assets and was soon to play a role in Offenbach as well—Pinson took charge of this project. He had initially assessed the collection in the Rothschild building but had not yet received approval for loans. He felt torn between his duty to provide the survivors with the books they needed and the fact that these books might eventually be lost to the broader Jewish community, as he explained to Hannah Arendt, with whom he corresponded frequently on Commission affairs. On the one hand, he observed Jewish camp residents' "craving" for books every day: "You should see with what zealous enthusiasm they pounce upon a book, what gleam of satisfaction and joy spreads over faces as they take a Hebrew or Yiddish book in their hands." On the other hand, he recognized the "responsibility we owe to world Jewry to see to it that proper disposition is made of all this material."[68] Nonetheless, Pinson decided to implement the proposed loans. After obtaining Clay's approval in January 1946, he helped Pomrenze select and sort a number of prayer books, religious law texts, and rabbinical volumes in addition to Yiddish and Hebrew fiction. In March 1946, he arranged the first loan of just under six thousand volumes, which were to be followed by more than thirteen thousand in April. Pinson repeatedly underlined the books' enthusiastic reception in the camps. Not only were the residents overwhelmed, but the camp's staff was able to do genuine educational and cultural work for the first time.[69] Full of gratitude for their successful collaboration, in late April 1946, Pinson wrote to Pomrenze just before the latter's departure: "Through your able und efficient organization and administration, through your intelligent understanding of all the problems involved and through your warm human sympathy you have made it possible for us to bring educational and cultural facilities to thousands of Jews who have hungered for such facilities for seven years."[70]

The Offenbach books were distributed to the DP camps in Bamberg, Belsen, Feldafing, Fürth, Landsberg, München-Neu-Freimann, Stuttgart, and Zeilsheim. As attested in numerous reports and memoirs, camp residents felt that books were as vital as food supplies.[71] Further, in September 1946, Bencowitz made sure that the Joint, now represented by Alexander Rosenberg, received fifty-one Torah scrolls for the Jewish New Year, which were distributed to various German Jewish and DP communities. The DPs themselves greatly appreciated the American authorities' efforts to cater to their intellectual and religious needs. Despite the huge challenges involved, on the initiative of a number of rabbis and the Joint, the first full postwar edition of the Talmud was published in 1948 by Winter Verlag in Heidelberg. This was formally presented to Lucius Clay, now military governor, in 1949. A dedication in the preface states,

> This edition of the Talmud is dedicated to the United States Army. The Army played a major role in the rescue of the Jewish people from total annihilation, and after the defeat of Hitler bore the major burden of sustaining the DPs of the Jewish faith. This special edition of the Talmud published in the very land where, but a short time ago, everything Jewish and of Jewish inspiration was anathema, will remain a symbol of the indestructibility of the Torah. The Jewish DPs will never forget the generous impulses and the unprecedented humanitarianism of the American forces, to whom they owe so much.[72]

But the cooperation between the depot and the Joint was not always harmonious. Later attempts to facilitate further loans met with obstructions and delays and raised tensions. Contrary to his assurances, Pinson had failed to compile precise inventory lists, obscuring the whereabouts of almost all of the twenty thousand volumes. Fulfilling the fears he had earlier expressed to Arendt, these books were now irretrievably lost to restitution. Like Pinson, the Joint had also sent Lucy Schildkret, known today under her married name of Dawidowicz, to Germany from New York in fall 1946 to carry out charitable work in the DP camps, and she took over Pinson's work in Offenbach in spring 1947. Her requests to get more books into the camps were met with an even more reluctant response. Key American officials had grown distrustful. After Bencowitz left the depot in winter 1946, his position was held for a brief period by the MFA&A officer Theodore A. Heinrich. He was succeeded by Joseph A. Horne, a civilian employee of the military government, in January 1947, who continued the negotiations with the Joint. In March 1947, he reported that Dawidowicz (still using her maiden name of Schildkret at the time) and Ernst Grumach had jointly selected books for lending, but the American administration was now far less accommodating.[73] In her reports to Max Weinreich, her superior and colleague in New York, Dawidowicz herself underlined her growing doubts that the books were in good hands at the Joint, even if they were desperately needed by DPs. There had, she felt, been too much personal enrichment, while not enough had been done to ensure the safety of the holdings.[74] As a result, just one more small loan was made in February 1948. This time it was the Board of Education and Culture that was borrowing the books. From February 1947 onward, this body established by the Joint, the Jewish Agency (JA), and the Central Committee of the Liberated Jews was responsible for all matters relating to culture and education in the DP camps.[75] The aforementioned loan provided the board with five thousand volumes in Yiddish, Hebrew, and German, which it distributed to Jews in need in the American occupation zone.[76] The debate on loans to DPs revealed a perceptual difference among those involved. Many of the international Jewish actors felt that safeguarding and salvaging the books and manuscripts over the long term was more important than provisioning destitute survivors in the transit camps. They feared that the few surviving printed works would be lost forever and were wary about exposing them to further danger by distributing them to camps in Germany that were earmarked for disbandment in the near future.

We can see how this belief in the great importance of saving books was translated into practical action if we look at the YIVO in New York. YIVO made the first successful request for restitution of Jewish property held at Offenbach that was not based on the territorial principle but allowed for the transfer of objects to the US. Initially opened in 1925 as a small division (the so-called Amerikaner Opteyl, the American department) of the institute established in Vilna the same year, following the German invasion of Poland, the German-Soviet partition, and the Nazis' subsequent seizure of the Vilna premises in 1941, the New York office had taken over the interim leadership of YIVO. This decision was at first disputed by the remaining staff in Vilna, but after the liberation of the city in 1944, it became increasingly clear that the institute and the world it represented had been utterly destroyed, so the New York division finally assumed all the headquarters' functions. It sought to preserve and commemorate the Vilna heritage and continue the work done there.[77] When founded in Vilna, YIVO symbolized Eastern European Jews' modernizing self-image and was regarded as an expression of a new Jewish historical consciousness that served as a substitute for religious Judaism.[78] During the second half of the 1920s, it rapidly developed into a lively locus of Jewish science and culture. Its most striking feature was its archive, unique to the region, which featured collections of historical documents, musical materials, books, manuscripts, and periodicals. YIVO's library with its more than forty thousand volumes not only housed the major scientific and literary writings as well as a press archive of ten thousand items in Yiddish; its archive also contained a vast collection of sources and items gathered by hundreds of so-called *zamlers*—individuals who voluntarily assembled materials of all sorts from their Jewish communities in order to preserve them for historical research. It was its unique setup that made YIVO famous as "the temple of Yiddish scholarship."[79] It served as a "national university, language academy, and library for a stateless Yiddish speaking Jewry,"[80] and its staff engaged in history, psychology, linguistics, ethnography, sociology, and literature, leading to many important publications. It also housed a bibliographic center that produced a registry of Yiddish printed materials.[81] Lucy Dawidowicz considered YIVO's work the realization of the Jewish historian Simon Dubnow's 1891 call to his Jewish contemporaries to "collect material for the construction of a history of the Jews in Poland and Russia" in order to preserve the Eastern European Jews' heritage.[82] What Dubnow sought to promote was collective work on the Jewish historical memory, which prompted his concern for the safeguarding of sources and documents. It was to this task that YIVO later devoted itself.[83] On a personal level too, Dubnow was an important figure for the newly established institute in Vilna. He attended the founding meeting of its "Historical Section" and was a key reference point for the Institute's self-understanding. After the Second World War, Dubnow's call for the securing of material and sources to safeguard the achievements and traditions of Eastern European Jewish culture took on an even deeper, and tragic, significance. The Eastern European archives and libraries had been almost entirely destroyed or plundered, while he himself had been murdered in Riga.[84]

In the summer of 1941, the ERR established one of its Eastern European centers in the YIVO building. Little by little, under the leadership of Nazi theologian Johannes Pohl, all the institute's holdings were inspected. Due to his knowledge of Hebrew, Pohl rapidly gained a reputation within the German Reich as an expert on Jewish literature and thus on "Judenforschung," or research on the Jews, and his work was mandated by the library of the Institute for Research on the Jewish Question in Frankfurt.[85] The YIVO collection was first shown in a vilifying propaganda exhibition entitled "The Culture of the Enemy" before being transferred to Frankfurt.[86] All the remaining, rejected parts of the holdings in Vilna were to be burned or misused for other purposes. During the associated operation, conscripted Jews such as Abraham Sutzkever from the Vilna ghetto, who had to carry out the sorting and shipping for the Germans, risked their lives to launch the campaign of salvage described in the introduction. Their commitment spared valuable objects and writings from destruction, including texts by Leo Tolstoy and Hayim Nahman Bialik. Most ritual objects, works of art, and books of Jewish provenance in Vilna were threatened by the Nazis' mania for destruction. Only smaller portions, originating in YIVO and the venerable Strashun community library,[87] made it to Berlin and Frankfurt. The Paper Brigade, which, in addition to Sutzkever, included the journalist and ghetto library chief Herman Kruk, the writer Shmerke Kaczerginski, and the linguist and translator Selig Kalmanowitsch, smuggled as many of the cultural treasures as possible from the institute to the ghetto, burying them in the ground and hiding them in walls, cellars, and caves.[88] After the war, the YIVO holdings were scattered across a number of locations in Vilna, making their discovery and recovery a laborious and painstaking process. After tracing most of them, Sutzkever managed to send certain volumes and objects to Western Europe and America in 1945, but many of the individual collections that had remained in the city were confiscated by the Soviets and were not returned to YIVO until 1996.

The Vilna YIVO holdings that had been sent to Frankfurt were later cached in the nearby town of Hungen along with other plundered materials. Before the war was over, Max Weinreich, head of the YIVO in New York—who had himself worked for years as the research director in the Vilna office but had managed to escape to the United States—had begun his investigations into the surviving collections. In 1942, he started to correspond with the American State Department and various Jewish organizations.[89] Shortly after the end of the war in Europe, he was already in a position to inform the American authorities that he believed there was YIVO property in Frankfurt, and he asserted the New York institute's claim to its restitution. Toward the end of June 1945, the military government's reparation, deliveries, and restitution division confirmed that YIVO books, manuscripts, and journals had been found in Hungen. A protracted discussion on the future of the collection now began between YIVO representatives in New York, especially Weinreich, and the American authorities, including Lucius Clay, who promised "careful consideration" of the case. At this point, there had been no official recognition of the institute in New York as the successor to that in Vilna. And in line with the legal conception outlined earlier, the city of Vilna was considered the claimant entitled to restitution. But officials in Offenbach, where all the holdings from Vilna had been sent, sought to delay their restitution to the city.[90]

In Offenbach, Koppel S. Pinson—and after him, Lucy Dawidowicz—tried to order and catalog these holdings within the Rosenberg material. During the sorting for the planned DP loan, they also sought to systematically scour the many volumes that could not be identified or were labeled "no owner" for books from Vilna. This blend of negotiations in the United States and practical initiatives at the depot ultimately proved successful. Two factors were crucial here. First, with the American authorities' approval, the YIVO in New York officially succeeded the Vilna institute. Second, the United States' decision not to recognize the Soviet Union's 1944 reoccupation of the Baltic countries also played an important role. This meant severing all diplomatic ties with the region, ultimately facilitating the authorized transfer of all the Vilna holdings to New York.[91] This included objects of Jewish provenance from Vilna in the Offenbach Depot that had been claimed by Polish restitution officers as Polish property. Given the decimated state of the Jewish communities there, their restitution to Poland was ultimately rejected by the American authorities. In Offenbach, it was once again Dawidowicz who expressed outrage at the possible transfer of material to Poland, thus helping prompt a reassessment. In a letter to Weinreich, she wrote, "There is some Polish major who wants all Polish publications (anything published in Poland) to be returned there. Horne asked me to tell him about Poland and I helped him maintain the opinion he already had, that there is no hope for renewed cultural life in Poland. There may be a Jewish community there, but he feels that no one will ever make use of the material."[92]

On June 18, 1947, under the supervision of Seymour Pomrenze—who had gone back to work in the National Archives in Washington in 1947 but had returned to Offenbach in June the same year specifically to help salvage the YIVO collections—a start was made on shipping just under eighty thousand objects via Bremen to New York. Weinreich had made contact with Pomrenze through the latter's brother, who was on the YIVO executive board, and had asked for his help because of his knowledge of the situation in Offenbach and his contacts with the American authorities.[93] In the course of the negotiations, however, YIVO requested more than just those materials directly attributable to it. It also filed claims to the Offenbach collections of the S. Anski Jewish Historical and Ethnographical Society of Vilna, the Jewish Teachers Institute of Vilna, and the Strashun Library in Vilna based on the argument that YIVO had enjoyed a close relationship with those institutions in every respect. Weinreich also claimed books from the private collections of S. Anski, Shlomo Bastomski, Judah Leib Cahan, Simon Dubnow, Selig Kalmanowitsch, Pinchas Kon, Alfred Landau, Moshe Lerer, Zalman Reyzen, and his own library, which he had been forced to leave behind in Vilna. Once again, he gained the support of Dawidowicz, who urged the senior depot staff to transfer all the books from Vilna to New York since most recovered parts of the collection had previously been entrusted to YIVO. The institute's staff argued that private libraries in Vilna had often been bequeathed or promised to YIVO in the 1930s prior to their owners' flight or deportation. The Community Library of Vilna, for example, was already considered part of the YIVO collection during the war. Dawidowicz also tried to back up her argument by stating that as late as 1940, YIVO staff had tried in vain to send the Strashun and YIVO libraries to Weinreich—who was then in Copenhagen and about to leave Europe—so he could escort them safely to America.[94] Ultimately, Joseph Horne and the military government were persuaded to embrace this comprehensive approach to the Vilna holdings, which were sent to New York and reunited in YIVO. After the successes in Offenbach, Dawidowicz and Pomrenze also went to Prague in order to recover further

YIVO holdings in German caches and have them shipped to New York, but this operation failed. They were able to locate YIVO's newspaper collection and other parts of the library in the vicinity of Prague, but they could not arrange for their transfer to the United States.[95]

Still, all in all, 420 cases of material were saved from dispersion in Offenbach and eventually sent to New York. Those involved saw this restitution to YIVO as a crucial step toward making a new beginning after the disaster of the war and as a milestone in Jews' efforts to start their lives again. The books were meant to preserve the memory of Jewish Vilna—regarded as "Lithuania's Jerusalem" before its violent destruction—in a special place where they would be accessible to contemporaries and secured for future generations. In a later essay, Lucy Dawidowicz poignantly described the meaning ascribed to their salvage: "When I first arrived in February 1947 at the Offenbach Archival Depot, a considerable portion of YIVO property had already been identified. [. . .] when my work was successfully completed [. . .] I witnessed the removal from the depot of some 420 cases of books and archives to the YIVO-Institute in New York. That experience was like a dream come true. [. . .] Finally, I had, in a very tangible way, rescued a part of Vilna, even if it consisted just of inanimate objects—books, mere pieces of paper, the tatters and shards of a civilization."[96]

Heirless Books

Most subsequent initiatives at the Offenbach Depot turned out to be far more complicated. Following the restitutions made during its first few years, the depot continued to house a vast number of objects and books of Jewish provenance whose exact origin and ownership had not been ascertained. The influx of materials from and to Eastern Europe or the Soviet-controlled zone in Germany caused particular problems. Cooperation with the Soviet authorities was limited, and in most cases, officials in the Soviet zone neither restituted the looted items found there nor handed them over to Offenbach. Instead, the Soviet government's so-called Trophy Brigades often took them to the Soviet Union to compensate for Soviet losses. Many works of art and books, regardless of their origin and earlier dispossession and theft, were transported to Minsk and Moscow and then dispatched throughout the Soviet Union.

Following the tremendous civilian and material losses incurred on Soviet territory during the Second World War as a result of the bloody German raids, many Soviets regarded this policy as entirely appropriate.[97] Officially, heirless Jewish assets and property in the Soviet realm were distributed to the various groups of victims of the Nazi regime—the disregard for their Jewish provenance dovetailing with the socialist ideal of neutralized ethnic affiliation. The Soviets hardly recognized any Jewish claim from western countries and refused to cooperate with most international Jewish actors or organizations, discrediting their activities as a front for American interests.[98]

Despite the increasing gulf between the Soviet and American perspectives, Soviet restitution officers were accredited to the Offenbach Archival Depot to identify stolen items of Soviet provenience there. The summer of 1946 saw the transfer of 1,055 crates of material from Offenbach to the Soviet Union. These contained the holdings of Communist Party headquarters and libraries, collections from city and university libraries, and Jewish property from former centers of Jewish life such as Odessa, Minsk, and Kiev. In total, as the depot's monthly report of August 1946 reveals, the restituted objects came from 310 libraries and institutions and 36 private households in the Soviet Union, while holdings from 226 Ukrainian and 161 Belarusian institutions were handed over to the Soviet officers at the same time.[99]

In the summer of that year, on assignment for the Hebrew University of Jerusalem, Gershom Scholem was making a research trip through Europe to assess the situation of looted cultural property for the university's Otzrot HaGolah ("Treasures of the Diaspora") committee. In this capacity, he also spent some months in Offenbach. As it happened, Scholem was working at the depot between June and August 1946 and was witness to the various transfers of crates of books to the Soviet Union and the preparatory work for transfers to Czechoslovakia and Poland.[100] He was convinced that the crates contained a huge number of items of Jewish ownership and was to become sharply critical of all restitution to Soviet-controlled areas. To raise awareness of what he believed to be an unjust and dangerous decision, in June 1946 he wrote a letter to the famous rabbi Leo Baeck in London, who he hoped might make a public intervention: "So far as I can tell, the American policy basically aims to return the vestiges of the Jewish collections, particularly those in Offenbach, to the governments of those countries where they originated—and not, say, to the Jewish people or their representatives. This means that a great many books will disappear back into Russia and Poland. We mustn't have any illusions about the future fate of these collections."[101] He made no bones about his preferred approach to restitution: "To put it in a nutshell, we believe that wherever the Jews migrate to, their books should go with them."[102] And he articulated similar views to officials in Offenbach. According to a report that summed up a conversation between Bencowitz, Scholem, and Pinson on the situation of the Eastern European holdings, Scholem expressed his dismay at the process of their restitution. It was quite certain, he stated here, that "books from Russia, including Jewish property" were being restituted to the Soviet Union without further consideration. Moreover, he believed that the situation of the "border countries, from Estonia to Slovakia," was just as difficult. While no clear decision had yet been made, there was a danger of even more extensive restitutions of Jewish property to the countries it had been stolen from. "We can't send Jewish books back to a country in which Jews are still being murdered," Scholem argued. But Washington, he contended, had as yet considered no alternative solution. Another problem was the impending transfer of responsibility for restitution to Germany. He feared that large sections of the collections would be "surreptitiously taken by the Germans for their libraries."[103] Scholem's misgivings are also evident in the travel report he completed upon his return. Here he focused on the situation in Czechoslovakia, highlighting that more than a quarter of a million precious Jewish books from Berlin had been cached in castles in northern Bohemia and faced possible plunder and theft. Neither American nor Jewish organizations had concerned themselves with these holdings as yet. Scholem saw a need for urgent action, but he also expressed his worries about the situation in Offenbach in general. In particular, he criticized the lack of special training for the German staff responsible for sorting through the holdings. Frustrated, he suggested that the American approach to restitution was helping scatter Jewish materials "to the four winds."[104] Scholem was convinced that the territorial principle should be annulled when it came to certain Jewish cases, demanding "that all collections whose legal owners no longer exist or can't be identified be delivered over to Jewish institutions," most probably the Hebrew University.[105]

Not much later, Weinreich and Dawidowicz addressed the issues emphasized by Scholem regarding the restitution of YIVO holdings. As they attempted to transfer all items from Vilna to New York, they too highlighted the grave consequences for global Jewry likely to flow from any return of materials to Poland or the Soviet Union. In a letter from May 1947, Dawidowicz tried to convince Joseph Horne of their point of view:

> We know that most Jewish institutions in Central and Eastern Europe were completely wiped out. Therefore it must be acknowledged that the establishment of individual ownership of books, especially from Eastern Europe, is, roughly speaking, 90 percent wasted effort. Large quantities of books have already been restituted to Poland and the Soviet Union, both countries where the Jewish population was largely decimated and where the revival of Jewish cultural institutions and the flourishing of Jewish culture are problematic. It is the opinion of the undersigned that the effort expended for further possible identification of property belonging to either country now is completely out of proportion to the ultimate use to which these books may be put, if returned.[106]

Jewish actors at the depot broadly agreed that there was limited scope for successful restitution in Eastern Europe. They anxiously followed reports of anti-Semitic riots in many places and became increasingly aware that war and annihilation had almost totally destroyed the Jewish infrastructure. Under these circumstances, the return of cultural property seemed out of the question. There were virtually no intact communities left that might have administered and used them. Rather than being available to Jews, venerable, centuries-old treasures were likely to disappear into state institutions.

But it was not just the collections from Eastern Europe that caused problems for depot staff. The large quantity of German and Austrian property—often taken or stolen from Jews before the war had started—also represented a major challenge to traditional jurisprudence. Their return was labeled "internal restitution." Hitherto international law had featured no regulations on states' robbery of their own citizens, so new solutions were required to avoid Jewish assets being transferred to the German or Austrian successor states. Senior staff at the depot and MFA&A representatives discussed various ways of resolving this problem. Some advocated for the large-scale transfer of these collections to the remaining or reestablished Jewish communities on German territory. Others called for the establishment of a site outside Germany to house the holdings as a whole. Another proposed solution was the creation of an international Jewish trust and thus the transfer of responsibility to representatives of the Jewish collective. Following several rounds of negotiations, the American military government finally concluded that the reestablished communities—whose size and composition no longer reflected pre-1933 realities—could gain no benefit from the remaining cultural property.[107] As many representatives of Jewish organizations outside Germany underlined again and again, the vast majority of German Jews who had survived Nazism saw their future in Palestine, the United States, and the United Kingdom rather than Germany.

In their efforts to secure cultural objects for Jewish communities and institutions abroad, actors in Offenbach found legal and illegal ways to respond to the Western Allies' indecisiveness and their jurisprudence, which seemed out of sync with Jewish realities after 1945. Gershom Scholem initially took an illegal approach, organizing the secret transfer of what he considered to be the most valuable documents and texts from Offenbach to Palestine. The five crates he filled mostly contained Hebrew-language rabbinical literature of the eighteenth and nineteenth centuries, including responsa, prayer texts, legal texts, Talmud manuscripts, commentaries, and exegetical writings from all over Europe as well as the death registers of several Jewish communities.[108] Herbert Friedman, chaplain in the American army and Joint employee, assisted Scholem in this cloak-and-dagger operation. On December 30, 1946, he collected Scholem's crates in the name of Koppel Pinson, though the latter was not involved in the proceedings, on the pretext that they were loans for DPs; no suspicions were raised. Friedman first took the crates from Offenbach to Paris in a Joint delivery truck. There, however, JA staff—responsible for logistics and the transport of Jewish property to Palestine—refused to accept them for fear of creating conflict with the American authorities. But they indicated to Friedman that he could add the books to a shipment containing Chaim Weizmann's private library, which was being sent from Antwerp to Haifa. Friedman did just that, separating out the books upon arrival at port and having them delivered to the Hebrew University on Mount Scopus in Jerusalem. The affair soon came to light. The American military government's property division, convinced that hugely valuable material had been taken out the country, demanded its return. However, after interventions from the army chaplain Philip Bernstein, who had succeeded Rifkind and served as adviser to the military governor on Jewish affairs between May 1946 and August 1947, and American-Jewish interest groups, particularly the JCR, Clay personally persuaded the authorities to allow the holdings to remain under the control of the American consulate in Palestine. Eventually they were transferred to the Jewish National and University Library in Jerusalem.[109] Scholem never had to answer to a court martial, and Friedman got off with a warning, though he resigned from his military rabbinate. Isaac Bencowitz, then head of the depot, was accused of helping the pair. He had himself been in Palestine in November and December 1946, where he had met with Scholem to discuss the transfer of the crates. In an attempt to explain and defend their actions, Scholem later reported that Bencowitz and the others involved "acted in good faith and in the best interest as to the preservation of these valuable documents of the Jewish past."[110] Shortly after the affair, Bencowitz left the Offenbach Depot and returned to the United States. Years later, Friedman described these events in his autobiographical account, *Roots of the Future*:

> These manuscripts, remnants of our people's past, at risk of destruction in the present, had been saved for the future, and I had been privileged to play a pivotal role in the adventure. [. . .] And so, in the end, the story does conclude happily. Rescued from the Nazi trap, brought to British Palestine, carried through the fire of the birth of Israel [. . .] and free at last, the manuscripts seemed like living beings, their course paralleling that of the Jewish people itself.[111]

Much like Dawidowicz and many other witnesses to proceedings at the Offenbach Depot, Friedman drew a parallel between the history of these materials and the fate of the European Jews and underlined the treasure's significance to the future of Jewish life and learning. It was this perspective, which most contemporaries involved shared, that allowed them to interpret this "theft" as the salvage of endangered objects for the sake of the Jewish collective and thus to view it as morally justified.[112]

In addition to YIVO and Joint staff, a number of Jewish politicians, diplomats, and representatives sought to preserve as many objects as possible by legal means. Members of nearly all the leading Jewish organizations active in Europe immediately after the war—envoys from the Joint, the JA, the American Jewish Conference (AJConf), and German Jewish groupings—visited the depot to find out how the work was proceeding and help shape the future of its holdings. Visitors included the French historian Léon Poliakov; Rabbi Leo Baeck, at Scholem's prompting; key actors in the restitution and indemnifications negotiations with Germany such as Saul Kagan and Max Kreutzberger; and a number of rabbis working for the Joint or within the American military and administrative apparatus. The American authorities ultimately responded to the realities of the situation and pressure from the various stakeholders, taking steps to improve the legal situation for Jewish claimants. In November 1947, the military government ratified law no. 59 on the restitution of identifiable assets. It included the requisite paragraphs permitting nonstate trusts to claim heirless items and assets, subverting the traditional territorial principle. The American military government initially stood alone in this endeavor—matching laws for the French and British zones came into force only later, and it proved impossible to agree on common interzonal rules in the Allied Control Council.[113]

This change in jurisdiction finally enabled the American actors at the collecting points to process numerous holdings. In February 1949, on the basis of this new legal framework, the JCR was officially authorized as the trustee for heirless, nonidentifiable Jewish cultural assets in the American occupation zone. Now in charge of these objects, the JCR made them available to Jewish communities and cultural centers worldwide.

In June 1946, the Offenbach Depot had housed more than one million books and ritual objects with an uncertain future. These included several thousand Torah scrolls, which were often too damaged for ritual purposes but served as reminders of their destroyed communities of origin. In legal terms, their future too was long shrouded in uncertainty, and in August 1946, Bencowitz proposed their transfer to the JTS in New York: "Because of the deep religious feeling attached to these scrolls made deeper and more tragic because of the association of this collection with the Jewish tragedy in Europe it should not be treated merely as property. It is recommended that excessive legality be dispensed with in favor of an early restoration of these toroth to competent authorities [. . .]. It is suggested that they be shipped to the Jewish Theological College [*sic*] in New York."[114] His proposal, including the idea of evading the letter of the law to achieve a solution appropriate to these objects' symbolic value, had to await the establishment of the JCR. It took charge of numerous Torah scrolls, silver objects, menorahs, and textiles from ruined European synagogues and distributed them across Israel, the United States, and the United Kingdom and, on a smaller scale, South America, South Africa, Western Europe, and Canada.[115]

As we saw earlier, in addition to the complicated legal situation of heirless and unidentifiable objects of Jewish provenance, it was their inspection, identification, and cataloging that caused the greatest problems. Now and then, the depot managed to attract experts like Dawidowicz and Scholem, who went out of their way to help read and classify the Judaica and Hebraica. But it was not until the appointment of the rabbi Severin Rochmann from Zeilsheim in March 1948 and of Arnold Schwimmer, a rabbinical student at the Offenbach Vocational College, in April the same year that this work was placed on an ongoing and stable basis. Under the leadership of Joseph Horne, the processing of the remaining Jewish material, almost all of which was hard to identify, was pursued with renewed vigor. By now, the process of restitution to countries and specific institutions was largely complete, and the depot personnel, made up of German employees from Frankfurt or Offenbach and DPs from nearby Zeilsheim, was reduced to a maximum of thirty individuals. In February 1949, James Kimball took over for Horne as director, and in March, he oversaw the first transfers of material to the JCR. He also supervised the closing of the depot, which was to be finalized in late June 1949. Remaining material was taken to the central collecting point in Wiesbaden for further processing.

Between March 1946 and June 1949, the depot's staff returned around 1.4 million books and objects to fourteen different countries; transferred 700,000 books to the Prussian State Library (Preußische Staatsbibliothek) in Berlin; dispatched 80,000 books, periodicals, archival holdings, and objects to the YIVO in New York; handed over 250,000 volumes to public authorities, military government offices, and German institutions; and sent around 80,000 objects to the JCR. Their Herculean efforts managed to reverse a small portion of the unprecedented looting campaign carried out by Rosenberg's task force and others.

Books as Vessels of Memory

From the outset, the Offenbach Depot attracted huge interest among Jewish contemporaries, who expressed enormous appreciation for its work; its impact and significance went far beyond its official purpose. This was essentially due to the objects it housed. Following the Jewish scriptural tradition, books and the written word always played an outstanding role in the construction of the Jewish collective self-understanding and identity. The German Jewish writer Lion Feuchtwanger neatly summed up the core of this phenomenon, which found its most iconic expressions in the notion of the Jews as "People of the Book" and Heinrich Heine's postulate of the book as "a portable fatherland": "They had no state, holding them together, no country, no soil, no king, no form of life in common. If in spite of this, they were one, more one than all the other peoples of the world, it was the Book that sweated them into unity. [. . .] They had dragged the Book with them through two thousand years. It was to them race, state, home, inheritance and possession."[116] What Feuchtwanger is referring to is above all the sacred text, the Torah, as the foundation of Jewish life and belonging, which served the scattered Jewish communities for centuries as a shared space and shared frame of reference. Under conditions of modernization, this framework expanded and became permeable—it was not just *the book*, but *books* that now functioned as a place of collective identity shared by all Jews. Propelled by periods of Jewish emancipation in Europe and ongoing secularization, the relationship of this "obstinately bookish people" to the text also became more worldly.[117] The scientification of thought ended the sacred text's role as the sole means of interpreting reality and history, ushering in a transformation: "The reverence previously felt for the sacred books was transferred to secular texts; the role that the collective religious service had played for the devout Jew was now played by the public library."[118] By the cusp of the twentieth century, the Jews' increasingly diverse textual territory had extended far beyond religious exegesis and laws to include a wide literary canon. Against this background, then, the book was both a vessel of the collectivity's history and memory and a substitute for a shared territory or homeland. These layers of meaning came to the fore in the Offenbach Depot in a special way. First, given the books' importance to questions of collective belonging, their preservation was regarded as vital to the collective's survival and its future. Every book that could be salvaged evoked a sense that Jewish tradition and history were being secured and carried on into the future. Second, the books assembled in Offenbach bore marks of the European Jews' annihilation. Every single volume in the depot conveyed the history of its origins and owners and the experience of Nazi depredation. Like monuments of remembrance, these books functioned as the symbolic gravestones of their owners murdered without a trace.[119] In this dual sense, the depot in Offenbach was both a graveyard or a "mortuary of books," as Lucy Dawidowicz put it,[120] and a stimulus to surviving Jews to *return to history* and reestablish their cultural life after 1945.

Both elements underpinned the devoted salvaging of books after the Second World War and the striking symbolic charge of this endeavor. In his essay "The Jewish Love of Books" (1944), the British-Jewish historian Cecil Roth—who played a critical role in the Jewish debate on the salvage of cultural property in the 1940s—bore witness to the existential meaning already ascribed to books during this time of attacks and destruction: "If anything excels the brutality with which Jews were treated during the past ages, it is the brutality with which their literature was tracked down, condemned, burned, destroyed."[121] Here the looting and destruction of books are virtually equated with the crimes committed against people. As the wave of destruction in Eastern Europe was reaching its apogee, though Roth was of course not fully aware of its scale, he resolved to do his utmost to ensure the recovery and restitution of stolen Jewish books, a clear sign of the threat many Jews perceived in the Nazis' systematic theft of cultural property. Later Holocaust historian Philip Friedman saw things in much the same way, referring to the "greatest book pogrom in Jewish history" and underlining the Nazis' "implacable warfare against the Jewish book."[122]

Leo Löwenthal, literary sociologist of the Frankfurt School, minced no words in describing the substance of the Nazi robbery and destruction of Jewish textual culture. For him, it amounted to the "expunging of memory, the expunging of the specific, the declaration of war on the individual, the relapse from the continuity of meaningful history into nothingness, chaos, and finally the transformation of historical space into brute nature."[123] This drastic interpretation helps us understand the urge to restitute books, on however limited a scale. It was the desire to reappropriate history and memory.

These examples reveal the significance attributed to the depot by most Jews involved in its work. Those who came to Offenbach felt as though they were standing amid the remnants of Jewish cultural life in Europe. Isaac Bencowitz described this immediate impression in his diary:

> I would walk into the loose document room to take a look at the things there and find it impossible to tear myself away from the fascinating pile of letters, folders and little personal bundles. [. . .] Books from the library which once had been in some distant town in Poland, or an extinct yeshiva. There was something sad and mournful about these volumes . . . as if they were whispering a tale of yearning and hope long since obliterated. I would pick up a badly worn Talmud with hundreds of names of many generations of students and scholars. Where were they now? Or rather, where were their ashes? [. . .] How dear all these tokens of love and gentle care must have been to someone and now they were so useless, destined to be burned, buried, or thrown away. All these things made my blood boil.[124]

The above-cited description of the depot's history by Severin Rochmann and Peter Leinekugel, with its highly idiosyncratic language and narrative form, also conveys the different attributions of meaning to this place, the books, their story and the possibility of salvaging them. In this account, the books in Offenbach are personalized. They are given faces and characteristics as their fate merges into that of their former owners:

> There were books from every part of both the old and new worlds. Some were clearly of an impressive age. One could see that many had been subject to regular use. But also that many had suffered a great deal [. . .]. While some books had been clothed in festive garb, nicely bound in vellum or leather, others were clad in simple working clothes. Their bindings were of plain cardboard, their corners and covers testifying to the passage of time or rough treatment. It was not just the Jews as people who were

despised and persecuted during the Hitler decade. The Jewish book too had to endure persecution; locked up in barns and cellars, it was exposed to all weathers. If this book could talk, it too would have plenty of sad tales to tell. Wrenched from the hands of those who bent over its pages of an evening by candlelight, when most people were at rest, and, poring over its lines, sought to grasp the wisdom of its teachings. Chucked into a sack or hurled into a vehicle, it later fell into the hands of those who regarded it with nothing but contempt and prejudice. Out of this book they wished to forge a sword to smite its previous owners. It was to serve its enemies. The book suffered the indignity of having sections and lines torn out to be falsely and misleadingly reprinted elsewhere.

Rochmann and Leinekugel tell of the Nazis' destruction and misuse of the books, but they also convey their hopes of a better future, which they associated with the restoration of the books in Offenbach: "But the suffering eventually came to an end. Retrieved from the cellars and dungeons, it saw the light again and is once again enjoying the fresh air and the care of those who wish to save it for later centuries, who wish to help it, if possible, find its earlier owner again or at least to fulfill the purpose for which it was created, namely to justify the glory of God, to acknowledge the path that leads to him, to promulgate that which helps human beings achieve peace."[125] For them, the books in Offenbach held out the prospect of the survival of Jewish traditions after the disaster. Their restitution became a powerful act that went far beyond the political-legal context. Rabbi Herbert Friedman evaluated the events at the depot in much the same way, expressing his euphoria in his account of the transfer of manuscripts and texts to Palestine, carried out in collaboration with Scholem: "Books! They form the soul of the Jewish people [. . .]. *Saving those books amounts to saving the People of the Book*, for the intellectual and spiritual messages they contain are the best guarantee of the people's continued physical existence."[126]

"Saving those books amounts to saving the People of the Book"—it is hard to imagine a clearer expression of the meaning attributed to the Offenbach operations. Friedman's perception was not based just on the notion of the constitutive force of text and writing in Judaism. An anthropological element also shines through. The tremendous efforts made by all those involved in the saving of books are an expression of the fusion, in spirit, of object and person. The lifeless books were ascribed human qualities, and for many, their return was a substitute for the impossible task of saving their former owners. In autobiographical remarks on her work in Offenbach, Lucy Dawidowicz describes this transference with great precision, underlining that saving the YIVO holdings helped her better process the trauma associated with her inability to get her friends and acquaintances out of Vilna: "The possibility that I might play a role, however minor, in the return of the YIVO library reawakened my old rescue fantasies. I no longer dreamed of rescuing Rivele and Kalman [friends from Vilna] from the flames of war, but now I had become obsessed with saving as many remnants as I could of the Vilna YIVO's books and manuscripts. I wanted to have a share in restoring them to their transplanted home in New York."[127]

Against this background, it comes as no surprise that the goal was to preserve every book, no matter how damaged it might be, and indeed every piece of paper originating from former Jewish collections the American soldiers found. For the Jewish staff in Offenbach, it would have seemed like another crime had they not made every effort to restore the books. They were to vouch for the memory of the dead, to give them back a place and thus hold out the prospect of a future. In other words, these remaining volumes were to secure the survival of the Jews as a collectivity.

The books' commemorative function was the second key element in debating the significance of their salvage. Once again, Dawidowicz captured this with great precision: "Since the Jewish culture which had flourished in Eastern Europe had been wiped out and since it was unlikely that Hebrew and Yiddish books would ever again be published there, every surviving book from that world had become a historical document, a cultural artefact, specimen, and testament of a murdered civilization."[128] A single sentence in a Swiss Jewish newspaper put this perception in a nutshell: "The fate of these millions of stolen and now retrieved books represents the fate of the European Jewry."[129] The idea that the Offenbach operation was of a special character and involved a profound obligation to commemorate the Holocaust was also articulated by American MFA&A officials such as Leslie Poste, who underscored that "the Depot operates as an American trusteeship for the millions of Jews destroyed by the Nazis. Through the depot have passed the remnants of age-old cultures, and particularly of a culture which survived despite the vicissitudes of interminable persecutions and periodic massacres. These books and objects were what was left of the hundreds of Jewish institutions of learning, of Jewish communities, wiped out by the Holocaust of Hitlerism. Few can fathom the depth of the Jewish tragedy of which these remnants stood as sad memorial."[130] But what shines through in his account is not just an awareness of the American military government's great responsibility to protect the Jewish cultural heritage. Poste also emphasizes that, in line with how the Americans saw themselves, the depot was to function as a trustee for the annihilated Jews—a role, as we have seen, that was later taken over by the JCR as a Jewish political advocacy group. The senior American depot staff's keen awareness of the legitimacy of the restitutions, and of the significance of the recovered assets to the Jewish collective, helped make the depot a veritable site of commemoration despite its brief existence. It was a *lieu de memoire* because here, in the form of cultural property, European Jewries' memory and history took on material form and also because it served as a disturbing monument to the destructive power of Nazi rule. It constituted no less than a temporary archive housing the Jewish cultural and spiritual heritage.[131]

The books stored in the depot not only conserved stocks of knowledge, experience, and memory but also conveyed the diverse histories of their places of origin, home institutions, and owners. For observers, the collection in the Offenbach Depot seemed to embody what Walter Benjamin had described when characterizing book collections as a "magic encyclopedia" of ages and landscapes, traditions and destinies.[132] And yet the nature of the place also shattered this constitutive connection between collection and memory since it differed profoundly from any traditional archive or library. The depot existed for just three years and was composed of the remnants of Nazi looting raids. Therefore, what it represented above all was death and annihilation. The objects were remnants of a world that had been brutally destroyed. They constituted the material testimony to the fact that the Holocaust had made it impossible to build on or reconstruct extinguished Jewish life. The trenchant semantic constructions of the Offenbach Depot highlight the efforts made to overcome this reality and create new meaning in an attempt to reestablish the continuity of history and a coherent historical narrative.[133] It was this need that prompted the frequent deployment of the trope of the "living book" and attempts to equate the saving of books and the saving of the Jewish collectivity, though this was a vision doomed to instant failure. Alongside moments of euphoria over the salvage of books, contemporary accounts are constantly pervaded by images of cemeteries, ghosts, death, and ashes. The multidirectional function attributed to the books remains unfulfilled. They can neither reconstruct past circumstances nor bridge the abyss opened up by the murder of six million Jews.

The collection in Offenbach had another innate quality that complicated the way this space was perceived. The objects had become part of a Nazi selection process that had determined their fate. Most of them were in Offenbach for a reason, Nazi strategic, ideological, and economic considerations having ensured their survival. This history too was inscribed in those parts of the looted collections that had evaded bombing, plunder, or concealment in caches and made it to Offenbach. The survival of a collection was rarely coincidental or arbitrary: The Nazis themselves had determined whether it was destroyed or confiscated. Joshua Starr, chief executive of the JCR in New York who worked at the Offenbach Depot from June 1948 to April 1949 on behalf of his organization, described this phenomenon: "Today when one handles a book stamped *Sichergestellt durch Einsatzstab RR*, he holds a mute witness of the final phase of a program designed to concentrate staggering facilities for the investigation of the Jewish past and present. [. . .] It is, as we shall see, largely to this bizarre program that we owe credit in the grim sense, for the survival of portions of Jewish property in central Europe."[134] Hannah Arendt later refers to the same paradox in her famous report *Eichmann in Jerusalem*, in which she describes the German authorities' painstaking approach to the looting and amassing of Jewish cultural property: "Incidentally, an eagerness to establish museums commemorating their enemies was very characteristic of the Nazis. During the war, several services competed bitterly for the honor of establishing anti-Jewish museums and libraries. We owe to this strange craze the salvage of many great cultural treasures of European Jewry."[135]

From a present-day perspective, it is not just the objects and their history that highlight the dimensions of the Nazi program of predation, and thus the scale of Nazi crimes as a whole, but also the progress reports produced by the depot administration in a monthly and later weekly rhythm. Lists were compiled, running to dozens of pages, of the names of looted institutions and individuals whose property was stored at Offenbach. Arranged alphabetically and by country of origin, these lists served chiefly as an ordering mechanism to make the restitution process as transparent as possible and facilitate the compilation of inventories. Beyond this practical function, the lists are of great historical value. Their stripped-down, catalog-like form provides a palpable sense of the systematic nature, geographical setting, and magnitude of Nazi cultural looting. And it is not just the looting that we find rendered so visible here—the underlying crimes are also evident at a glance. The eye scans down a seemingly endless series of names, libraries, and places that had been wiped out when these lists were compiled.[136] A similar impression emerges from the albums containing photographs of ex libris and stamps. What they represent is not so much continuity and order as a sense of emptiness—foregrounding the void created by the annihilation of the European Jews' cultural and spiritual worlds.

Between 1946 and 1949, an institution emerged in Offenbach that was to convey the complex challenges, possibilities, and aporias of Jewish memory-formation after the Holocaust.[137] It represented a place in which past, present, and future seemed to overlap. The objects there told of a Jewish world in Europe that was no more, and they resembled in their chaotic and fragmentary state the ruined continent of the present day. At the same time, restitution and distribution endowed them with a role in the future. The US-based JCR did its best to ensure and shape with the help of these objects a new, postwar Jewish cultural life. The next chapter explores these initiatives, which were intended to continue the work begun in Offenbach.

2

Envisioning a Future

American-Jewish Politics of Restitution

Negotiations during World War II

By the early 1940s, Jewish activists across the world had already begun to contemplate the issue of restorative justice in response to the Nazi terror. While the war raged on, the United States in particular saw the formation of a number of groups that dedicated themselves to different aspects of the Jewish condition in Europe. Virtually all individuals involved had one thing in common: they were focused on the future. Their priority was to prepare for the postwar order. It was the preconditions for Jewish participation in possible peace negotiations and the preparation of claims for compensation and restitution against Germany, rather than the present situation, that dominated the agendas of existing or newly founded political forums. A lot of activists began to draw up plans for peacetime on the basis of the strategies, misjudgments, and successes of Jewish diplomacy and politics after the First World War. One of them was Salo Wittmayer Baron, who was to become a leading figure in postwar Jewish efforts to salvage and restitute looted cultural property as head of the JCR. By 1942, he was already publicizing the looting and destruction of the European Jews' cultural landscape, underscoring the collective obligation to reconstruct it after the conclusion of a peace settlement. Baron's key concern was to explore options for securing Jewish life in the postwar world: "The rebuilding of the destroyed religious, educational and cultural institutions and the reawakening of the vast creative cultural energies of European Jewry will, in any case, remain principally a specific Jewish communal obligation. [. . .] It seems most advisable now to work along two lines and to seek for a two-fold program of action: one relating to the intermediary reconstruction period after the war, and the other looking toward more permanent solutions."[1]

Here, Baron, together with other Jewish scholars in the United States, laid the groundwork for later efforts to salvage looted and displaced Jewish cultural assets. The problems of Jewish cultural property—which were to become so pressing for the leadership of the Offenbach Depot just a few years later—were already being considered at this early stage, well beyond Europe's borders. In the early 1940s, several groups and individuals played an important role in the development and perspectives of what was to become the JCR. The most significant was the Conference on Jewish Relations (CJR), created in New York in the early 1930s by Salo W. Baron and Morris Raphael Cohen. It was under its aegis that the JCR's predecessor, the Commission on European Jewish Cultural Reconstruction (Commission), came into being in mid-1944. The latter body received resources and personnel from the CJR, which was in turn partly funded by the American Jewish Committee (AJC), an organization that also did much to set its agenda.[2]

During the war, Baron and Cohen, like many other central figures in the later JCR, were part of a broader network of engaged politicians and lawyers from the leading Jewish organizations of the time. All of them were committed to ensuring justice for Jews in the postwar world. The most prominent organizations in this field were the World Jewish Congress (WJC) and its think tank, the Institute of Jewish Affairs, established in February 1941 in New York.[3] Led by Jacob Robinson and later his brother Nehemia, its crucial contributions to redefining the premises of the political and legal recognition of Jews made this institute a key authority for everyone concerned with restitution and reparations. Jacob and Nehemia Robinson were already championing Jewish collective rights and treaties protecting minorities in Europe in the interwar period. In 1940, the two brothers fled from Lithuania to the United States, where they continued their political work. Over the course of the 1940s, like most politically engaged Jews in America, their frame of reference for evaluations of the present and future was the situation of Europe's Jews since the First World War. Though the associated political concepts were severely shaken by events in Europe and transformed on many levels, when it came to compensation and restitution, Jewish jurists often built directly on interwar experiences, attempting to formulate Jewish collective rights that might be recognized within the framework of international jurisprudence.[4]

The institute was not the only body to concern itself with these topics. Before the end of the war, the AJConf (convened in 1943 to represent the interests of a number of Jewish American organizations) and the American Jewish Congress (or AJCON, active since 1918 and a champion of Jewish rights in the context of the Versailles peace treaties) had also considered possible collective claims for reparations and compensation against Germany after any Allied victory. Jewish scholars and activists in Palestine and the United Kingdom were contemplating similar issues as well—most prominently Siegfried Moses, Cecil Roth, Chaim Weizmann, and Salomon Adler-Rudel, whose contributions were noted and debated in the United States.[5]

Baron and Cohen were immersed in this variety of ideas and opinions on Jewish participation in the construction of the postwar order, and it was a major stimulus for their political initiatives. We can grasp the nature of their activities in the CJR, and the Commission to which it gave rise, only if we examine the surrounding networks and their discursive emphases and thus the broader context of Jewish politics in America during the Second World War. Regardless of the political factions they represented, two overriding themes dominated the many Jewish organizations' plans for the future as discussed in the early 1940s. Their declared goal was, first, Jews' legal recognition as a collectivity and, second, the reconstruction of European Jewries and their sociocultural worlds. The key topics here were reconstruction, restitution, compensation, and welfare, but also emigration and the Jewish future in Europe more generally. Both themes, recognition and reconstruction, later formed the foundation for the JCR's mission. Baron and his colleagues built directly on the legal and political goals developed by the American-Jewish organizations during the war. But they tried to achieve them with the tools of the historian and the philosopher rather than the legal and political instruments deployed by most of their counterparts.

The international legal recognition of the Jewish people as a collectivity increasingly rose up the agenda of Jewish politics beyond the reach of German power. Many felt that the Jewish response to the German attack on the entire Jewish people must also be collective in nature. In light of the Nazis' systematic robbery, Aryanization, plunder, and destruction of Jewish property, Jewish campaigners working for the aforementioned organizations were determined to construct a Jewish legal subject capable of filing claims for restitution and reparations on a nonnational basis.[6] The quantity of assets involved was far from clear during the war. But there was little doubt that the persecution and destruction were of a severity likely to overwhelm the existing tools of international law. The "Inter-Allied Declaration" signed in London in January 1943 gave the Jewish organizations' campaign new impetus, with the signatory states announcing that, after an Allied victory, all property transfers and acts of dispossession within the German occupied areas would be declared null and void, even if they appeared to have been legal. As we saw in the case of the Offenbach Depot, there was an urgent need for an internationally competent form of Jewish representation: if states alone were involved in European restitution programs, Jews risked being shut out. Consonant with later discussions in Offenbach, by 1943, Jewish claimants were already wondering on what legal basis they might file claims against their own state, including émigré German Jews' claims against Germany. By declaring war not just on other countries but on its own Jewish citizens, and consequently the Jewish people as such, Germany had de facto destroyed the traditional modes of warfare, which had previously formed the basis for international agreements on war and peace. This new situation required new legal strategies in response.

After consulting with both Jacob and Nehemia Robinson, Nahum Goldmann, one of the chief negotiators after the war on all matters relating to recognition of Jewish rights and restitution, had already publicly considered these issues in November 1941 at the WJC's first Pan-American Conference in Baltimore, deriving Jewish claims for reparations from the German war against the Jewish people.[7] In the summer of 1943, in a pioneering essay on restitution, Ernest Munz—a Jewish lawyer from Vienna who had fled to the United States in 1941 and was later on the Commission staff—also highlighted the necessity to recognize the robbery of Jews in Europe as a specific form of warfare that required new legal measures and "collective action" by Jews vis-à-vis Germany.[8] To define the Jewish collectivity, stakeholders tended to refer to the "Jewish people" as the entity in need of recognition. But they had quite different ideas about just what this meant. Some regarded this entity as constituted chiefly through the collective experience of persecution. For others, collectivity centered on religious affiliation. Still others understood it as a national group that could be defined in transterritorial or (in Zionist models) territorial terms. The boundaries between these definitions were often fluid.[9] For those who couched their arguments in Zionist terms, the Jewish settlement in Palestine should be the Jewish people's natural center, and therefore, its representatives ought to lead negotiations with the Germans and the Allies. In addition to their overriding objective of giving the polity in Palestine state form and thus solving the legal and international question of the Jews' recognition once and for all, from the early 1940s on, Moses and Weizmann called for the JA to be appointed legal representative of the Jewish people. Moses expressed this aspiration in his important study *Jewish Post-War Claims* of 1944, which was to become one of the pioneering works preparing for reparation negotiations with Germany. Here, he identified the JA as the sole legal, moral, and political representative of the Jews of Palestine, which should enter into a coalition with globally active Jewish organizations to create "a representative body capable of action on behalf of the Jewish People" worldwide.[10] This idea was based on the desire to establish a collectivity that could stand on an equal basis alongside other national entities, putting it in a position to make legal claims: "Jews who have emigrated to Palestine and other countries should be recognized as nationals of a nation that has been at war with Germany since 1933. Insofar as it may be necessary for the presentation and realization of Jewish claims to reparations, these Jews as well as the bodies representing the Jewish People, should be granted the same rights in respect of the regulation of compensations as will be afforded to the nations united in the war against Hitler and the subjects of those nations."[11]

Moses's ideas were a key source of inspiration for Gershom Scholem, who later served on the JCR board of directors, and other prominent members of the Hebrew University of Jerusalem—who were quick to explore issues of cultural restitution in particular. In line with Moses's arguments, they too equated the Jewish people with the Yishuv (the pre-state community) in Palestine in their 1944 discussions with the Allies. On this basis, they asserted its claim to represent the Jews as a whole and its status as legal successor to the European Jewries.[12]

Following her flight to the United States in 1941, Hannah Arendt was to work full-time for the Commission and the later JCR in New York from 1944 onward. She was one of those individuals who, in reaction to the German persecution of the Jews, adopted a rather universalistic position on the Jewish collectivity, seeking to lay the foundations for a united form of Jewish resistance. In view of the Nazis' goal of annihilating all Jews everywhere, Arendt perceived a collective Jewish response as an existential imperative. As she saw it, this required a Jewish self-image that was independent of territorial ties, applied beyond a purely religious framework, and encompassed Jews worldwide. In April 1942, Arendt wrote to Gershom Scholem in Jerusalem, with whom she had been acquainted since the 1930s and who was to become a close colleague at the JCR just a few years later: "I never believed in the Two World Theory: that of Zion and the Diaspora. The events of the past few years have really proven that Jews are one people."[13] As Arendt saw it, a Jewish army must be established to guarantee an active, visible form of collective defense. On several occasions in her columns for the German Jewish émigré journal *Aufbau*, composed between 1942 and 1944, Arendt made impassioned calls for the establishment of such an army and called on the Jewish people "to take their political fate into their own hands"[14] and bolster the prospect of Jews having a say in postwar negotiations through "participation in the war with full and equal rights, that is, a Jewish army."[15] Arendt too embraced the argument that every idea developed with reference to the present must be combined with consideration of future options—she supported Jews' active participation in war chiefly because she believed it would enhance their postwar negotiating position.

Despite their different political backgrounds, Salo W. Baron and Nehemia Robinson also supported the idea of a universal perspective on the Jewish collectivity that reflected the realities of diasporic Jewish life. Robinson's perspectives were rooted in the Eastern European approach to Jewish nationality known as *Gegenwartsarbeit*, prompting him to champion the idea of a representative legal entity, beyond territorial constraints, that could speak for all Jews worldwide.[16] During the war, Baron called for American leadership on these issues of representation because he believed that it was incumbent upon American Jews, more than anyone else, to champion the interests of the Jewish people: "The present war has placed in its [the American Jewry's] hands undisputed leadership of world Jewry [. . .]. The enormity of the relief and migration problems confronting European Jewry at the end of the hostilities will be so great as to overtax the resources of the entire Jewish people.

[. . .] Undoubtedly some international action of unprecedented magnitude will be required to salvage the hundreds of millions of suffering humanity in Europe and Asia. But the extent to which such international action will take cognizance of the Jewish sufferers will depend largely on American Jewry."[17] This leadership role, however, was based more on pragmatic considerations than hierarchical thinking—Baron was convinced that the whole of the Jewish people, be it in Israel or the Diaspora, was constituted by a shared history and shared historical consciousness and must therefore seek to achieve common objectives and a united approach to shaping the future.[18] This is what underpinned his own political initiative, which was intended to benefit Jews worldwide and promote the later JCR as the representative of all Jewries. Nehemia Robinson presented the different views held by members of the Institute of Jewish Affairs in his famous 1944 study *Indemnification and Reparations: Jewish Aspects*, in which he put forward a detailed plan for postwar jurisprudence focusing on Jewish representatives' participation in negotiations and Jewish claims to compensation and restitution. He too expressed these ideas as aspirations shared by the Jewish people as a whole, whose representatives, he believed, must be recognized as equal to governments: "The property of extinguished families and legal persons, communities and organizations must be disposed of in favor of the Jewish people [. . .]. There is no doubt that the transfer of the equivalent of the property or the compensation funds and the disposition of heirless communal property is a difficult task, but it can be solved if entrusted to an organization of international scope entitled to deal with the governments concerned on equal footing."[19]

While Hannah Arendt, Nehemia Robinson, Salo W. Baron, Morris Raphael Cohen, Ernest Munz, and Nahum Goldmann came from very different backgrounds, they all shared a transterritorial understanding of the Jewish collectivity as a historically, religiously, or nationally constituted community and attempted to build its legal claims on these bases.

Within the overall context of Jewish political debates during the Second World War, however, differing views on the significance, future, and location of the Jewish collectivity certainly led to tensions over *who* might represent this people. The main dividing line ran not just between Zionist and diasporic claims to representation but between different political organizations. The associated conflicts were to continue until well after the war. It was partly because of them that the first step toward satisfying the calls for a representative body (beyond the sovereign form of representation assumed by the state of Israel) was taken only in 1948 with the establishment of the JRSO, which focused on heirless Jewish property, and its subsidiary, the JCR. Despite this delay, the uniting of all the aforementioned organizations in the JRSO and JCR was a considerable achievement. Despite the legal obstacles, after the war, the American government decided—through precisely the kind of institutionalized representation demanded by Robinson—to endow the Jewish people itself with the status of collective legal heir to this legacy. Apart from the preparatory discussions and interventions, what expedited this decision more than anything else was probably the overwhelming mass of heirless property, objects, and real estate generated by the annihilation of the Jews and found by the Allied forces on German or German-occupied territory.[20]

The second aspect to planning for the future, one closely bound up with recognition and representation, was the attempt to rebuild Jewish life after the war. The associated debate proceeded under the heading of "reconstruction," which centered on the restoration of the European Jewish communities' previous structures and thus a return to the status quo ante or envisaged a new beginning in a new place. By 1940 at the latest, virtually every statement, speech, strategy paper, and text produced by the Jewish organizations was working with this term, though the different factions had different ideas about its ramifications. Whether reconstruction ought to be pursued in Europe or in the new centers of Jewish life—the United States and Palestine—depended on the observer's point of view and the timing of the discussion.[21] At the beginning of the war, many commentators still considered it possible to reconstruct the communities that had existed in Europe, and it was primarily Zionists who saw Palestine as the only hope for a Jewish future. But mounting awareness of the scale of the European Jews' annihilation made reconstruction in Europe seem increasingly unlikely.

The annual report of the AJC of 1941 was already identifying the need to "engage in efforts for post-war reconstruction and rehabilitation of the plundered and uprooted Jewish victims of Nazi tyranny."[22] In February 1943, its members thus urged upon the "United Nations and upon those who shall frame the terms of peace the relief from the havoc and ruin inflicted by the barbarism on millions [...] especially Jews, their reparation, rehabilitation and the complete restoration of their equal civil and religious rights."[23] But it was the Research Institute on Peace and Post-War Problems, established by the AJC in November 1940, that considered this issue in the greatest depth.[24] The institute was of significance to the emergence of the JCR because Baron and especially Cohen were involved in it and formulated elements of their later political work there. Cohen was one of the founding fathers of this research initiative and supervised its activities together with the Belgian social scientist Max Gottschalk. In his essay "Jewish Studies of Peace and Post-war Problems" of 1941, Cohen outlined the program planned for the institute: "Under no conditions must we fall into Hitler's deliberate trap of paralyzing us by inducing feelings of terror or else benumbing uncertainty. Our problem is thus: How can we escape this trap [...]? Obviously only by fearless and painstaking study of the actual condition and drift of world affairs, and by such preparation for the different eventualities that only a well informed understanding can foresee."[25]

Once again, it was planning for the future that stood center stage. The institute sought to provide the necessary research to better understand the current situation but primarily to draw up plans of action and catalogs of demands for the postwar period. According to Cohen, the preparatory work should focus on three key areas. First, "Relief and Reconstruction"—in other words, measures to promote rehabilitation of survivors and salvage of the European Jews' "remaining resources." Second, "Migration and Colonization," including all the different aspects of flight, migration, and settlement in new places in terms of not just practical organization but also legal, social, and political conditions. Third, he called for rigorous study of the "Political, Economic, and Cultural Status" of the Jews after the war's end. Among other things, this required the implementation of an international jurisprudence that would guarantee universal human rights for all groups regardless of ethnicity and origin.[26] The members of the institute (many of whom later worked at the Commission) carried out a remarkable program of research to address the catalog of issues identified by Cohen.[27] In 1943, under the overall heading of "Jewish Post War Problems," Abraham Duker and Max Gottschalk implemented an eight-part study program, bringing together the issues discussed there in a monograph published in New York in

1945.[28] Referring explicitly to experiences gained in the First World War and the interwar period in their analysis of the strengths and weaknesses of Jewish politics from 1914 onward, the authors discussed the situation in Europe and presented plans for a postwar order. Here Gottschalk and Duker used the term *reconstruction* to refer to the realities of rebuilding Jewish life after the war, giving special emphasis to the role of culture and tradition because of its outstanding meaning for guaranteeing the Jews' long-term survival.[29] In addition to the study by Duker and Gottschalk, the research institute published a number of shorter texts dedicated to various aspects of the—anticipated—postwar reality and especially its pressing legal aspects.[30]

In their key speeches and texts, Jacob and Nehemia Robinson and Siegfried Moses expressed the same ideas about restoration and reconstruction. On the first page of the preface to his brother's study *Indemnification and Reparations*, Jacob Robinson pointed out that political, economic, and social reconstruction and security for the Jews must constitute the core of a just postwar politics: "The present study is concerned with the situation of the Jewish people and their needs. Its aim is to show what can and ought to be done to rehabilitate the Jews in the countries where they were persecuted and despoiled."[31] In the study itself, Nehemia Robinson tried to tease out the legal preconditions for such rehabilitation in Europe and provide concrete political proposals on how to implement it. Moses took a different approach. He too referred to the reconstruction of Jewish life with the help of reparations to be secured from Germany, but what he had in mind was clearly reconstruction in Palestine.[32] Finally, the AJConf, which saw itself as a democratically elected American corporation dedicated to saving the European Jews, preparing postwar demands, and fostering the Zionist project in Palestine, published its "Program for Postwar Jewish Reconstruction" shortly before the end of the war. This articulated the aspiration to banish all forms of anti-Semitism, help surviving European Jews immigrate to Palestine and ensure their postwar rights, push for war crimes trials, and facilitate the restitution of stolen property.[33] That Baron chose to use the term *reconstruction* in the name of his commission in 1944 was therefore no coincidence: it directly reflected these debates. The ideas trading under the name of "reconstruction" were one of the core elements in the political projects pursued by Jewish organizations in the 1940s and thus in the development of the JCR. First of all, the term highlights participants' difficulties in dealing directly with the disaster unfolding in Europe. The focus on "writing for the 'Day after Tomorrow'"[34]—as Günther Anders once described his work as an exiled Jewish author in France and the United States—applied equally to the activities of Jewish organizations in America.[35] The reality of Nazi annihilation, violence, and destruction defied imagination and was incompatible with most participants' perceptual horizon, forged prior to National Socialism.[36] A number of essays by Cohen, for example, demonstrate that the actual threat was beyond anything he envisaged. In 1941, he certainly assumed that Hitler would cause terrible suffering but that it would prove impossible to simply wipe out large numbers of people: "And if the history of the Jews since the Hadrianic persecutions be any guide, it is reasonable to assume that there will be Jews in Europe after Hitler's days are over. [. . .] For a thorough examination of Hitler's general policies shows that they have little originality, that they are all but a brutal intensification of plans and measures previously discussed or even in part carried out in Germany since the reaction that followed the Napoleonic wars."[37]

Many of his contemporaries argued in much the same way as Cohen. Even if they faced up to the emerging threats—and later realities—of annihilation, they generally fit them into explanatory models anchored in the Jewish historical experience hitherto. Integrating the logic of Nazi persecution into the narrative of a continuous Jewish history of suffering seemed to reduce the associated danger to a manageable scale. Oscar Karbach, a later member of the Commission, aptly criticized this attitude in a 1945 review of the previously cited volume by Duker and Gottschalk: "[The Book] is astonishingly successful in underemphasizing the decisive tragedy of the annihilation of the European Jewries."[38] Baron's texts from the early 1940s evince similar forms of rationalization and future orientation while also being captive to the political explanatory models of the past. In both his essays published in the *Contemporary Jewish Record*, "Reflections on the Future of the Jews of Europe" and the previously cited "What War Has Meant to Community Life," he not only underlined American Jews' responsibility to lead the effort to help the embattled Jews of Europe but also outlined an action plan to safeguard Jewish life after the war. He provided no further detail on the requisite aid but emphasized that the lack of preparation for what might be a sudden peace could be a major blunder: one need only think of the undesirable developments that occurred after the First World War due to inadequate Jewish representation in the peace negotiations.[39] At this point in time, Baron seemed unable to recognize the current reality of persecution and its impending intensification in Europe. Two years earlier, in 1940, he had even imagined that—given the historical experience of Europe's multinational empires—the kind of imperial Germany envisaged by the Nazis would ultimately offer Jews greater security than an ethnonational constitution: "It has been an old historic experience that the Jews suffered more heavily in purely national states than in countries of multiple nationality. [. . .] Germany's nationalist spirit draws the country irresistibly into military adventures. Should it win and conquer large territories, it would lose its national homogeneity and become a state of multiple nationality, which, incidentally, might cool its anti-Semitic zest."[40]

Baron's flawed assessments, which seem astonishing from a present-day perspective, are unsurprising within the logic of the time. At this point, it was impossible to foresee the scale of the coming annihilation. Moreover (and as was true for most of the politically active Jews in America), his arguments were embedded in the historical and political ideas that held sway in the interwar period—and concepts of Jewish politics that derived from them. He thus sought to integrate his present into schemata provided by this experiential framework. Protection for minorities and the pressing "national questions"; the potential for Jews to acquire an unambiguous legal status without their own state; and a new approach to international jurisprudence that might enduringly safeguard peace and human rights and bring perpetrators to court: it was to this spectrum of topics that Baron, and most other politically active, US-based Jewish scholars of the time, devoted themselves.[41] In the early 1940s, many of them were still assuming that the European Jewry would survive the Nazi threat just as it had survived other pogroms and expulsion plans emanating from the gentile environment. This allowed them to focus on rebuilding survivors' lives after the war. These Jewish actors, operating "out of the firing line"[42] were ultimately concerned not so much with *saving* people in the sense of active intervention (regardless of how much—given the specific features of Nazi terror and the systematic campaign of annihilation—American

Jews could in fact have intervened to save their European counterparts) but with *preserving* Europe's age-old Jewish worlds.[43] Baron articulates this perception as early as 1940. In the previously cited essay on the future of the European Jews, he writes, "One realizes that at present there still are some three quarters of the Jewish people left [in the United States, Soviet Union, Latin America, and the British Dominions] who might assist the remaining suffering quarter *not only through direct relief but also in permanent reconstruction.*"[44]

This striving to maintain and preserve was inscribed in the concept of reconstruction. Within this conceptual framework, sustaining the people, which was identified as the core of Jewish affairs, tended to mean addressing—in an abstract and long-term way—a future for the Jews in general rather than saving particular Jews under threat. The key participants thus dedicated themselves to preparing for restitution, safeguarding the Jewish cultural and intellectual legacy, maintaining traditions, and rebuilding Jewish communities in the United States and Palestine in light of the European Jews' predicament. This is precisely what Baron envisaged: "Europe is likely to emerge after the next peace treaty in a state of utter economic collapse [. . .] shattered European Jewry may, in the course of fewer years than we now dare to hope, reconstruct its existence on a basis more solid than that upon which it had lived during the present generation. But moral obligation [. . .] will require that the Jewish communities still left relatively intact should unite in furthering these reconstructive endeavors."[45] The "reconstructive endeavors" Baron and the CJR wanted to focus on were obviously very specific. They were convinced that "the new stimuli given to Jewish learning in a much-neglected field and the refinement of new methods [as proposed by the CJR] would in themselves represent a highly significant contribution to Jewish culture, which, in the long run, may assist the Jewish people in its struggle for survival perhaps to an even higher degree than any direct political or economic action."[46] Only against this background can we understand the broad attention given to the recovery of expropriated, dislocated, and vandalized cultural property. By 1933, the Polish-Jewish jurist Raphael Lemkin was already discussing the specific role played by the spoliation of cultural treasures within attempts to destroy entire groups, underlining the crucial importance of the phenomenon:

An attack targeting a collectivity can also take the form of systematic and organized destruction of the art and cultural heritage in which the unique genius and achievement of a collectivity are revealed in fields of science, arts and literature. The contribution of any particular collectivity to world culture as a whole, forms the wealth of all of humanity, even while exhibiting unique characteristics. Thus, the destruction of a work of art of any nation must be regarded as acts of vandalism directed against world culture. The author [of the crime] causes not only the immediate irrevocable losses of the destroyed work as property and as the culture of the collectivity directly concerned (whose unique genius contributed to the creation of this work); it is also all humanity which experiences a loss by this act of vandalism.[47]

What Lemkin conceptualized here is what he later termed "cultural genocide."[48] He made it very clear that the destruction of its cultural assets is an attack on a collective's, or even humanity's, essence. And it is this understanding that led Jewish individuals to put such emphasis on cultural restitution. They were eager to ensure the survival of Jewish tradition and history, the constitutive grounds of the collective self. The historian Dalia Ofer describes this prevailing vision in relation to postwar Palestine: "Rescue was seen not only as the direct and real act of saving lives [...], but included all actions that would ensure the future of the Jews as a people [...]. Rescue now included reconstruction."[49] A close look at the debates of the early 1940s reveals the same diagnosis during this era, beyond the borders of Palestine.

*　*　*

This realm of ideas and discussions had a direct impact on the genesis of the JCR. Baron sought to fulfill the obligation to maintain the European Jews' religious, spiritual, and cultural heritage through the work of the Commission. This sense of obligation was anchored in the deep-rooted conviction, shared by Baron and Cohen, that there was an urgent need for scholars and intellectuals to mobilize in an organized way in response to developments in Germany from 1933 onward. As early as April 1933, Baron published a farsighted appeal in the *New York Times* in an attempt to raise awareness of the new, dangerous situation for Jews in Germany after Hitler's rise to power. He called for international

"Jewish Action" and underlined the global significance of these events: "The recent occurrences in Germany show how national hysteria can violate the most fundamental human rights of the Jews. [. . .] Only the formal acknowledgement of the question's international character and the adoption of common measures for the entire Jewish people can help establish more peaceful conditions between the Jews and their neighbors in many lands."[50]

By the next summer, Cohen and Baron were already corresponding about possible responses. Cohen summed up the main points: "It occurs to me that some permanent organization of professional people, teachers, students, doctors, lawyers, artists and other intellectual workers and educated people—all the classes can, on the basis of their own experience, sympathetically understand what is happening to our Jewish brethren—is needed to combat the permanent forces that are trying to destroy the Jewish people."[51]

Inspired by motives that recall the German-Jewish Defense (Abwehrkampf) of the late 1920s and early 1930s,[52] they began their joint campaign of mobilization. They strove to utilize their profession to combat German anti-Semitic propaganda, nurturing empirical research and source-based historical accounts. Their liberal political stance dovetailed with their conviction that by spreading knowledge, and thus facilitating sounder judgments, it might prove possible to create a more humane and tolerant future.[53] Their vision was realized through a circle of New York intellectuals who belonged to a number of competing Jewish factions, all of whom agreed that the growth of education could engender a more positive perspective on the Jews in the modern world. In line with earlier initiatives launched by their Jewish contemporaries in Europe, the goal was to disseminate sound demographic and historical data on the Jews in response to anti-Semitic polemics.[54] Cohen described the idea underpinning this coalition of New York scholars and professionals in his autobiography: "We were united in thinking that in days of bitter stress for the Jews over most of the world there was a great need for an organization that would be devoted primarily to the business of fact-finding so that our attitude and policies might be based on the most reliable information and not on cant or illusion."[55]

The group met at the New School—which was considered a progressive place and seemed particularly close to Europe as home to the

University in Exile, which had been established by the school's president Alvin Johnson in 1933 to support European refugee scholars—and was soon calling itself the Conference on Jewish Relations (CJR): "'The Conference on Jewish Relations' is the name that best represents the attitude of our membership. We shall subjoin a motto indicating that ours is an association of men and women in the liberal professions devoted to the ascertainment and dissemination of the truth in regard to the relations between Jews and their fellow citizens."[56] The CJR first aroused public interest through a 1935 conference on the history of anti-Semitism from an anthropological and history-of-law perspective. In addition to Baron, some important scholars of the time such as Hans Kohn, Franz Boas, Israel Wechsler, Edward Sapir, and Marvin Lowenthal participated and laid the groundwork for the well-regarded anthology by Koppel Pinson, *Essays on Antisemitism*, which was published in 1942.[57] The analyses of Judeophobia at the conference extended all the way back to antiquity but rarely touched on the present. When contemporary anti-Semitism was discussed at all, its portrayals primarily attested to these scholars' struggle to grasp its racial character, which underpinned the Nazi mania for destruction and the redemptive element of Nazi ideology at the time.[58] In the wake of the conference, the CJR was officially established, and its mission spelled out, in spring 1936 in New York. With motives akin to those of the later research institute of the AJC and the Institute of Jewish Affairs, it sought to improve relations between Jews and non-Jews and respond to the increasing Jew-baiting and propaganda in Germany. As evident in Baron's memorandum previously cited, this goal was to be achieved through publications and studies—"answering the lies of Goebbels"[59]—while also sensitizing the American public to developments in Europe and the Jews' situation.[60] Albert Einstein and Harold Laski spoke at the founding meeting, and Henry Morgenthau pushed for donations; Harry A. Wolfson, Felix Frankfurter, and Monroe Deutsch attended early meetings to help raise public awareness of the CJR's mission.[61] Financed by private contributions, the CJR subsequently appointed a number of working groups to investigate the economic, social, and demographic status of American Jews, the legal situation of Jews in Germany, and issues of anti-Semitism. It soon numbered more than seven hundred members and was involved in a very broad range of activities.[62] In a speech to the CJR in 1937, Cohen underlined that the organization regarded empirical research and the promotion of knowledge as its most important tasks, being convinced of "the ancient insight that where there is no vision the people perish."[63] This conviction also stimulated the CJR's further professionalization through the founding of its journal *Jewish Social Studies* in January 1939. Koppel Pinson, Theodor Gaster, and Joshua Starr made up the editorial team, while Salo W. Baron, Morris Cohen, Hans Kohn, and later Koppel Pinson were acting publishers. They aimed to provide a journal "devoted to the scholarly exploration of the social aspects of Jewish life past and present."[64] Another motive was to help combat anti-Semitism and counteract Nazi propaganda, which they feared might influence American public sentiment toward Jews. Once again, these scholars felt that nurturing American Jewish research initiatives was essential at this time of crisis: "The destruction of important centers of Jewish learning in Eastern and Central Europe makes it imperative that the United States, which is the largest and richest Jewish community in the world today, should do its share to see to it that Jewish studies and research do not perish."[65] A large network of Jewish scholars rapidly grew up around this journal, many of whom cooperated with or supported the JCR a few years later. Most of its early contributors had fled Europe, such as Hannah Arendt, Adolf Kober, Jacob Lestchinsky, Raphael Mahler, Zosa Szajkowski, Max Weinreich, and Bernard Weinryb. *Jewish Social Studies* was soon to develop into a leading and respected scholarly forum in the United States.[66]

The outbreak of the Second World War prompted discussions within the CJR as elsewhere on how to shape the postwar order. In 1940, Cohen stated that it was important to actively prepare for peacetime policies. He regarded the empirical documentation of Jewish social and demographic reality in America as a means of preparing for incoming refugees and paving the way for their professional integration.[67] The CJR's focus on the collection of information and data had direct consequences for the later work of the Commission. Very much in the tradition of its parent organization, many of those involved in the newly set up Commission saw their main task as gathering documentary material that would enable them to initiate the process of cultural restitution in Europe.

All these attempts at intervention had the same ultimate objectives. For the most part, however, the plans so meticulously drawn up by those involved in the CJR, and other organizations and institutes in the same field, were on paper only. The individuals involved tried to respond to the challenges of their time with the tools of science and research and to shape the future in light of historical and political experiences—a reflection of their origins, education, and self-image. As early as 1942, in one of her columns in *Aufbau*, Hannah Arendt was making trenchant remarks on the risks associated with this attitude, excoriating the leading American-Jewish organizations: "With scientific meticulousness [they have been] busy preparing us for peace" rather than taking an active approach by pushing for the establishment of a Jewish army. Arendt continued,

> And so we too are being prepared "unpolitically" for peace. It is true that a discussion about the goals of peace always tends to arise during a war—and so far it has always turned out that the only goals of peace that are realized are those already implemented in war and the way in which it is fought. But so far no people has ever come up with the idea of trying to replace participation in a war with *dreaming* in advance about participation in a peace conference. This is a scholarly idea, and we like to hope that our scholars will not succeed in turning a "people of the book" into a people of papers. Because as long as a Jewish army remains on paper, the best collections of materials in the world are just stacks of dead paper.[68]

But the Jewish army was to remain on paper only, along with a vast number of other plans, organizational templates, and strategic ideas generated by the many-layered activities of Jewish organizations and individuals as they grappled with National Socialism's persecution of the Jews and with the war. While their eyes may have been fixed on the future and in some ways closed to the present, the American Jews' indefatigable engagement in response to events in Europe flatly contradicts the claim, often found in the research, that they were indifferent to the fate of their European brethren. Quite the reverse: the scale of their activities attests to the tremendous sense of responsibility felt by the broadest array of politicians, scholars, rabbis, and lawyers vis-à-vis the embattled Jews of Europe in the early 1940s.

The restitution of Jewish property that had fallen victim to Nazi looting was central to all the aforementioned political forums and their plans. Restitution was regarded as crucial to reestablishing law, justice, and stability. Against the background of the anticipatory schemes outlined above, the Commission, founded within the CJR in summer 1944 by Baron and Cohen (which laid the legal and organizational foundation for the work of the JCR, which began to operate in 1947), sought to create a representative Jewish body to pursue the recognition of the Jewish collectivity and campaign for the reconstruction of prewar Jewish life in Europe. But it was to be a number of years before the JCR was legally authorized by the American government. Arendt spoke prophetically in 1944: "It would be foolish to believe that peace will be easier for us than a war, in which, right to the end, we fought as allies but were never recognized as one of the Allied Nations."[69] In some ways, at least, Arendt was quite right, as evident in the tremendous efforts made from 1944 onward by the members and appointees of the Commission, and by Arendt herself, to achieve its recognition as trust for Jewish cultural property and ensure the latter's safekeeping in Europe.

The Commission on European Jewish Cultural Reconstruction

Surprisingly, it was in the UK rather than the US that the first initiative for Jewish cultural restitution took on an institutional form. In April 1943, under the auspices of the Jewish Historical Society of England, a committee was set up to promote the reconstruction of the Jewish libraries, museums, and archives that had been affected by Nazi plunder and destruction: the Committee on the Restoration of Continental Jewish Museums, Libraries, and Archives (Committee on Restoration). Under the chairmanship of Cecil Roth, this body brought together Jewish scholars such as Norman Bentwich, Oscar Rabinowicz, Franz Kobler, Ernst G. Lowenthal, and Adolph G. Brotman to discuss the restitution of stolen Jewish cultural property. They aimed to present their findings to the Allied powers in the form of a resolution and establish the committee as key interlocutor for all issues relating to the cultural restitution of Jewish property in Europe.[70] In his opening address to the founding conference on April 11, 1943, in London, Roth brought home to his audience the scale and consequences of the Nazis' cultural raids and called for immediate action to salvage the items involved and return them to their owners.[71] Where the owners could not be identified, Roth proposed that these items be stored at the Hebrew University in Jerusalem.

Roth explained that his UK-based committee was best placed to take charge of the salvage of Jewish cultural heritage because of the special role of the Jewish Historical Society as virtually the only Jewish scientific body still active in Europe.[72] These discussions occurred not long after the signing of the "Inter-Allied Declaration" in London, which undoubtedly helped inspire the committee's demands. Roth's plans came to the notice of Nazi Germany. In September 1943, the anti-Semitic weekly *Der Stürmer* published a sneering commentary on the committee's establishment and its aspiration to transfer looted cultural property to the Hebrew University or claim indemnification for lost collections, demonstrating once again the significance of theft and plunder in German politics—the Nazis carefully monitored every countervailing measure and calibrated their own approach accordingly.[73]

Roth knew he could count on support for his project from New York. Just four days after the conference in London, he made contact with Baron, informing him of the resolutions that had been adopted and asking for his appraisal. Baron explained that the CJR was making plans similar to those of the London Committee and that the Joint had established a division dedicated to the same issues under Abraham Neuman; he emphasized that the goal must be to ensure cooperation between these different bodies.[74] But it was a number of years before this was achieved. The relationship between the British and American interest groups was pervaded by a sense of rivalry, while the political issues thrown up by the process of restitution long remained contentious. Nonetheless, over the course of 1943, the CJR in New York agreed that the reconstruction of Jewish culture in Europe must be its top priority. The CJR, composed mainly of academics in the humanities and social sciences, seemed made for this task.[75] In December of the same year, at an in-house conference, the CJR executive secretary Theodor Gaster presented a program for the reestablishment of cultural life in Europe that adumbrated the core objectives and future structure of the Commission. The CJR resolved to establish three subcommittees dedicated to (1) the reconstruction of Jewish cultural institutions in Europe, (2) Jewish education in Europe, and (3) surveying the European-Jewish communities, collecting "all information available from émigré sources concerning the assets, structure, etc. of German communities, as of 1933." The first subcommittee set out to advise the Allied nations "on the rebuilding of such institutions as have been destroyed," to serve as trustee "to administer cultural institutions formerly owned by communities which have since been dispersed," and to present claims "for indemnities in respect of Jewish cultural properties."[76] In the summer of 1944, correspondence between Baron and several members of Jewish organizations began to refer to the CJR Reconstruction Committee. At this point, Baron shared responsibility for the Committee primarily with Gaster, who from 1945 on concurrently headed the Hebraic Section of the Library of Congress in Washington, DC. They jointly appointed a group made up of members of the CJR and other organizations, including Hannah Arendt, Raphael Mahler, Max Weinreich, and Horace Kallen, whose work was partly funded by organizations such as the AJC and the Emergency Committee in Aid of Displaced Foreign Scholars.[77] A text composed by Gaster in September 1944 outlined the tasks and profile of the group, now known as the Commission on European Jewish Cultural Reconstruction: "The Conference of Jewish Relations has recently set up a commission of leading scholars and educators in this country for the Cultural Reconstruction of European Jewry after the war. [. . .] The Commission is intended to serve as a central co-ordinating body for all activities in this field."[78]

Initially, then, the Commission's work revolved around advice, education, and research, with a particular focus on the latter. Unlike the English Committee on Restoration, its members thus set about meeting the obligation already articulated by Baron in 1942 to foster cultural reconstruction in Europe rather than abroad.[79] Baron discussed this obligation and its practical implementation in his essay "The Spiritual Reconstruction of European Jewry," which appeared in the first issue of the monthly journal *Commentary* in 1945.[80] Once again, he explained the special role of the non-European Jewish communities—particularly in the United States—in supporting the surviving Jews of Europe and the necessity for a "spiritual resurgence" after the disaster. As he saw it, books and literature must play a key role in this new beginning. Not only was there a need to provide the "shattered remnants of European Jewry" with books and religious texts, all their possessions having been lost, but the salvage of the looted libraries was also crucial in light of a pronounced Jewish bibliophilia.[81] Here he made much the same argument as the staff and visitors at the Offenbach Depot, underlining the profound significance of salvaging and restoring books due to their special status in the collective Jewish identity. Baron aimed to provide an advisory service for the Allied soldiers who had been tasked with finding and safeguarding stolen libraries. His and the CJR's goal was to restitute stolen property to its owners and ensure that it was allocated in such a way as to advance the "general cultural reconstruction of European Jewry."[82] He was obviously aware that such allocation was a difficult undertaking due to the changed political, social, and cultural realities. He thus underlined the duty of Jewish political organizations to help out and highlighted the steps already taken by the CJR and similar initiatives in Palestine and the United Kingdom, which he wished to turn into coordinated action.[83]

Three working groups, created by the Commission in June 1945, were to lay the groundwork for the salvage and restitution of Jewish cultural property in Europe. Initially the largest and most important group was the Research Committee, led by Alexander Marx of the JTS in New York, which was composed of a permanent staff and an advisory body. Hannah Arendt, herself employed full-time at the Commission since early 1945, headed the research staff and guided their work. The second working group, the Committee on Cooperation, presided over by Horace Kallen of the New School, sought to establish structures of cooperation with other Jewish and non-Jewish organizations and institutions. The third and later the most significant group, the Legal Committee, was dedicated to reworking and improving restitution laws. It was headed by Jerome Michael, Baron's colleague at the Columbia Law School, and like the Research Committee, it consisted of permanent and honorary staff. Beyond the fields of activity, there was a growing circle of registered members at the Commission who were on hand to provide advice and support. This group was composed of around seventy individuals, many of whom were acquainted with Baron and recruited from various Jewish organizations: Nehemia Robinson, Simon Federbusch, Gerhard Jacoby and Oscar Karbach from the WJC, Jacob Landau from the Jewish Telegraphic Agency, Max Gottschalk, Abraham Duker and Simon Segal from the AJC, Leo Jung and Nathan Reich from the Joint, Jacob Shatzky and Max Weinreich from YIVO, and Eugen Täubler from the Hebrew Union College (HUC). Over time, this circle was to expand to include other personalities, with the later JCR gathering together many leading figures in Jewish public life of the 1940s and 1950s in the United States. As the director of the Commission, Salo W. Baron was able to shape and had the final say on all its activities, and he used his extensive personal network to promote its interests. The Commission received funding from the Joint, the JA, the AJC, the American Association for Jewish Education, and the B'nai B'rith. In addition, the Guggenheim Foundation and Rockefeller Foundation awarded grants to Commission staff, while offices and materials were made available by the CJR.[84]

The Commission's seemingly solid structures should not obscure the fact that it had to cope with persistently meager budgets and that initially it was just one of several initiatives being pursued by the Hebrew University, the Committee on Restoration, the WJC, and the Royal Library of Copenhagen. What was to distinguish the Commission and, crucially, pave the way for its formal recognition later on was its impressive research preparing for restitution. As announced in its first programs, from fall 1944 onward, members of its staff had set about gaining a detailed picture of the Jewish cultural landscape as it existed before the Nazis' campaign of robbery and destruction. The idea behind this tremendous research endeavor was that a comprehensive overview would be indispensable to filing specific restitution claims.[85] The Commission not only established a working basis for the search for looted property and its identification but also, quite literally, created an archive of Europe's devastated Jewish culture.

Textual Monuments

Building on a tradition established by the CJR, the members of the Commission initially sought to counter the boundless destruction through empirical research as well. In order to "investigate the manifold, complex problems of the cultural reconstruction of European Jewry after the devastation of the Second World War"—to quote Baron[86]— the Research Committee under Alexander Marx and Hannah Arendt decided to publish lists documenting cultural institutions and collections of Jewish cultural property in Europe before the war in as complete a form as possible. This comprehensive inventory of all Jewish museum holdings, schools, scientific bodies, rabbinical seminaries, libraries, publishers, journals, and important private collections was intended to render visible the wealth of Jewish cultural treasures that had existed in Europe for centuries. Key activists in New York soon realized that there was a lack of precise information on the assets existing prior to 1939 and their location, greatly hindering the search for these objects and their restitution.[87] In Germany too, most of the MFA&A officers and military government members active in this field complained that the lack of reliable evidence was severely hampering the discovery and identification of Jewish collections.[88] The Research Committee was keen to help remedy this. Its advisers included Aron Freimann, former director of the Frankfurt City Library; Rahel Wischnitzer, former curator of the Jewish Museum Berlin; and her husband, Mark Wischnitzer, who had been secretary-general of the Relief Organization of German Jews (Hilfsverein der deutschen Juden); Max Weinreich; Jacob Shatzky; Joshua Bloch of the Jewish division of New York Public Library; and Bernard Dov Weinryb, director of the Jewish Teachers' Seminary. The staff consisted of Hannah Arendt, Adolf Kober, Raphael Mahler, Nathan Eck, and Herbert Strauss, and it was their responsibility to compile and process all gathered data. They created overviews of all accessible European library catalogs and previously existing Jewish journals in Western and Central Europe, made a collection of newspaper excerpts on relevant topics with the help of the AJC library, and surveyed refugees from Europe and members of the Jewish *Landsmanshaftn* (homeland associations).[89] For the most part, however, they got their information from around 250 standardized questionnaires conceived by Arendt and her colleagues and sent to exiled Jewish scholars, publicists, journalists, rabbis, social workers, librarians, artists, and members of American-Jewish organizations as well as personnel working in the occupation zones in Germany. The respondents had to provide information on collections and institutes in Europe and their holdings, rare items, administration, budget, and staff. They were also asked for information on the present state of assets and on non-Jewish institutions in Europe that housed Jewish cultural property.[90] The Research Committee made contact with the Hebrew University of Jerusalem, which was compiling its own list of Jewish-European cultural goods. Some of its entries were used, but for the most part, upon perusal, the researchers in America discarded the list in light of major lacunae and shortcomings.[91] Through its tireless efforts, between 1945 and 1948, the Research Committee ultimately drew up five lists, which were published as supplements to *Jewish Social Studies*.[92] The fact that Baron and the CJR could present this work in an established and acknowledged journal was critical to the project's success. The published lists covered the following fields: first, so-called Jewish cultural treasures, which included libraries, museums, archives, and private collections; second, Jewish schools, adult educational institutions, and rabbinical seminaries; third, journals from all over Europe; and fourth, Jewish publishers. The fifth list expanded on and corrected earlier entries, providing new and more detailed information, and it was published under the title "Addenda and Corrigenda."

The composition of the research group, including staff of varying backgrounds and education, was intended to ensure coverage of as much of Jewish Europe as possible. Hannah Arendt was mostly responsible for Western Europe; historians such as Raphael Mahler (who had dropped out due to illness by October 1945) and Adolf Kober, in consultation with Bernard Weinryb, professor of Eastern European Jewish economic and social history, were entrusted with the Central and Eastern European countries. Nathan Eck, later on the staff of the Yad Vashem research and remembrance center in Jerusalem, also worked on Eastern Europe for the Committee. Baron particularly valued his involvement because he had previously been a member of the Polish underground; Baron perceived him as a "living testimony to the tenacity with which East-European Jewry pursued its cultural and educational interests under the most harrowing conditions."[93] Beyond their authors, the lists identify a few other individuals involved in their preparation. Mention is made of Nehemia Robinson and Rabbi S. Fischer, who contributed detailed information on Jewish publishing and journals in Lithuania, Romania, and Hungary.[94] In addition, the sources show that Berlin-based philologist Ernst Grumach provided important details. He was a long-standing friend of Hannah Arendt and had worked as a forced laborer in the RSHA. He was already collaborating with the staff of the Offenbach Depot.[95] Despite their sometimes competing interests, even the staff of the WJC and the Committee on Restoration in London provided valuable advice.[96] For example, Oscar Rabinowicz, a key figure on the Committee on Restoration under Cecil Roth and later a member of the JCR executive board, sent a paper with detailed information for the list of corrections, which was included as a section in its own right.[97]

Every conceivable resource was used to obtain as complete a picture as possible of Jewish cultural life before the devastation wrought by the Nazis. The five lists contained several thousand entries from more than nineteen European countries, from Norway to Greece and from Belgium to the Soviet Union—"all of them [. . .] reflected the richness and variety of Jewish cultural life on the European continent before the curtain of history was pulled down upon it."[98] In addition to this past-oriented research, the Research Committee in New York was concurrently attempting to compile an index detailing the current situation of Jewish cultural property, institutions, and educational establishments; in combination with the lists, this was to form the working basis for later restitution claims. The staff collected demographic data on the Jewish population and Jewish DPs in Europe and documented evidence of all newly established or reestablished Jewish schools as well as the whereabouts of stolen cultural property.[99]

The Commission's research had far greater ramifications than initially envisaged. The documents cautiously referred to as "Tentative Lists" are of significance on a number of levels. Contemporaries already regarded them as valuable sources for historical research on European-Jewish cultural and intellectual history. In his introductory remarks to each list, Baron emphasized their value to future research, thus attributing an importance to them that went beyond their immediate function. Herbert Strauss too underlined the lists' relevance to Jewish historiography. In a letter to Baron, he remarked that the lists brought out the diversity of cultural activities in Jewish Europe, giving the reader, for example, an impressive sense of the vitality of Jewish publishing in Poland and France.[100] A press release published in January 1947, in which the Commission set out its mission and called for help in collecting the correct data, provides particularly striking testimony to the great value placed on the lists:

> In addition to the sad and complicated task of salvaging and recovering what is left of a once flourishing Jewish cultural life on the European continent, the Commission on European Jewish Cultural Reconstruction previously made valuable contributions. Its research staff, after more than a year's painstaking research published two Tentative Lists, one of cultural treasures and the other of educational institutions in former

Axis-occupied countries. [. . .] Their momentum is highly estimated, by scholars and laymen who are writing the history of a period of proud spiritual achievements in the Jewish past, as a balance sheet of the spiritual losses suffered by the Jewish world through the comparably short period of the reign of madness.[101]

This communication also hints at the impact this documentary project was having beyond its utility for historical research. The lists were attaining the status of a monument. The systematic compiling of information on the institutions and other key components of Jewish culture in Europe was tantamount to the creation of an archive of documentation and remembrance. This detailed portrayal of the European Jewish cultural realm was the first of its kind and to this day serves as an important store of knowledge. In addition to the reconstruction of the past, and thus its preservation, the Tentative Lists convey the brutality and violence of National Socialism: their blank spaces are in a sense their disturbing focal point. In a similar way, as we have seen, the catalogs produced at the Offenbach Archival Depot articulated the void left by an obliterated world in the schematic form of figures, numbers, and facts. The representation of both the irretrievable past and the magnitude of destruction distinguish the Tentative Lists as outstanding historical testimony.

Seen from this perspective, the Commission's research fits into the larger context of postwar initiatives launched by many Jewish organizations and Jewish survivors, who set themselves similar tasks: providing a precise description of Nazi crimes, assessing acts of destruction, and making preemptive, offensive efforts to counter any attempts by the perpetrators and those not involved to hush up or repress the Nazi past.[102] Most prominently, this was a significant motive for the Jewish Historical Commissions active in a number of European countries. As early as 1943, they had begun to collect oral testimony and any documentary evidence of Nazi crimes in order to lay the groundwork for war crimes trials and compensation claims; at the same time, their work generated some initial tools of historical research, new rituals, and new ways of remembering the dead.[103] In much the same way, the lists compiled under the leadership of Hannah Arendt were an attempt to meet this obligation to record and commemorate the atrocities. They concurrently established a form of order, returning the unstructured, chaotic "remnants" of Jewish culture in Europe to their original context. They thus have not just a documentary but also a constructive function, expressing the goal pursued by Baron through the Commission of reappropriating the Jewish historical and cultural space.

Despite their increasingly significant symbolic, historical, and commemorative value, the lists always retained their practical utility. They became the basis for the work of the many individuals employed in the depots and collecting points in Europe and for the activities of the American military government, and they were of crucial significance to cooperation with American government officials when it came to the Commission's formal recognition. Upon receiving the first list while working in the DP camps and the Offenbach Depot, Koppel Pinson, long a close confident of Baron as coeditor of *Jewish Social Studies* and himself a member of the Commission, expressed his enthusiasm in a letter to Arendt: "You have done a wonderful job and as one of the people here put it, you gave us a catalogue for the Offenbach Collection."[104] It was Pinson who passed the list on to Seymour Pomrenze, first director of the depot. The latter was so impressed by the list that he increasingly promoted the Commission's interests in his dealings with the agencies of the State Department. In May 1946, Pomrenze wrote to Baron, "When Prof. Pinson gave me a copy of the list of treasures put out by your commission I said to him here is the Agency which can be the instrument of *geulah* [redemption] for these treasures."[105] The list circulated both in the various subdivisions of the MFA&A and within the American military government's restitution division.[106] And in his correspondence with the officials of the MFA&A and Isaac Bencowitz, second director of the depot in Offenbach, Max Weinreich used the first list as proof of the ownership of the Vilna YIVO holdings.[107] Arendt also sent the lists to the Jewish communities in the American zone to aid with the identification of cultural property and books, to the rabbis working for the military government, to Jewish journalists in Europe, to key organizations such as the Joint and the JA, which were the main advocates of Jewish interests in Europe, and to American libraries that did not subscribe to *Jewish Social Studies*.[108]

The lists were thus to play an important role in planning the Commission's subsequent activities as well.[109] In line with its self-image as an advisory body during the first phase of its work, for the time being, the lists were to be passed to the United Nations and to those political organs that had dedicated themselves to protecting cultural property, in order to support their work: "It is planned to have the Commission serve as the central research and co-ordinating body for all American activities in the field of Jewish cultural reconstruction [. . . and] to constitute [. . .] an Advisory Council to the United Nations in the restoration and/ or reconstruction of the cultural aspects of European Jewish life."[110]

Before long, the focus of the Commission's work increasingly shifted to its own active role in the restitution process. Once again, the lists were of great significance. It was not just Pomrenze who saw them as an embodiment of the Commission's professionalism, prompting him to support its plans henceforth. Officials at the State Department, who received the lists along with the Commission's application for the role of trustee for heirless Jewish cultural property, were also extremely impressed by them.[111]

In addition to the many strategic advantages the Commission had gained through its comprehensive research work, one thing had become abundantly clear: there was a vast amount of scattered and "homeless" cultural property of Jewish provenance in Europe whose owners and heirs had been murdered or could no longer be found, whose institutions of origin had been plundered and destroyed, and whose communities of origin had no realistic prospect of being reestablished. This was the point of departure for the wide-ranging discussions among those Jewish intellectuals keen to preserve this heritage. Who could undertake the search and salvage operations? How was the objects' future to be decided? How could one ever reconstruct anything that resembled the world before 1933? For all those involved, these issues threw up one of the most complicated questions of post-Holocaust Jewish life: Was there any prospect at all of reestablishing Jewish life and Jewish culture in Europe, or had the reality of annihilation rendered such ideas null and void?

Rebuilding Jewish Culture

Commission members' ideas about strategy and about the organization's role in shaping the future of Jewish culture were always bound up with general debates on the prospects for Jewish life after the Holocaust. All of them struggled to find an answer to the question of how best to reconstruct the European-Jewish cultural landscape. Numerous reports from Germany and Europe reached New York, strengthening the conviction that increasingly held sway there—namely, that the future of the Jews must be pursued elsewhere and that it was therefore vital to transfer surviving cultural property from Europe to the new centers of Jewish life. Above all, this view was reinforced by the near-innumerable heirless objects of Jewish provenance collected at Offenbach and other sites. It was becoming increasingly clear that the Germans' war of annihilation had left an enormous discrepancy between the surviving cultural property and the individuals who might have been able to make use of them. New solutions had to be found beyond traditional forms of restoration. For the key advocates in New York, the issue of a just form of restitution was thus intimately bound up with the future location of the European Jewries, and this in turn was a core element of the general discourse among Jews after 1945. The moral and political issues of the time forced their way into the legal debate.

Initially, Baron and the Commission were quite clear about how best to approach the "where" and "how" of cultural reconstruction: it must be fostered locally. Early in 1945, Baron began by calling for the normalization of the European Jews' situation and for the renewal of institutional and community life with outside help. Communities in the process of reestablishing themselves must be provided with the necessary resources, while their infrastructure must be restored with the support of American welfare organizations.[112] But this idea was soon overtaken by reality. First, the New York YIVO was a key source of information for the Commission; as early as 1942, Max Weinreich and his colleagues were searching for the remains of their Vilna predecessor and were therefore in contact with the American authorities and other information-providers in Europe. At the end of the war, they were among the first to know about the finds in Hungen and the establishment of the Offenbach Depot, passing this news on to the Commission executive board. Weinreich was convinced that all the book holdings on Jewish culture, religion, and history, including those from national and city collections, must be removed from Germany and distributed to Jewish institutions across the world. Under no circumstances could they remain where they were.[113] The second key source for the Commission was Rabbi Philip Bernstein, later adviser to the American military government. When the war ended, he was already in constant contact with his predecessors in Germany, had a precise grasp of current developments locally, and kept Baron up to date. In numerous letters and reports, he described the situation, pushing for the implementation of an action plan to salvage cultural property. As early as July 1945—in light of information from Rabbi Judah Nadich, the first adviser to the military government—he was able to report on the Americans' difficulties in dealing with Jewish cultural treasures and their idea of setting up collecting depots to identify and return material to their "pre-Hitler owners."[114] In addition to the data provided by Bernstein and Nadich, a report from March 1946 by the Jewish captain Abraham Aaroni, who worked for the American military government in Frankfurt, also set out in detail the urgent need for Jewish scholars to aid the work of the collecting points and depots.[115] Finally, at a relatively early stage, the Hebrew University of Jerusalem sent Gershom Scholem and Abraham Yaari to the American occupation zone in an effort to obtain reliable reports, which were also sent to New York.[116]

From April to August 1946, Scholem pursued his mission to prepare for the future work of the university's Otzrot HaGolah group with respect to cultural property. Like the university representatives that succeeded him, after his experience in Germany and the former German-occupied areas, he confirmed his initial assessment that the university must assume the trusteeship of every locatable object and that as many of the Jewish cultural and ritual objects as possible should be taken to Palestine. Scholem and the other members of the Otzrot HaGolah wished to support the Yishuv in building a new center of Jewish cultural life, gain sovereignty over the emerging culture of Holocaust remembrance, and become the prime inheritor of the European Jewry.[117] In mid-1945, this was an attitude held by many Jews, far beyond the borders of Palestine. A symposium in London held at the time on "The Future of the Jews" brought together politicians, scholars, and writers. Most agreed that a "return to [the] slaughterhouse" of Germany was out of the question, that it was unclear whether there could be a future for Jews anywhere in Europe, and that the only sustainable prospect for Jewish life lay in the development of Palestine.[118]

The rejection of Europe, and particularly Germany, as a future home for the Jewish people opened up much potential for conflict among Jews over the role of the Jewish communities now emerging in Germany.[119] Should one support their reconstruction in places where, as Robert Weltsch bluntly put it, there was a lingering stench of "gas chambers and torture chambers,"[120] let alone enrich the tiny communities by entrusting to them large amounts of salvaged cultural property? On his trip to Germany in late 1945, Weltsch was directly exposed to the debates surrounding the American approach to restituting the looted collection created by the ERR. He later expressed his indignation:

> Take for example the library of the rabbinical seminary in Breslau, or of the Lehranstalt für die Wissenschaft des Judentums in Berlin. Can we, that is, the Jewish world, accept the view that Breslau or Berlin has a right to the return of these books? These Jewish educational establishments and communities no longer exist! Who should be considered their legal successor? This is already a question of a Jewish-political nature, and one of the first importance. Eretz Yisrael must be assigned a fitting role here. We must win over global public opinion to the idea that Eretz Yisrael is the cultural center of the Jewish people, where the now ownerless cultural property stolen from the Jews must find its legitimate home.[121]

And Weltsch soon had an unambiguous view of those he managed to meet in the Jewish communities of Germany: "The fact is that there is no trace of continuity, that is, of any connection with Jewish life before the war. The people are ignorant of the simplest things, of which every German Jew was well aware in 1938 [. . .] In other words: these remnants of the German Jewry are complete outsiders that just happened to be left over here."[122]

A year later, in the course of her work at the Offenbach Archival Depot, Lucy Dawidowicz (then Schildkret) gave a similar assessment: "German-Jewish institutions, if reconstituted as Gemeindes [sic], [. . .] no longer have the same composition or serve the same number of constituents. Because of the systematic extermination of Jewish professionals, we do not believe that there are at present among the Jews living within the German economy such persons as can make proper use of valuable books."[123]

By July 1945, Hannah Arendt had already warned Baron of the risk that the German Jewish communities might be recognized as the legal heirs to cultural goods.[124] Most Jewish international organizations active outside Europe—their members themselves often of German origin—felt it would be highly unjust if the American restitution authorities recognized the few small German Jewish communities as claimants to this valuable material and were keen to see this option ruled out unconditionally. A strategy paper produced by the Commission in the spring of 1946 stated that the group of Jews now in Germany had no legal right to recovered cultural objects because a far larger number of surviving German Jews were now living in New York, Tel Aviv, and London.[125] The politically active Zionist and trained lawyer Georg Landauer, who was involved in the debates about restorative justice in Palestine/Israel at the time, later summed up the view dominant among Jews worldwide, underlining that there was "no reconstruction that might supersede destruction," while the "impoverished Jewish life in Germany [could not represent] any continuation of more than fourteen centuries of German Jewry."[126] Here he highlighted one of the thorniest legal issues in the aftermath of the war—namely, whether the reestablished communities in Germany should in fact be regarded as the same as the ones that existed in 1933. With regard to community property as well as heirless German Jewish assets, the communities taking shape after 1945 were entitled to file claims only if they could be recognized as identical to their predecessors. Surrendering goods to a Jewish trustee rather than Jewish communities in Germany, as both the Commission and the Hebrew University wanted, could be justified only if one assumed that these communities had nothing in common, apart from their name, with those existing before their enforced dissolution. This was the thrust of the arguments put forward by the JRSO, which was officially appointed in 1948 to administer heirless Jewish assets and property (excepting cultural property) in the American zone.[127] A brochure prepared by the JRSO executives at the German headquarters in Nuremberg summarizes their position. Here they declared that the size, composition, and form of the new communities did not create an identity with the earlier ones, while the assets that had formerly been at the disposal of six hundred thousand Jews in Germany could not be entrusted to the twenty-three thousand Jews now living there, of whom, moreover, more than 40 percent were of non-German origin. As a compromise, however, the JRSO proposed that these communities be furnished with capital and ritual objects to help ensure their survival and cover their needs.[128] By 1948, the American military government, along with the relevant authorities in the United States, was viewing these communities' role in much the same way as the JRSO and other Jewish representatives: "It does not seem proper to consider the communities where some Jews have survived the successors to the communities or organizations that existed at the same places prior to the Nazi regime because not only their number is [sic] only a small percentage of their former number, but, also, the composition of the people seems, in most instances, to be entirely different from those that formerly belonged to these communities."[129]

The competition that generally existed between the interests of the communities in Germany and those of Jewish organizations elsewhere developed into a persistent problem for restitution policy, hampering the establishment of the Jewish successor organizations and trusts.[130] Also linked with these communities' problematic legal status was the question of how best to deal with the unprecedented German case of the systematic robbery of one's own citizens and what to do about heirless property, issues that had already been raised with respect to the Offenbach Depot. In the American occupation zone, the military government's law 52 on the blocking and control of property in the German Reich and its organizations—a second, amended version of which was ratified in July 1945—resolved some of these problems by decreeing that all stolen goods, whether of German or other origin, must initially come under American supervision and jurisdiction. Only upon submission of unambiguous evidence of ownership—the task of the restitution officers registered at the Offenbach Depot—were these goods released for restitution. This procedure was often problematic in the case of formerly German Jewish property. Implementing the restitution measures to which the Americans had committed themselves through this law presupposed "the existence of a claimant. In cases in which an entire family was killed in the concentration camps or gas chambers and has been deprived of all heirs, no such claimant existed."[131] In cases involving the former property of German Jewish citizens who could not be found or had been murdered, it was Germany that would have acted as administrator according to the escheat doctrine of common law. In the absence of legal heirs, this called for property to revert to the state. Jewish advocacy groups regarded this as outrageous because it "would mean to reward them [the Germans] for the extermination of the Jews."[132]

It was this legal situation that compelled American-Jewish emissaries to intervene in a more targeted way. Members of the JRSO, along with Commission officials, attempted to persuade the American authorities to transform individual claims into collective claims. Just as Nehemia Robinson had envisaged in his pioneering study in 1944, as so-called successor organizations (ones that formally succeed to the inheritance of the murdered), both groups thus strove to gain the right to file claims to and administer the property involved on behalf of the Jewish collectivity: "The creation [of the] successor organizations is the inevitable consequence of the Nazis' persecution of the Jews. [. . .] Where a bleak silence reigns over scenes of carnage, this is the voice demanding atonement for the wrongs committed. [. . .] Hence it is in the successor organization, which serves no special interests [. . .] and is intended to prevent the ongoing alienation of property under the pretext of Nazi law for want of legally effective claims, that the idea of restitution has found its clearest and most unconditional expression."[133]

The dilemma with which the international Jewish organizations struggled was that while the Americans certainly acknowledged the moral justification for restitution and compensation, they failed to provide the political and legal means of achieving them. At the Paris Conference on Reparations of November and December 1945, the Allies had granted those persecuted by the Nazis a special status, resolving to use gold bullion found by the Allied armed forces on German territory, along with an additional twenty-five million dollars, for the rehabilitation and settlement of stateless victims, thus signaling their sympathy for Jewish claims. In legal terms, however, these provisions initially had no effect on restitution and compensation.[134]

Beyond the complicated legal status of stolen Jewish goods in the American occupation zone, Commission members were also deeply concerned about Jewish cultural treasures elsewhere, especially in Eastern Europe.[135] Officials responsible for collection and restitution in Germany constantly complained about the lack of experts capable of identifying material. Furthermore, many of the cultural goods outside the depot were at risk of being carried off or illegally sold or falling into disrepair. With growing concern, Commission members in New York learned of the black market trade in valuable materials and the use of papers and parchments from Jewish estates as scrap paper. Seymour Pomrenze reported to them that in Łódź, Poland, fish was on sale at markets wrapped in pages from the Talmud; some time later Arendt stated that she had been offered five Jewish gravestones through the Budapest black market.[136]

In addition, like the officials in Offenbach, Commission members struggled to work effectively with the Soviet military leadership. The authorized Soviet officials made no distinction in their confiscation policy between German goods and goods looted by Germans, creating an ever-present risk that stolen Jewish assets would be subjected to displacement once again. Accounts of the confiscation of Jewish property in the Soviet occupation zone and in other areas of Soviet influence regularly did the rounds. In 1946, Scholem told of a supposed Soviet plan to establish an oriental library in Samarkand and Tashkent, for which a Russian restitution officer in Offenbach was to file claims to Jewish holdings.[137] Furthermore, the Soviet military government and Soviet authorities refused to cooperate with Jewish nonstate organizations. The Soviet leadership took the view that the restitution of stolen goods should take place in their countries of origin so they could be of benefit to the victims of the Nazi regime without distinction. There was no recognition of any special "Jewish case."[138] Keen to do all they could to prevent the transfer of goods into the Soviet Union and the rest of Eastern Europe (even on a legal basis), the Jewish interest groups campaigned for an end to the restitution of items to Polish and Soviet officers on the basis of the territorial principle. They also drew up plans to salvage stolen goods in the Soviet zone. In both cases, many individuals were convinced that the assets and treasures would not make it back into Jewish ownership but would end up as state property that would never benefit a single Jew. In March 1946, Pinson expressed his fears to the chair of the Otzrot HaGolah in Jerusalem: "There is a very immediate and grave danger that the Soviet Union may make claim to everything that comes from Russia, Poland, Lithuania, the Baltic States, Czechoslovakia and Russian occupied Germany, regardless of legal ownership. In such a case our headquarters in Berlin would be forced to bow to these claims and the greatest bulk of the collection would be lost to us all."[139]

It was to a large degree as a result of this clearly dire predicament that the participants in the Commission agreed to push for the transfer of most material out of Germany: "Our idea [. . .] is to get all the non-identifiable parts of the collection [OAD] out of Europe into the U.S.A. as soon as possible. In the U.S.A. our research department [Commission] can better carry on its work and a more just and equitable distribution and restitution can be made."[140] Very similar arguments were put forward by Salo W. Baron and eminent scholars of the Hebrew University (including Judah Magnes, Gershom Scholem, Ben-Zion Dinur, and Martin Buber) at a September 1946 meeting in Jerusalem. While there was a total lack of agreement on how to proceed, everyone agreed that cultural goods must without fail be taken out of Germany and Czechoslovakia, another location where large quantities of looted items were to be found. Gershom Scholem spoke bluntly of the dangers posed by "the Russians, who [would] hand over nothing to the benefit of the Jews" and had already taken objects to the Soviet Union while also emphasizing that "this danger exists to no lesser a degree when it comes to the Germans themselves." It was thus "impossible to leave the collections in Germany."[141]

Throughout 1946, the Commission's Legal Committee worked intensely to resolve the outstanding issues: the idea was to strengthen the Commission's international authority and presence through closer cooperation with other groups and institutions, particularly those in Palestine. It was also proposed to submit to the State Department a memorandum advocating the case for the Commission's authorization as trustee of heirless Jewish cultural goods, with the power to transfer goods out of Germany.[142] This was submitted to the State Department in June 1946. Eight pages long and composed by Jerome Michael, the memorandum set out the organization's status; its core ideas and key concerns; the situation of "Jewish religious and cultural treasures" in Europe, particularly the large quantities of heirless objects; the value of these cultural treasures to the Jewish people; and a detailed plan for their redistribution to Jewries worldwide. The paper envisaged the Commission as part of a board of advisers to the American military government that, along with the Hebrew University in Jerusalem and the Synagogue Council, which represented the various Jewish denominations in the United States, would be consulted on matters of restitution and the allocation of property to facilitate recognition of "the special and exclusive interest of the Jewish people in these objects." There was no reference as yet to its own potential role as trustee. In analogy to the discussions of the early 1940s, here "the Jewish people" was taken to mean the ethnic collectivity of the Jews throughout the world, a group characterized by a shared religion and historical experience. The Commission also called for compensation for the many destroyed Jewish collections formerly held by German and Austrian cultural institutions and libraries. The final point in the memorandum underlined the risks entailed in the impending postoccupation transfer of responsibility for restitution to the German authorities and requested a change of approach: "To entrust the disposition of these objects to the German land governments or other German agencies is to desecrate them and gratuitously to offend deeply the Jewish people."[143] The first Tentative List was appended to the letter to provide an impression of the dimensions and significance of the theft of cultural property and thus underline the need for bespoke regulation of their salvage: "The instrumentalities, the tangible products, and the physical embodiment of this long, devoted, and often heroic spiritual and intellectual activity [the long-term historical development of Jewish religious, scientific and cultural institutions all over Europe] were books, manuscripts, Torah scrolls and other religious and cultural objects which constitute a priceless heritage and one of the proudest possessions of the Jewish people."[144] The goal of the memorandum was to convince the American authorities to help draw up plans for the "preservation and ultimate disposition of the Jewish religious and cultural treasures which are still to be found in Germany and Austria" in order to "save them for mankind in general and the Jewish people in particular."[145] The memorandum was accompanied by a letter from Philip Bernstein to the commander-in-chief of the American armed forces and then military governor in Germany, Joseph T. McNarney. In it, Bernstein too emphasized the urgency of the issues raised, highlighting the complexity and significance of the political and legal decisions required to resolve them: "In fact, Jewish scholars all over the world— and particularly in the United States and Palestine—are the rightful heirs of such treasures. But the laws presently under consideration by military authorities do not place these collections in a separate category. [...] general legislation overlooks a special case."[146] Bernstein regarded the provision of advice to the military government by the Commission as an important step toward the appropriate treatment of the "special case" of Jewish property.

In light of changes suggested by State Department staff and the assistant secretary of state John H. Hilldring, on behalf of the Commission, Michael submitted a second, improved version of the paper on August 26, 1946. The most important change was that now the Commission no longer presented itself as an adviser to the military government but instead acted as the official representative of collective Jewish claims to stolen cultural property in Europe. To this end, the plan was to establish a corporation consisting of the AJConf, the Joint, the AJC, the Synagogue Council, the American Federation of Jews from Germany, the WJC, and the Hebrew University, which could be expanded later if necessary. According to this plan, the new corporation would be entrusted with the safekeeping and allocation of all heirless and nonidentifiable objects, ensuring that they benefited Jewries across the world. Michael called for special arrangements to be made with respect to Poland and the Soviet Union as the sites of the grossest misalignment between the quantity of discovered objects and the number of local survivors. The new corporation would thus aim to take charge of almost all items stolen from Eastern Europe and would return them to their countries of origin only if they were demonstrably necessary for the securing of the religious and cultural life of the Jews resident there. The practical implementation of these tasks should initially be the responsibility of a small group of experts who could travel to Europe and begin searching for, inspecting, cataloging, returning, and reallocating items. The American military government was asked to grant unimpeded access to every depot and collecting point and freedom of movement within the occupation zone. All the costs of this undertaking would be borne by the German states.[147]

Astonishingly, after the submission of this memorandum, which already mentions key elements of the later agreements between what was then the JCR and the American government, it took more than two more years for the JCR to be recognized as the trustee. This was due, first, to the complexity of decision-making processes within the American administration: both the State and War Department, and the occupation government in Germany, had to be convinced of this proposal. Second, cooperation between the various Jewish interest groups—within the corporative structure adopted by the JCR from 1947 onward—entailed a number of problems that had to be solved before articles of incorporation could be drawn up. State Department officials were concerned about how the transfer of responsibility for goods to which Michael aspired might be viewed in Germany: "It gives the impression of an act of revenge on the part of the Jews using the American Army and American Officials as a reverse version of the Einsatzstab Rosenberg." In the same vein, the demand for "restitution-in-kind"—the transfer of cultural treasures of Jewish provenance belonging to German museums and collections to Jewish bodies in the Yishuv and elsewhere as a form of compensation for the losses suffered—was dismissed with the argument that this contravened both Allied policy and the Hague Convention. The activities of potential successor and trust organizations must, according to departmental officials, be strictly controlled: "Jewish organizations [. . .] could loot with the assistance of United States troops, German public museums, libraries and archives, of any cultural treasures which, in the opinion of the personnel of the Jewish mission, had a Jewish character. It is contrary to elementary principles of justice." Nonetheless, State Department officials seemed convinced of the Commission's integrity. Keen to achieve a common solution for all Western occupation zones, they initially proposed consulting the Commission on how best to integrate its plans into the legislation of the Allied Control Council in Berlin.[148] In a letter to the military government of September 1946, meanwhile, the War Department declared itself ready to consent to all the Commission's proposals, pending the agreement of the military government and a positive reaction from the British and French.[149] The response from the military government was initially guarded. Its assumption was that Allied law permitted no role for nonstate or nonmilitary corporations, and it would therefore be necessary to uphold the bilateral agreements with specific countries. Lester Born, MFA&A archive officer within the military government's restitution division, expressed major reservations about evaluating the "Jewish case" entirely separately from all others. He thought it right for Jews to file their claims as citizens of countries that were entitled to restitution. Furthermore, for him, Jewish cultural treasures were always also part of the cultural heritage of their country of origin, and in his eyes, this legitimized sending

them back there.[150] His appraisal was typical of many of those working for the American military government and its Allied counterparts
who dealt with restitution. Above all, though, the military government
underlined that it was vital to ensure that the future Jewish trust comprehensively represent all Jewish aspirations—special attention must be
paid to the interests of German and European Jews still living in Europe.
Like the other authorities, the military government balked at the idea of
taking compensatory cultural items from Germany, viewing it as tantamount to destroying the German cultural landscape (the "cultural rape
of Germany").[151]

The Commission had influential backers in the State Department,
and they played a major part in its ultimately successful attempts to
gain authorization. Thanks to his close contacts with members of staff
at the MFA&A and the Library of Congress, Seymour Pomrenze was
to become a crucial source of support. At a meeting with Hannah
Arendt, Horace Kallen, and Simon Federbusch in June 1946, he pledged
the Commission his assistance as soon as it had, first, applied for the
status of a nonprofit organization of the United Nations and in the state
of New York (enabling it to act as an international corporation), second,
established a depot where it could store the transferred holdings, third,
persuaded the Library in Washington to act as a partner in logistical
matters, and fourth, achieved unity among the various Jewish organizations and their conflicting views.[152] Judah Magnes, president of the
Hebrew University, also expressed his support for Jerome Michael's proposals by sending a series of letters to the State Department.[153] This was
mainly because the university had itself made numerous unsuccessful
attempts to attain the status of trust. Since Israel did not yet exist as a
state and had not existed during the period of Nazi looting, and because
the Nazi campaign of spoliation had obviously not affected property in
Palestine, it was virtually out of the question for the university to play
a leading role in the legal procedure of restitution. Its aspirations also
came to nothing because the Western Allied military governments as
well as other Jewish individuals feared that if it gained trust status it
would be likely to allocate goods solely to Palestine/Israel. Pinson put
this to Magnes in stark terms in a letter of March 1946, going so far as
to state that if the Hebrew University were the sole actor in the field of
restitution, it would hamper the success of Jewish initiatives: "Official

claims or representations at this time from Palestine, a country from which no part of this collection has come and which, unfortunately, is not recognized as possessing any legal claims in restitution proceedings, would only serve to stimulate or incite Russian claims. May I assure you that we here on the spot are doing all we can to preserve the collection, and that the interests of the Hebrew University in Jerusalem are very close to the hearts of us all."[154]

Many key figures agreed that the Hebrew University should be one of the main repositories of salvaged objects, but most American-Jewish representatives advocated the equitable distribution of goods to a number of countries. Magnes embraced a collective approach and supported the Commission in his communications with the State Department, greatly increasing its prospects of recognition—his advocacy being seen as evidence of unity between the Jews of Palestine and the Diaspora. Lucius Clay, then deputy to the military governor McNarney, was also well-disposed toward the Commission's aspirations and was dedicated in his pursuit of a positive outcome for Jewish cultural goods in the American occupation zone.[155] On December 1, 1946, the Waldorf Astoria hotel in New York was the scene of a meeting between Clay, Salo W. Baron, Jerome Michael, Alexander Marx, Aron Freimann of the Commission, and Wolf Blattberg of the WJC, where they discussed how to proceed. Clay again pushed for greater inclusion of European-Jewish and German Jewish representatives. The meeting focused chiefly on the legal options available to nonstate actors and on how a future law on restitution might apply to cultural goods.[156] Clay then began to step up his efforts to effectuate a law of this kind that would recognize Jewish claims. In March 1947, he succeeded McNarney as military governor and initiated a comprehensive discussion of the issue of restitution with the German state governments and the Allied Control Council. His plans for a joint resolution came to grief due to the Allies' irreconcilable positions and the state governments' desire to transfer responsibility for restitution to German courts and authorities. In the face of this opposition, Clay had little choice but to implement a solution for the American zone alone. In November 1947, the new military law 59 on the restitution of identifiable property was passed, clarifying the approach to restitution in this zone and permitting the appointment of trust organizations to file nonstate claims.[157] In his memoirs, Clay relates his struggle over the law and its significance: "After months of fruitless effort to obtain a quadripartite law and also a bipartite law, United States Military Government enacted for the United States Zone a law which provided for the restitution of identifiable property taken by Germany by duress [. . .]. To ensure that the property of the Jewish people who were killed in Germany and left no heirs would not benefit German holders, a Jewish successor agency, formed by recognized world Jewish organizations, was authorized to claim and receive their property, including valuable cultural property."[158]

Among the Western Allies, the Americans were the quickest to formulate a comprehensive policy to address the specific situation of stolen goods of Jewish origin. Most scholars explain this in light of the fact that the Americans had no need to pursue compensation to cover their own losses during the war or to deal with the aftereffects of German occupation because—in contrast to their European counterparts—their national territory had been unaffected.[159] A secondary explanation highlights the Americans' special sensitivity to the predicament of those persecuted by the Nazis. This is put down to the diverse range of Jewish political initiatives in the United States, which had emerged in part because it was the destination of the largest wave of refugees from Europe. Perhaps even more significant than these factors, however, was that the softening of the territorial principle meant that the United States and Palestine could obtain cultural goods while countries such as France and especially the Eastern European nations had to forego some of the objects formerly located there. Because Jewish art and cultural goods were often considered part of a given nation's cultural heritage, the debate on their future inevitably caused friction.

As a result, in addition to its copious work on the Tentative Lists, the first phase of the Commission's activities involved legal negotiations relating to the constitution of the JCR, its recognition by the Allies, and more far-reaching questions about the future of Jewish life. Plans for the literal postwar reconstruction of European Jewish communities and institutions had been superseded by plans to commemorate the dead and preserve the European-Jewish cultural legacy abroad. Despite this shift of perspective, however, the same term continued to be used for JCR operations. *Reconstruction* finally encompassed everything associated with the reestablishment of Jewish life after the Holocaust. According to the leading perspective in Israel, this semantic shift went so far that reconstruction was seen as an element in a "process of redemption" bound up with the foundation of the Jewish state, imbuing the term with a new significance for the future of the Jewish people in that country. The issues of salvaging, preserving, and incorporating the cultural heritage into the Israeli realm were expertly integrated into the dominant historical narrative that accompanied the construction of the early Israeli self-image; here, the prevailing perception was of the "Holocaust as an inevitable outcome of the Jewish exilic situation and of the return to Eretz Yisrael as the ultimate act of redemption."[160] If one presupposed that the Jewish people and Israel would become as one, and that Israel was developing into the hub of Jewish life—an assumption that amounted to a more or less unambiguous rejection of the Diaspora—there could be no doubt that heirless assets and property must find their future home there. Within this frame of interpretation, according to the historian Hannah Yablonka, Zionism represented "the only hope for salvation and rebuilding what was left of the Jewish population of Europe."[161] Through the Zionist lens, reconstruction could only take place in Israel. It was there that most survivors of the Holocaust went to find a new home, and it was there that the remnants of their property and that of the murdered must be transferred as well. Those active within the Jewish Diaspora shared this view only to a limited degree. Cecil Roth, for example, who championed the Hebrew University's interests, discussed the problem of cultural rebuilding in Palestine and the United States in his essay "Jewish Culture: Renaissance or Ice Age?" of 1947. From an Anglo-Saxon perspective, he described the "starving" of Diaspora culture through what he calls a "cultural inferiority complex" and a focus on Palestine, something he considered every bit as dangerous as excessive assimilation into the surrounding culture.[162] He thus called for a renaissance of Jewish culture in both Palestine and the Diaspora—with his main emphasis being on the United Kingdom, the United States, and other countries outside of continental Europe. A few years after the war, the Committee on Restoration, which had still unambiguously viewed Palestine as the target destination for every recoverable fragment of the European-Jewish cultural heritage in 1944, had also changed its view. As he observed the emergence of the Jewish state, Roth became convinced that salvaged cultural goods must strengthen not just the Yishuv but the Diaspora as well, and here he pushed for the United Kingdom to play a major role in negotiations on the Jewish heritage, his goal being to make it the third center of Jewish life alongside the United States and Palestine/Israel.[163] With an eye on the future, in his introduction to the first Tentative List, Salo W. Baron explained the changed meaning of the term *reconstruction* for Jewish life: "The term 'cultural reconstruction' is not to be interpreted in any too narrow sense. [. . .] In view of the wholesale destruction of Jewish life and property by the Nazis, reconstruction of Jewish cultural institutions cannot possibly mean mechanical restoration in their original form or, in all cases, to their previous locations. The Commission [. . .] may seek to help redistribute the Jewish cultural treasures in accordance with the needs created by the new situation of world Jewry."[164] Understanding that former centers of scholarship and publishing, academic institutions, and rabbinical seminaries had been irretrievably destroyed, Baron and his colleagues advanced the idea of establishing the United States as a central space for Jewish culture and thought. The transfer of knowledge and ideas through the migration of material remnants from Europe to the United States and the fruitful integration of former cultural and educational traditions into the American context became Baron's enduring preoccupation.

Not least, this shift away from the Commission's original concept found expression in the organization's reconstitution as a corporation made up of several institutions, named Jewish Cultural Reconstruction, Inc., in April 1947. In contrast to its predecessor, the JCR did not include the word *European* in its title. The spatial perspective had shifted. There was no point in systematic reconstruction in the absence of those to whom it would have meant something. From 1946 onward, the Commission executive board had expressed an increasingly clear view of where the locus of Jewish life ought to be: "Europe is no longer, and it is very unlikely that it can again become, a center of Jewish spiritual and cultural activity. The great centers of such activity are now, and will continue to be, Palestine and the United States, where so many thousands of the survivors of European Jews have found refuge."[165] The JCR's Hebrew name allowed the changed perception of reconstruction to shine through even more clearly. Labels on the volumes allocated by the JCR to Israel later bore the inscription *Tekumah Latrabut Israel* (resurrection of Jewish culture), almost entirely undoing the original idea of returning stolen property to its earlier ownership and thus to its previous setting as typically entailed in restitution. Here restitution meant a new beginning, and with respect to cultural activities, it specifically meant a new beginning for the Jewish community in the *Altneuland* of Israel. But some obstacles still had to be overcome before any objects could be distributed to the new centers of Jewish life. The key challenges were the formation of a sustainable corporative structure and the legal negotiations that preceded the conclusion of the "Frankfurt Agreement," which authorized the JCR as trust.

Creating Networks

The competition between the various Jewish and non-Jewish initiatives described earlier impeded concerted action and slowed institutions' attainment of trust status. One highly controversial rival initiative on European soil was launched by the Royal Library in Copenhagen. As early as 1945—due to its neutral location and its famous collection, which had suffered no damage during the war—its representatives were envisioning the library as a locus for heirless books of Jewish provenance and called for the establishment of a Jewish memorial collection. Its promoters projected a World Jewish Library in Copenhagen that would make its holdings available to researchers from all over the globe.[166] With backing from UNESCO, which had been founded shortly before, Raphael Edelmann, head librarian of its Judaica division (consisting most prominently of the Rabbi David Simonsen collection), argued vigorously for this solution in proposals presented to the American occupation authorities and various Jewish advocates, causing outrage among the latter. Jerome Michael urged him to instead support the Commission's project and keep in mind the Jews' special situation: "There is a deeper reason why we feel that these plundered Jewish libraries should be handed over direct to the Jewish people without the intermediary of any organization. The Jewish people have suffered in the war spiritually and materially more than any other community; and we want therefore that these books, the precipitate of the labors of generations of Jewish scholars, be restored without unnecessary delay to the Jewish people. Unfortunately the lives of six million Jewish victims cannot be restored. But these books belong to the Jewish people, and to its scholars and students."[167] In the same vein, Judah Magnes wrote to Edelmann in January 1947, seeking to convince him to abandon the idea and instead support the Jewish salvage initiatives: "It would—if I may be allowed to speak frankly—be a real demonstration of your Government's sense of generosity and its genuine understanding of the plight of the Jewish people if they were to support a plan, which has been agreed upon by recognized agencies of the Jewish people, rather than to oppose it through a plan of their own."[168] For Magnes and those of like mind, the time seemed anything but ripe for a "universal" European approach to heirless Jewish books; rejecting Edelmann's proposal, they were determined to ensure Jewish ownership of all heirless cultural remnants on the continent. In a letter to his friend Hugo Bergman, who was also helping salvage books and religious objects from Europe, Gershom Scholem was uncompromising: "As you (may) know, the peculiar activities of this Dr. Edelmann, who tried to steal the property of the Jewish people for the Danish government in order to boost his own profile (though he failed in this!), have raised our suspicions. [. . .] I'm sure you realize that we have absolutely no intention of supporting Dr. Edelmann's plans in any form [. . .]. I'm convinced that there is no objective reason to accumulate valuable books in a place such as Copenhagen that is devoid of any real Jewish life."[169] Edelmann's plan was thwarted as a result of this fierce opposition. UNESCO, prominently backed by the United States, dropped the plan for a Jewish library in Europe. But the initiative had rekindled the debate on whether—and if so, where and how—there might be post-Holocaust Jewish life in Europe. Most Jewish representatives' blunt rejection of the Copenhagen plan was testimony to their virtually unanimous view of the issue.

The second major non-Jewish library that was involved in every debate and whose representatives took part in months of discussions on potential cooperation was the Library of Congress in Washington. As early as December 1945, Theodor Gaster of the Commission had underscored the benefits of cooperation and even proposed the library as an independent agency to administer heirless European holdings.[170] He envisaged himself playing a key role here. Similarly, in the summer of 1946, the head of the Library of Congress mission, Reuben Peiss, suggested to Lucius Clay that the four victorious powers ought to administer the holdings found in their zones and allow the various national libraries to allocate nonrestitutable items.[171] At first, the other Commission members were also persuaded that the Library of Congress should play the kind of role suggested by Gaster, and they endeavored to provide support as an adviser on Jewish affairs. But the more Baron and the executive board intervened actively in the restitution procedures, the more they shifted away from their original vision, conceding the library a purely logistical role in their dealings with the American authorities. The deciding factor here was the moral and political argument, already put to Raphael Edelmann by Jerome Michael, that the disaster that had befallen Europe's Jews made it both impossible and undesirable to entrust the administration of the Jewish heritage to non-Jewish institutions.

The imperative, then, was to join forces and dismantle the barriers between the various Jewish initiatives. Network building was entrusted mainly to the Commission's Cooperation Committee under the leadership of Horace Kallen. Two aspects were important here: first, forging links with other organizations and institutions, covering as many Jewish factions and geographical areas as possible that were prepared to work together within a corporative structure under the chairmanship of Salo W. Baron; second, cooperation with the JRSO, which was emerging in a parallel process. JRSO registered as a corporation in the state of New York in May 1947, integrating the JA, the Joint, the AJConf, the AJC, the Board of Deputies of British Jews, the CRIF, the Council, the Central Committee of Liberated Jews in the American Zone of Germany, the WJC and the recently founded JCR. Between June and August 1948, it began operating as the official Jewish successor organization for the American occupation zone in Germany.[172] It took laborious discussions to establish the Commission as a key agent of heirless Jewish cultural property under the aegis of JRSO. There were disagreements about its leadership, the different groups invited to join feared their interests would be neglected if they were subordinated to Baron's organization, and there were conflicting views on where to finally locate cultural treasures. Cooperation between the Commission and representatives of the AJC, AJConf, and the Synagogue Council went fairly smoothly; they supported and funded it from the outset. In early 1947, efforts were made to persuade Rabbi Leo Baeck to join the Commission. Once the State Department and military government had made recognition of the Commission conditional on improved integration of

German Jewish and European Jewish representatives, it was an obvious step to ask the chair of the Council for the Protection of the Rights and Interests of Jews from Germany—later the Council of Jews from Germany (hereafter: the Council)—to become a member. After some initial hesitation, Baeck agreed.[173]

The Commission's relationship to the Hebrew University of Jerusalem, the Committee on Restoration, and the World Jewish Congress was more complicated in nature. The Congress was the only competing initiative on American soil. The Commission certainly consulted Nehemia and Jacob Robinson as legal and political advisers, basing its concept of restitution on the principle of collective claims put forward by the Institute of Jewish Affairs. Both Robinsons were directly involved in the Commission's work and are listed as members. The same applies to Simon Federbusch, who had agreed to become a member separate from his work in the WJC. But initially, the WJC still insisted on pursuing its own projects to salvage Jewish cultural goods.[174] In 1945, WJC representatives were still suggesting that Baron ought to join Federbusch's Committee on the Recovery of Jewish Cultural Property and that the latter would be entirely responsible for the practical implementation of the Commission's ideas. The high-profile and politically engaged Rabbi Stephen S. Wise, president of the WJC since its establishment in 1936, also rejected the idea of participating in the Commission because of the near-identical project being pursued by the WJC.[175] In June 1946, the Commission asked the WJC for financial aid, but this was curtly rejected with reference to its own plans.[176] Jerome Michael then turned to the executive board and Nahum Goldmann, who succeeded Wise as president in 1949. Goldmann ultimately reined in all of Federbusch's unilateral activities and ordered him to work together with Baron on issues of cultural restitution. It was agreed that the WJC should use its diplomatic contacts to negotiate the fate of Jewish cultural goods in Poland and Czechoslovakia in particular—where the Commission could make little headway due to resistance from the local authorities.[177]

Cooperation with the Hebrew University went more smoothly because its representatives quickly realized that no member of the Commission was in any doubt that it would play the leading role in the allocation of goods. University members soon grasped their poor prospects of winning over the Allies in Germany if they tried to act alone, the legal basis for those activities being even weaker than that of the American interest groups. It therefore made sense to abandon its exclusive approach and ally itself with the Commission. In contrast to the WJC, the university's close personal contacts with its New York colleagues smoothed the way for cooperation.

As we saw earlier, Cecil Roth's Committee on Restoration ultimately hoped to establish itself as an independent European advisory body with respect to Jewish cultural heritage. There were repeated misunderstandings and communication problems between the Commission and Roth's Committee, chiefly due to the Americans' preeminent role in the restitution process. This conflict was obviously an expression of the broader transition occurring in the Jewish world at the time, which saw the shift of Jewish centers away from Europe to the United States and Palestine. Evidently due to financial problems and in the awareness that it was in a far weaker position vis-à-vis the American military government, the Committee too shifted its stance and signed a contractual agreement on cooperation. In March 1947, after consulting with the Hebrew University, Oskar Rabinowitz, later member of the JCR executive board, requested the Committee's incorporation into the JCR, though Baron approved this only in January 1948.[178]

When it came to their objectives and key ideas, the various individuals involved agreed on far more than was apparent at first sight, and the Commission's established status (relatively secure funding, a large network, recognition by the American authorities, high-profile supporters) ultimately helped ensure a joint approach. On April 30, 1947, through a deed of incorporation in the state of New York, the following bodies came together as the Jewish Cultural Reconstruction, Inc. (JCR): the AJC, the AJConf, the Commission, the Council, the Hebrew University, the Synagogue Council, and the World Jewish Congress. The new organization's mission statement set out its responsibilities in three sections: first, to "locate, identify, salvage, [. . .] preserve, repair, protect, [and] catalogue" books, manuscripts and ritual objects; second, to work as a successor organization "to institute and prosecute claims for the recovery of, or compensation for Jewish religious and cultural objects"; and third, to distribute the goods in its charge in such "a way as to best serve and promote the spiritual and cultural needs and interests of the Jewish people in particular and of mankind in general, and especially

the spiritual and cultural needs of the victims of Nazi or Fascist persecution." The signatories undertook to fulfill these responsibilities on the
basis of the legal requirements of the United States.[179]

By the time the American authorities finally authorized the JCR as
trustee in February 1949, it had gained several other members: the Agu-
das Israel World Organization, the American Federation of Jews from
Central Europe, the Joint, the Anglo-Jewish Association, the Board of
Deputies of British Jews, the Committee on Restoration, the JA, and
the Committee Representing the Interests of the Jewish Communities
of Germany (initially in the American Occupation Zone, known as Interessenvertretung der jüdischen Gemeinden und Kultusvereinigungen
in der amerikanischen Besatzungszone).[180] The final body to be integrated into the JCR in December 1949 was the French Alliance Israélite
Universelle, JCR members having repeatedly complained about the lack
of French representation.[181] The JCR had thus not only succeeded in
besting and incorporating its competitors while securing its status as
sole Jewish interest group in the field of cultural restitution but had also
managed to unite under one banner all the important Jewish organizations of the day and thus the various factions of world Jewry. Apart from
the Commission executive board's efforts, this was probably achieved
chiefly because, for all those involved, preservation of the meager remnants of Jewish cultural life in Europe was an existential matter.

The legal and financial framework for the JCR's work was to be provided through its ties to the JRSO. Cooperation made a great deal of
sense given that both organizations had the same goal—namely, to establish the Jewish people as collective heirs to the remaining heirless goods
in Germany. Cooperation was also favored by the representatives of the
American government. In response to the Commission's proposals, US
officials had suggested that it was best to wait until the JRSO had been authorized and then proceed in cooperation with it.[182] Precisely because the
two organizations' spheres of activity overlapped, the American officials
regarded their fusion as conducive to their success.[183] The Commission
endorsed this proposal. In early 1947, in a letter to Isaiah Kenen of the AJ-
Conf chiefly concerned with financial issues, Baron also mulled whether

to organize a membership corporation under New York law with some
such name as the Jewish Cultural Reconstruction Corporation. This

corporation [. . .] will be given powers sufficiently varied and broad to enable it to act either as the Restitution Commission's [JRSO] agent with respect to confiscated cultural property [. . .] or as the trustee of the cultural property, in the event that there shall be a separate trustee for such property. [. . .] In the event that there shall be a single trusteeship for all confiscated property, the Restitution Commission shall irrevocably designate the Reconstruction Commission as the trustee's agent to perform, in the Trustee's name and on the Trustee's behalf, the duties and functions of the trustee with respect to cultural property.[184]

The JCR executive board later backed such cooperation as well, so in June 1947, the JCR and JRSO signed an agreement setting out their different responsibilities, which was also signed by the Joint and the JA as the JRSO's future sponsors: "You will distribute such Jewish cultural property as you may succeed in recovering among Jewish communities throughout the world in such manner as will in your judgment best serve the religious and cultural needs and interests of the Jewish people. [. . .] To the best of your ability you will act as the Commission's [JRSO] agent in relation to cultural property and, as such, will promptly undertake necessary and appropriate measures in order to discover, claim, acquire, receive, hold, maintain, and dispose of such property."[185]

In August, this agreement came into force, laying the groundwork for the two organizations' joint endeavors.[186] As a result, the JCR too now received financial support from the Joint and JA.[187] On June 23, 1948, the JRSO gained formal recognition as the successor organization with responsibility for Jewish property in the American occupation zone after the two organizations had jointly negotiated the final steps in the process, while the JCR was authorized as its agent on February 15, 1949.

3

Reconstructing Jewish Culture

The New Map of Jewish Life after 1945

The Salvage of Jewish Cultural Property from Germany

An Agreement in Frankfurt

On February 15, 1949, in the Frankfurt headquarters of the American military government, Orren McJunkins, head of the OMGUS restitution division, Benjamin Ferencz, JRSO director general in Germany, and Joshua Starr, executive secretary of the JCR, signed the agreement establishing the JCR as official Jewish trustee. Henceforth the JCR bore responsibility for, and rights to, heirless and nonidentifiable cultural goods of Jewish provenance in the American zone. The preconditions for this had been created, first, through the recognition, in June 1948, of the JRSO on the basis of implementing regulation 3 to military government law 59[1] and, second, through fulfillment of the US authorities' requirement that the JCR enhance its international character and integrate German Jewish interest groups.

The decisive factor was the pressure emanating from the US military government, particularly from Lucius Clay. He had increasingly sought to dispel the doubts of the State and War Department by emphasizing the complicated situation in the American-controlled collecting points for stolen cultural property, which still housed hundreds of thousands of heirless Jewish items—a problem crying out for rapid resolution.[2] But initially, the Department of the Army suspended all negotiations between the military government and the JCR,[3] as the State Department saw a need for further discussion within the US administration.[4] The pressure to act increased again only due to the planned conclusion of the cultural restitution program in December 1948 and the gradual transfer of responsibility to the German state governments.[5] But before a contract could be signed, the precise areas of responsibility of the JRSO and JCR had still to be determined. Regardless of the negotiations with JCR, the JRSO had resumed its work as a Jewish successor organization in the American occupation zone in summer 1948 and could now take charge of, restitute, or in some cases sell former Jewish property to support Jewish welfare organizations and communities across the world. It took care of private and public Jewish real estate and property assets in Germany.[6] The JCR, meanwhile, was not just to act as administrator of heirless Jewish cultural property originating in Germany but was also permitted to file claims to objects from other countries. Strictly speaking, then, the JCR was not so much a successor organization as a trust—a status that did much to determine its character, enabling it to act as a representative of the entire Jewish collectivity rather than just German Jews. In a letter to Eli Rock, who was the member of the JCR board of directors representing the Joint, Hannah Arendt underlined this difference and its significance: "Although JCR acted as the cultural agent of JRSO, it was not founded as a German Jewish successor organization, but laid claim to all heirless Jewish cultural property found on German territory on behalf of the Jewish people."[7] This legal construction allowed the JCR to administer all stolen cultural property whose owners were no longer alive or could no longer be ascertained or whose institutions of origin had been destroyed, regardless of its territorial origin. The decision to extend JCR's remit was made chiefly because of the Eastern European collections on German soil: if there was to be any hope of ensuring the return of Jewish cultural property to Jewish ownership, it was vital to overcome the limitations imposed by the territorialism of traditional restitution law. The "Frankfurt Agreement" established between the JCR and OMGUS eliminated this restriction and officially conferred on the JCR the rights to confiscated and stolen cultural property from all over Europe found in the American zone: "Jewish Cultural Properties, separated from owning individuals and organizations in Europe during the period of Nazi Rule, taken into the custody by the U.S. Military Government in occupied Germany, [. . .] are transferred herewith to JCR, Inc. [. . .] The JCR will act as trustee in receiving this property for the Jewish people and in distributing it to such public or quasi-public religious, cultural, or educational institutions as it sees fit to be used in the interest of perpetuating Jewish art and culture."[8]

What the protagonists of the Jewish organizations had been fighting for since the early 1940s was thus cast into a legally binding agreement—namely, the recognition of a nonstate Jewish organization to pursue the interests of the Jewish collectivity within postwar restitution. In this context, it is remarkable that—in contrast to the much bigger and more famous Claims Conference, which got off the ground not much later—the JCR combined the interests of Diaspora Jews and those in Israel. The stipulation that goods would be transferred to the JCR on the condition of their exclusive use to maintain the collective Jewish cultural heritage referred to all Jews worldwide, thus recognizing the needs of those living in Israel and the rest of the world on an equal basis.[9] The only reference made to earlier restitution agreements was the proposition that if legitimate claims were filed by former owners, the JCR undertook to return their property to them. The agreement encompassed books, archival materials and documents, Torah scrolls, ritual objects of fabric, precious metal and stone, paintings, selected furniture, and other property agreed upon by the parties responsible. The JCR pledged to organize the distribution of these materials; their sale was prohibited, particularly in the case of ritual objects, while the costs of the entire process of packaging, stowage, crating, and shipments to the German border or a warehouse were to be borne by the German state governments as "occupation costs."[10]

However marginal it may appear within the overall history of postwar restitution and despite all the limits imposed, the agreement must be considered a revolutionary success of Jewish diplomacy. Crucially, the JCR formulated a program representing the needs of all Jewries, thus integrating the different factions across the world. The all-encompassing experience of persecution and annihilation had virtually imposed this collective approach. The JCR thus championed Jewish interests and, for the first time in history, ensured that the Jewish collectivity could figure as a recognized legal subject within international law beyond the status of national minority. The organization mediated between the old antagonisms within the Jewish world, which continued to flare up from time to time, and the new ones generated by the geographical and demographic shifts after 1945. It succeeded in doing so because all those involved had a shared interest in preserving the few remaining treasures. There is reason to view this cultural restitution process as a prelude to subsequent extensive accords on restitution and compensation between Germany and Jewish representative bodies, which finally reached their conclusion in the 1952 Luxembourg Agreement. The nearly forgotten agreements signed by American officials on the one hand and the JRSO and JCR on the other had set the course for what was "undoubtedly the largest program of compensation in human history,"[11] as negotiated between the state of Israel, the Claims Conference, and the Federal Republic of Germany in the Dutch town of Wassenaar. In recognition of the exceptional degree of persecution suffered by Jews under National Socialism, both the Luxembourg Agreement and, earlier, the authorization of the JRSO and JCR endowed the Jewish collectivity with a new legal status and constructed a nonstate legal successor while categorizing Nazi confiscations as an element in the policy of annihilation.[12]

Before the official agreement, the JCR had already begun to fulfill its future role by becoming a corporation, and in October 1947, its leadership resolved that a small group of representatives would travel to the American zone in Germany and begin work. Joshua Starr set off for Europe in spring 1948, and from then on, he furnished the members of the JCR with all necessary information. He visited the Offenbach Archival Depot, gained a sense of the situation there, and negotiated with the director at the time, Joseph Horne. Starr succeeded in getting Horne interested in the JCR's cause. The prospect of resolving the unclear status of the masses of objects for which the JCR would be responsible made Horne one's of its key supporters.[13] During his stay in Europe, Starr visited Offenbach on numerous occasions. He underlined the gravity of the situation to the various members of the military government, sought to prevent the return of collections whose future seemed uncertain, and helped identify and catalog Jewish and especially Hebrew books in the depot.[14] In addition to his activities at the depot, Starr negotiated with the JCR's local Jewish partner organizations and with German authorities and institutions to obtain information on their holdings and suspected stolen materials. Without specific instruction from the JCR, he also made contact with the Committee Representing the Interests of the Jewish Communities and Religious Associations in Germany (Interessenvertretung der jüdischen Gemeinden und Kultusvereinigungen in Deutschland). Following a meeting in Munich with Philipp Auerbach, Bavarian state commissioner for the racially, religiously, and politically persecuted, and Rabbi Aaron Orenstein, the most important members of the Interessenvertretung, Starr reported to Baron that they had reached agreement on cooperation and there were no further obstacles to the latter's membership of the JCR. Starr had little inkling of the problems this cooperation was to entail; these reached a serious level only after the JCR's work in the American zone had properly taken off. Auerbach, himself a member of JRSO's board of directors, became an at times fierce critic of the policy of exportation and compensation pursued by the JRSO and JCR.[15] Joshua Starr was also the first to report in detail on the situation in Austria, which he visited in August 1948 to speak with community representatives from Vienna and assess the progress of restitution. Overall, he felt, neither the investigations into objects' whereabouts nor restitution seemed to have gotten very far.[16] Following a brief stay in New York in January 1949, Starr returned to Europe to conclude the "Frankfurt Agreement" on behalf of the JCR.

During the same period, the JCR's structure and communicative system were being established in New York. In addition to the board of directors, made up of two individuals from each member organization and presided over by the six officers of the corporation, an advisory committee dealing with all issues relating to the allocation and distribution of goods and, from May 1949, an executive committee intended to operate between meetings of the board of directors were created. So-called field directors were to be sent to Germany and other parts of Europe to coordinate the organization's work at the local level. To handle the material to be delivered from Europe, the JCR established two large collecting depots in Brooklyn for interim storage. At the time of its official recognition, JCR's officers were Salo W. Baron, president; Leo Baeck, Simon Federbusch, Gershom Scholem, Alan Stroock, vice presidents; and Jerome Michael, chairman of the board of directors. David Rosenstein acted as treasurer, Joshua Starr as executive secretary, and Max Gruenewald as secretary, with Hannah Arendt taking over for Starr in June 1949. The advisory committee was composed of rabbis and scholars from the major Jewish research institutions in the United States,[17] while the executive committee was composed of representatives from each corporation member.

The Offenbach Operation

Once the agreement had been signed, the JCR gradually implemented its ideas on the reordering of Jewish cultural life in the wake of Nazi rule.

The American officials had signed up to the near-complete removal of the amassed cultural treasures from Europe, sharing the view that there was little prospect of any revival of Jewish culture there, particularly in Germany. With respect to Jewish knowledge and tradition, the idea was that future sites of learning, study, research, collection, preservation, and commemoration were to emerge and grow in other places with the help of the salvaged books and objects. First, though, the priority was to sort, allocate, and distribute the collections in Offenbach and Wiesbaden while launching a systematic search for stolen goods in Germany. In addition to Joshua Starr, five members of the JCR were sent to the American central collecting points. Ernst G. Lowenthal, representative of the British Jewish Relief Unit and the Committee on Restoration and a member of the Council, worked at both depots from April 1949 to March 1951. Later, he occupied a key position at the Jewish successor organization established in 1950 in the British zone (the Jewish Trust Corporation; JTC). Rabbi Bernard Heller worked in Germany from February to September 1949. Shlomo Shunami, chief librarian at the National and University Library in Jerusalem, worked in Offenbach and Wiesbaden for the JCR and the Hebrew University from March to November 1949. In his capacity as the director of the Bezalel Museum in Jerusalem, Mordechai Narkiss dealt with the art and ritual objects in the depots. Finally, Meir Ben-Horin worked in Wiesbaden from July to October 1950. Hannah Arendt went to Germany twice in her capacity as JCR executive secretary, but rather than the depots, her primary focus was on negotiating with Jewish communities and the German authorities.

In late June 1949, the Offenbach Archival Depot was officially closed. By then, the JCR had taken charge of just under nine hundred Torah scrolls and more than 250,000 volumes of Jewish provenance in addition to journals and those sections of the library established by the Nazi Stürmer publishing house in Nuremberg—consisting of materials stolen from Jewish private households and institutions—that remained in the depot. While the OAD was prepared for its dissolution, the books and objects were already on their way to the United Kingdom, Israel, South Africa, and the United States. Around ten thousand books were entrusted to bodies representing the Jewish communities in Germany in order to cover their needs. In connection with the American military government's gradual withdrawal from Germany, and to save costs, all remaining holdings from Offenbach were transferred to the large collecting point at the State Museum in Wiesbaden.[18] As they concluded their activities in Offenbach, the senior staff at the depot organized a farewell celebration that was held on May 31 and attended by a number of JCR and JRSO members. Two years earlier, Lucy Dawidowicz had reported with consternation on the ceremony marking the depot's first anniversary, which she deemed inappropriate amid the piled-up remnants of willfully destroyed Jewish culture. In contrast, in his farewell speech to the German staff, Bernard Heller made a number of generous remarks on the atmosphere in the depot and on the symbolic significance of its work. He praised the efforts of the German assistants, interpreting them as an important act of rapprochement and reconciliation between Jews and Germans. And while he admitted in his report to New York that the Jewish DPs working in the depot and the German staff had celebrated separately all afternoon, he concluded his speech on-site with an optimistic summary: "May this commingling of German and Jewish workers spell the beginning of peace, and amity and goodwill between the peoples we represent. May it be taken as an assurance that never again will such misdeeds be allowed to be reenacted."[19] That Heller's conciliatory stance was somewhat out of sync with the views of JCR officials is evident in the New York staff's truncation of his official report on the conclusion of the depot's activities (which was sent to all members); they also augmented it with some of the less benign passages from his speech.

Holdings in the Offenbach Depot that were transferred to Wiesbaden were chiefly those with an uncertain future. These included Hermann Cohen's private library; the Raphael Kirchheim collection from Frankfurt am Main; the library of the Israelite Religious School (Israelitische Religionsschule) in Frankfurt; the Wünsche collection from Dresden; sections of the libraries of the Jewish Theological Seminary in Breslau and the Hochschule für die Wissenschaft des Judentums in Berlin; holdings from community libraries in Berlin, Darmstadt, Frankfurt, and Königsberg; and the so-called Baltic Collection, which included more than thirty thousand volumes. The latter comprised all the identifiable books of Jewish provenance from the Baltic region, such as the comprehensive holdings of the Mapu Library in Kaunas, yeshivot libraries from Slabodka (present-day Vilijampolė) and Kaunas, and large collections from Riga, Vilna, and Tallinn.[20] While doing his research in Offenbach Starr had already determined that most of their institutions of origin no longer existed. In July 1949, after protracted discussions between the American military government, officials at the State Department, and the JCR, an addendum to the "Frankfurt Agreement" conferred full responsibility for the Baltic Collection on the JCR on the proviso that it identify as many owners as possible and initiate restitutions as necessary.[21] This agreement was reached because, like the JCR, the American government concluded that the "almost complete disorganization of Jewish cultural and community life in Eastern Europe in comparison to 1939, render restitution on basis [of] existing principles of questionable value."[22] This decision, to the benefit of the JCR, was no doubt partly made due to the logic of the Cold War. As had already occurred with respect to the YIVO, the Americans refused to transfer or restitute goods to the Baltic countries due to their annexation by the Soviet Union. In compliance with the regulations, the JCR stored the Baltic books in the Joint warehouse in Paris for two years, while the Mapu Library holdings, along with forty-five crates of yeshivot holdings, were sent to the JNUL in Jerusalem for fiduciary administration since a number of Baltic yeshivot had been reestablished in Israel.[23] Lists of identifiable owners were distributed to leading Jewish institutions and also published.[24] Once it was clear that there was no significant potential for restitution—partly because the JCR deliberately included in the lists only private and no public Baltic assets[25]—in June 1951, the decision was made to distribute the rest of the items, along with a request that all recipients document and keep them separately to facilitate the settling of any subsequent claims. Against the wishes of Arendt and the JCR leadership, who wanted to transfer a large number of books to the Joint as a gesture of thanks for the close cooperation, which would have meant leaving them in Europe, the majority of members decided that the books should be shipped in equal parts to the United States and Israel, while only a far smaller proportion would go to the communities and institutions of Western Europe.[26]

But the United States' hardening stance toward the Soviet Union was not entirely good news for JCR employees in Germany. They feared the resumption of armed conflict and were highly critical of the Americans' progressive surrender of responsibility to the West German authorities.

The background to this was the new U.S. political strategy of rehabilitating West Germany and rapidly integrating it into the Western alliances to form a bulwark against the Eastern bloc. Jewish representatives were naturally suspicious of the reorientation away from a strict policy of "reeducation" and reappraisal of Nazi crimes to an integrative, diplomatic approach to West Germany with a focus on democratization and strategic partnership. This turn had a discernible impact on the field of restitution, in which it was impossible to predict whether the German authorities would live up to American standards.[27] Bernard Heller expressed these concerns in September 1949, shortly before concluding his work in Germany: "The foundation of the Restitution Program is Law 59. Considering, however, the political conditions consequent to the tension between the East and West and the latter's eagerness to woo and win the Germans to its side, this law assumed the form not of granite stone but of a crumbling chunk of clay. [. . .] We are working on a terrain where the ground under us is gradually sinking and out of its deep bowel a sudden violent eruption may break out at any time."[28]

JCR staff feared that under German authority, the restitution law and the "Frankfurt Agreement" might cease to apply or be curtailed, particularly when it came to the many objects of German Jewish origin still stored in the Wiesbaden Depot, which they were determined to get out of Germany at all costs. Fears often discussed in the abstract now took on concrete form: the goods might ultimately fall into the hands of the former perpetrators rather than returning to Jewish ownership. Against this background, Lowenthal, Heller, Narkiss, and Shunami stepped up their efforts in Wiesbaden and other American collecting points that still housed Jewish cultural property.

Two collections now in Wiesbaden confronted JCR workers with particular challenges: first, a collection of more than ten thousand partially fragmented ritual objects and hundreds of Torah scrolls and, second, tens of thousands of volumes from private Jewish collections. Prior to his return to the United States, Starr had pushed for an expert in art and ritual objects to be sent from Israel to Offenbach to categorize the materials there and determine their value, utility, and potential for future use. Ultimately, it was Narkiss who was to be chiefly responsible for this work.[29] In Wiesbaden, he and Heller sorted and cataloged Seder Plates, Torah arks and crowns, lamps, silver and gold goblets, menorot,

Hanukkah lamps, and fabrics for use in religious services. They continued to distinguish between usable ceremonial objects and those whose only function could be as museum pieces. The Bezalel Museum in Jerusalem was granted first choice of objects. In addition, the JCR advisory committee had decided to transfer six hundred still usable Torah scrolls held by the Joint to individual communities in Israel.[30] Several thousand objects and scrolls, however, were in very poor condition, and here Hannah Arendt recognized a specific hallmark of the Nazis' approach to ritual objects: "Unlike the books which had been pretty well preserved by the Nazis, the Torah Scrolls and ritual objects bear the all too visible marks of willful destruction. More than 3,000 of the 10,000 objects can no longer be regarded as objects at all; they are merely fragments, not only beyond repair, but sometimes even beyond recognition."[31] Her observation highlights again the different notions and aims embedded in Nazi theft and material destruction in relation to Jewish history and memory: valuable books, documents, and works of art were stolen and preserved with the goal of usurping them entirely or cutting them off their original background. Objects that were visibly linked with the traditions and religion of Judaism were far more likely to fall prey to destruction at the hands of the Rosenberg task force and others wishing to eliminate them from European space and memory altogether.[32]

Of the several thousand heavily damaged objects and Torah scrolls, several hundred were painstakingly restored by a group of Eastern European specialists at the Joint in Paris. Many objects, however, could no longer be saved, so in line with Jewish ritual, their remnants were laid to rest in Israel and the United States. For America, the Synagogue Council arranged a public ceremony attended by Baron and performed by Rabbi Simon Kramer, president of the Council, on January 13, 1952, at the Beth-El Cemetery in Paramus, New Jersey. A makeshift gravestone bore the inscription "Holy Religious Objects from Nazi-Looted European Synagogues."[33] Just how seriously the salvage and adequate treatment of ceremonial objects were felt to be is also evident in the harsh reaction to another way in which JCR and JRSO officials treated unusable silver objects. In June 1949, at the behest of Saul Kagan, twenty-five crates of such objects were sent to Sheffield, England, where they were to be melted down and sold in order to support welfare projects for the survivors, and immigrants arriving in Israel. Most JCR officers and Cecil Roth in

particular expressed disapproval at this procedure and the nontranspar-
ent decision-making process that had preceded it.[34] The procedure was
clearly painful for Heller, who compared the melting to the incineration
of human beings in death camp crematoria.[35] As we saw in connection
with the Offenbach Archival Depot, the issues thrown up by the restoration process were rooted in the much broader trauma suffered as
a result of the impossibility of rescuing people from the Nazis earlier.
The vanishing of further objects had to be prevented at all costs; so little
remained of the cultural wealth of the European Jewries that additional
losses seemed unbearable to most contemporaries; the imperative was
to collect, save, and conserve every fragment, no matter how small. In
this sense, the JCR's official policy differed markedly from that of the
JRSO, which repeatedly sold objects, land, real estate, and other assets
for which it was responsible in order to provide financial support for
survivors of the Holocaust. JCR's approach to movable cultural property,
which it perceived to have historical and identity-forming value, was the
exact opposite: it resolved not to sell a single item. Ultimately, the JCR
distributed a total of just under eight thousand intact objects. In addition to communities in Israel, the beneficiaries of this legacy were to be
found chiefly in the United States, the United Kingdom, South Africa,
Canada, Argentina, and Peru, in addition to the Jews in Western European served by the Joint.[36]

The second step taken at the Wiesbaden collecting point, which took
several months to implement, involved the large quantity of books from
private Jewish households, which had to be dealt with in compliance
with OMGUS requirements. Around 45,000 such volumes accumulated
in Wiesbaden between early 1949 and mid-1950. The JCR—represented
by Arendt, Ben-Horin, and Lowenthal—came to an agreement with the
American officials that attempts would be made to find all owners of
at least six surviving volumes and return the books to them if possible.
By fall 1951, 16,500 books were thus removed from the depot and stored
along with the Baltic books at the Joint depots in Paris and Antwerp. It
was possible to identify around 830 owners by means of ex libris and
other evidence in the volumes; like the owners of the Baltic books, from
April 1951 on, they were listed in relevant, widely distributed Jewish
newspapers such as *Aufbau* and the *Jewish Chronicle*. Under the heading
"Books are looking for their owners," the JCR published page upon page

of owners' names and information on the number of volumes originating in their private collections, stating that it was willing to return them if their ownership could be proved to their "satisfaction."[37] About 450 individuals subsequently contacted the JCR in New York; 225 of them were recognized as legitimate claimants and went on to receive almost five thousand books. From then on, requests from private individuals searching for their families' or communities' property piled up in the JCR office, but the organization had insufficient personnel to take care of them all. Many requests were passed on to the Central Filing Agency (Zentralmeldeamt) in Bad Nauheim, which processed all private claims for compensation and restitution in the American zone and had already relayed a number of private claims to the Offenbach Depot.[38] Some of those who contacted JCR were well-known figures attempting to ascertain the fate of their stolen private library or the libraries of other Jewish scholars. For example, Jewish lawyer Guido Kisch, cousin of the famous journalist and writer Egon Erwin Kisch, contacted the JCR and urged it to ensure the transfer of the 113 volumes to the German department at the University of Lund that had belonged to Agathe Lasch, a professor of German philology in Hamburg before the Nazi takeover who was murdered after her deportation to Riga in 1942. Members of the department in Sweden had gone to great lengths to save her, though ultimately in vain. The JCR agreed to this proposal on the condition that any heirs to Lasch's estate must give their consent and supported the books' donation as a gesture of symbolic thanks to the university.[39]

The remains of large private collections whose owners or rightful heirs could not be found were divided between the United States, Latin America, and Israel. Almost thirteen thousand volumes were transferred to YIVO, its branch in Buenos Aires, the HUC, and a number of communities and the Colegio Israelita de México in Mexico City; all other books, together with those left in the Paris Depot, were sent to the JNUL and to smaller libraries in Israel.[40]

Throughout 1950, the sorting and allocation of the holdings of German Jewish institutions at the Wiesbaden collecting point also came to an end, work mostly supervised by Lowenthal. A large portion of the archival materials arriving there were allocated to Israel, the majority view being that its needs were greatest. In the case of newspapers, meanwhile, priority was given to the United States, while rare items were divided fairly equally between the two countries. The United Kingdom also received a small portion of the holdings.[41] After several extensions, the collecting point finally wound up its work on July 1, 1951. The remaining objects were transferred to the largest central collecting point under American administration, located in Munich, Lowenthal and Ben-Horin of the JCR ended their work in Wiesbaden, the JRSO in Nuremberg took charge of the remaining Jewish objects, and the site itself was transformed back into the Hesse State Museum. A crucial part of JCR operations in Germany was completed—what remained were many open questions about Jewish cultural treasures outside the protected spaces in Offenbach and Wiesbaden.

Opposing Visions: JCR and the German Jewish Communities

JCR staff now increasingly turned to new tasks, intensifying the search for cultural property throughout Germany and fostering cooperation with the German authorities and the senior staff of libraries and archives. In addition, the board of directors promoted a comprehensive microfilm project encompassing archival materials, documents, and Hebrew manuscripts in German institutions.[42]

Outside of the American-administered collecting points, the key representative of JCR was Hannah Arendt, who returned to Germany for the first time after her forced emigration. Between December 1949 and March 1950, she traveled throughout the country to inspect holdings, negotiate with German institutions, conclude agreements with German Jewish communities, and help stimulate the further restitution of objects. Often she remained in one place no longer than two days. By car or train she traveled through Germany, meticulously searching for looted items and displaying a combative spirit as she dealt with often uncooperative personnel. In a letter home to her husband Heinrich Blücher, she described her situation laconically: "It's a damned mess I've let myself in for here. But it's worth the trouble."[43] Her former academic teacher Karl Jaspers, close confidante of Arendt since her university days with whom she had resumed contact and whom she visited in Basel during this journey, praised her commitment in a note sent to Blücher after her visit: "Your Hannah is unbelievably lively. So far in her venture all doors have opened, so that her success feels a little uncanny even to her. [. . .] When not only trust and standing one's ground, but also the momentum of creative action, are as apparent as they are in Hannah, one becomes more courageous oneself."[44] But Arendt had little choice but to be courageous as she constantly came up against the boundaries imposed on her by the German authorities. Yet another area of conflict arose in connection with the reestablished Jewish communities in Germany. Against most international predictions, Jewish communities reemerged in Germany, and they often saw themselves as the legal heirs to recovered Jewish property. The JRSO and JCR, like most international Jewish organizations, struggled to understand Jews who opted to reconstruct Jewish life in the "land of the perpetrators" and rarely saw any good reason for property assets to remain there. Their views were only reinforced by the fact that between 1945 and 1947, around 250,000 Holocaust survivors, desperate to immigrate to the new Jewish centers outside Europe, found themselves in Germany, Italy, and Austria after emerging from concentration camps, hiding places, and their temporary shelters in the Soviet Union; most of them were accommodated in DP camps supervised by the US Army and the UN Relief and Rehabilitation Administration. For the JRSO and JCR, after this transitional phase of vibrant Jewish life on "bloodstained soil," Jewish life in Germany (and most other central and Eastern European places) would be over.[45] Several international bodies called for Jews who had resumed residence in Germany to be excluded from Jewish organizations or even disputed their belonging to the Jewish people—in sum, many of their outraged brethren pursued a "politics of total isolation."[46] All major initiatives pursued by the Joint, the JA, and most other committees and organizations active in Germany and Europe after 1945 sought to provide emergency relief for survivors and facilitate emigration and resettlement. In this context, there was hardly any room for reemerging communities.[47] The JCR actively contributed to this internal Jewish dispute. Hannah Arendt wrote to Gertrud Jaspers as early as May 1946: "But I don't know either how one can stand to live there [in Germany] as a Jew in a society that doesn't even deign to speak about 'our' problem— and today that means our dead."[48] Despite all the positive experiences that Arendt also reported, her trip to Germany was to reinforce this aversion. In many places and on many occasions, her sense of now belonging to—and wanting to belong to—the United States rather than Germany was painfully reconfirmed. This conviction, which she was never to revise, had to do with the past but also with her present impression of the country and its inhabitants. "Do you know how right you were never to want to come back here again?" she asked Blücher in one of her letters and carried on explaining: "The lump of sentimentality that begins to rise gets stuck in one's throat. The Germans are living off lifelong illusions and stupidity. The latter stinks to the skies."[49] On Arendt's second trip to Germany in 1952, nothing much had changed. Again she wrote to her husband: "There are many 'returnees' here from America [. . .]. But don't let this tempt you; we would have a hard time putting up with this masked ball of the '20s, which resembles Proust's death ball to a hair."[50] At the JRSO and JCR, visions of the end of Jewish life in Germany nurtured the old fears. Hannah Arendt confirmed those concerns after taking part in a meeting of the Bavarian State Association of Jewish Communities (Bayerischer Landesverband jüdischer Gemeinden) in January 1950, and despite contrary developments already in evidence, she concluded that "with the probable extinction of the German communities over the next few years their cultural property will automatically pass to the German state. It is thus clear that every German authority must have an interest in cultural property being restituted to the Jewish communities and *not* to the JRSO/JCR."[51]

Many community members, meanwhile, accused the JCR and JRSO of self-enrichment and corruption. They felt disadvantaged in the process of distribution and in some cases even saw themselves as victims of a second round of looting. Arendt was, for example, confronted with accusations from the Munich community that the JCR was administering money into its own pockets, selling books in New York, and breaking "ceremonial objects in order to sell them as scrap metal."[52] It was not just in view of these misinterpretations that Arendt concluded that the communities were one of the greatest obstacles to the JCR's work. Her assessment was also based on the conduct of many of the community representatives she met who rarely took a positive view of the JCR's activities. Certainly, all JCR members emphasized that the small remnant of Jews in Germany must be furnished with the bare necessities, but they were not prepared to relinquish to them more than was necessary. With reference to the communities in Mainz and Worms, whose recognition as rightful heirs to the Jewish cultural property present in the area was being negotiated with the French authorities, Meir Ben-Horin minced no words in outlining how things stood following the official recognition of these claims: "At the moment, the post-war congregations are recognized as legal successors. This means that the 3,000–5,000 books in the Mainz congregational library, the ceremonial objects in the Mainz museum, and the objects saved from destruction in Worms, including the two Machsorim of 1272, as well as the property of nazi-dissolved associations, foundations, societies, all legally belong at present to the 65 members—mostly old widows—of the Mainz congregation."[53]

In the opinion of the JCR, this assessment applied to almost all German communities and their cultural treasures. In addition, the Nazi policy of dispersal of looted objects meant that after the war, Jewish cultural property often appeared in places it did not originate from, but—for practical reasons—it was returned from the Allies to the closest community at hand. As a result, objects often ended up in communities they did not belong to. In light of this, in May 1949, the directors of the JCR decided that with the help of the Council, the German communities themselves must be called upon to research the provenance of all items allocated to them in order to prove that they were in their rightful place.[54] One exception seems to have been JCR's negotiations with the communities in Nuremberg and Marburg. The Jews in Nuremberg relinquished without hesitation all the material in their possession, chiefly salvaged sections of the Nazi Stürmer collection, to Koppel Pinson and the Offenbach Depot.[55] The Marburg community followed suit, remarking to the JCR that there were no German Jews left in the city and that the community consisted of Eastern European refugees who made no claim to the material found there.[56] In general, despite all the concerns and criticism on both sides, the JCR's work with the communities in Germany went more smoothly than that of the JRSO. Because the latter dealt almost exclusively with German congregational property and also proposed to administer it, the field of conflict was more extensive than in the case of the JCR.[57] But one fact that provoked the relevant communities' ire seemed to apply more to the JCR than the JRSO: its board of directors was focused on the interests of émigré Jews worldwide—the JCR itself, of course, consisted almost entirely of emigrants. They were convinced that the Jewish people as a whole was much better served when property was taken out of Germany even if local communities might suffer as a result.

This ambivalent relationship between the JCR and community members in Germany with respect to post-Holocaust Jewish life is particularly evident if we look at the JCR's efforts in Berlin and Frankfurt, former centers of German Jewish culture. Conditions in Berlin were particularly difficult for JCR officials because of its division into four administrative zones; the Allies had failed to agree to a common approach, so laws on restitution were sector-specific. The JCR's most important informant in the city was again Ernst Grumach.[58] Hannah Arendt, Joshua Starr, and Gershom Scholem asked him to help find and restitute collections, his forced labor in the RSHA having endowed him with detailed knowledge of the whereabouts of the looted cultural property concentrated in Berlin. Arendt knew Grumach from her school days in Königsberg and their student years in Marburg, where they had been close acquaintances, so she could easily establish contact with him to advance her own work and that of her colleagues. After a number of talks with Grumach in April 1949, Joshua Starr submitted the first coherent report on the situation of cultural property in Berlin, supplemented by a second report produced by Arendt following her arrival there in February 1950.[59] In addition to the sections of the Berlin congregational libraries looted by the RSHA and eventually stored in the Offenbach Depot, which had been passed to the JCR for fiduciary administration,[60] according to both reports, there were still substantial collections in Berlin that the JCR ought to take charge of as soon as possible. These consisted of parts of the Gesamtarchiv of the German Jews, which had apparently survived among the remnants of the archive of the Reich Association of Jews in Germany, paintings and handicraft from the Jewish Museum Berlin (Jüdisches Museum Berlin), remains of the congregational library of the Oranienburger Straße synagogue, and Nazi-looted volumes stored there from Amsterdam, Mantua, Białystok, Posen, and Breslau. In Berlin, Arendt also found books from the Hochschule für die Wissenschaft des Judentums and a number of private libraries. Further recovered items included a collection of silver and ceremonial objects from all over Germany stored in the Joachimstaler Straße community building, archival holdings of the Reich Office of Genealogy (Reichssippenamt) with materials from Breslau and Vienna communities, and a portion of YIVO properties. Arendt also discovered around one thousand Torah scrolls, some of them heavily damaged, in the Weißensee Cemetery.

The main problem facing the JCR was that the majority of treasures were stored in the eastern sector of the city. Arendt reported, "Transportation from the Russian into one of the western sectors is not impossible, but depends entirely upon good will of the Berlin community and is, indeed, a rather dangerous affair. Every office in the Eastern sector, Jewish or non-Jewish, is infested with agents."[61] She therefore recommended working as closely as possible with rabbi Steven Schwarzschild, who had left Berlin in 1939 and returned there from the United States in September 1948 to do his best to meet the needs of the city's entire Jewish community—which, according to Arendt, was "the most difficult position in all Germany."[62] In July 1945, approximately 6 to 7,000 Jews were left of more than 160,000, and they reestablished the community with its center in Oranienburger Straße—a "fractious, divided congregation."[63] Their numbers grew as Jewish refugees arrived from the East and were housed in camps in Mariendorf and Schlachtensee, but most of them left Berlin soon after. By 1948, about 2,000 Jews lived in the Eastern parts and roughly 7,000 in the Western parts of the city. Since rabbi Schwarzschild was responsible for all of them, the community—as his daughter recalls—"transcended the division between the Russian occupation Zone, [. . .] and the Western Zones."[64] Still, cooperation with this uprooted Berlin community proved highly problematic for the JCR. This was because, among other things, the Israeli representatives—above all Gershom Scholem, Schlomo Shunami, and Alexander Bein—pursued their own interests in their dealings with the community, wishing to obtain the remnants of the Gesamtarchiv for the newly established institutions in Jerusalem. Despite the joint efforts being made within the JCR, competing projects suddenly emerged that confused the local interlocutors and slowed things down: the various responsibilities and interests had become impenetrable to community representatives. Another problem was that books and documents were frequently dispersed across the city. Certain volumes were returned to their owners or bequeathed to city libraries, and a number of community members stated that a large portion of documents was passed to the Berlin municipal authorities. But the main issue causing friction between the JCR and the community was the collection of books found by Arendt in its center on Oranienburger Straße, on whose size and provenance the sources present an ambiguous picture. After Arendt's alarmed report, the JCR, with the help of the first Tentative List, attempted to demonstrate that the holdings did not belong in Berlin. The board of directors therefore decided to offer parts of the remaining collections in Wiesbaden in exchange because Schwarzschild and prominent members of the community had repeatedly underlined their need for prayer books and other religious texts. To initiate the exchange, the JCR compiled a list of claims and sent five thousand books from the Wiesbaden collecting point to the community.

But the Berliners failed to respond, and JCR staff were never able to ascertain precisely how many and which books actually remained in the Oranienburger Straße building. Heinz Galinski, head of the community, had in fact become so enraged with the JCR over the course of the negotiations that he publicly announced that there was no library in the community center at all. In an official note sent to the JCR, he declared that the opposite was true, asserting that reports from Starr, Scholem, Bein, Arendt, and Heller were based on a mistake: the books they had seen, he contended, were not the property of the community or from any other Jewish source and had to be transferred back to the municipality. Contradicting their reports, he stated, "Our congregational library is empty. [. . .] Our people hunger for spiritual goods and we urgently request your help [. . .]."[65] As early as December 1946, another representative of the community in Berlin, Berthold Breslauer, the only person other than Grumach to have survived the RSHA forced labor unit, had sent a similar account to the Offenbach Depot, requesting that twenty-five thousand books from the depot be sent to Berlin because the community there had lost its precious holdings to RSHA plunder:

> The loss [of our] library is tremendously painful for us. The Jewish community of Berlin, which is currently being reestablished, requires not just material sources of support but above all spiritual ones. It is an ancient and hallowed tradition in Judaism that communities dedicate themselves to the cultivation of the sciences and regard the maintenance of libraries as their special duty. We too wish to contribute to this task and reestablish a community library. It would help further the scholarship on Judaism and the specific history of the German Jews and be generally accessible. A public library of this kind in Berlin is all the more necessary given that our members' private libraries have been lost due to the Nazi authorities' acts of violence and the bombing raids.[66]

For a short time, Ernst Grumach and Berthold Breslauer had envisaged that Berlin could become a center for Jewish thought and culture again. Both knew that a substantial number of books from the vast collection of volumes looted by the RSHA were still to be found in the city, and they wanted them to stay there as the "nucleus of a new Jewish central library [under the auspices of the Berlin Jewish Community] to which, if prevailing circumstances allow, other scientific and cultural institutes could be affiliated"[67] The authorities in Offenbach and in Berlin, along with most international Jewish organizations and activists, rejected this plan. Grumach too was increasingly doubtful.[68] In contrast, Galinski was pushing and championed Jewish community life in Germany. He was prepared to fight for it: "I have always represented the point of view that the Wannsee Conference cannot be the last word in the life of the Jewish community in Germany. Therefore, I participated with a few others to restore the Jewish community in Berlin. I have never been one of those who considered the community here as a liquidation community, but rather I have endeavored to give back to the survivors the belief in a restored, new life."[69] By the time JCR representatives concluded their operations in Germany, it had proved impossible for them to obtain unambiguous information on the Berlin holdings, which Arendt had seen with her own eyes, or to get hold of the books she had claimed. Whether some of these books had been part of the former RSHA collection and been brought clandestinely to the premises of the community or originated somewhere else, and where they were transported to later, remain open questions to this day.[70] In the JCR's official final report of 1952, however, Arendt remarked that the five thousand volumes distributed to Jewish institutions in Argentina had included numerous books originally held by the Berlin Jewish community, but it is no longer possible to determine whether the books came directly from Berlin or from the holdings at the Offenbach Depot. Furthermore, three hundred Torah scrolls from Berlin, which the JCR obtained "only by the skin of [its] teeth," were sent to Israel and the United States.[71]

Despite all the problems with the community, Arendt was euphoric about Berlin when she contemplated the situation of Germany as a whole: "Berlin: [. . .], from Spandau to Neukölln is one big field of rubble; nothing recognizable [. . .]. But: what still exists, are the Berliners. Unchanged, marvelous, humane, humorous, clever, lightening-clever even. It's the first time I feel that I've come home. [. . .] now I understand why quite a few people in the West have said, time and again, that the only place they'd want to live is in Berlin. Only here can you still find the real Germany."[72] But for the JCR, it was undoubtedly a profoundly challenging setting. Though the JRSO as a successor organization had been granted responsibility for all Western sectors in October 1949,[73] the city was a tense matrix characterized by a comparatively strong community, four Allied parties each with their own views on restitution, hardening Cold War fronts running through the city, and often intransigent German authorities and institutions. Above all, Berlin exposed JCR staff to the full impact of the Nazis' frenzied destruction of its rich Jewish cultural life. The tremendous variety of Jewish cultural and educational institutions, the diverse worlds of reading, learning, and thinking that the city had offered prior to 1933, had shrunk to a barely recognizable remnant.[74]

After Berlin, the more than thirty-thousand-strong Jewish community in Frankfurt am Main had been the second largest in Germany before 1933. Numerous art and cultural treasures, such as the large collection of Hebraica and Judaica at the university and the important ritual objects and rare items in the Museum of Jewish Antiquities (Museum Jüdischer Altertümer),[75] made the city a center of Jewish culture in the interwar period. During the war, Alfred Rosenberg's Institute for Research on the Jewish Question accumulated a tremendous amount of Jewish cultural property in the city, endowing it with an extraordinarily high concentration of valuable goods. After the war, Guido Schönberger, a former curator of the Frankfurt Historical Museum (Historisches Museum Frankfurt), who had become professor of art history at New York University and member of staff at the Jewish Museum of New York, made contact with the Frankfurt museums. He discovered that a large portion of the silver and ritual objects confiscated or saved during the November pogroms of 1938 had ended up in his former German institutional home, now known as the Frankfurter Stadtgeschichtliches Museum.[76] Arendt and others assessed the collection. The Frankfurt community reconstituted in summer 1945 and officially reestablished in January 1947 with approximately 650 members. Its heads insisted on the return of objects of recognizable Frankfurt provenance, and was granted first refusal.[77] The JCR took charge of the remaining items. In the late summer of 1951, Schönberger himself traveled to Frankfurt to supervise the distribution of the objects designated for restitution by the JCR, a process that inspired great controversy. Some pieces were transferred to the JTC. This British counterpart of the JRSO appointed in June 1950, which was responsible for heirless Jewish property in the British zone, made the objects available to the local communities there. But when it came to most treasures in this collection—as typical of JCR's distribution of ceremonial and art objects—the Bezalel Museum in Jerusalem was to be given first choice. This approach garnered heavy criticism. British and American corporation members objected to this preferential treatment and felt that Diaspora interests were being neglected. In July 1951, JCR officers therefore decided to conduct a written vote among all members, which resulted in a new practice: Schönberger—on behalf of the United States—was allowed first refusal of the Frankfurt silverware, while the United Kingdom was also to receive special attention in the distribution process.[78] Schönberger sought out objects that the Jewish Museum of New York was especially keen to obtain, but most items were ultimately transferred to Israel. In a letter to the Frankfurt art historian Albert Rapp, who was the only former curator to resume his post at the museum after 1945, Schönberger described the New York collection, enriched in this way, as symbolic "compensation" for the ruined Frankfurt Museum of Jewish Antiquities. Unlike his colleagues at the JCR, time and again Schönberger emphasized his sympathy for the situation of the Frankfurt museums, underlining their positive role in the safeguarding of Jewish cultural property under National Socialism. He tried to build on his time in Frankfurt before 1938 by reactivating his personal and professional ties to the city.[79] Frankfurt was in many ways a special case in the history of efforts to rebuild Jewish life after the Holocaust; it soon developed into a small but significant center with prominent Jewish intellectuals, politicians, and entrepreneurs. Not only is its first mayor, Walter Kolb, famously remembered for his outspoken invitation to the former Jewish citizens of the city to return; its proximity to the American Military Forces headquarters also proved attractive to many Jewish displaced persons and returnees.

In the summer of 1950, another important JCR operation began in Frankfurt—namely, negotiations on the more than one hundred thousand books transferred from Offenbach to the Hesse state government by military government staff on the assumption that they were of non-Jewish provenance. Only later did it emerge that much of the collection was originally private or communal Jewish property. The JCR thus negotiated with Hanns Wilhelm Eppelsheimer, director of Frankfurt University Library, and Erwin Stein, Hesse minister of education and cultural affairs, in an attempt to find a solution. The Frankfurt community received most of the property found bearing the stamp of the former "Israelitische Religionsgemeinschaft" and added these to its reestablished library in the Philanthropin (a former Jewish school building), which held thirteen thousand books by the summer of 1950.[80] Gershom Scholem made a special trip to Frankfurt to inspect the books, stashed in two large rooms of a bunker on Wittelsbacher Allee, and suggest a way forward. He was surprised by the high quality of these holdings, which included valuable seventeenth- and eighteenth-century Judaica along with brochures and journals, all of which he was determined to take to Israel.[81] In October, it was agreed that the Judaica would be transferred directly to the JCR and thus secured for Israel. The rest was to be distributed equally between the JCR and libraries in the state of Hesse. Lowenthal supervised the sorting in the bunker. In total, two-thirds of the Judaica and books from the "bunker collection" entrusted to the JCR went to Israel, and the rest, chiefly journals, went to the United States for worldwide distribution.[82] Time and again, the negotiations pursued by Arendt and Scholem on these holdings were viewed as evidence of positive cooperation between a German institution and the JCR. Within Germany, however, the chief librarian Eppelsheimer was to remain an exception in his support for such initiatives.

Claiming Property in the British and the French Zones

One key problem for the JCR's work throughout Germany was the differing laws on heirless property in the various occupation zones.[83] To overcome the obstacles this threw up, intensive efforts were made to persuade officials in the British and French zones that a Jewish trust organization was the only way of achieving the just restitution of cultural property. The JCR board of directors and other Jewish representatives had long complained that no restitution laws on the American model had been implemented in either zone. Both the British and French military governments essentially believed that, regardless of the composition, size, and structure of reemerging Jewish communities, recovered items should be entrusted to their administration and very little material should be removed from Germany.[84] The European Allies were also more reluctant than the Americans to make a distinction between Jewish and non-Jewish victims, arguing that this would be a continuation of Nazi ideology. Nor were they immediately won over by the idea of an international Jewish trust or successor organization. The United Kingdom was initially concerned that recognition of such a body might lend indirect support to the Zionist project in Palestine, thus stimulating illegal immigration. After the foundation of the state of Israel in 1948, British fears focused more on possible competition between Jewish claims of ownership and the Polish ones presented so ardently to the UK. In view of the incidental concentration of looted Polish property in the British zone, the British government tended to favor a universal, standardized approach to restitution issues and was keen to avoid the impression that Jews were receiving preferential treatment—fearing similar demands from the Poles, which could no longer be met due to the Cold War. The British restitution law for Germany was thus passed only in May 1949, and it did not provide for a foreign—that is, mainly American—Jewish successor organization to take charge of heirless property. British reluctance to aid the Jewish cause in this respect spurred several representatives of Jewish organizations to action: the international lawyer Sir Norman Bentwich, president of the United Restitution Organization in London, which had been dedicated to pursuing all private Jewish compensation and restitution claims worldwide since 1948, was a fierce critic of the British stance. Also a member of the Committee on Restoration and the Otzrot HaGolah, in August 1949, he managed to obtain the consent of British parliamentary under the secretary of state, Arthur Henderson, for the establishment of a successor organization. But the process of defining its responsibilities and granting it authority, particularly vis-à-vis the communities—which had hitherto functioned as legal successors to their prewar antecedents in the British zone—dragged on until the appointment of the JTC in June 1950.[85] This required the British government to abandon the approach to restitution it had already implemented in cooperation with the German state governments. In line with the views of the Allied High

Commissioners, it now recognized that the existing Jewish communities did not represent the survivors of their prewar counterparts, as most of them now lived outside Germany. Still, it urged the JTC to recognize the needs of German communities more than the JRSO had done.[86]

The JCR now attempted to conclude a contract with the JTC, independently and via Cecil Roth, and proposed to function as its agent for cultural goods on the model of its cooperation with the JRSO. But this project came to grief, first, due to the British government's hesitant stance toward the international organizations and, second, as a result of the competition once again flaring up between the British and American representatives. Cecil Roth and Oscar Rabinowicz were keen to ensure their committee's primacy in the cultural sphere, defying the American organizations' "supremacy." As early as July 1950, Roth had presented the JTC with a detailed plan for activities in the British zone that gave his committee a more prominent role than the JCR.[87] The relationship between the British members of the JCR and their American counterparts had grown increasingly fraught because the Committee on Restoration essentially shared the view that the United Kingdom was being shortchanged by the JCR advisory committee when it came to the distribution of materials.[88] Eventually, JCR gave in: informed by Arendt's and Ben-Horin's reports, most members were convinced that there was no prospect of recovering major treasures in the British zone anyway and that the British Foreign Office was providing neither symbolic nor financial support for the successor organizations, so Baron had no qualms about announcing the cessation of JCR activities in the British zone. Given Lowenthal's involvement in the British successor organization and the cooperation with Cecil Roth, he felt that JCR know-how was sufficiently represented there.[89] The quantity of books and ritual objects from the British zone restituted by the JTC was in fact quite small. Though Ernst G. Lowenthal traveled "from the Danish border to Bonn and from Aachen to Goslar" carrying out a systematic search for such objects, his success was limited.[90] Only in Hamburg were there sufficient quantities of works in silver as well as library and ritual treasures to arouse international interest.[91] There Lowenthal established a storage site, which he did not "dare" to call a "collecting point" since it was so small but which still functioned as his base for supervising the restitution process.[92] The Jewish communities reestablished in the British zone were permitted to choose objects from among the heirless goods as needed, while the remainder was usually transferred to the Hebrew University.[93] One prominent case was resolved through cooperation between the JCR and JTC. After long-drawn-out negotiations with the community and JTC, around four hundred paintings held by the Jewish Museum Berlin—which had been discovered in 1946 in a cellar in the British sector formerly used by the Reich Chamber of Culture (Reichs-kulturkammer) and which the Nazis had planned to use as the basis for a condemnatory exhibition—were distributed on the basis of proposals drawn up by the former museum director Franz Landsberger. As typical in the case of valuable art objects, the JRSO assumed overall responsibility for these holdings. The organization managed to identify a number of private owners who had made loans to the Jewish Museum, while the rest was divided between the Bezalel Museum, the Jewish Museum New York and the HUC, and in response to claims filed by the JTC, a small number of select European museums.[94]

Different conditions initially pertained in the French zone, home to cultural treasures with a rich and centuries-old tradition, particularly in Worms, which had developed into something of a "Jewish pilgrimage site" after the war.[95] The French government advocated an overarching approach to heirless property, perceiving successor organizations' ethnic or religious links as fundamentally discriminatory and contrary to the law.[96] Representatives of Jewish interests were forced to struggle with a restitution law that provided no bespoke regulation of their specific claims but instead required all recoverable assets (including those arising from the sale of heirless property) to flow into a general fund that was used for compensation or, as in the British zone, that provided for restitution to the local communities in Germany. The relevant ordinance, no. 120, had come into force on the same day as the restitution law for the American zone on November 10, 1947.[97] The Joint in Paris, headed by Jerome Jacobson, tried to persuade the French authorities to agree to the establishment of a Jewish successor organization, but initially the legal situation in the French zone did not permit this. This prompted a series of concerned missives from Arendt to the JCR in New York and Ger-shom Scholem in Jerusalem.[98] There was, she felt, a risk that the valuable collections in Mainz and Worms might pass to the small number of Jews that made up the communities there. Furthermore, the Freiburg

University Library, for example, contained holdings from twenty private Jewish households, to which no individual claims had been made, prompting its director to declare to Arendt that he wanted to keep them for the library. From France itself, Arendt reported that there too, Jewish organizations and institutions had been granted no legal right to heirless holdings.[99] After an attempt by the JRSO to establish a branch office in the French zone had been rejected on the basis that there must be no supremacy of the American military government in the Western zones, representatives of the French government and Jewish spokespersons finally agreed to the establishment of a branch office of the British JTC in the French zone.[100] But the so-called Branche Française, headquartered in Mainz and Freiburg im Breisgau, began its work only in May 1952. At the behest of the French authorities, it was administered by its own committee in Paris, the Conseil d'Administration, chaired by Baron Guy de Rothschild and made up of members of French and international organizations as well as German communities.[101]

As Meir Ben-Horin saw it, the French approach did not augur well. He anticipated that amid the major controversies engendered by restitution in the French zone, cultural goods would receive little attention.[102] And a number of restitution cases did in fact take several years to resolve. Just over one thousand volumes from the private Jewish libraries now in the Freiburg University Library were transferred to the Branche Française in 1954, while a small number were restituted to their owners. Most of the looted books in Freiburg, originally numbering more than eleven thousand, had been sold, given away, or pulped by the end of the war.[103] The fragmentary collections in Worms were the object of a legal dispute lasting almost two years, from 1952 to 1954, between the Branche Française on the one hand and the Worms City Archive and City Museum on the other, the latter two institutions being headed by Friedrich Illert, with whom Arendt had previously negotiated. Illert had already rejected three individual requests from American-Jewish museums when the Branche Française filed its claim to the collections. After 1945, the reestablished Mainz community had acted as legal successor to the one in Worms, providing the Worms City Museum with objects and archival materials on loan. In 1954, a legal settlement was reached, but it triggered further court proceedings and appeals because Illert wished to keep the material in Worms. He initiated legal proceedings based on the West German "Act to Prevent the Exodus of German Cultural Property," which came into force in August 1955, aiming to convince the judges that the material was of great historical value to Worms— far beyond the city's Jewish history. Following vigorous interventions, for example by the Israel Mission in Cologne, his case was dismissed because cultural goods from churches and recognized religious communities were not subject to this law. In the end, an amicable agreement was reached. Parts of the collection were to stay in Worms, such as the material remains of the ruined Worms synagogue, select prayer books, and ritual objects, while the records of the community, some rare imperial documents, the two-volume Machzor manuscript of 1273, Torah scrolls, *mappoth* (ritual textiles), and other Judaica were transferred to Israel by the Branche Française.[104] The objects in the Mainz Museum of Jewish Antiquities (Mainzer Museum für jüdische Altertümer), which had been plundered and destroyed by the Nazis, meanwhile, were not restituted to the successor organization. The collection of the Mainz Jewish Community Library also remained in place; in 1955, community members entrusted it to the Mainz University Library on long-term loan, where it is stored to this day under the heading "Jewish Library." The cases of Worms and Frankfurt show that the German authorities and institutions also had a say in restitution procedures. For Jewish stakeholders, negotiations with the latter were often an uphill struggle: they generally encountered a lack of sympathy and a prevailing sense of resentment at the Allies' and Jewish organizations' restitution policies.

En Route to the Luxembourg Agreement

In summer 1949, in his role as the chair of the JCR executive board, Jerome Michael traveled to Europe to get a sense of the situation there, particularly in Germany. He noted that the German institutions and individuals benefiting from looted items were complying only haltingly with the requirement to report such materials to the American occupying authorities as stipulated in article 73 of restitution law no. 59.[105] Hannah Arendt too drew attention to this problem. She considered the application of this article to cultural property particularly problematic since it required only items to a value of more than one thousand German marks to be reported, which made "recovery from private owners almost hopeless."[106] The JCR had no choice but to focus on major German cultural institutions such as libraries and archives. Arendt saw it as the main task of JCR outside the collection points to search for further looted and displaced properties and force librarians, archivists, and local or state authorities to initiate systematic research into the issue. During her stay in Germany, in collaboration with the Polish librarian Mordechai Bernstein and the JCR staff members Lowenthal and Narkiss, she initiated the steps needed to achieve this. Bernstein sifted through archives and libraries, Narkiss and Lowenthal searched for art and ritual objects in museums in all the Western zones, and Arendt herself negotiated with the German authorities.[107] Often, however, they lacked a legal basis for official searches and were therefore dependent on the cooperation of German personnel.[108] Following a phase of fairly detailed research in various libraries and archives and her failed attempt to find and question personnel who had worked in such institutions under the Nazis, Arendt moved up the institutional ladder with a request for support. She persuaded Gustav Hofmann, secretary-general of the Bavarian State Library (Bayerische Staatsbibliothek) in Munich and first president of the Association of German Librarians (Verein deutscher Bibliothekare) after 1945, to publish an appeal to all German libraries, which she submitted in draft form, to report any Jewish property in their holdings. The text appeared in early 1950 in the German library's bulletin *Nachrichten für wissenschaftliche Bibliotheken*:

There is every reason to believe that German public libraries still house plenty of once confiscated property of Jewish provenance. Hitherto only fragments of the major collections of former Jewish communities and scientific institutes, theological seminaries and so on have come to light. The main items of relevance here are Judaica and Hebraica of all kinds (books, incunabula, manuscripts and archival materials), which poured into German libraries after the war from evacuation depots, along with holdings of former Nazi institutes or organizations, which were incorporated into libraries following their liquidation. Also significant are collections offered for purchase by libraries (particularly their Oriental departments) by state or Nazi party authorities after 1938 and especially after 1940. The Jewish Cultural Reconstruction, Inc., Wiesbaden, State Museum, now requests the identification and reporting of any holdings of this kind present in German libraries. In the case of Bavarian libraries reports should be made to the Bavarian State Office for Restitution (Bayerisches Landesamt für Wiedergutmachung), Munich, Arcisstraße 11.[109]

A small but very important modification to Arendt's proposal related to the final line of the appeal. Naturally, Arendt had called for reports of all holdings to be made to the JRSO in Nuremberg. The fact that the published text instead requested that material found in Bavaria be reported to the State Office was down to its head and Arendt's adversary, Philipp Auerbach. Evidently, he had initially assured Arendt of his cooperation but behind her back had ensured that it was not the JRSO/JCR but his own office that would function as interlocutor. As mentioned before, Auerbach's attitude toward the JCR fluctuated. When responsibility for restitution began to pass to German authorities and the JCR leadership's focus therefore shifted from the Americans to representatives of the German states, he had often played an intermediary role and succeeded in opening certain doors. With his help, for example, Arendt approached Dieter Sattler, Bavarian state secretary for the fine arts, with a request for support. Turning to the ministries of education and culture, she sought to establish a legal foundation for appeals to German cultural institutions to search for cultural treasures of Jewish provenance and report them to the JCR. Sattler responded positively, referring Arendt to his superior, the Bavarian minister of culture and education Alois Hundhammer, who also chaired the Standing Conference of the Ministers of Education and Cultural Affairs of the States in the Federal Republic of Germany (Ständige Konferenz der Kultusminister der Länder in der Bundesrepublik) in order to expedite her project. After consulting with Auerbach, Hofmann, Sattler, and Hans Ludwig Held of the Munich City Library, in January 1950, Arendt sent a memorandum to Hundhammer. It indicated that the JCR would like to see "an appeal to all state and municipal libraries, university institutes, archives, and museums, to make the most careful examination of their stocks" and a "decree [. . .] providing a legal basis for this voluntary action and instructing all librarians and archive and museum officials of the three Western zones to submit periodic reports." On behalf of JCR's directors, Arendt requested that the Standing Conference consider this matter and regard the JCR in

Wiesbaden as the central agency for the collection of relevant information and reports. Arendt appended to her memorandum the Tentative List of Jewish Cultural Treasures, underlining how little material had so far been found given how much had existed prior to 1933. She was convinced that German institutions still held among their wartime acquisitions "at least part of the cultural treasures of the German Jews," which could be made "accessible again to the Jewish educated and scholarly world."[110] In the summer of 1950, Meir Ben-Horin, who continued the negotiations after Arendt's return to the US, reported that the German authorities had failed to embrace the various initiatives. Once again, he attempted to convince Hundhammer to pass a law enabling Jewish organizations to examine German holdings.[111] But these efforts too came to nothing. In July, State Secretary Sattler officially informed Hannah Arendt that this was a matter for the State Office for Restitution and Controlled Assets (Landesamt für Vermögensverwaltung und Wiedergutmachung) and thus lay outside his ministry's remit. Decision-making authority thus reverted to Philipp Auerbach, who deliberately tried to undermine the work of the JCR and JRSO by filing claims to recovered cultural goods himself.[112] Because Auerbach, much like Galinski in Berlin, was primarily interested in rebuilding the Bavarian communities and helping local survivors, he was reluctant to support the removal of cultural and ritual objects. In addition to Arendt, who often complained about his behavior, Meir Ben-Horin pointed to the opposing perspectives of Auerbach and JCR/JRSO: "In general, it appears that all Jewish cultural property in Bavaria is blocked by Mr. Auerbach who commands many Bavarian key positions. In what is apparently designated to be a demonstration of German patriotism, he takes an offensive position vis-à-vis the 'international' Jewish organizations and prevents German authorities from cooperating with the Jewish organizations."[113]

Nonetheless, the JCR chalked up a number of successes. Arendt also sent the memorandum to Erwin Stein, Hesse minister of education and culture, and Clemens von Brentano di Tremezzo, head of the Baden State Chancellery in Freiburg. Hesse was eager to set a good example by issuing a decree on the recovery of cultural goods that other states might emulate, and the state's Ministry of Education and Culture did so in January 1951. It is likely that this success was a result of the JCR's smooth cooperation with the Frankfurt City and University Library,

Hanns Wilhelm Eppelsheimer, and the city councilors, while the strong American presence in Hesse also played a role.[114] In accordance with this decree, the West German Library (Westdeutsche Bibliothek), established in Marburg in 1949 using the holdings of the former Prussian State Library (Preußische Staatsbibliothek), transferred three thousand Yiddish books from Eastern Europe to the JCR, most of which were then allocated to the Eastern European émigré communities in Chile and Brazil.[115]

During her second journey to Germany from March to August 1952, Arendt managed to persuade other states in what used to be the American zone of the need for a decree of this kind. In his role as the head of the JNUL, Curt Wormann supported Arendt's mission, especially in Berlin. Arendt reported that at a meeting held with the Berlin Senator Joachim Tiburtius, Fritz Moser of the Senate for Education, and Mayor Ernst Reuter, Tiburtius felt moved to declare, "We shall not permit Hessen [sic] to do better than Berlin."[116] But this did not settle the matter. Later, Moser presented legal concerns about JCR's role and the prospect of enforcing such a decree. To resolve the matter, Benjamin Ferencz of the JRSO got involved, but ultimately it seems that no decree was issued in Berlin. After a slew of meetings and negotiations, however, despite great initial resistance in Stuttgart and Munich, Baden-Württemberg and Bavaria issued decrees requesting the reporting of cultural goods.[117]

Arendt remained persistent and engaged throughout, though she often underlined to her husband the difficult and unpleasant nature of her work for the JCR in Germany. In fact, she and Baron had even greater goals in mind. Once the states of the former American zone had finally expressed support for the idea, the JCR was keen to see the implementation of a federal law obligating German institutions to inspect their collections and report any looted items. Its representatives sought to achieve this goal through direct correspondence with the Federal Ministry of the Interior (Bundesministerium des Innern) in Bonn while also publicizing it with the help of delegates to the Claims Conference and the Israeli delegation to the negotiations on the Luxembourg Agreement in Wassenaar and the Hague. Scholem and Wormann from Israel also lent their support. In the spring of 1952, Scholem wrote to the Israeli delegation, underlining, in the name of the JCR, the need for federal legislation on the restitution of Jewish cultural property. Above all, he demanded a form of loss compensation that would entail the transfer of books held by German institutions to help complete Israeli collections. For example, he pushed for Hebrew documents, select microfilms, and the Munich Talmud manuscript to be surrendered to the JNUL. He shared Wormann's view that such "restitution in kind" ought to be obligatory for Germany as a form of "moral restitution."[118] To lend these demands more weight, at a meeting in Nuremberg in May 1952, Arendt and Wormann discussed with Ferencz and Ernst Katzenstein of the JRSO whether it would be helpful to ask Moshe Sharett, Israeli foreign minister and head of the Israeli delegation in Wassenaar, to bring up the topic of cultural goods during the general negotiations on restitution and—in light of the tremendous losses caused by Germany—propose the surrender of compensatory collections to Israel.[119] By September 1952, however, Arendt had informed the JCR board of directors that the German libraries were refusing to surrender their Hebraica, though in some cases, they were at least prepared to produce microfilms for the JNUL.[120]

To increase awareness of their concerns, Salo Baron also approached Nahum Goldman, chair of the Claims Conference, and Carl Gussone, senior official in the Cultural Department of the German Federal Ministry of the Interior. He again emphasized to Goldman that the allocation of cultural treasures was of more use and value to Jews across the world than compensation payments. The requested compensatory goods could, he asserted, function as a "gesture of genuine goodwill" on the part of the Germans, "who would suffer no real deprivation."[121] Finally, in August 1952, Baron approached the federal government directly with the JCR's request for a nationwide law. But Baron no longer addressed the issue of compensation in kind, as by this point it evidently seemed unlikely to materialize. Rather, he quoted the decree issued by the state of Hesse in January 1951 and requested that it be used as a template for a federal law. Despite the fact that "cultural affairs [were] a matter for the states," he and his colleagues were convinced that the entire process would be expedited by a circular from the ministry to every state instructing them to "speed up their search for Jewish cultural items" and convey any discoveries or lack of such to the JCR/JRSO. Like Arendt before him, he attached a copy of the Tentative List to underscore "that the largest part" of German Jewish treasures was "still missing, both quantitatively and especially qualitatively." He further noted that "there are strong indications that a considerable part of such objects are still available in German public libraries, museums and archives," mentioning German librarians who had themselves assured Hannah Arendt that "considerable holdings of Jewish cultural property since the Nazi period, some of which came from non-German countries, are still among the unpacked and uncatalogued materials in the libraries."[122] Arendt again sought to build pressure for such a law from two other angles as well. On several occasions she spoke with Franz Böhm, appointed by German chancellor Konrad Adenauer to head the German delegation in Wassenaar, and gained his support for her cause. Böhm, meanwhile, believed that the best approach was to begin by implementing as many state-level decrees as possible to facilitate later action at the federal level.[123] Second, Arendt communicated repeatedly with Ferencz; as the head of the JRSO, he was a member of the Claims Conference's delegation and she hoped he would help advance the JCR's interests. The British and French zones were particularly troublesome because neither Jerome Jacobson nor Charles Kapralik of the JTC had put enough effort into negotiations with state-level representatives. Ferencz was not convinced the JCR's demands should be integrated into the negotiations in the Netherlands and saw little realistic prospect of further state-level decrees. Furthermore, he believed it impossible to exert pressure on the Soviet zone, as there was already too much resistance to the JCR in general to expect any great successes there. He was proven right—just as the Genocide Convention ratified by the United Nations did not include Article III on cultural genocide, so the Luxembourg Agreement featured no bespoke passage on cultural property and no federal law requiring a systematic search for stolen items was passed. It took another fifty years for such a decree to be ratified in Germany. The time did not seem ripe for an acknowledgement of the meaning and repercussions of the Jewish cultural destruction in Europe.

For Baron and Arendt, the only way to continue their work within the framework of German restitution and compensation, as achieved through the Luxembourg Agreement in September 1952, was to contribute to the Claims Conference. At the request of Nahum Goldmann, Baron took over chairmanship of the Conference's Advisory Committee on Cultural Applications, while Arendt became a member. Both focused their efforts here primarily on supporting Jewish cultural institutions worldwide with the help of funds received from Germany. The JCR as an organization, however, did not take part in the Claims Conference since all its constituent organizations, with the exception of the Hebrew University of Jerusalem, were already independent members.

Starting in March 1952, the JCR gradually began to wind itself up. Over the summer, the organization declared its tasks in Europe complete and its scope for action exhausted, and Hannah Arendt wrote a tabulated final report on its activities.[124] Despite this, the members of the corporation continued to meet until 1954 to discuss specific matters addressed to it and advance the microfilm project that was to be the JCR's last official endeavor. Once it had become clear that there was no chance of obtaining the archival and rare materials that were German property, the JCR initiated a project to microfilm relevant documents, but this largely came to grief due to a lack of funds.[125] Attempts to gain the financial support of the Ford Foundation came to nothing. Hopes of obtaining support from the relevant German city archives and museums were also disappointed. By 1954, a number of small pilot projects had been completed, but it proved impossible to raise the funds necessary to obtaining full access to the material. In April 1954, the JCR executive board gave it one last try by applying for financial resources at the Claims Conference, but this proposal was also rejected. Ultimately, the idea was left entirely in the hands of the Israeli partners who were following similar projects throughout Europe.[126] Baron's activities for the Claims Conference also came to an end following numerous differences of opinion. Goldmann had dissolved the Committee on Cultural Applications by March 1954, and Judah Shapiro, previously cultural director of the Joint in Paris, took over as head of its Cultural Department.[127]

By mid-1952 at the latest, the search for and salvage of looted cultural property in Germany was no longer taking place within the institutional framework of the JCR. In West Germany, the ongoing search for material and receipt of recovered objects were now primarily the task of the JNUL, in the shape of its librarian Shlomo Shunami, who continued to make regular trips there until his death.[128] Officially, the JCR was not dissolved until February 1977, though by then it had long existed on paper only.[129] While its last active phase was characterized by failures, this in no way detracts from the JCR's importance. In collaboration with the JRSO, it had paved the way for the negotiations in Wassenaar, both bodies having managed to achieve recognition as nonstate organizations within the framework of international law; this was later crucial to the Claims Conference as well. And what is more, for once, the JCR framework allowed all the Jewish political factions to speak with one voice—the urgency of the situation helping overcome the old divisions and dissonances that had often plagued Jewish political activities. The integration of all the different stakeholders in the Diaspora, plus those of the Yishuv, in one political entity was an outstanding achievement of Baron's commission. The work done by the JCR and JRSO was thus of great political and symbolic significance. It was an important expression of a proactive approach and a symbol of the defense of the Nazis' victims, who gained attention, a voice, and representation through these organizations' efforts. The JCR's success can also be expressed in figures. It distributed just under five hundred thousand books and between eight thousand and ten thousand ritual objects to institutions and communities across the world in an effort to ensure the continuity of Jewish cultural and spiritual life, foster the development of new centers of research and commemoration and the ongoing development of existing ones, and support community activities.[130] The fact that the work stimulated by the JCR in West Germany was discontinued, and that it was not until the late 1990s that systematic research began on looted property in European libraries and museums, is one of the elements of postwar history requiring reappraisal in its own right.

New Topographies: The Distribution of Heirless Cultural Treasures

If we were to mark every place that received books and objects from the JCR—synagogues, community centers, yeshivot, universities, colleges, schools, libraries, museums, archives, foundations, old people's homes, hospitals, kibbutzim, and other research institutions and archives—on a world map, we would gain a fairly complete overview of the geographical centers and peripheries of Jewish life after 1945. If the Commission members had sought to conserve and archive the old spatial structure of the former Jewish world in Europe with the help of the Tentative Lists, JCR's distribution policy now reflected the new topography of Jewish life. Following the great waves of refugees and migrants, it was no longer Europe but Israel and the United States that constituted the new centers. Treasures were sent to those places where, as those involved saw it, they could secure, facilitate, and enrich the future of Jewish learning and research, cultural, and liturgical activities. This applied above all to Israel, which required most support to develop its cultural infrastructure. "In general, Israel needs all books it can get," as Meir Ben-Horin summed up the situation shortly after the state's foundation, suggesting that "we ought not to look for recipients; the more we can send to Israel the better."[131] In most cases, both the JCR advisory committee and its executive board shared this view. A strategy paper of January 1949 setting out allocation guidelines concluded that the JNUL in Jerusalem should in principle be granted first choice of book collections, while the Bezalel Museum ought to enjoy the same privilege when it came to applied art and ritual objects. An agreement on allocation reached by the advisory committee with respect to the holdings in Offenbach, which (with a few exceptions) applied to all other objects as well, provided for around 40 percent of a given holding to be transferred to Israel, 40 percent to the United States, and the remaining 20 percent to the rest of the world, with special consideration being given to the United Kingdom.[132] Through this allocation formula, the JCR aimed to ensure that Israel was well supplied with items while also satisfying the needs of the steadily growing Jewish communities in the United States. In addition, it was agreed that Jews in Germany would receive specific parts of collections; beyond this, European beneficiaries were to be identified and supplied by the Joint. Nonetheless, the allocation process sometimes created frictions between JCR members. While some, like Ben-Horin, called for as much material as possible to be transferred to Israel, others felt constantly disadvantaged and highlighted the needs of the Diaspora Jewries. The advisory committee—like the specially appointed allocations committee—often had to coordinate decisions with the executive board in the face of considerable opposition.[133]

Distribution to communities and institutions in Western Europe was organized by Judah Shapiro, director of the Joint's Department for Cultural and Educational Reconstruction in Paris. There were frequent discussions about the utility of this process: in much the same way as in Germany, it was uncertain whether the beneficiaries would in fact remain in Europe. Hannah Arendt, for example, declared in a letter to Baron that "the whole Jewish cultural life in Western Europe is based on and carried out by Eastern European refugees. These will certainly leave the countries in a few years; in France, only very few people are naturalized, and it is not likely that the present practice will change in the favor of refugees. Even people who arrived in the twenties are still in the same uncertain situation as before. [. . .] The refugees, on the other hand, as long as they are in Europe need books. And this is especially true for the orthodox people."[134]

In the end, around eight thousand volumes were given to France. They were surrendered to the Alliance, the French consistory in Paris, individual communities and colleges, and the Centre de Documentation Juive Contemporaine, which was initiated by Isaac Schneersohn in 1943 and established as a research and commemoration center after the war. Some books and journals were also made available to the Bibliothèque Nationale de France in Paris for its Judaica department. In March 1949, the JCR board of directors had agreed that non-Jewish libraries featuring large amounts of Judaica that had suffered German raids could also inform the JCR of their needs.[135] Via the Joint, JCR holdings also went to Jewish schools and libraries in Brussels and Antwerp and to libraries, educational institutions, and communities in the Netherlands and Italy, such as the Collegio Rabbinico Italiano in Rome. Communities in nearby Mediterranean states were also supplied by the Joint, with a small number of books being sent to Casablanca, Algiers, and Tehran for use in communal and school libraries.[136]

Much anger was caused by the JCR executive board's decision to surrender nearly half of the collections of the community and Rabbinical Seminary in Breslau—found at the Offenbach Archival Depot—to the Swiss Federation of Jewish Communities (Schweizerischer Israelitischer Gemeindebund) in Zurich.[137] A number of Swiss communities had repeatedly requested books. In addition, after a brief visit to Switzerland in the spring of 1949, Bernard Heller wrote to Baron that he was convinced that the Swiss Jews would play a key role in the reemergence of Jewish culture and education in Western Europe and recommended that their needs be taken into account.[138] This proposed transfer of materials was justified by the argument that it was right for at least a portion of these books to remain in Europe. Scholem and other Israelis opposed this idea, first, because despite its fragmentary character, they were keen to avoid dividing up the collection any further and, second, because they did not recognize their utility to the Jewish institutions in Switzerland. Shlomo Shunami expressed his concerns to Hannah Arendt in a letter of November 1950: "To the Jews in Switzerland numbering ca. 20,000 without higher institutions of learning [. . .] this collection, representing one of the most scholarly research libraries in the Jewish world, would mean an 'embarras de richesse' and I wonder if they could cope with it."[139] Repeated exhortations from the Israeli members of the JCR, however, did nothing to change this decision. In the spring of 1950, the Swiss Federation received seventy-three boxes from Wiesbaden containing just under six thousand volumes of the Breslau collection. Contrary to the JCR's stipulation that the books must be kept in one location, they were divided between Zurich, Geneva, and Basel—partly based on the argument that the greater part of the collection had in any case gone to Israel rather than Switzerland and the lot was therefore already divided.[140]

There was no transfer of books or objects to Eastern Europe. The JCR's vehement rejection of any surrender of material to Poland and other former centers of Jewish cultural life was based on realities on the ground in the wake of the Nazi occupation. To some extent, it was also a response to the virulent anti-Semitism in Eastern Europe in the first few years after the war as well as to the ongoing nationalization of private property. And yet this meant ignoring the initiatives of local Jewish groupings, institutions, and remnant communities that sought to rebuild Jewish infrastructure in Eastern Europe.[141] Of particular importance was the emergence of the Central Jewish Library in Warsaw; its holdings were collected by the Central Committee of Polish Jews and representatives of the Jewish congregations in Poland and merged with the collections of the Central Jewish Historical Commission headed by Philip Friedman, which later became the Jewish Historical Institute in Warsaw.[142] By 1949, a veritable research library had thus emerged in Warsaw, described in euphoric terms by the historian Isaiah Trunk, himself a member of the Jewish Historical Commission, as "one of the largest and most important libraries in Europe." Trunk emphasized that the Polish government had done much to support the project of a central Jewish library.[143] In much the same way as the soldiers of the MFA&A in German territory, Polish Jews active in various groups had gathered together looted, dislocated, and cached collections from throughout Poland, concentrating them in Warsaw. Michael Sylberberg, a Jewish community representative in Poland in the first few years after the war, provided a comprehensive account of this in a 1949 article in the *Jewish Chronicle* entitled "Saving Jewish Treasures in Poland":

> The Jews did everything possible, throughout the occupation, to save as much as they could. In the worst days of the fighting despite extreme personal danger, they carried off and hid Scrolls of the Law and religious books of all kinds. In many cities and towns, the last Jews, before they were forced to leave, hid the sacred articles collected over centuries. As a result, we have, since the end of the war, found scrolls of Law, books, paintings and other articles hidden throughout Poland in attics and cellars and even buried underground. [. . .] The first thing we did after liberation was to search among the ruins of the Warsaw Ghetto. But we had little hope. [. . .] We continued our search. We felt convinced that there must be many more valuables buried under the ruins or hidden in cellars. And sure enough, in a cellar under the ruins, we found a large collection of religious and other books which has become the basis of the new collection of the Central Jewish library in Warsaw. [. . .] From the moment the Central Jewish Library opened in Warsaw, it received hundreds of letters from Polish institutions and individuals reporting the existence of collections of Jewish books in various parts of the country. [. . .] in many towns and villages, we found large stores of religious books, which have been taken over partly by individual communities, and partly by the Council of Jewish Communities.[144]

Sylberberg also mentions a major collection in Posen, gathered there by German soldiers, which included holdings from Warsaw communal libraries and the Breslau theological seminary. This collection, he stated, was entrusted to the care of the Central Library, but much of it was later surrendered to Israel because the Jewish community in Poland was too small to justifiably claim it. The vast majority of Jewish activists in Poland agreed that the books' future would be best safeguarded in Israel. Sylberberg concluded, "They will be a small monument to the memory of the three million Jews of Poland who perished. And Jews in Palestine, as they pore over these books will draw from the learning and knowledge, and will continue the golden chain of what was once the rich Jewish life of Poland."[145] An essay by Jewish historian Ephraim Kupfer from this period also refers to the collections of manuscripts brought together in Warsaw, which included writings and incunabula from the fourteenth to seventeenth centuries along with documents from communities in Vienna, Berlin, Breslau and the former Theological Seminary (Israelitisch-Theologische Lehranstalt) in Vienna. These, he explained, had been recovered by the "heroic Red Army."[146] Their history, however, reflected another facet of the postwar situation in Poland: holdings demonstrably from outside the country were often not returned but instead declared state property and left in Warsaw, albeit in the Jewish Historical Institute, where some remain to this day.[147] These snapshots of the Polish-Jewish situation after 1945 show that the rather one-sided view of conditions there typically held by JCR members was not entirely appropriate and that certain fears expressed about state confiscations, especially by Hugo Bergman and Gershom Scholem, essentially reflected their goal of concentrating holdings in Israel. Certainly, reports from Poland were conspicuously ideological. And the later development of the Jewish Historical Institute in Warsaw, which increasingly espoused the imposed Marxist-Leninist historical outlook, confirmed the validity of certain concerns.[148] Nonetheless, it was manifestly not the case that all Jewish materials accumulated by soldiers and government representatives in Eastern Europe were being taken to Moscow and were lost to the Jewish community. The JCR, however, strictly upheld the principle that no books must be sent to Eastern Europe. As far as we can tell from the documentary evidence, not a single volume of the Baltic Collection of which the JCR had taken charge had made it back to Estonia, Lithuania, or Latvia. If we examine subsequent historical developments, this decision now appears more far-sighted than at the time it was taken. The already small Jewish communities lost even more members as a result of later waves of Jewish emigration following anti-Semitic attacks in the wake of the Slánský trial of 1952 in Czechoslovakia and the unrest of 1968 throughout Eastern Europe.[149]

The JCR received several requests from northern Europe, above all from communities in Sweden, where many Jewish refugees from Central and Eastern Europe had fled. Few received an affirmative response. Just under seven hundred books from the institutional German Jewish holdings were transported from Wiesbaden to Sweden, while the Oslo Synagogue in Norway and several communities in Denmark received a small number of prayer books. In addition to the JCR's general reluctance to allow books to remain in Europe, its dogged opposition, shared by the Otzrot HaGolah, to attempts by Raphael Edelmann in Copenhagen to develop a special collection of Jewish materials in the city's Royal Library, was another factor in its refusal to allocate no more than absolutely necessary to Scandinavia.[150]

The JCR's allocation policy granted a special place to the United Kingdom. Oscar Rabinowicz, Ernst G. Lowenthal, and Cecil Roth of the Committee on Restoration repeatedly underlined the great needs of British institutions and communities, often feeling disadvantaged—as representatives of one of the major communities of Jewish emigrants—in comparison to the United States. At the same time, a number of German Jewish émigré scholars in the United Kingdom were pushing for certain holdings, such as those of the Hochschule für die Wissenschaft des Judentums, to be sent to London in their entirety. They justified this on the basis that several leading figures in German Jewish spiritual life had immigrated to the United Kingdom. Under the leadership of Rabbi Leo Baeck, head of both the Council and the Society of Jewish Studies, which had been established in London in early 1947 and sought to safeguard the Hochschule's intellectual legacy, attempts were made to persuade JCR's board of directors to establish a German Jewish memorial library in London. The idea mirrored identical plans put forward by German Jewish emigrants in the United States (above all Eugen Täubler, Max Gruenewald, and Rudolf Callmann). Whether such a library would find a better home in London or the United States was the subject of numerous discussions. Members of the Council subgroup in New York known as the American Federation of the Jews from Germany were also eager to create a library with German holdings. Both groups, however, agreed that the holdings must be kept together and under no circumstances divided up. In this spirit, Baeck approached Baron in April 1949 and asked him to consider the interests of émigré German Jews in general:

> The former German Jews, which constitute an articulate element in the United States, England and South America ought to receive a share in the cultural property, which at one time belonged to their congregations and institutions. Nor is this claim a merely sentimental one. It expresses

the fact that the bonds still exist, and with them, a deeply felt conscious-ness of their heritage. [. . .] Their interest, and the interest of those who work in the field of Jewish research, can be clearly defined. It comprises the area of what is known as Wissenschaft des Judentums, the publica-tions of the Academy der Wissenschaft des Judentums, and of the rab-binical Seminaries.[151]

This request was granted but only partially. After a long struggle, German Jewish advocates in the United States succeeded in obtaining from the JCR certain components of German collections, already pres-ent in the JCR depot in New York, for a Memorial Library that would, as they envisaged, be housed within the Institute of Religion.[152] But its establishment came to grief due to the uncooperative behavior of the institute itself, which was not prepared to furnish the items with their own visible section. The institute also declined to house and give spe-cial attention to the Stürmer collection from Nuremberg, which was therefore entrusted to the Yeshiva University in New York. Because of the American Jewish institutions' reluctance to cooperate and lack of interest, JCR began to pay more attention to the proposals emanat-ing from the United Kingdom. Baeck wished to concentrate virtually all the remaining volumes and documents of German Jewish collec-tions in London but was successful only with respect to the fragments of the library of the Hochschule. After the JCR's directors had made their decision on this, Max Gruenewald in the US concluded bitterly, "The Jews from Germany have been closed out of their own inheritance, sometimes with forethought and design. [. . .] Sometimes our own friends have been helpful and instrumental in establishing a new legal rule: Everyone may establish a title of ownership—except the former ones."[153] Much like the members of Jewish communities in Germany, some émigré German Jews also felt that the JCR had betrayed them and was failing to honor their needs, though they shared its conviction that objects and books must on no account remain in Germany. But the dispersal of such items to multiple locations rankled them. Eventually, their desire to maintain the German Jewish intellectual legacy and create a space for the commemoration of its exponents was satisfied in another form. Under the leadership of Siegfried Moses, the Israeli section of the Council consisting of Gershom Scholem, Martin Buber,

Hugo Bergman, Curt Wormann, Georg Landauer, and Ernst Simon secured financial support from the Claims Conference and established the Leo Baeck Institute in Jerusalem in 1955. The West German compensation payments enabled them to create an institute that, together with its branch offices, opened the same year in New York and London; it was to become probably the most important monument to the German Jewries and their scholarly tradition after 1945. Here again, the holdings salvaged by the JCR played a substantial role since quite a few of the distributed volumes ended up in one of the LBI's branches. A total of just under twenty thousand books and around three hundred ritual objects were transferred to the United Kingdom. With the help of the Committee on Restoration and the Jewish Historical Society of England, they were allocated to a number of libraries, including the Wiener Library for the Study of Holocaust and Genocide, the Mocatta Library for Jewish Studies at University College London, Manchester University Library, and the British Library as well as Leo Baeck's Society of Jewish Studies, the Jews' College, and a number of yeshivot. These holdings chiefly consisted of German Judaica, journals, documents from German communities, silver objects, and Torah scrolls.[154]

All books and objects not distributed directly to Europe or Israel were initially transferred to a JCR depot in Brooklyn. Between 1949 and 1951, this depot was supervised by Jack Novack and Rabbi Severin Rochman, the latter having previously overseen the sorting and cataloging of Jewish holdings in Offenbach. They were responsible for the inspection and packaging of the books and their dispatch to Australia, Canada, Central and South America, and South Africa. The recipient institutions met the transportation costs themselves. In most countries, this transfer of materials attracted a great deal of attention from Jewish communities and institutions. For example, the Canadian Jewish Congress, which supervised the distribution of the around two thousand volumes and ritual objects allocated to Canada, had a label created for every book as a reminder of its history and that of its former owners: "This book was once the property of a Jew, victim of the Great Massacre in Europe. The Nazis who seized this book eventually destroyed the owner. It has been recovered by the Jewish people, and reverently placed in this institution by the Canadian Jewish Congress, as a memorial to those who gave their lives for the sanctification of the Holy Name."[155] The formulation of this brief text is interesting because it identifies the Jews as a collectivity as the agent of restitution. In this account, it was not the staff of the JCR, an organization, but the Jewish people itself that had recovered the books. The process of search and salvage was thus envisaged as a collective act involving all Jews worldwide. The JCR leadership disliked this portrayal since it ignored the concrete work done by those involved. Time and again such cases engendered frictions when recipients resisted the explicit requirement to furnish books with ex libris, and ritual objects with labels, produced by the JCR to highlight their origins and the history of their salvage. Often the ex libris and stamps on the first few pages of books originating in Europe told the entire history of their ownership, robbery, and restitution: many volumes bore identificatory information concerning their former owners, the stamps and classification marks of the German institutions that had stolen them, a stamp from the Offenbach Archival Depot—sometimes with the MFA&A's supplementary note "Desinf. Sept. 1945," highlighting the books' disinfection in Frankfurt—as well as ex libris provided by the JCR and, sometimes, another label inserted by the recipient. The JCR leadership was eager for these commemorative traces to remain visible.

In South Africa too, books were given bespoke ex libris. The African Jewish Board of Deputies created a label reminiscent of its Canadian counterpart: "This book, once in Jewish ownership, then looted by the Nazis, and now restored to Jewish hands, is a silent witness to the martyrdom of the six million Jews who perished *Al kedushat ha-shem* [sanctify his name]. May their memory inspire us to keep alight the flame of Jewish learning and Jewish life."[156] In addition to the more than seven thousand volumes and periodicals distributed by the South African Board to congregations, universities, and Jewish organizations in both major cities and rural areas, around 150 lamps, goblets, and textiles from European synagogues were also sent there and divided between Johannesburg, Cape Town, and Durban. In February 1954, an exhibition of these objects was organized in Johannesburg and later in the Old Synagogue of Cape Town. They were subsequently entrusted to the newly established Jewish museums in these two cities, forming the basis for their collections.[157] These books, however, were forgotten and remained unused until 1989, when a number of volumes came to light again due to an accidental find in Cape Town; the search then began for the other parts of the collection. In 1999, around two hundred recovered books were listed and put on display as the Nazi Looted Books collection in the Jewish Studies Library of the University of Cape Town.[158]

Other key beneficiaries of JCR allocations were the Central and South American countries, particularly Jewish communities in Argentina, Bolivia, Brazil, Chile, Costa Rica, Curaçao, Ecuador, Mexico, Uruguay, and Venezuela. It was Argentina and Brazil, countries with important Jewish communities that had been growing steadily since 1492 and were home to many Eastern European Jews who had migrated and fled there from the late nineteenth century, that benefited most. The transfer of books and objects to these countries was carried out by the WJC's Department of Culture and Education on behalf of the JCR. With respect to this procedure and the enthusiasm of the South American beneficiary communities, a memorandum by Wolf Blattberg, member of the JCR and director of the department from 1950 on, stated, "The response of our affiliates and the central organizations thus far has been very favorable, and even enthusiastic. They are very eager to have the books and cultural objects to enlarge their existing libraries or to open new libraries in places where there are none at present. They feel such libraries will give a great impulse to their cultural life. They are well aware, also, that these books, apart from their cultural importance, have a high sentimental value as they constitute the heritage of the once great Jewish communities of Europe."[159]

Despite British resistance to the dispersal of German Jewish collections, a number of these holdings were transferred to Central and South America, including parts of the Berlin Community Library and the Breslau Seminary Library. A number of Breslau holdings were surrendered to the Jewish Community Central Committee in Mexico City (Comité Central de la Comunidad Judía de México) in 1950, which established a Judaica library with the help of approximately one thousand volumes, though later it transferred these as a "memorial" to the local Ashkenazi community, which retains them to this day.[160] One of the key Jewish institutions in Buenos Aires, the Asociación Mutual Israelita Argentina community center, which also houses, for example, the Argentinian branch of YIVO, received most of the more than five thousand volumes dispatched to Argentina. With these, the center was to establish one of the largest Jewish libraries of the Diaspora.[161] Due to the large number of Eastern European, Yiddish-speaking immigrants there, Argentina and other South American countries were supplied primarily with Yiddish journals, newspapers, and books and Orthodox liturgical objects. The tremendous gratitude expressed by several South American communities to the JCR was described by Hannah Arendt in a report, which quotes an example: "We wish to express to you [JCR] our sincerest gratitude for the invaluable treasures our library has received and to assure you that the best use shall be made of them for the benefit of the cultural reconstruction of our people [. . .] we have received such a valuable gift that words cannot express it."[162]

JCR allocations mostly flowed from Europe to the United States and Israel. The transfer of every object and every volume from the ruined and disintegrating world to the new world—and this chiefly meant the young Jewish state of Israel rather than the United States—fulfilled the predictions made by many Jewish observers before Germany's surrender: the reconstruction and revitalization of Jewish culture was taking place outside Europe. In the awareness of the Holocaust's destructive impact on European-Jewish history, Arendt described the objects and collections dispatched to a different place as "the last remnants of an era which has ended."[163] The salvage of the remaining cultural goods entailed an element of a new beginning and of a spatial shift away from their European origins and communities, but it was also a means of enduringly commemorating this European past and its destruction. Every salvaged book seemed to symbolize a new dawn for Jewish life in a new location while also constituting vessels of time and memory that preserved the knowledge and traditions of the past.

More than one hundred Jewish and non-Jewish institutions and communities in the United States received books and objects from the JCR, including major academic libraries such as those of Columbia, New York, Harvard, and Yale universities, the New York Public Library, and the Library of Congress in Washington, DC.[164] More than forty yeshivot across the country were supplied with journals and books, with distribution in this case being entrusted to the Torah Umesorah society, established in New York in 1944, which was dedicated to the cultivation and advancement of Jewish life.[165] In addition, every major Jewish teaching institution received documents from the JCR collections. The Synagogue Council, the Yeshiva University New York, and its Jewish

Museum are particularly worthy of mention, either because they played a crucial role or because of the quantity of objects they received. The Synagogue Council, for example, was responsible for ascertaining the needs of the communities and distributed the still usable religious items, including prayer books and textiles. Above all else, it was mainly so-called immigrant communities that were the intended beneficiaries—in other words, those that had relocated to the United States from Europe over the course of the war or afterward.[166]

The Yeshiva University, meanwhile, provided the JCR with space to store books for which there was insufficient room in the depot but that were still to be distributed, and contrary to the wishes of Cecil Roth it received the partial holdings, which had been collected in Offenbach, of the Nazi Stürmer publishing house. At the end of the war, the MFA&A surrendered this library partly to the Nuremberg Israelite Community (Nürnberger Israelitische Gemeinde) and to the Nuremberg Municipal Library, but the entire community immigrated to Palestine, dividing their part of the collection between the Library and Koppel Pinson. The latter then took his portion to Offenbach. In the course of this process, numerous Hebrew books from the Stürmer collection clearly ended up in Palestine as well. In his 1957 article "The Fate of the Jewish Book during the Nazi Era," Philip Friedman refers to several thousand books from Nuremberg; along with agricultural implements from the farm of Julius Streicher, publisher and editor of the *Stürmer* newspaper, these were sent to a kibbutz made up of young Holocaust survivors in Palestine via the MFA&A. In this way, Friedman stated, "the treasures collected by the rapacious and ruthless *Judenfresser* eventually came to serve a noble purpose—the trainings of his victims, the youthful pioneers, for *hakhsharah* [preparation] to [sic] Israel. This presage of a brighter tomorrow is a happy augury for the 'People of the Book.'"[167]

The portions of the Stürmer library collection sent to New York in 1950 comprised around six thousand volumes (of a total of fifteen thousand), most of them Hebraica and rabbinical literature. The JCR demanded that Yeshiva University provide them with a section of their own because, as Friedman had already made clear, they were a striking reminder of the Nazis' policy of theft and confiscation. Many volumes bore annotations made by Streicher's staff. Furthermore, to a significant extent, the collection had been created with the direct help of the

German population. Many Germans had responded to Streicher's appeals in the *Stürmer* and sent books stolen from neighbors and institutions to Nuremberg from all over the German Empire to support his anti-Semitic propaganda.[168] Initially, however, Yeshiva University displeased the JCR by failing to follow its instructions, neither making the collection accessible nor making any public mention of the JCR's role in bringing it to the United States. Only after repeated admonitions by Arendt and Baron was the collection put on public display and opened for research.[169] Yeshiva University received more than ten thousand books in total from the JCR.[170]

The staff of the Jewish Museum in New York, established in 1904 as part of the JTS, responded to the JCR quite differently. By the summer of 1950, they had organized several exhibitions of the ritual objects and works of art entrusted to them.[171] For the museum, which was still very small at the time, the arrival of these European cultural treasures necessitated a process of redefinition. Stephen S. Kayser, first curator of the museum, housed since 1944 in a building donated by the Warburg family, declared that after the Holocaust, it had been transformed from a "museum of Jewish religious objects and Jewish art" into a "silent and yet highly eloquent memorial to Europe's Jews."[172] For a time, the museum's basement served the JCR as a temporary warehouse for all the ritual and art objects arriving in New York. The museum retained around two hundred objects, while the others, including very old and valuable treasures, were distributed to other museums and university collections—more than ten in total. The fact that so many different institutions and groups in the United States received books and objects from the JCR attests in a special way to the diversity of the country's Jewish community, which had existed long before the Second World War but which gained a new role and a new voice among Jews worldwide after 1945. Though no one was in any doubt about the importance of the Hebrew University among the heirs to European Jewish cultural property, key JCR figures resident in the United States were particularly keen to bolster the American-Jewish cultural infrastructure. Israel's political status was still uncertain, while the United States was now home to many émigré scholars from Europe who—like those involved in JCR's mission—could make direct use of the books, manuscripts, and objects.

Just under two hundred thousand books, more than 3,300 ritual objects, and around one thousand Torah scrolls, and thus the greater part of the cultural property recovered in Germany, was shipped by the JCR to Israel.[173] Here, unlike in the United States, there existed two central institutions that could house them: the Bezalel Museum in Jerusalem, whose holdings now form part of the Israel Museum, and the Jewish National and University Library, today's National Library of Israel.

The members of the library's staff on the Otzrot HaGolah committee showed great dedication, cooperating with the JCR but also seeking out book holdings and collections in Europe on their own initiative and soliciting donations and transfers of material to the library. They formed the core of Israeli efforts to salvage European cultural treasures.

Building the New State

Israel and the European Jewish Cultural Heritage

As soon as the Nazi persecution of Jews in Germany and Austria began, leading Jewish figures in Palestine started to discuss the future of their cultural property and book collections. The library holdings from Europe that had been arriving in Jerusalem regularly since 1933—preemptively saved from German seizure—were, so to speak, material witnesses to and portents of the threats facing Jewish culture in the expanding area under German domination.[1] During this period, the first port of call for European book and manuscript collections was already the Jewish National and University Library. The library, still in embryonic form in the 1930s, formed a sort of safe haven for that which was being wantonly destroyed in Europe—like the Offenbach Archival Depot later on, it symbolized a kind of antithesis of the Nazis' policy of confiscation and burning.[2] A predecessor to the library had existed since the early 1890s, having been established as a national library in 1892 by the B'nai B'rith Lodge with the help of the collections of the scholar Elizer Ben-Yehuda and the physician Josef Chasanowicz from Białystok. Chasanowicz was a staunch believer in the book's powerful and fundamental role in the Jewish tradition: "We, the people of the book, must honor and watch over the book. We, the ancient wanderers, must find a dwelling place for our books. We, the people of history, must not allow the chain of our history to be broken. We must preserve for the future all that which our spirit created in the past."[3]

In 1918, the library then officially came under the authority of the World Zionist Organization, which expanded it to create the JNUL. Its first director, appointed in 1920, was the philosopher Hugo S. Bergman from Prague, who expedited its development and expansion in the present-day university grounds on Mount Scopus in Jerusalem. During his tenure, Gershom Scholem was employed at the library after his arrival in Palestine in 1923, taking on the systematic cataloging of Hebraica. After the establishment of the university in 1925, the library was incorporated into the new institution, and in 1930, it moved into the Wolffsohn Building on the university grounds. When Bergman left his position to become the dean of the Hebrew University in 1935, Gotthold Weil, head of the Oriental Department of the Prussian State Library of Berlin before his forced emigration, succeeded him as director. The tradition of German Jewish leadership of the library continued during the period of Israel's foundation as a state: after the war, in 1946, Curt Wormann, also from Berlin, became its new director. And it was he who supervised the salvage and restitution of European collections. These tasks had to be pursued in a context in which the library's own situation had changed dramatically. In the wake of the War of Independence of 1948, the building on Mount Scopus was no longer accessible to the Jewish population because the territory was declared an enclave, partly under Israeli control, partly under Jordanian control and supervised by the UN. With soldiers' help, certain volumes were gradually transferred to the western part of the city, where an interim library—a "library in Exile" as it was called by its administrators—was established in the Collegium Terra Sancta and smaller premises nearby. But a large part of the holdings remained in the Mt. Scopus enclave and was barely accessible. This situation did not change until the opening, in 1960, of the JNUL building on the new Hebrew University campus in the Givat Ram district.[4]

Hugo Bergman was to be one of the first in Palestine to put forward concrete plans to salvage Jewish libraries in Europe, and by 1942, he was already pushing for a joint effort by the Hebrew University and JNUL to this end.[5] Judah Magnes, the university's first president, provided him with much support, and after the war, Magnes became a driving force in the negotiations with the Allied military authorities in Europe. He also publicized the scandal of Nazi cultural raids, thus underlining the urgent need for action. At a time when the Jewish books of Europe were under severe threat and much of the Jewish intellectual tradition faced liquidation along with them, the previously quoted words of the library's founding father, Chasanowicz, took on a nearly prophetic significance. It had become more pressing than ever to find a place where the books could be preserved for the future. Given *Eretz Israel*'s determination to be recognized as the national and spiritual center of the entire Jewish collectivity, the JNUL seemed an apt setting for both the salvage and administration of European Jewish cultural objects.

On Magnes's initiative, by November 1944, the Jewish Telegraphic Agency had announced that the Hebrew University had taken the first steps to rescuing looted Jewish cultural and art treasures discovered in Munich for the Jewish people. Negotiations, it was stated, were being held with the relevant departments of the United Nations, which was being established at the time, on the potential transfer of all yet-to-be-recovered items to the JNUL and the Hebrew University's Museum of Jewish Antiquities.[6] These "first steps" mainly consisted in the activities of the aforementioned Committee for the Salvaging of Diaspora Treasures (*Ha-va' ad le-hazalat ozrot ha-golah*), which was appointed in spring 1944 under Magnes's leadership. Made up of members of the university and library, this body was dedicated to salvaging and returning stolen cultural property of Jewish provenance in Europe. The semantic core of the term *Otzroth HaGolah* can no longer be definitively decoded because the Hebrew word *golah* is used in different ways in different contexts.[7] But we can work on the assumption that committee members were convinced that the Jewish settlement in Palestine was a means of overcoming a diasporic existence bound up with marginalization and persecution and potentially total destruction.[8] This perspective pointed the way to the future in the old-new home while also making it possible to call, without reservation, for the transfer of all goods to the prestate Yishuv and later to Israel. Ultimately, as the Committee—and most Jews in the Yishuv—saw it, the land of Israel ought to be the successor and "historical, material, moral, and legal heir of the murdered millions" in Europe.[9]

The primarily German Jewish members of the Otzrot HaGolah, however, did not endorse the demand, which dominated Israeli public discourse in the late 1940s, for total renunciation of Jewish life in Europe—an existence generally associated with passivity, overassimilation, and a loss of connection to Jewish traditions.[10] Given their personal history and education, often completed at German universities, they held positive views of European academic cultures and felt it absolutely necessary to establish the Hebrew University in the tradition of European, even German, institutions of higher learning. This explains their overwhelming commitment to salvaging the material heritage from Europe;

they were keenly aware of the scholarly and historical value of these books, documents, and art objects to their own intellectual canon. They thus occupied a "dissonant" position within the developing cultural and scholarly institutions of Israel.[11] Most of the members had come to Palestine before the Nazis seized power but had not broken entirely with German cultural traditions, retaining them in their language, habitus, and lifestyle. Hugo Bergman wrote to his friend Robert Weltsch in 1928, "Spiritually we live in Germany, not here."[12] This was to change during the war and after, as the German members of the Hebrew University found their feet in Israel and Hebrew and engaged in the country's cultural and academic development. They often lost their positive attitude toward their country of origin as they became aware of the horrors unleashed by Germany.[13] Nonetheless, they tried to create a space for remnants of European and German tradition in Israel. This group of German Jewish scholars in Jerusalem always lived, according to David Myers, in a state of tension "between the enduring legacy of German scholarship and the new Zionist cause."[14] Given this ambivalent sense of belonging, pulled between preservation of their German roots and transition to their new Israeli identity, the first generation of professors at the Hebrew University were predestined to act as the administrators of the European Jewry's cultural legacy.

The Otzrot HaGolah Committee

From spring 1944 onward, the Otzrot HaGolah committee brought together prominent professors at the Hebrew University, among them Simha Assaf, Hugo Bergman, Martin Buber, Ben-Zion Dinur, Yehoshua Gutman and Gershom Scholem, JNUL directors Weil and Wormann, and Werner Senator, who was appointed administrative head of the Hebrew University in 1949. When the war was over, Magnes and the committee entered into negotiations with key figures and institutions in the Allied administrative apparatus in an attempt to gain their support for the salvaging and return of Jewish cultural property in Europe. Magnes minced no words in addressing the British high commissioner for Palestine, Alan G. Cunningham, introducing the idea of the Hebrew University as a prominent party to the negotiations: "We feel that it is a requirement of historic justice that the Hebrew University and the Jewish National and

University Library in Jerusalem be made the repository of these remains of Jewish culture which have fortunately been saved for the world. [...] We feel that we can well be regarded as the spokesmen of the Jewish people in this regard."[15]

In this missive, we can discern the central arguments that would be put forward as the negotiations continued. First, emphasis was placed on historical justice in an attempt to lay the groundwork for an international acceptance of the rights of Jewish educational and cultural institutions in Palestine/Israel. The claims formulated here lacked an incontestable legal basis since there was no state in Israel/Palestine that might be invoked as legal representative or identified as a direct victim of Nazi looting. It was thus necessary to place "soft" moral arguments front and center. Again and again, the committee's letters and reports referred to "historical justice," a "natural and elementary sense of justice," and a "moral obligation" in order to back up the Yishuv's claims and especially those of the institutions located there vis-à-vis Germany. The second crucial argument related to the legal representation of the Jewish people. Like the representatives of the Commission and JCR in the United States, Jewish spokespersons in the Yishuv argued that recognition of a nonstate form of representation for the Jewish collectivity was a prerequisite for fair restitution laws. It was taken for granted that the Yishuv or Israel had a right to claim this role as the only legitimate national and cultural representative of the entire Jewish people. Together with the later president of Israel Chaim Weizmann, Magnes attempted to persuade the American administration that the Yishuv should be sole representative with respect to cultural restitution. In July 1945, they requested the transfer of all nonidentifiable objects found by the MFA&A in Germany and the former occupied areas, justifying this in light of the fact that the Hebrew University was the "the one university and the highest seat of learning of the Jewish people." The goal was to "serve as the authorized repository for the Jewish libraries, historical documents, Jewish art objects as well as the anti-Semitic collections which the allied forces have come upon in Germany and Austria." Concluding their letter, Magnes and Weizmann appealed to the Allies' humanistic ideals, which they presented as favorable to their interests.[16] Simon Rifkind, adviser to the American military government, was a strong supporter of Magnes's application for trust status and repeatedly pushed for this to be granted, though he always met with a negative response.[17]

As a result, the scholars in Jerusalem sought to rework their strategy. In early 1946, the Otzrot HaGolah legal advisory board, which consisted of the renowned jurists Norman Bentwich, Nathan Feinberg, and Abraham Chaim Freimann, set out the legal and political foundations for the committee's future work in greater detail. Like the New York–based Commission, the legal board expressed opposition to territorially based restitution laws and the escheat doctrine. Their main criticism was that this right of inheritance would help ensure that stolen property remained in Germany—an offense against elementary principles of justice. In a comprehensive memorandum they underlined, "German penal law in the interwar period stipulated that a murderer can never become the rightful owner of the murdered party's property. In line with this principle, the German state cannot be recognized as owner of the assets of Jews murdered at its hands."[18]

In their deliberations, the Jerusalem legal experts sought to establish a more just legal framework for restitution, one that called for the recognition of the Jewish people as a subject in the negotiations instead of the German state. To back up their arguments, they first made a historical point, referring to the (unsuccessful) attempt, already incorporated into the Treaty of Sèvres of 1920, to confirm the collective right of Armenians to the property stolen from them by Turkey.[19] Second, they pointed to the nature of the crime itself to underscore the necessity for new legal standards. As the lawyers saw it, the war waged by the Germans was not directed against individual Jews but against the Jewish people (in the original Hebrew: *am haJehudi*) as a whole and therefore constituted an act of genocide. This understanding was also recognized in the verdict of the International Military Tribunal in Nuremberg. Hence, as they saw it, acknowledgement of the Nazis' genocidal actions was a fundamental prerequisite for reformulating restitution laws and opened up the possibility of rendering the Jewish people an independent claimant. Here they were referring to the Jewish people (in the original Hebrew: *am Israel*) that was now experiencing a renaissance "in the Land of the Fathers" and had a "unique and vital connection to the treasures of its culture," which meant that it had the right and a duty to preserve them. To strengthen their case,

Bentwich, Feinberg, and Freimann firmly rejected the idea of reconstructing the European congregations and were convinced that "the emergence of fictitious entities that appropriate the name of earlier communities and file claims in their name must be opposed." With respect to the prominent role of the Hebrew University and the JNUL and their suitability for administration and trusteeship, the memo stated that the Committee members considered it their "sacred duty" to nurture the Jewish cultural legacy and play a part in the "resurrection and strengthening" of the Jewish people in Israel and the rest of the world. It claimed that both institutions possessed the infrastructure, administrative apparatus, and personnel necessary to this end and all the key prerequisites for the potential restitution and maintenance of cultural property. It also emphasized that international cooperation with Jewish organizations was desirable in order to establish a "united front" made up of all scholarly and cultural organizations. The memorandum ends by underlining that obtaining compensatory goods from German libraries and archives in the form of Hebrew manuscripts and rare materials would also be one of the Otzrot HaGolah committee's declared goals.[20] The hallmarks of this report are its Zionist thumbprint and its plea—which mirrored those made by many Jewish politicians and experts in international law across the world in the early 1940s—for recognition of a common form of legal representation for Jews regardless of their countries of origin. In much the same way as Jerome Michael and Salo W. Baron of the Commission, the memo drew on the preparatory work done by Siegfried Moses, Nahum Goldmann, and Chaim Weizmann with respect to restitution and indemnification policies.

Before the negotiations with the JCR and the cooperation under its leadership began, then, the activists in Jerusalem had been eager to obtain a monopoly on cultural restitution. There could be no mistaking Magnes's aspiration in this regard vis-à-vis the competing initiatives in the United States:

> We are to be the chief country for the absorption of the living human beings who have escaped from Nazi persecution [. . .]. By the same token we should be the trustee of these spiritual goods which destroyed German Jewry left behind. It will be nothing less than disgraceful if there were any competition between Jewish organizations for the receipt of

books, manuscripts and other collections. [. . .] We are [. . .] anxious that the Jews of the world should recognize that it is our duty to establish our spiritual and moral claim to be in the direct line of succession to the Jewish culture and scholarship of European Jewry.[21]

This claim of a "direct line of succession" between the Jewish institutions of the Yishuv and the "Jewish culture and scholarship of European Jewry" was aimed in two directions: the Allied forces implementing restitution procedures as well as the Jewish organizations with parallel goals in the United States needed to be convinced that the Hebrew University ought to play a central role. The JA supported this stance.[22] But among other Jewish individuals involved, this approach soon faced considerable opposition. During Magnes's visits to New York in early summer 1946 and at Baron's meeting with the members of the Otzrot HaGolah committee in Jerusalem in September the same year, it was already evident that only a joint approach would have any chance of winning over the Allies. A skeptical view of the Otzrot HaGolah committee's aspiration for *Eretz Israel* to act as sole representative was not only inspired by the uncertain political situation in Palestine; American government officials (before emancipating themselves from the views of the Allied Control Council in late 1947 and issuing their zone-wide restitution law no. 59) wished to avoid snubbing their British allies, who were eager to control migration as well as the transfer of property to their mandated territory in Palestine in a delicate situation in which the region's future status remained unclear.

In view of these various obstacles, the scholars in Jerusalem reframed their claims and instead sought to obtain the most influential role possible within the JCR. They achieved most of their goals. Another position paper, published by the Jerusalem committee in January 1948, presented a compromise while still placing the university at the center of attention: "Historical justice requires that the scholarly work of destroyed Jewish institutions of learning and Jewish communities be continued in Jewish institutions throughout the world, but especially in the Holy Land, here the Jewish tradition of learning has now its main living center. [. . .] The Hebrew University is confident that the other institutions represented in Jewish Cultural Reconstruction Inc. will be ready to grant priority in this respect to the Hebrew University, which represents not only itself but all the institutions of learning and the communities of Palestine."[23]

The demand already articulated by Scholem in his 1946 letter to Leo Baeck was to be fulfilled through cooperation with the JCR—namely, that wherever the Jews went their books should go too.[24] The large number of European immigrants clamoring to migrate to Palestine was highlighted to underline the need to transfer as many books and ritual or art objects as possible to the territory.[25] What led to disagreements between the JCR and their partners in Jerusalem was not so much the latter's Zionist line of argument, which was shared by the majority of Jews living outside Israel, but practical matters. There were divergent views on the composition of the group that was to pursue their objectives in Europe, there was initial disagreement over how best to approach Czechoslovakia and other Eastern European countries, and there were bitter disputes over the allocation formula used by the JCR. Time and again, gray areas emerged in which the Otzrot HaGolah committee acted independently, keeping the JCR at arm's length even when the latter was directly affected. This had already occurred before the official foundation of the corporation when Gershom Scholem, on his first trip to Europe on behalf of the university in 1946, initiated the illegal transfer of boxes containing rare items from the Offenbach Depot to Palestine. American officials estimated the objects' value at several million dollars and requested their return, the case being considered by the highest level of the military authorities.[26] When the JCR had finally been established and became actively involved in this affair, its board proposed that the boxes remain in Jerusalem on the condition that they would be inspected and restituted to former owners if necessary. Scholem too sought to limit the damage, emphasizing that he had previously come to an understanding with Koppel Pinson and the depot director Isaac Bencowitz about his plans, with all agreeing that it was best to get the material out of Germany as quickly as possible because they considered it "dangerous to leave these documents in the hands of a German staff for a longer period."[27] The JCR's proposed solution was ultimately incorporated into the so-called Addendum I to the "Frankfurt Agreement" and ratified on April 5, 1949.[28] Internally, the members of the JCR board of directors—at the meetings in New York the Otzrot HaGolah was mostly represented by Leo Schwarz, High Salpeter, Benjamin Halpern, and other members of the American Friends of the Hebrew University committee—agreed that Curt Wormann, along with his deputy Isaachar Joel, would identify objects and initiate any necessary restitution. The American officials approved of this course of action, and the manuscripts were transferred to the Jerusalem library, later becoming the legal property of Israel.

In two more cases, the Hebrew University–based group was to act independently of the JCR: in the protracted and complicated negotiations on the Jewish book holdings discovered in Czechoslovakia and Poland and with respect to the restitution of remnants of the Gesamtarchiv of the German Jews.

Initiatives in Prague

Soon after the war, those involved in the search for looted cultural property discovered that precious items were located outside the American zone: large quantities had been taken to a number of Bohemian castles and the Theresienstadt concentration camp in 1943.[29] In the spring of 1945, a disturbing reality became apparent: in the region spanning the Czech cities of Prague and Terezín and the town of Mimoň, only a small remnant of the large prewar Jewish population had survived, while a huge, almost unmanageable number of books of Jewish provenance remained. Most of them were stored in the Prague Jewish Museum, founded in 1906. After the occupation of Prague, the Nazis had used it to host defaming exhibitions of Jewish life and culture and turned it into a large storage depot for booty stolen from Jewish communities and private individuals throughout Bohemia and Moravia. This contained more than one hundred thousand books that had been looked after by Jewish professionals forced to run the museum.[30] Two libraries had also been set up in the Theresienstadt concentration camp. In the "Ghetto Library," which could be used by internees and was headed by Emil Utitz, a philosophy professor from Prague, about 180,000 volumes taken from Jewish communities, private households, and expellees were found after the liberation. A second, concealed SS depot housed about sixty thousand valuable items of Judaica and archival documents from all over Central and Eastern Europe, formerly stored in the Berlin RSHA.[31] Eventually, the bulk of the looted collection held by Berlin's RSHA was found in several castles near the small town of

Mimoň in northern Bohemia, having been transported there by German soldiers to protect it from bombardment. These holdings contained some of the most valuable and renowned European Jewish libraries.[32]

By January 1946, the Hebrew University had already been made aware of this thanks to a letter from Zeev Scheck and Robert Weinberger of the Council of the Jewish Communities of Bohemia and Moravia-Silesia (Rat der Jüdischen Kultusgemeinden Böhmen und Mähren) in Prague. The letter provided detailed information on how many books of Jewish origin were being kept in the Jewish Museum in Prague at this point under the control of the Czechoslovak government.[33] Both of the letter's authors were survivors of Theresienstadt and were able to describe the situation there in light of personal experience. They highlighted in particular the book collection from RSHA Berlin housed in the camp, which had been looked after by a book acquisition unit, whose members had sorted and cataloged the precious Judaica and Hebraica. After the camp's liberation, most of the books from both holdings in Theresienstadt ended up in the museum or were surrendered to the Prague congregation. In the museum, the books were merged with the existing library, which had been established under Nazi supervision and had been headed by Hebraist Mojssch Woskin-Nahartabi, who was later murdered in Auschwitz. After the war, Hana Volavková, Otto Muneles, and the later famous writer H. G. Adler, themselves among the few survivors of the wartime museum and the camp, together with a small staff took care of its holdings and worked to ensure its reestablishment. Weinberger and Scheck were greatly concerned about the collection's fate and feared its loss since it seemed that all collections had come under government control in mid-1945.[34] They concluded their letter with an exhortation and request: "As we see it, there is only one setting and one location to which these books, some of which originate in the famous libraries of Jewish scholars, ought to be restituted, namely Jerusalem. [. . .] Only there can the books still fulfill their intended purpose." "With the blessing of Zion," Weinberger and Scheck thus called on the university to approach the government of Czechoslovakia and the Council of the Jewish Communities and fight to obtain these books and art objects.[35] At the time this letter was written, the still young Zeev Scheck—later a senior official in the Western Europe Division of the Israeli Foreign Ministry, where he was concerned, among other things, with demands for reparations and restitution vis-à-vis West Germany—was soon to depart for Palestine and would take with him a box containing important documents.[36] Having arrived in Jerusalem and enrolled in the Hebrew University, he became a member of the Otzrot HaGolah committee and later traveled back to Prague to negotiate on behalf of the university.

The first members of the university to be sent to Europe, however, in the spring of 1946, were Abraham Yaari and Gershom Scholem, and an array of tasks awaited them there. They arrived in Paris in April but were initially unable to continue on either to Germany or Czechoslovakia for want of the requisite permit. They failed in their attempts to influence the Joint and, via Philip Bernstein, the military government, and Yaari flew back to Israel having achieved nothing. Scholem complained to Magnes, "I feel depressed about the failure to get where I want to be [. . .]. There must be something going wrong with the whole system—people suspecting us of some sinister motive, of which we are unaware."[37] Magnes, holding talks in New York with Baron (among others) at the time, approached the State Department and ultimately succeeded in gaining Scholem entry to Germany in July. The latter made good use of the interim period, visiting Switzerland, Vienna, Prague, and Bratislava on a semilegal basis. He reached Prague in June 1946 and began three weeks of fraught negotiations with representatives of the congregations there, staff at the Jewish Museum, and the government authorities. Scholem confirmed the situation described by Scheck and Weinberger. It seemed to him that the Nazis had sent the evidently most valuable and high-quality books for storage to Prague and the surrounding area. Meanwhile, he was shocked by the state of the city, which left him in no doubt that Jewish life had been completely wiped out in what had been one of its cultural centers. With bitter sarcasm, he declared that there was no longer any need for a single Jewish book in Prague, as there were no more than ten people left with a knowledge of Hebrew.[38] Shattered by what he had experienced, he wrote to his friend Siegmund Hurwitz, a Kabbalah researcher in Switzerland, "I am sitting here in a hotel, feeling a bit lost [. . .]. Yesterday I walked alone for an hour through the old Jewish cemetery. It filled me with inexpressible emotion, and I could not hold back my tears. I fear nothing will remain here but the cemetery and a synagogue, which has now become a museum."[39]

This only increased his commitment, as he was convinced of the urgent need for action. Scholem gained permission from the Council of Jewish Communities, which was responsible for the administration of the books from Theresienstadt now in Prague, to transfer a number of them to Jerusalem. But he had to make sure that the representatives of the German Jews, who were earmarked as heirs to the collection, the Ministries of Education and Social Affairs, and the staff of the Jewish Museum gave their consent.[40] Against this background, Scholem tried to gain the support of Irgun Olei Merkaz (which represented German Jews in Palestine) and Leo Baeck, who had himself been interned in Theresienstadt, for the Hebrew University's endeavors in Prague.[41] Under no circumstances did he want the Jewish congregations in Germany to be involved in this decision. He refused to accept that they had any right to identify themselves as the legal heirs or successors to the German Jews—either in Germany or Czechoslovakia—and regarded them as illegitimate bodies. Indeed, he did not even recognize their members as Jews. The minutes of his negotiations in Prague quote him as follows: "I recognize that it makes sense in this regard to submit possible claims by the Olej Maaraf Europa [*sic*] in Palestine and the Council of German Jews in England, and we may be able to facilitate these. Under no circumstances [should] the Jewish people negotiate officially with the small groups of only de facto existing congregations in Germany, which in some cases consist only of quasi-Jews, as legitimate representatives of the German Jewry." Finally, he reinforced this point with a dramatic assessment of the situation of the German Jews: "German Jewry either died in Auschwitz and Theresienstadt or lives on in the shape of its representatives in other countries and above all in Eretz Israel."[42] Scholem won practical support from Samuel Sharp, a WJC spokesman newly arrived in Prague, who supervised the book-transfer project on site after Scholem's departure. The Council provided Scholem with a written statement permitting the Hebrew University to take charge of holdings of German Jewish provenance in Czechoslovakia, enabling him to approach the Council of the Jewish Community in Prague and its president Ernst (Arnošt) Frischer with clear-cut demands:

We are convinced that these cultural goods ought to be collected in those places where there is vibrant Jewish life and, therefore, the possibility

that these items will be put to good use, while also being available to researchers and serving the development of the religious and cultural needs
of the Jewish community—not least because in Palestine the interest in
these works is not limited to specialists but attracts lively interest from
the broadest circles of the Jewish population. In my opinion, these books,
which were transported to this state's territory by the Nazis and ended
up here by chance must be regarded as a holding alien to the Jews here.
[. . .] Here these books can in no way even begin to fulfill their proper
purpose, as they will in Palestine. I therefore believe these books belong
in the spiritual center of the Jewish community, quite apart from the fact
that in Palestine many German Jews, and especially those most interested
in Judaism, have put down roots and the great intellectual tradition of
German Judaism will continue to be cultivated there. [. . .] I will not
omit to mention that Jewish Prague, which played such a glorious role in
the past, once again has an opportunity, in continuance of its traditions,
to do an inestimable service to Jewish intellectual life by salvaging the
spiritual goods of Judaism and allowing them to make a living and fruitful impact.[43]

As mentioned before, these German traditions were highly contested
in the Yishuv itself and were subject to attack in public and academic
debates, but this played no role in Scholem's practical perspective. He
left Prague in the belief that he had set the course for the transfer of
select parts of the Theresienstadt holdings, but it was to be four years
before they were finally shipped, and this required the negotiating acu-
men of three further emissaries from the Hebrew University. Scholem
continued to negotiate in Bratislava, where he found important books
of Jewish provenance, which he also claimed for the JNUL. In this case
too, the Czechoslovak government initially opposed the transfer of
materials, instead wishing to use the one hundred thousand books to
supply the resident Jewish congregations. But according to Scholem,
their representatives were mostly Zionists and supported his cause.
He therefore proposed the selection of six thousand books for Jerusalem
and their shipment via Paris to Haifa.[44] Only later, during his ten-day
stay in Berlin, did Ernst Grumach brief him on the remaining RSHA
collections in Niemes Castle and other Bohemian castles. Scholem
immediately passed this news on to Sharp in Prague, as he suspected

that Niemes (Mimoň) housed the "the most important collection which remains of the great Nazi loot."[45]

From November 1946 onward, Hugo Bergman continued Scholem's work in Prague.[46] As he himself hailed from the city, the university in Jerusalem hoped that his knowledge of the language and a large network of local contacts would lead to further negotiating successes, including with respect to the collections in Niemes Castle, which were viewed as especially valuable.[47] Upon arrival, he quickly concluded that his activities were under threat, chiefly from the sudden intervention of the American military government and the Commission, which wished to transfer all recovered material to the American occupation zone in order to restitute it from there. Arguing that neither the government of Czechoslovakia nor the Jews resident there had "any legal or moral rights to retain these objects," Jerome Michael had again approached John H. Hilldring at the American State Department in August to request their transfer. Around the same time, Hilldring received a letter from Scholem setting out the plans of the Hebrew University. Beyond the conflicting views on responsibilities and justifiable claims, the main issue at stake here was that most treasures' ownership was unclear because they represented "internal loot"—in other words, objects stolen from Germans by Germans that were still awaiting an incontestable legal ruling on their restitution.[48] Ultimately, the Commission and the Hebrew University reached an agreement and managed to cooperate rather than impeding one another. This, however, did not prevent the emergence of other parties wishing to take charge of the collections in Prague. By 1951, the United Nations Relief and Rehabilitation Administration (UNRRA) had received more than sixty-five thousand Jewish prayer books to supply refugees in Europe from the Prague holdings, while the Joint bought more than twenty thousand books from the Theresienstadt collection for DP camps in Austria.[49] While Bergman was still in Prague, another Czech negotiating party appeared on the scene: the Prague University Library, which had been appointed by the government to take charge of the recovered castle collections. Bergman was the first spokesperson from Jerusalem to travel to Niemes himself to assess the situation there with his own eyes. He found not only Yiddish books and a newspaper collection from the Vilna YIVO but also parts of the Congregational Library of Berlin and the Berlin Hochschule für die Wissenschaft des Judentums library, the private collection of Sigmund Seeligmann, and that of librarian Werner Kraft, who had fled to Jerusalem in 1934.[50] Bergman confirmed the sad picture of Jewish Prague painted by Scholem. Much shaken, he reported, "It is hard to witness the vibrant life of Prague. Jewish life is vibrant here too, but only on the steps of the Palestine Office and the other aid agencies. A people of wanderers and the homeless!"[51] Compared with Scholem, Bergman was able to establish a much closer relationship with the local representatives from the community and museum. Nonetheless, at the end of his stay many questions remained open and it was not until the summer of the next year that the next two emissaries of the Hebrew University could resume the work begun in Prague.

These were Hugo Bergman's brother Arthur Bergman, who went to Prague for three months, and Zeev Scheck, the initiator of the transfer of materials, who returned to the city to ensure its implementation over a ten-month period. Prior to the arrival of these Hebrew University representatives, two other important figures went to Prague to inspect the books there. Working for the Joint in Munich and at the Offenbach Depot, Lucy Schildkret (Dawidowicz) was focused on advancing restitution in connection with YIVO in addition to her work supplying materials to those in need, while the former Depot director Seymour Pomrenze was sent to Prague by YIVO itself. Neither was able to travel to Niemes, but in collaboration with the Council of Jewish Communities and with the support of the American consulate, they did what they could to restitute the YIVO newspaper and journal holdings recovered there to New York. In negotiations held in March 1947, Dawidowicz also pushed for DP camps in Austria to receive further book donations without the Joint having to pay for them. She was particularly struck by the disinterest and hostile behavior of the Czechoslovak authorities, which clearly saw no need for restitution. With much indignation, she wrote to the Depot head Joseph Horne: "On the whole, no attempt has been made to sort the books and locate the owners. [. . .] The Czech government generally has a negative attitude towards the question of restitution and has in certain instances labeled the desire of persons or organizations for return of their property as 'Fascist,' 'bourgeois,' or whatever is the appropriate term at that particular time."[52]

In the opinion of Dawidowicz, Pomrenze, and Max Weinreich, the official authorization for the transfer of YIVO property from Germany granted in the spring of 1947 ought to facilitate the removal of such property from Czechoslovakia as well. Following the dispatch of the books and archival materials from Offenbach, Pomrenze traveled directly to Prague to lay the groundwork for the shipment of materials there. But he could not fulfill his mission. A memorandum sent from Prague in July certainly shows that at this point in time, some material from the Bohemian castles had arrived in Prague and an agreement had been reached with the Council of Jewish Communities that YIVO property could be prepared for transfer to the United States. However, the available sources leave us in the dark about whether this transfer actually occurred despite the state authorities' fundamental opposition to restitution to the West and, if so, how this might have happened. What we do know is that YIVO New York was unable to obtain any of the holdings Hugo Bergman had mentioned after his visit to the castle.[53] Arthur Bergman and Scheck confirmed the extreme difficulties involved in any form of cultural restitution within the Czech context. They started negotiations practically from scratch because the government was now demanding compensation payments of one million crowns for the removal of the material selected by Scholem and Hugo Bergman from the Theresienstadt holdings, had initiated a comprehensive cataloging process, proposed to surrender duplicates and only made available books of German ownership for selection. Such seemingly arbitrary decisions slowed things down tremendously. After many of those involved had been bribed with money and cigarettes, Arthur Bergman was able to select just under twenty thousand volumes and have them stored at a haulage company in the main Prague railroad station. According to his report, this lot included "old Bible editions, old liturgy, Venetian Talmud, Basel Talmud, rabbinical literature, old Oriental prints, collections of the Rabbinical Seminary and responsa, modern-day Talmud commentaries, old editions of the [De]Cisoren, Rambam [Maimonides] and Shulchan Aruch, [a] large number of old prints and, when it comes to Judaica, mainly biblical commentaries and ancient theological literature."[54] In addition, Bergman initiated the transfer of the large quantity of books, manuscripts, archival materials, and journals in the castles, above all Niemes, to Prague with the help of a military convoy. He too was dismayed by the situation in Niemes Castle: "In a number of rooms and on several floors there lay mountains of books furnished with labels indicating who they had belonged to. In one huge hall—the YWO [*sic*] books—tall as a man and scattered across the entire room, it is virtually impossible to identify even one book, an unimaginable picture of devastation!" The staff of the Prague University Library had begun to sort the individual collections but had to leave out Judaica due to a lack of linguistic knowledge. Since no storage site could be found in Prague, Bergman decided to store the books in the mortuary of the Jewish cemetery in the Smíchov-Malvazinka district. In the summer of 1947, a situation arose in Prague that was not dissimilar to that in Offenbach: stacks of books in the thousands with an unclear future were stored in cramped quarters—in this case, in a real mortuary.

Another year was to pass before the selected books from the castles and the Theresienstadt collection were sent to Antwerp then dispatched to Israel. During this period, Scheck and Menachem Mendel Schneurson, who was working for the Otzrot HaGolah committee in Poland, managed to ensure that the books recovered in Prague from the Rabbinical Seminary in Breslau, together with eighty thousand volumes of rabbinical literature from Poland, were surrendered to the state of Israel as an official donation.[55] In order to take more materials than declared out of the country, the desired books and manuscripts in Prague were provided with fake inventories, manuscripts were hidden in crates of books, and misleading valuations were prepared for the customs authorities. This facilitated the shipment from Prague of a first consignment, supervised by Scheck, in January and a second in October 1948, together containing a total of around fifty thousand books, documents, and manuscripts.[56] These boxes, however, reached Jerusalem only in 1950, as it was thought to be safer to store them in the Joint depot in Antwerp during the Israeli War of Independence. Small portions of the other books of Jewish provenance in Prague were surrendered to the WJC, the rest mostly being allocated to various Czech and Slovak institutions. Many volumes and objects are still to be found in the Prague Jewish Museum, where detailed research is gradually establishing their provenance.[57]

Israeli Initiatives in Germany

After 1945, quite a few members of the Otzrot HaGolah committee visited Germany and—often under great psychological strain—dedicated themselves to the salvage and restitution of cultural property. Gershom Scholem often related to friends and colleagues the painful character of his trips to Germany. This direct confrontation with the perpetrating society and with the scale of the destruction wrought by the Nazis on Jewish Europe had a traumatic effect on the Jewish emissaries, though it also reinforced their resolve to leave the Germans as little of the Jewish cultural legacy as possible. Scholem's attempts to influence German authorities and institutions and to obtain a donation of books to Israel from the German Publishers and Booksellers Association (Börsenverein des deutschen Buchhandels) were largely independent of the work he carried out in collaboration with the JCR. He also laid the groundwork for the restitution of archival materials from the various occupation zones to the Central Archive for the History of the Jewish People in Jerusalem on a fairly independent basis.

Scholem's efforts to obtain the compensatory material from German museums and libraries demanded by the Otzrot HaGolah generally failed. The main focus of his attention here were Hebrew texts held by the State Library in Munich (Münchner Staatsbibliothek), especially the particularly valuable *Codex Hebraicus 95* of 1343, which is the only existing near-complete manuscript of the Babylonian Talmud. On a number of occasions, he sought to persuade Gustav Hofmann, its director, and Hans Ludwig Held, head of the Munich City Library (Münchner Stadtbibliothek), to surrender materials as a form of compensation—"as a first step toward bridging the awful abyss that has been created between the two peoples."[58] Scholem tried to come to a similar agreement with Hanns Wilhelm Eppelsheimer in Frankfurt in light of the valuable Judaica and Hebraica he assumed to still be there. The famous Frankfurt collection, cataloged by Aron Freimann in 1920 and 1932, in its majority represented donations to the city and university libraries from Jewish patrons, so a Jewish claim seemed more than justified.[59] He was unsuccessful in both cases. As the city councilors and library representatives saw things, given its illustrious status, the remaining collection of Judaica, most of which was in German, ought to stay in Frankfurt. The collection was fragmented because some of its prints and manuscripts had been incinerated during the war, while in 1950, others had been passed to the formerly Frankfurt-based Jewish Levi family in New York, who received them as compensation for their aryanized and destroyed properties in the city center. Sections believed lost only reappeared in 1963 in one of the library's document storage bunkers. Nehemiah Aloni, who later traveled on behalf of the Institute for Hebrew Manuscripts from Israel to Frankfurt as Scholem's successor to lay claim to the valuable Hebraica in German libraries, or at least to get them microfilmed, came at the wrong time and gained nothing.[60] Nor was the Munich Talmud manuscript ever surrendered. Extensive demands for compensation from Germany did not succeed, and Scholem's efforts often came up against a brick wall. In 1948, he stated to Joshua Starr that, following a brief period of opening, the Germans' "hearts" had hardened once again and there was virtually no prospect of concessions from them.[61]

The agreement he negotiated with the German Publishers and Booksellers Association on a regular donation of books to Israel must have been only a small consolation given his strenuous, tilting-at-windmills efforts to win over German institutions and authorities. Fritz Moser, spokesperson for the Berlin Senate, submitted Scholem's request for book donations to the president of the association, arguing that such a donation could "make a significant contribution to reconciliation with Israel and in a sense provide the cultural equivalent of the olive tree donation initiated by Hamburg Senate Director Erich Lüth."[62] But Scholem's initiative was also slowed down because it was still uncertain whether Israel would respond positively to or even accept a donation, so further negotiations were postponed until the conclusion of the Luxembourg Agreement. After its ratification, Israel did assent to annual donations from the German publishers in the context of the awarding of the Peace Prize of the German Book Trade on September 24, 1952. Israeli Foreign Minister Moshe Sharett, and the Israeli consul in Munich, Eliahu Kurt Livneh, both gave their consent. Scholem, however, who had paved the way for the donation in collaboration with the association's executive secretary, the Heidelberg-based publisher Lambert Schneider, did not attend the ceremony in Frankfurt's Paulskirche. The leadership of the Hebrew University requested that he stay away. Werner Senator set out the motives for this decision in a letter to Scholem that attests to the ambivalent Israeli attitude toward any kind of concession to West Germany, even if it was to Israel's benefit, and to the tense debate on such decisions in Israel during the postwar period:

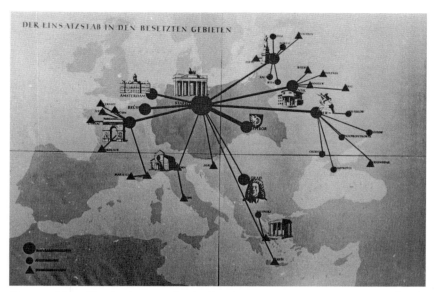

Figure 1. Map of looting locations by the Nazi Party ERR, 1940–1945. Courtesy of Yad Vashem Archives, Jerusalem (Isaac Bencowitz Album).

Figure 2. Storage of looted archival materials from Smolensk in a Benedictine monastery, Vilna, 1943. Courtesy of Yad Vashem Archives, Jerusalem (Isaac Bencowitz Album).

Figure 3. Sorting of the YIVO library in Vilna by forced laborers of the ERR. Courtesy of Yad Vashem Archives, Jerusalem (Isaac Bencowitz Album).

Figure 4. The packing and transporting of looted materials from Vilna by the ERR, April 1943. Courtesy of Yad Vashem Archives, Jerusalem (Isaac Bencowitz Album).

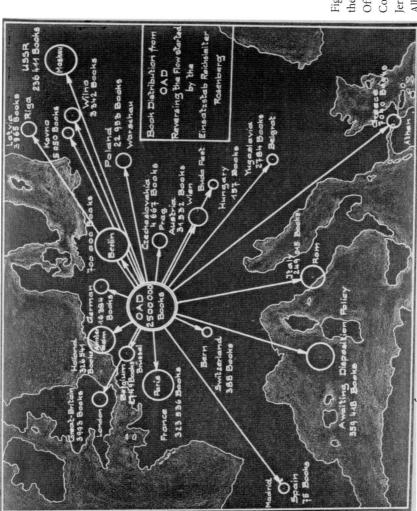

Figure 5. Map of the MFA&A on the distribution of books from Offenbach Archival Depot, 1946. Courtesy of Yad Vashem Archives, Jerusalem (Isaac Bencowitz Album).

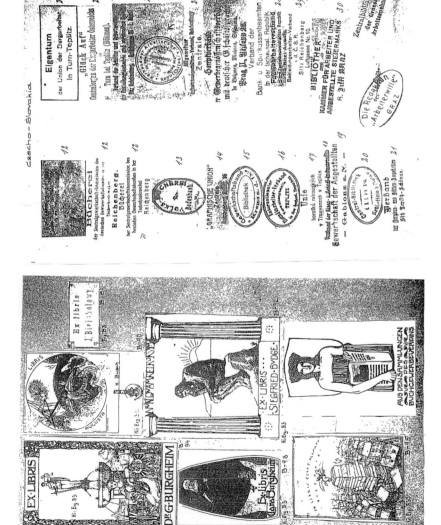

Figure 6. Library stamps and ex libris (bookplates) from the Offenbach Archival Depot, 1946. © National Archives and Records Administration, College Park, MD (RG 260, M1942, roll 12: Library Markings; roll 13: Ex-Libris; Isaac Bencowitz Albums).

Unidentifiable books.
300 000 of them awaiting final sorting and unknown ultimate destination.
Hebrew books. 55.0 per cent
German language, Hebrew religions and historical subjects. 9.3 "
German language, classical literature. 17.0 "
Russian language, Jewish cultural subjects. 2.0 "
Various other languages, Jewish cultural subjects. 8.6 "
Various other languages, general subjects. 8.1 "

Figure 7. Books of Jewish provenance in the Offenbach Archival Depot that could not be definitively identified, 1946. Courtesy of Yad Vashem Archives, Jerusalem (Isaac Bencowitz Album).

Figure 8. Employees in front of the Offenbach Archival Depot building, 1946.
Courtesy of Yad Vashem Archives, Jerusalem (Isaac Bencowitz Album).

Figure 9. Employees of the Offenbach Archival Depot sorting through books, 1946.
Courtesy of Yad Vashem Archives, Jerusalem (Isaac Bencowitz Album).

Figure 10. The conservation and restoration workshop for books in the Offenbach Archival Depot, 1946. Courtesy of Yad Vashem Archives, Jerusalem (Isaac Bencowitz Album).

Figure 11. Employees of the Offenbach Archival Depot packing books, 1946. Courtesy of Yad Vashem Archives, Jerusalem (Isaac Bencowitz Album).

Figure 12. The American military rabbi Isaiah Rachowsky working in the Offenbach Archival Depot. Courtesy of Yad Vashem Archives, Jerusalem (Isaac Bencowitz Album).

Figure 13. Koppel S. Pinson (middle) chooses materials from the Offenbach Archival Depot to loan to the Displaced Persons camps, 1946. Courtesy of Yad Vashem Archives, Jerusalem (Isaac Bencowitz Album).

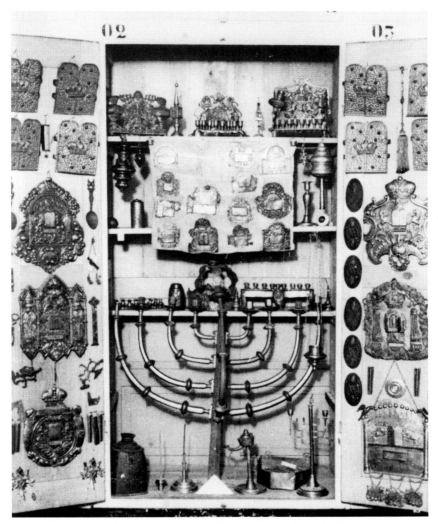

Figure 14. A cabinet for a silver menorah, Torah plates, and ritual objects in the Offenbach Archival Depot, 1946. Courtesy of United States Holocaust Memorial Museum, Washington, DC.

Figure 15. A room for synagogue textiles in the Offenbach Archival Depot, 1946. Courtesy of United States Holocaust Memorial Museum, Washington, DC.

Figure 16. Torah scrolls in the Offenbach Archival Depot, 1946. Courtesy of Yad Vashem Archives, Jerusalem (Isaac Bencowitz Album).

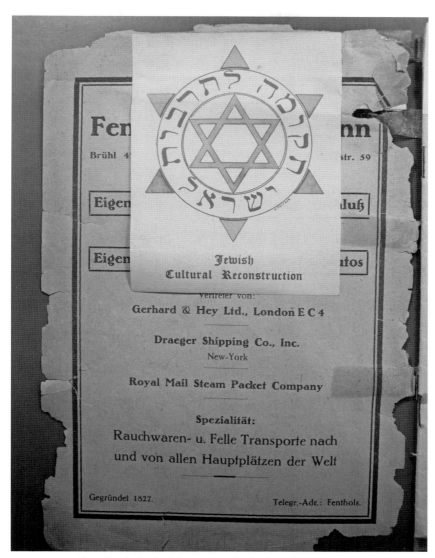

Figure 17. Ex libris (bookplate) of the JCR. © Elisabeth Gallas

Figure 18. The burial of ruined Torah scrolls from the inventory of objects looted by the ERR, carried out for the JCR by Salo W. Baron (second from the left) and the Synagogue Council of America, Paramus, NJ, January 13, 1952. Courtesy of the Department of Special Collections, Stanford University Libraries, Stanford, CA.

Figure 19. Dinner (a so-called *Testimonial Dinner*) for the employees of the JCR at the Schreiber restaurant in New York, December 21, 1951. From left to right: Wolf Blattberg, Philip Friedman, Irwin Weintroub, Joseph Reider, Aaron Margalit, Lawrence Marwick, Chaim Wormann, Alexander Marx, Salo W. Baron, Hannah Arendt, Jacob Novak-Schwimmer, Isaac E. Kiev, M. Gruber, Isaac Goldberg, Jacob Dienstag, Sylvia Landress, David Rosenstein; in front: Dr. Popper. Courtesy of the Department of Special Collections, Stanford University Libraries, Stanford, CA.

Figure 20. Lucy S. Dawidowicz in Prague, March 1947. Courtesy of Laurie Sapakoff Cohen, private collection.

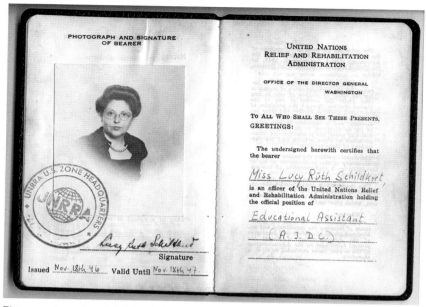

Figure 21. Lucy Ruth Schildkret's (Dawidowicz) United Nations Relief and Rehabilitation Administration (UNRRA) ID card for traveling to Germany as an employee of the American Jewish Joint Distribution Committee, 1946/47. Courtesy of American Jewish Historical Society, Newton Center, MA and NY.

Figure 22. Gershom Scholem at the Offenbach Archival Depot, July/August 1946. Courtesy of Yad Vashem Archives, Jerusalem (Isaac Bencowitz Album).

Figure 23. Hannah Arendt (1906–1975), July 1, 1958. Courtesy of ullstein bild.

Figure 24. Salo W. Baron (1895–1989). Courtesy of Leo Baeck Institute, New York.

You [will] understand that for our part neither we nor the Foreign Ministry is keen to add to the conspicuousness of the event in the Paulskirche. The presence of a University representative at this ceremony would however signify a special [. . .] emphasis. [. . .] But we would be very pleased if you would take the opportunity to speak to Lambert Schneider and to express to him in the name of the University our thanks for this act [. . .] but to make it clear to him [. . .] that the whole problem of German-Jewish relations is still a very difficult and delicate one and that it is better to achieve normalization cautiously and gradually than to proceed in a hasty and imprudent way.[63]

Curt Wormann, meanwhile, was critical of the practical process of selection for the book donation and felt that too little had been asked of the Germans.[64] But Scholem's negotiating successes seem to contradict this: he managed to ensure that the German booksellers committed to an annual donation of books to a value of ten thousand marks. In public, however, in accordance with an explicit request from the library's heads in Jerusalem, this commitment was to remain essentially invisible in order to deny Germany any opportunity to crow about the donation. Scholem took a different view on this. He was in fact aggrieved at how little publicity events of this kind received in Germany: "The truth is quite different and far more bitter: no one is interested in these things and they receive absolutely no publicity."[65] The tensions that marked German-Israeli negotiations in the early 1950s are clearly apparent in this essentially peripheral incident. Certainly, there were a number of advocates of cooperation with the German government and German institutions in Israel, chiefly motivated by recognition that without it there was little prospect of reparations, restitution, or compensation. Many of them were also aware of the importance of material support and payments in a phase of nation-building from scratch. And yet the political sphere and public opinion were pervaded by a marked tendency to emphasize distance from Germany and the rejection of any form of cooperation or diplomatic relations. As a result, even the Israeli consul appointed in Munich was not authorized to make contact with German authorities and communicated solely with the Allies.[66]

These polarities were evident in much the same way in the negotiations between the Germans and Israelis on restitution of the Judaica and archival documents in Worms.

In 1954, when the JTC's attempts to reach agreement with top officials in the city were in danger of failing, Chaim Yahil of the Israel Mission in Cologne addressed an impressive statement to its mayor aimed at restarting the negotiations. Yahil began by emphasizing the consequences of National Socialism and its regime of terror for Jewish life in Europe and Germany: "As a result of Nazism, Jews in Europe—and certainly in Germany—have ceased to be a vibrant, creative community with a promising future. We can consider Jewish history in Germany and most European countries over and done with." This sober résumé led him to conclude that even though it was necessary to consider the needs of the few remaining congregations in Germany, they would never "again play that role in the life of the Jewish people as a whole [. . .] that German Jewry played over a thousand-year history of shifting fortunes." In contrast, Yahil highlighted the achievements of the newly established state of Israel as the "original homeland of the Jewish people." Supporting this polity, which had "absorbed the greater part of the survivors of Nazi persecution and given them a new homeland," was a more urgent task than ever in view of the destruction of the "old centers of Jewish culture in Europe." The cultural goods, he argued, were not only important to Israel's cultural development but also did not belong in Germany, the actions of its people in recent times having disqualified them as the "custodians of Jewish spiritual treasures." Instead, his hope was that "German authorities would transfer ownership of Jewish cultural relics to the Jewish spiritual center in Israel as a sign of understanding for the hardships of a community in the initial stages of its development, such as the famous Darmstadt Haggadah or the Talmud manuscript in the Munich University Library." Underscoring his opposition to the decisions in Worms, Yahil closed his appeal by contrasting the possible uses of the treasures within the newly established world of Jewish research and teaching in Israel and their miserable fate as museum pieces in Germany.[67] As unofficial Israeli ambassador in Germany, Yahil was surely channeling the views of the Otzrot Hagolah committee, as he succeeded in affirming the new order of Jewish life, with Israel as its center, while also managing not to deny the imperative of carrying on European intellectual traditions there. The case of Worms impacted on both countries' official policies: the parties involved ultimately succeeded in reaching an agreement and indirectly confirmed the prospects outlined by Yahil.[68]

Another crucial goal of Israeli intervention in Germany was the salvage of archival materials, above all the precious remains of Jewish community archives. Just as Yahil argued in the case of Worms, in other cases too, the transfer of Jewish archival material to Israel was framed by the idea that Jewish life in Europe, especially Germany, was over and its material remnants should therefore help ensure a Jewish future in Israel. But gathering together most archival material in Israel was no easy task.[69] When it came to the Gesamtarchiv—the most important repository of the records of the German Jewish communities, associations, and organizations, established in 1905—the point of departure was even more complicated than usual because the vast majority of its holdings were dispersed in Soviet-controlled areas. This greatly impeded all negotiations. The Israeli representatives pursued independent initiatives not just in order to advance Israeli claims to the documents but also because they were convinced that an American organization had no chance of negotiating successfully with East German and Soviet officials—the intensifying Cold War made such cooperation impossible. In a letter to Arendt, Scholem described the difficult deliberations between Julius Meyer, representative of the East Berlin Jewish community, the government spokesperson Otto Korfes (head of the Archives Department of the GDR Ministry of the Interior), and Alexander Bein of the Zionist Archives in Jerusalem (known from 1956 as the Central Zionist Archives) as clearly pervaded by the conflict between the two political blocks:

> There can be but little doubt that no headway can be made by JCR in that matter because the authorities of the Deutsche Volksrepublik will not allow such material to be given to JCR owing to its formally American character. [. . .] If there is any hope to get the material it will be only for Israel. The Central Zionist Archives [sic] in Jerusalem are in charge of these negotiations and I am afraid that the only thing that could be achieved by competition is that nothing would be obtained at all. It is the same case that we had in Prague only that the political situation has since become much more precarious as the anti-American line of policy has become more outspoken.[70]

From Jacob Jacobson, former head of the Gesamtarchiv, who had been forced to supervise its looted holdings in the Reich Office of Genealogy prior to his deportation to Theresienstadt, Scholem had obtained more detailed information about the dispersal of its materials. Parts remained in the original location of the Gesamtarchiv in what was now East Berlin (Oranienburger Straße). The genealogical section had been relocated to Rathsfeld Castle in Thuringia during the war, where it was microfilmed, but the originals were destroyed. A third part had already been transferred to the Prussian Privy State Archives (Geheimes Staatsarchiv) in Potsdam by 1943 and was later sent by Soviet soldiers to a storage site in Merseburg, south of Berlin.[71] Much as in Prague, Alexander Bein and Gershom Scholem, along with representatives of the Berlin community, then sought—at least for the files in the Oranienburger Straße premises—to find an unofficial means of transfer. These archival materials, which had not been cataloged and were unknown to the government, were gradually transferred to the community center in West Berlin before being sent on to Jerusalem. In this way, by 1951, fifty boxes containing documents from the Gesamtarchiv had made it to the Jewish Historical General Archives (from 1969 known as the Central Archive for the History of the Jewish People) in Jerusalem. When it came to the cataloged records stored in Merseburg, Israeli emissaries had to continue negotiating on the official level. One of the thorniest problems was that while the GDR regime was willing to carry out an official act of "reparation" by transferring material to Jewish communities, it refused to cooperate with Israel and dismissed the country, in line with Soviet doctrine, as a "spearhead of imperialism" in the Middle East. The USSR itself had supported the founding of Israel just a few years before, interpreting it as an antiimperialist struggle against the British Mandate, but since the 1950s, attacks on Israel with an anti-Semitic undertone had been par for the course. Israel, meanwhile, was unwilling to recognize public proclamations of "reparations" from the German side, so its representatives had a tightrope to walk if they were to succeed in obtaining the documents.[72] Thanks to repeated requests by Julius Meyer, the congregation ultimately managed to ensure the material's transfer from Merseburg to Berlin in 1950, but its subsequent dispatch to Israel was not permitted. By 1958, with the tireless assistance of Alexander Bein, Israel's "foreign minister of archives,"[73] a few sections were taken to West Berlin, which reached Jerusalem after some delay. But the greater part was returned to the Prussian Privy State Archives in Potsdam. Since the reunification of Germany, these materials have been kept in the Centrum Judaicum in Berlin, while other holdings are still housed in the Special Archive in Moscow and in the Jewish Historical Institute in Warsaw.

Scholem, Bein, and Georg Herlitz managed to ensure that various other sections of the community archives left West Germany for Israel. These included congregational records from Hamburg, which, after several years of effort by the JTC and Jerusalem-based Jewish advocates, were divided between Hamburg and Jerusalem and microfilmed; congregational records from Königsberg that had ended up in Göttingen after the war and were also obtained by the JTC and Bein; and Bavarian congregational records, which were restituted to Jerusalem on the basis of the decree negotiated by Hannah Arendt and a claim filed by the JRSO—in the face of strong opposition from the Bavarian State Association of Jewish Communities and its spokesperson, Philipp Auerbach. Various document collections from Hesse, Rhineland-Palatinate, and Baden-Württemberg were either claimed for Israel by the JCR or unilaterally claimed by representatives of Israeli archives such as the Jewish Historical General Archives director Daniel Cohen.[74] The extraordinary commitment of the archivists involved led to a notable success within the overall mission of transferring the greatest possible quantity of archival material out of Germany, much of it of central significance to European Jewish history.

Once the JCR had finished its work in Germany, the Hebrew University continued to take independent action, sometimes by order of the Israeli Ministry for Religious Affairs. JNUL's chief librarian Shlomo Shunami in particular, who became head of the Otzrot HaGolah committee in 1950, devoted himself to the search for books and incunabula for the rest of his life. His tireless efforts even inspired the author and poet Lea Goldberg to write a play centered on him and his "hunt for books": *Baʾalat haArmon* (*Lady of the Castle*), which was first performed in Tel Aviv in 1956 and whose plot was based on the historical events of the cultural restitution mission. Protagonist Michael Sand, inspired by Shunami, searches for looted books in an old castle in Eastern Europe while on a mission to save Jewish children after the Second World War.

The search for books is carried out in parallel to the search for children, and both are deployed as metaphors for past and future. The significance of the salvaged remnants of the lost world of Jewish Europe to Israel's national self-image and their function within the Israelis' newly forming historical consciousness constitute the central theme in Goldberg's play, demonstrating their relevance to the collective mentality that emerged at the time of Israel's foundation.[75]

In addition to his activities at the Offenbach and Wiesbaden collecting points and his investigations throughout Germany, Shlomo Shunami was active all over Europe. With the assistance of Yehuda Leib Bilor of the Ministry for Religious Affairs and Ernst Daniel Goldschmidt of the JNUL, he regularly traveled throughout Austria, Hungary, Romania, Italy, the Netherlands, France, and Yugoslavia into the late 1970s in an attempt to find more prints, manuscripts, books, Torah scrolls, and archival materials.[76] According to the Israeli historian Dov Schidorsky, of a total of around one million books that Israel obtained from Europe, around eight hundred thousand made it to the country thanks to Shunami's activities.[77] It was in Austria that he chalked up his greatest successes, building on the results of Scholem's negotiations in the summer of 1946. Talks with the Jewish Community of Vienna and the Austrian National Library (Österreichische Nationalbibliothek) ultimately led to the transfer of tens of thousands of volumes to Jerusalem.[78] Shortly after the war, the Jewish community in Vienna had recovered sections of its holdings from various sources and could partially rebuild its old library.[79] Scholem himself had already spoken to the congregational leaders in Vienna and staff at the National Library, which he suspected held important Jewish looted materials, and they agreed to a transfer of books to Jerusalem.[80] As a result of the enduring Soviet presence in Austria and the unclear legal situation of Jewish cultural property in Vienna, however, negotiations proved difficult for Shunami despite the JRSO's support. He did at least manage to ensure that between 1952 and 1954, certain parts of the collections stashed in the Tanzenberg monastic estate, which had been earmarked for the planned Nazi Hohe Schule university, and books from the congregational library were transferred to Jerusalem.[81] For Shunami, the Tanzenberg holdings, which were under British authority, had special significance because this was a looted collection created for the "leaders of the NSDAP." Around 75 percent of the recovered community library was dispatched to Jerusalem, while the near-complete community archives from Vienna were transferred to the CAHJP on long-term loan. The quantity of material from Austria that ended up in Israeli institutions is considered extraordinary, and Shunami acclaimed this achievement time and again. Today, it entails potential for conflict: the Jewish Community in Vienna, which has grown steadily over the decades, has requested the return of archival materials and documents from Israel for its own use.[82]

In Hungary too, Shunami achieved a number of successes. Despite opposition from the Hungarian government, he won for Jerusalem the valuable library of Rabbi Immanuel Loew, consisting of twenty-five thousand volumes and archival materials, which the Jewish community of Szeged had promised to the first Israeli prime minister, David Ben-Gurion, as a gift marking Israel's foundation as a state.[83] All in all, Shunami's dedication ensured the transfer of more than thirty thousand books and documents to the JNUL from Italy, Yugoslavia, the Netherlands, and Romania. He often expressed his delight at the European communities' willingness to cooperate and requested that the JA and Israeli Foreign Ministry support them in turn. But he failed to obtain the papers of the renowned rabbi David Kaufmann from Budapest and achieve his most important objective: recovery of the precious looted incunabula, rare items, and prints still thought to be hidden in German caches. Until the end of his life, Shunami remained convinced that the most valuable treasures were yet to be recovered.[84]

European Memory Objects in Israel

The arrival of salvaged cultural treasures and ritual objects in Israel triggered a range of emotions among the recipients. The books and objects were welcomed joyfully, their rescue celebrated as virtually miraculous, yet they were surrounded by an aura of sorrow that enveloped those involved. In most cases, attempts were made to bridge this chasm by placing the salvage of cultural goods on par with the saving of survivors from Europe and endowing them with a sacred aura. So with respect to these objects, reference was often made to salvation, redemption, and returning home. From this perspective, the individual book—which preserved the intellectual traditions of a vanished world while bearing visible signs of the Nazis' destructive intent—had now made it to the "safe haven" of Israel, homeland of the Jewish people, where it was endowed with new purpose. Here salvaged books performed many tasks: they maintained a connection to a lost past, to lost people, to the world of yesterday; they were memorials to the dead; and they preserved knowledge, tradition, and thought that many Israeli individuals believed would help lay the spiritual and cultural foundation for the Jewish collective in Israel.

In their new setting, these books and objects were not just to function as the materialized memory of European Jewry but came to substitute for the world that had been destroyed, a world that was supposed to find a new home in Israel. In contrast to the millions of dead, therefore, they lit a beacon of hope. In his autobiographical novel *A Tale of Love and Darkness*, the Israeli writer Amos Oz depicts, from a universal perspective, the imaginative world that gave rise to such patterns of thinking and emotions: "When I was little, my ambition was to grow up to be a book. Not a writer. People can be killed like ants. Writers are not hard to kill either. But not books: however systematically you try to destroy them, there is always a chance that a copy will survive and continue to enjoy a shelf-life in some corner of an out-of-the-way library somewhere, in Reykjavik, Valladolid or Vancouver."[85]

This idea took on a concrete form in ceremonies and exhibitions in Israel, which served to welcome the salvaged objects in a variety of ways. In the spring and summer of 1950, the Bezalel Museum in Jerusalem put the Judaica and synagogue materials selected by its director Mordechai Narkiss and provided by the JCR on public display.[86] These objects were a testimony to Nazi violence and destruction but also to a successful history of salvage. A review of the exhibition in the Jewish newspaper *Der Weg* demonstrates the way contemporaries perceived the history of rescued objects and their mnemonic qualities. After describing the intricate path taken by one silver Torah ornament from Poland, the author resumes: "One piece of 3,000, all of them 'remnants plucked from the fire.' The 400 fine specimens (of the 3,000) currently on display in the Bezalel are from Poland, Hungary, Romania, Greece and above all from Germany itself and they consist of: lamps and goblets, Torah ornaments and Seder bowls, megilloth and implements of the chevrot kadisha for washing the dead, mementos of the great era of German Jewry (commemorative coins) and moving handicrafts from the besieged ghettos in Poland. A powerful exhibition."[87] His text highlights the objects' memorial function; their salvage is placed in a sacred context, and their arrival in Jerusalem is described as akin to redemption. As relics of an irretrievably lost past, the objects from Europe now arrived at the museum in Israel. In some cases, this was the first time they had been placed in such a context, their ritual function being superseded by a commemorative one.[88]

The Israeli Ministry for Religious Affairs took a different approach to the numerous Torah fragments that made it from Europe to Israel. It erected a genizah (hiding or burial place) for them on the holy site of Mount Zion in Jerusalem, which is recognized as the tomb of King David. This storage site, comparable to a burial chamber, was to serve as a place of mourning for the murdered European Jews. When the fragments arrived from Europe, a military convoy and a procession of mourners escorted them from the port in Haifa to the memorial site, and religious services were held in their honor. In the immediate vicinity of this site, the ashes of murdered Jews from the crematoria of German death camps were also laid to rest in December 1949, and together, both burial places formed the basis for the Chamber of the Holocaust, a religious memorial established in 1948.[89] There could scarcely be any clearer testimony to the existential charge of the salvage process. While Jewish law requires the burial rather than the destruction of sacred books and scrolls that are no longer usable, the spatial proximity of the genizah to the site of the murdered's remains and the similarity of the act performed to mark their arrival attested to the outstanding importance and special treatment of the material remnants. In the late 1940s and early 1950s, prior to the establishment of the Yad Vashem remembrance center, Mount Zion was used for religious commemoration of the Holocaust in Israel. On certain Jewish holidays, commemorative ceremonies were carried out here, the sources indicating that they attracted up to twenty thousand attendees.[90] Looking back over events in Israel in the 1950s, Salo Baron mentioned festivities marking the arrival of shipments of cultural goods from Europe on the streets of Jerusalem and Tel Aviv: "On two or three occasions, they even made a festival 'otzrot hagolah,' treasures of the dispersion arriving. With marches in Jerusalem and Tel

Aviv—singing and so on. Each time a shipment arrived it was publicized in the papers. They were very happy to get anything."[91]

The degree of public attention that these activities received distinguishes the situation in Israel from that in other countries across the world. In December 1950, Curt Wormann contributed an enthusiastic report to the *Jüdisches Gemeindeblatt* on the "great book treasures" from Europe whose impending arrival had been announced. He further outlined the quantity to be expected and highlighted that many institutions would benefit from these books because the plan was to make them available to "every library in the country," enriching the cultural life of Israel as whole.[92] In addition to their commemorative and scholarly value, the books, works of art, Judaica, and ritual objects from Europe also had a highly practical significance. For example, in a letter to Salo Baron, Werner Senator explained that the salvage of Jewish art collections for Israel was particularly important because there was as yet no art history department at the university, and it was thus impossible to ensure the "aesthetic and ethical education of the people." The heritage from Europe was expected to help fill this gap.[93] Numerous small libraries throughout the country, as well as a number of newly established kibbutzim—some made up of survivors from Europe—were to receive a basic stock of books with the help of the rescued collections. The most important holdings, however, remained in Jerusalem. The JNUL received several outstanding collections, among them the entire private estate of the philosopher Hermann Cohen found in Offenbach, as well as the recovered volumes of Raphael Kirchheim's Frankfurt library; the library of Karl August Wünsche, originally located in Dresden; and the Mapu library from Kaunas.[94]

Israeli allocation policy, however, did not always meet with the JCR's approval. On several occasions, Hannah Arendt warned Otzrot HaGolah representatives that it was crucial to develop a transparent allocation system, to appoint a committee to ensure this, and to respect the numerous communities' and institutions' desire for fair and equal participation, including museums, archives, memorial sites, colleges, schools, city libraries, and kibbutzim.[95] As a result, in early 1950, an advisory body was appointed in Israel to deal with the distribution of cultural property. It included representatives of the city of Tel Aviv, the Histadrut trade union, the JA, the Chief Rabbinate, the Ministry for

Religious Affairs, the Ministry of Education, the Zionist Archive, the Ministry of Defense, the Society for the Advancement of Science, and the Association of Local Councils in addition to JNUL representatives.[96] It is surely no exaggeration to state that in some respects, the transfer of cultural property from Europe was a key component and motor of the emerging scholarly and cultural infrastructure in Israel. As dissatisfied as Otzrot HaGolah representatives often were with the finds made, suspecting there was a far greater quantity of looted items in Germany and in German caches in former German-occupied areas, the history of salvage must be regarded as a success from an Israeli perspective. Thanks to worldwide support and the tireless engagement of all those involved, what had come to pass was something no one had truly dared hope when the war ended: a portion of the European Jews' spiritual heritage had been saved and could be preserved and used in future. This material provided a key to understanding the European-Jewish culture inherent in Israel, a polity that "drew on Europe" but was not "in Europe,"[97] and opened up a viable future for research and teaching as well as religious practice and commemorative activities. From this vantage point, the salvage of European cultural treasures was a perhaps small but nonetheless meaningful part of the project of ensuring a Jewish future after the Holocaust, a project now taking off through the establishment of the state of Israel.

5

Taking Action in Dark Times

*The Commitment of Hannah Arendt, Salo W. Baron,
Lucy S. Dawidowicz, and Gershom Scholem*

For Hannah Arendt, Salo W. Baron, Lucy Dawidowicz, and Gershom Scholem—today the best-known protagonists of postwar Jewish initiatives to salvage looted cultural goods—their efforts to advance cultural restitution was much more than just a temporary task. It was their work for JCR and YIVO that first confronted all four individuals, in a concrete way, with the consequences of the Holocaust. It shaped their view of what had happened and had a lasting impact on their understanding of its significance to Jewish life in general. As they sought to achieve restitution, these scholars learned how the Nazi cultural raids had unfolded and how they were organized, furnishing them with comprehensive insights into the Nazis' political practices and key elements of their policy of destruction and annihilation. Early trips to a postwar Europe in a state of material and moral collapse compelled them to face the immediate past of war and Nazi terror, while the search for and salvage of books and objects stimulated discussions on memory and the Jewish future. Their political and personal experiences molded their view of events that—in a wide range of ways—left behind traces in their historical thinking. Important later writings, particularly those of Arendt and Dawidowicz, echo some of the questions that have determined their work for both organizations. Baron's and Scholem's long-lasting scholarly and cultural activities in the United States and Israel as well as their ways to respond to the Holocaust were shaped by these specific experiences.

The four scholars differed fundamentally in terms of their generation, background, self-image, and political vision. Nonetheless, all regarded their shared rescue mission as an existential duty. The political arena of cultural restitution created an opportunity to preserve fragments of European-Jewish tradition and history. On the one hand, this enabled these scholars to shape the ongoing and future life of the Jewish collectivity in its new centers outside Europe. On the other hand, as discussed earlier, the negotiations that ultimately resulted in a more just concept of restitution allowed them, in a supposedly peripheral sphere, to advance a central goal of Jewish politics: to ensure Jews' participation in international law and thus their international political recognition. Besides the general aims that all four shared, the motives underlying their commitment were very different. Scholem linked his engagement closely with his Zionist aspirations. In particular, he viewed the acquisition of precious Judaica from Europe as a vital component of nation-building in *Eretz Israel*. Dawidowicz, meanwhile, saw the transfer of the dislocated YIVO holdings to the United States as a means of perpetuating and transmitting the lost Jewish worlds of Vilna, a way of preserving part of the old world in the new. Arendt was determined to participate actively in Jewish politics, while her work for the JCR gave her important insights into the character of Nazi rule, which she was busy researching for her magnum opus on totalitarianism. Finally, in the JCR, Baron found an important forum for the advancement of his goals of institutionalizing and promoting Jewish spiritual and cultural life within the US.

*   *   *

Between 1942 and 1944, the scholars in New York and Jerusalem later involved in cultural restitution became aware of the practices of annihilation unfolding in Europe. With the help of Lucy Dawidowicz, senior YIVO figures searched for the dislocated library and archival collection of the original institute in Vilna. Salo Baron and Hannah Arendt, meanwhile, initiated their cooperation in the Commission in the summer of 1944. And in Jerusalem, Scholem met with other Hebrew University personnel to create the Otzrot HaGolah working group. Based in the United States or Palestine, all four protagonists sought to determine the prospects for a political initiative to salvage the looted treasures, each of them bringing differing political views and biographies.

Born in Tarnów in 1895, Salo Wittmayer Baron came from a middle-class family, deeply rooted in Jewish traditions, in the Habsburg monarchy's crownland of Galicia. After his studies in Lwów, he moved to

Vienna; there, in addition to his ordination as rabbi, he obtained three doctorates in politics, history, and law in the early 1920s. By 1926, he had immigrated to New York, where he took up an invitation from the eminent rabbi Steven S. Wise to teach at the Jewish Institute of Religion. Baron fully established himself in the United States after assuming the first American chair in Jewish history, literature, and institutions at Columbia University in 1930. Concurrently, through his multifaceted engagement in political and charitable organizations, he managed to build up a broad intellectual and political network. In this process, the "multilingual, well-travelled European, the sophisticated intellectual who knew Berlin and Vienna and Kraków," became "an American."[1] Beginning in 1933, Baron's position and responsibilities within the American-Jewish public sphere fostered his political mobilization in opposition to anti-Semitic propaganda and his calls for greater attention to be paid to developments in Europe.[2] Significantly, his sensitivity to the political processes unfolding there prompted him to make a research trip to Germany in the summer of 1933. The insights he gained in Hamburg, Bremen, Frankfurt, Berlin, and Breslau intensified his concerns about developments under Hitler, particularly when it came to the Jews, and lent new impetus to his political initiatives in the United States.[3] Baron's leading role in the Conference on Jewish Relations, officially established in 1936, and the *Jewish Social Studies* journal, a quarterly first published in 1939, along with his work for the National Jewish Welfare Board, are examples of the different ways in which he sought to respond during this period to the growing threats facing the European Jews.[4] In addition, Baron became an important interlocutor for Jewish scholars who had immigrated to the United States. He helped many of them secure invitations, visas, affidavits, and passage to the United States, communicating with the authorities in support of their cases and providing them with an initial point of contact in New York.[5] He also played this role for Hannah Arendt, who sought him out on the recommendation of the famous rabbi and historian Ismar Elbogen immediately after her arrival in 1941. It was not long before he had helped her achieve her first English-language publication and arranged her first job in the United States by employing her at the Commission.[6] Toward the end of the war, Baron focused his political efforts on the preservation of the European Jewries' cultural heritage. Specifically, he sought to lay the groundwork for the provision of aid for the revival of European-Jewish congregations and institutions. On a practical level, his commitment complimented what Baron was in the process of developing as his particular view of Jewish history, one that was increasingly turning into a historical school of thought. Since the mid-1920s, he had focused his attention on the historical preconditions for the Jews' survival over the centuries. This prompted him to concentrate on their social history as a collectivity, rather than on the history of the leading exponents of Jewish tradition and their scholarship. Against the tendency to write what he famously referred to as the "lachrymose history" of the Jews, which focused solely on Jewish suffering, he sought to highlight the many different forms of Jewish action, creativity, and organization in non-Jewish environments in various places over time.[7] His convictions clearly provided the framework for his political ideas during and after the war. The catastrophic news of the destruction and annihilation of the European Jews did not prevent him from cultivating a certain optimism, enabling him, even beyond the 1940s, to keep faith in the Jews' capacity for survival. This is particularly evident in his essays from this period.[8] In 1940, he indicated to his colleague and friend Alexander Marx that he was depressed by the "international situation," which was having an adverse effect on his writing, but he still cleaved to the belief that it was possible to exercise a positive influence on events in Europe.[9] Baron's biographer, Robert Liberles, explains this faith partly in light of his personal situation. Throughout the war, he states, Baron had remained hopeful that his parents and sister, whom he could not persuade to leave Tarnów, had survived. It was not until several months after the German capitulation that he received news of their deaths.[10] After this, Baron increasingly abandoned the position—one he was still advocating in early 1945—that Jewish life ought to be reestablished in Europe and that a strong European-Jewish community could rise again. Henceforth, he focused with even greater commitment on the development of American Jewish community life. Rather than retreating into reflection and spirituality, as one might have expected given his profession, Baron found a way to deal with the disaster in Europe through his tireless work for the Commission and the JCR, devoting almost half of his weekly working hours to these and other political and philanthropic initiatives intended to help Jews.[11] He was the engine and heart of the JCR, whose members were predominantly recruited from among his personal network and helped him implement his ideas. Baron gave his all to make a success of the JCR's mission.

Gershom Scholem, born in Berlin in 1897, felt drawn to *Eretz Israel* at young age. Marking a critical distance from his bourgeois, assimilated, secular German Jewish parents, after completing studies in mathematics, philosophy, and Semitic languages, he had emigrated from Germany to Palestine by 1923. He thus experienced the Second World War and the Holocaust from the perspective of Jerusalem. The realities unfolding in Europe first impinged on his life directly when he received news that his close friend Walter Benjamin, on the run from the Nazis, had committed suicide near the French-Spanish border. Like Benjamin, Hannah Arendt too was living in southern France at the time and was in contact with both men. After distressing experiences of expulsion from Germany, exile in Paris, statelessness, internment in the French internment camp of Gurs, and fortuitous escape, Arendt now endured a period of profound uncertainty as she waited for a transit visa in order to travel to Lisbon and obtain safe passage to New York. In 1940, she wrote to Scholem from the French city of Montauban with the shattering news of Benjamin's death, expressing her dark presentiments of the disasters to come: "Walter Benjamin took his own life on September 29 in Portbou on the Spanish frontier. [. . .] Jews are dying in Europe and are being buried like dogs."[12] For both of them, Benjamin's death meant the loss of an inspiring thinker and important friend. At the same time, they considered it an unmistakable sign that Europe's Jews faced a hopeless future.[13]

The Nazis' war on the European Jews moved geographically close to Palestine when General Rommel and his German Italian troops advanced toward the territory of the Yishuv as part of the Axis North Africa campaign. In the fall of 1942, however, they were beaten and repulsed by British soldiers under the field marshal Bernard Montgomery in the battle of El Alamein, Egypt. While this removed the direct threat to the Jews of Palestine, uncertainty and fear persisted in view of the disastrous situation in Europe.[14] Scholem related this to Arendt in a letter of 1942: "Over time we've lived through some quite anxious days, and now it appears as if the miracle indeed has happened and Palestine will be spared. [. . .] But of course, what else may yet go to wrack and ruin—that is still unimaginable."[15]

Scholem described his nagging sense of unease again in another letter to Arendt in December 1943: "We don't know what sort of revelations we will encounter about the state of the Jewish people in Europe, though one gets ill just thinking about what we already know."[16] This prediction was to come true for Scholem on a personal level more literally than even he perhaps imagined at the time. Concrete knowledge of the mass murder of the European Jews, a development of which he became increasingly aware, had a highly destructive impact on him. His wartime accounts are testimony to his despair and turmoil.[17] Hitherto, Scholem had focused mainly on the project, so close to his heart, of building a new Jewish existence in Palestine resembling the conception of Ahad Ha'am. The latter's idea of cultural Zionism stressed Palestine as the Jews' spiritual-cultural center, as a means of renouncing the assimilated Western European way of life, and as a new vehicle for developing a modern Jewish consciousness rooted in tradition, one that would in turn impact the Jews in the Diaspora. Scholem had grave doubts that this project would succeed. Since the 1929 Arab uprising, he had been increasingly pessimistic. His fears grew over time, as becomes evident in one of his letters to Arendt in spring 1942: "The moral atmosphere here in this country is calamitous, giving rise to the gloomiest thoughts regarding the fate of our local work here."[18] Fears for the Zionist endeavor intensified as ever more dreadful news poured in from Europe; the prospects of establishing a Jewish national entity seemed poor.[19]

By the end of the war, Scholem had shifted position and was now publicly defending the foundation of a state in Israel as the only means of securing Jewish life in a world pervaded by lethal anti-Semitism. Nonetheless, he kept his distance from the political realm and concentrated on fostering the country's scholarly and cultural development. As a result, he soon occupied an outstanding position within its intellectual life. With the inauguration of the chair of Jewish Mysticism within the Hebrew University's Institute of Jewish Studies—an institute Scholem himself played a significant role in developing—and through his efforts to breathe new life into the entire field of Jewish history, he made a major contribution to the university's emerging profile.[20] The development and institutionalization of the National and University Library in Jerusalem were also projects close to his heart ever since, in the mid-1920s, he had formulated a new method for cataloging and systematizing its Judaica

collection, which is still in use. Through the efforts of the Otzrot HaGolah committee, which Scholem did much to sustain, the library received
hundreds of thousands of books and documents from Europe, and ultimately, he bequeathed his private library, comprising more than thirty
thousand volumes, to the JNUL as well.[21] If Israel was to have a future as
a vibrant state, and particularly if it was to be built on solid intellectual
foundations, then according to Scholem it was not just crucial that as
many Jews as possible emigrate there; it was just as important to ensure
that Israel acquired the cultural and spiritual legacy of the European
Jews, enabling this heritage to bear fruit. The first steps toward establishing the university as a repository and trust for the books and art objects
of Europe's murdered Jews, taken by Judah Magnes in 1944, expressed
Scholem's vision.

Hannah Arendt, born in the German city of Hannover in 1906 to
assimilated, bourgeois parents much like Scholem's, observed events in
Europe from the perspective of an emigrant who had fled to the United
States after being driven out of Germany. In spring 1941 she managed
to escape via Portugal to New York with her husband Heinrich Blücher,
and later she arranged safe passage for her mother Martha Arendt as
well. Having arrived in the United States, she sought to gain an academic foothold in light of her outstanding degrees in philosophy, theol-
ogy, and philology. First, though, she learned English and with the help
of various contacts—above all Baron—tried to build up her professional
and social life in this new world. Arendt started to write for the journal
Aufbau, which catered chiefly to émigré German Jews, and in 1942, she
began to teach modern European history at Brooklyn College. While
still in France, Arendt had begun to engage with Jewish politics. As the
threats to Europe's Jews mounted, she had increasingly shifted focus
away from individual and toward collective constructions of belonging
and, consonant with the Eastern European tradition, came to regard the
Jews as a distinct national and political group that must act as such and
assert its rights.[22] In the same vein, she continued after her arrival in
New York—for example, with her impassionate call for the raising of
a Jewish Army as an act of collective defense, which drew her closer
to Zionist circles in the United States. In May 1942, she participated in
the famous Biltmore Conference, where David Ben-Gurion called for a
Jewish commonwealth in Mandatory Palestine and an unlimited right

to Jewish immigration. But Arendt was soon to distance herself from the nationalistic elements of political Zionism, which she accused of ignoring the lot of the Arab population in Palestine and disregarding the Zionist project's fateful dependency on the major powers' goodwill.[23] It was during these months of intense political debate in American-Jewish circles that Arendt was first confronted with news of the ultimate genocide of the European Jews, and she described this moment in poignant detail later on in her famous interview with Günter Gaus:

> What was decisive was the day we learned about Auschwitz. [. . .] That was in 1943. [. . .] That was the real shock. [. . .] It was really as if an abyss had opened. Because we had the idea that amends could somehow be made for everything else [. . .]. But not for this. *This ought not to have happened.* And I don't mean just the number of victims. I mean the method, the fabrication of corpses and so on [. . .]. This should not have happened. Something happened there to which we cannot reconcile ourselves.[24]

But the impossibility of coping with what had happened did not paralyze Hannah Arendt—quite the opposite. Looking back, Alfred Kazin, a New York–based writer and Arendt's friend, described her as driven and indefatigable during this period, obsessed with the search for answers: "Hitler's war was the central fact in the dark shadowy Morningside Drive apartment where she [Arendt] and her feisty husband, Heinrich Bluecher, now lived [. . .]. Hannah never stopped thinking. [. . .] How did *it* happen? How had it all happened? How had this modern age happened?"[25]

In 1947, Arendt was still describing her state of mind in much the same way in a letter to her friend and mentor, the German Zionist Kurt Blumenfeld, who lived in Jerusalem from 1933 onward: "I simply cannot get over the factories of annihilation [. . .]. I have my own kind of melancholy, which I can only fight my way out of through thinking."[26] This concept of thinking as a way of surviving and dealing with the burdens of her time may explain her ceaseless writing. After her columns for *Aufbau*, beginning in 1944, she wrote many articles and essays for American Jewish journals: texts that enable us to trace the different ways in which she approached the political situation and its consequences.[27]

All appear to have been guided by Arendt's dogged attempts "at under-standing, what at first and even at second glance appeared simply out-rageous."[28] This quest to understand virtually became the basis of her postwar existence: "Understanding [. . .] is an unending activity by which, in constant change and variation, we come to terms with and rec-oncile ourselves to reality, that is, try to be at home in the world. [. . .] to understand totalitarianism is not to condone anything, but to reconcile ourselves to a world in which such things are possible at all."[29]

She had also stressed this conviction to Scholem, to whom she wrote that the "metaphysical shock" triggered by the news from Europe made striving for "a clear glimpse into the catastrophe" unavoidable—but she believed that only a very few were prepared to undertake this journey.[30] This quest was consonant not only with her thinking and writing but also with her work for the Commission and later the JCR.[31] Once again, it was Kazin who recognized more clearly than many others the impor-tance of this work to Arendt's life after the war: "When I met her in the late forties she was a blazing Jew, working round the clock for Jewish Cultural Reconstruction."[32] But Arendt's commitment to the JCR was not only a political endeavor; the research she conducted for the Com-mission, especially while she was drawing up the Tentative Lists, gave Arendt important insights into the functional principles of Nazi rule. In this context, she came to view the scale and significance of cultural theft as an explicit part of the Nazi project of annihilation. Arendt's in-tensive work on the seizure of goods and dispossession on behalf of the Commission gave her a concrete sense of the complex structures of the Nazi system, providing key reference points for her concurrent re-search, which was to culminate in her great study *The Origins of Totali-tarianism*. In its third chapter, when describing the structural character of totalitarian forms of rule and their central features, she referred sev-eral times to the robbery of the Jews and to Nazi scholarship as the ben-eficiary of dispossessed books and documents.[33]

In addition, in her work for the Commission, Arendt saw an oppor-tunity to achieve political objectives that she believed were imperative in view of the terrible news from Europe. Arendt simply felt compelled to intervene by prevailing realities: "There are certain extreme situations where you have to act," as she explained in retrospect with reference to the 1930s and 1940s.[34] From this perspective, Arendt's activities in the postwar period must be observed, on the one hand, as a key element in her process of understanding and as part of her attempt "to be at home in the world" again. On the other hand, she was well aware of the limits of this approach and expressed this aporia of thinking and acting in response to the catastrophe as early as 1944: "For systematic mass murder [. . .] strains not only the imagination of human beings, but also the framework and categories of our political thought and action. [. . .] There is no political method for dealing with German mass crimes [. . .]. Just as there is no political solution within human capacity for the crime of administrative mass murder."[35]

Lucy Dawidowicz's confrontation with the Holocaust and her path toward cultural restitution resembled that of Arendt in terms of their dynamics, but they occurred in a different milieu and in light of different questions. Born under the name Schildkret in New York in 1915, Dawidowicz grew up in a family of Polish Jewish origin. In addition to the standard American school education, she completed a traditional Jewish education at the Sholem Aleichem College in New York before devoting herself to the study of English literature at the city's Hunter College. Finally, at the suggestion of Jacob Shatzky, her most influential teacher in the Jewish school, in 1938, she began a year of research at the YIVO in Vilna within the framework of the institute's Aspiratur program, intensifying her relationship with the *Yiddishland*.[36] Just a few weeks before Germany's attack on Poland, Dawidowicz left Vilna and was able to travel back unscathed to New York, where she decided to work for the local YIVO. As its members learned of the monstrous events in Europe, they were forced to watch the annihilation of the institute's frame of reference—indeed, its very substance. During the war years, Dawidowicz worked as assistant to the institute head Max Weinreich, who had managed to flee Vilna via Copenhagen in 1939 as he happened to be attending a conference there when the war broke out. He was never to return to Poland. Over the next few years, the institute in New York functioned as a gathering place for many Eastern European immigrants who had managed to save themselves and who brought with them important information about the situation in Europe. In addition, YIVO maintained its own close links with the Polish underground and the Polish exile government in London, so its staff members were among the first to receive detailed information on German death camps and mass shootings in Poland and the Soviet Union. In her autobiography, Dawidowicz recalled, "Being at the YIVO, I probably knew more than most other American Jews about what was happening to the European Jews. [. . .] We were witnessing the end of the world. [. . .] None of us had seen the heavens turn black, but in Europe I knew the earth was red with Jewish blood."[37]

As she herself explained, her personal reaction oscillated between disbelief and a desire for revenge: "It was past my fathoming how even fanatical anti-Semites could become mass murderers. [. . .] We were aware of our impotence. Powerless to avenge the murder of the Jews, we fell a-cursing like Hamlet unable to avenge his father's murder."[38] One of the most important tasks pursued by YIVO during this period, in part because more active means of intervening in Europe were infeasible, was the quest to identify the whereabouts of the Vilna YIVO's material remains. Those involved seem to have associated this activity with virtually religious hopes of salvation. Looking back, Dawidowicz described this phase of anxiety and hope in emphatic terms: "Finding the library would be a token of redemption. [. . .] The recovery of the looted art treasures gave us hope."[39] The protracted search for the dispersed books ultimately led to Frankfurt and Prague, and to the poet Abraham Sutzkever, who was one of the few survivors of the Vilna ghetto. Together with a few other inmates, he had managed to save some YIVO book holdings under the most difficult of circumstances.[40] These developments became a crucial source of meaning during a period otherwise pervaded by shock and terror at reports from Europe, which were worsening by the day: "Our intentness in searching for YIVO's library helped to sustain us then against the horrors of the camps, horrors which we had internalized from accounts we had read back in 1944."[41] This sense of salvation was to intensify when Dawidowicz directly encountered the salvaged holdings from Vilna during her trip to Germany from 1946 to 1947.

Amid the Ruins of History: Travels to Europe

Dawidowicz arrived in Germany in October 1946 on behalf of the American Jewish Joint Distribution Committee. During the first few months, she primarily helped provision Jewish Displaced Persons in

Munich, but her focus soon shifted to researching the remnants of the YIVO Institute. She had been encouraged to take up a post in Germany by Koppel Pinson, who was cooperating closely with the Commission and YIVO. He himself worked for the Joint between 1945 and 1946 in the American occupation zone and was keen to employ Dawidowicz as an education officer. She accepted the challenge. In Munich, she was responsible for obtaining licenses for Yiddish-language DP newspapers, procuring printing presses and paper, and securing supplies of school-books and other materials for DP camp schools along with religious texts and prayer books. She also helped Jewish students obtain scholar-ships for study in the United States. During the course of her work, she managed to ensure that DP newspapers were produced and printed in the former publishing house of the Nazi paper *Völkischer Beobachter*, now home to the *Neue Zeitung* published by the American military gov-ernment—a "grotesque historical irony," as Dawidowicz later put it.[42] Overall, her impression of Germany and the Germans was pervaded by distrust and disapproval: she did not believe that anti-Semitic convic-tions could have disappeared overnight. Particularly in her activities for the DPs, she often had no choice but to work with German authorities and institutions, something that greatly rankled her: "I hated the Ger-mans and hated to do business with them. [. . .] I was convinced that Munich, as indeed all of Germany, was aswarm with former Nazi Party members and sympathizers, all at liberty, their minds still filled with the lurid anti-Semitism in which they had been indoctrinated for over twelve years."[43]

More affecting yet, according to Dawidowicz's own accounts, was her work at the Offenbach Depot.[44] Tasked with continuing the selection, begun by Koppel Pinson, of material to be lent to DP camp libraries, she quickly discovered her true mission: identification of the Vilna holdings found at the depot. Under Dawidowicz's leadership, the efforts begun in New York to locate the collection, and the subsequent tough negotia-tions on their restitution, were brought to a successful conclusion: sev-eral thousand books, documents, and manuscripts, brought to Frankfurt by the ERR, passed once again into YIVO's possession. Dawidowicz took up her post in Offenbach in February 1947 and began to systematically sort the vast mass of so-called unidentifiable Jewish book collections and those holdings of Jewish origin categorized as heirless. When she arrived in Offenbach, the many Yiddish- and Hebrew-language papers, journals, books, and manuscripts had received virtually no attention (with the exception of the efforts of Pinson and Scholem, who had worked at the depot in the summer before her arrival). As she inspected the books, Dawidowicz found ever more volumes and documents from Vilna. In her memoir she recalls, that 175 ex libris were discovered in Offenbach, indicating a Lithuanian origin.[45] By June 1947, Dawidowicz had sorted, organized, stacked, identified, and cataloged just under 180,000 books and several crates of papers and documents at the depot, giving her direct exposure to the extreme level of destruction.[46] Every book reminded her of the murdered; she felt confronted by both the final, fragmentary traces of European Jewry and the eminent material witnesses to the crime committed against them: "The smell of death emanated from these hundreds of thousands of books and religious objects—orphaned and homeless mute survivors of their murdered owners. Like the human survivors, these inanimate remnants of a once-thriving civilization had found temporary and comfortless shelter in the land of Amalek. The sight of the massed inert objects chilled me."[47]

Time and again, Dawidowicz drew a parallel between the Jewish survivors, the "saved remnant" (*Sherit HaPletah*)[48] hoping to leave Germany, and the books, which she regarded equally as a "saved remnant" awaiting transfer to a new and better place. Her equation of the history of the books and the history of human beings led her to anthropomorphize inanimate objects: "At last, the YIVO books, like survivors with visas and travel permits, would soon be en route to a new home and a new life."[49] This perception of material objects also reflects Dawidowicz's hopes that salvaging the remnants of Jewish Vilna could provide them with future relevance. Clearly this was a mission to counter the Nazis' destruction of YIVO and its world. When her work in Offenbach was over, however, she understood that this had been rendered impossible due to the sheer scale of devastation and destruction. She was forced to recognize that Jewish Vilna had been reduced to scraps of paper and vestiges of memory that could never again yield any kind of whole.

Gershom Scholem's trip through Europe from April to August 1946, which took him as well to the Offenbach Depot, had a similarly decisive impact on his perception of the Holocaust and its consequences. His journey put him under tremendous strain, and he returned to Jerusalem a psychologically broken man. In his intellectual biography of Scholem, Noam Zadoff quotes the striking assessment of Scholem's state of mind made later by his wife, Fania Scholem:

> He returned to the Land of Israel physically exhausted and mentally depressed. He would lie down for most of the day, doing nothing, hardly speaking with anyone, and only occasionally repeat sentences like: "The Jewish people has been murdered, has ceased to exist, only smoldering stumps are left, with no strength or direction. Their source of nourishment no longer exists, the people has been cut off at the root. And we in Israel, a handful of people, the remnant (sheerit hapletah). Will we really find the strength to build the creative, free society, not materialistic, for the sake of whose formation we came here? Maybe we won't succeed in the task and we will degenerate, because we are bereft of our nation, we are orphaned." He was prostrate on his bed, going from couch to couch in his house, without finding repose for himself. Scholem refused to be consoled and he only became himself again and recovered a year later.[50]

Scholem was left utterly drained by his exposure to the few remaining scraps of a centuries-old Jewish culture now in a state of misery and emptiness, his experience of profound destruction, and his confrontation with the Germans who had carried it out. Over and above this trauma, he also had to cope with the death of his mother during his time in Germany. His travel journal bears ample testimony to the situation he found himself in: "Everything is sad and is becoming ever sadder. [. . .] Every little step here hurts for a long time. [. . .] Something within me has been shattered, something of my creativity and strength, and I am very depressed. This mission bereaved me and has not brought me the inner redemption I had envisaged."[51]

Scholem too had traveled to Germany with certain hopes. But the reality of the devastation that confronted him there exceeded all his previous imaginings, and he was disappointed at the correspondingly limited potential to salvage books and manuscripts. Only fragments of the formerly extensive corpus of texts central to Jewish intellectual history in Europe were ultimately found.[52] During this journey, Scholem gained a comprehensive impression of postwar Europe, having traveled from Paris via Zurich, Vienna, Prague, and Bratislava to Frankfurt,

Heidelberg, Munich, and Berlin. But he was to do more than take stock of Jewish library and archival collections. He also visited Jewish survivors in a number of DP camps, met Walter Benjamin's sister Dora in Switzerland shortly before her death, prayed with Jews in makeshift prayer houses in Berlin and Munich, negotiated with rabbis on the future of these Jews and their books, and debated with both members of international Jewish organizations and representatives of German cultural institutions.[53] This confronted him with the sometimes conflicting experiences and political outlooks of these different groups, and once again he perceived the hopelessness of the situation in more drastic terms than he had done from the perspective of Jerusalem. While traveling, Scholem became increasingly convinced that there would be no place in Germany for either Jews or their cultural and spiritual remains and that it was thus necessary, without restriction, to initiate the transfer of all recoverable material and encourage the remaining Jews to emigrate. In his newspaper article "Besuch bei den Juden in Deutschland" (Visiting the Jews in Germany, 1946), he drew a gloomy picture of efforts to rebuild Jewish life there. He confirmed the tendency of Jews in Germany to distance themselves from "things Jewish": "the scale of ignorance" defied imagination and interest was "negligible."[54] He then described the difficulty of their situation, as there was little opportunity to make an income outside the black market. Overall, his views resembled those of some local congregation members, whose drastic assessment he quoted: "The Jews will not remain here. Those who do are lost to Judaism. There can be no new beginning here." According to Scholem, the same went for survivors in the DP camps who had come to Germany from Eastern Europe as a result of their "unfortunate geographical position." Their situation too, he stated, was demoralizing and discouraging, and only immigration to Palestine could now offer them any hope. Letters written by Scholem following his return to Jerusalem also attest to the discontent, pain, and sorrow that his journey had caused him and that his wife Fania described so poignantly. To his close colleague Siegmund Hurwitz in Switzerland, he wrote, "I have to tell you that I arrived here from Paris in a state of utter exhaustion; the moment it was all over the extreme, prolonged nervous tension in Europe and all the little things that go with it burst to the surface, leaving me weak and incapable of doing anything [. . .]. It will be a long time before I have processed the many impressions arising from this trip to Europe."[55] His tone was similarly deflated in communication with his acquaintance Ernst Grumach, whom he had met in Berlin to discuss the whereabouts of books stolen for the RSHA: "The journey and the entire heavy burden of impressions have truly exhausted me. I was severely run down for two months."[56] Eventually, he also articulated his thoughts on Germany and his condition during and after his journey in detail to Hannah Arendt: "I was so worn out when I returned from Europe that I immediately collapsed into a heap, and I'm only now slowly recovering. [. . .] For over six months or more what I've been doing or experiencing has pushed scholarship into a *very* distant corner. That I wrote neither to you nor to anyone else during my time in Europe just goes to show how incapable I was of lifting my pen. What I saw didn't exactly stir up my desire to write but instead ended up adding considerably to my melancholy."[57] His condition was worsened by his growing anxiety over the future of the Jewish collective consciousness. In his letter to Arendt, he continued, "My experiences in Europe were very gloomy and depressing [. . .]. In my opinion, there is a catastrophic chasm opening up between various Jewish communities in Europe, America, and Palestine. There is no overcoming this through any conceivable theory. Everything is falling apart, and people don't understand one another." Scholem feared that the unity of the Jewish people was threatened by the experience of the Holocaust and the Jews' further dispersal across the world. This was bound up with the fear that, due to its problematic security, legal, and supply situation, Palestine would fail to become the go-to location for most European survivors, denying Zionists their most important objective. At the end of his letter to Arendt, in a shattered state, he wrote, "I'm afraid that this trip broke my heart, if I have such a thing (as I presume). In any event, I left behind in Europe all my hopes. I'd really like to know where I could recover this hope." While preparing for his journey, Scholem had anticipated that concrete involvement in the salvage of cultural treasures would bring him some relief from the agony unleashed within him by the dire situation in which Jews found themselves. And yet the opposite had happened—"these were among my bitterest moments."[58]

Hannah Arendt's first trip to Germany, which she began in late 1949 on behalf of the JCR, would augment her understanding of the principles of Nazi rule and leave a mark on her personally. While engaged in a meticulous search for Jewish cultural property, she also sought to find traces of the Germany that had once been her home. But the reality she encountered reinforced her view that she would never be able to live there again.[59] Her impressions of postwar Germany from 1949 to 1950 generally confirmed the picture she had constructed before her arrival. In response to Scholem after his devastating journey, she concluded, "You are no doubt right about Germany. [. . .] The blabber just like in 1932—the ridiculous talk of forging forward amid the ruins—is bad; even worse is the lack of vitality, the absence of rage, of fury."[60] This assessment was reinforced by what she herself saw during her first trip back. In the analysis of contemporary Germany she composed after it, "The Aftermath of Nazi Rule. Report from Germany," published in *Commentary* in 1950, she made virtually identical remarks on the situation there: "But nowhere is this nightmare of destruction and horror less felt and less talked about than in Germany itself. A lack of response is evident everywhere, and it is difficult to say whether this signifies a half-conscious refusal to yield to grief or a genuine inability to feel. Amid the ruins, Germans mail each other picture postcards still showing the cathedrals and market places, the public buildings and bridges that no longer exist."[61] She also referred to the absence of rage among the Germans, which she considered symptomatic of German behavior: "The only conceivable alternative to the denazification program would have been a revolution—the outbreak of the German people's spontaneous wrath against all those they knew to be prominent members of the Nazi regime. [. . .] But the revolution did not come to pass [. . .]. This wrath does not exist today, and apparently it has never existed."[62]

During their trips to Germany, Scholem and Arendt both felt that virtually all the Germans they met lacked empathy, were heartless, and failed to take responsibility while also suppressing the crimes that had been committed. The social climate seemed poisoned. Scholem was unable to grasp how Jews could "breathe in this air" and described the atmosphere as "most sticky."[63] Arendt agreed: "Germany is terrible. I'm haunted by this place; I'm filled with inner revulsion. Disgust. Every conversation I have leaves a bad taste in my mouth."[64] She also sensed an alarming tendency toward the persistence of anti-Semitic and Nazi convictions. In this regard, she wrote to Salo Baron: "The renazification of Germany is frightening. SS people who are now returning from the internment camps have great amounts of money in their pockets [...] the atmosphere is frightful."[65] Her close confidante Hilde Fränkel received similar accounts from Arendt. Since she was suffering from a serious illness in New York at the time, she was, apart from Blücher, the only private individual to whom Arendt regularly wrote from Germany: "Right now, the Nazis (known as *Mitläufer* [followers]) are resuming all their old positions, while behaving as if they had a self-evident right to them. In Heidelberg I have just been told that all that is now meant by the 'politically persecuted,' whom the whole world is trying to rehabilitate, is Nazis. It is a fantastical situation."[66]

The key source of Dawidowicz's, Scholem's, and Arendt's drastic assessments of Germany was their work at the American collecting points and with numerous German cultural institutions, ministries, and authorities, which put them into direct contact with German personnel. This often led to confrontation with individuals who had managed to seamlessly continue their careers after the demise of National Socialism or whose political convictions were simply an unknown quantity. This was a particularly onerous problem for Arendt because she was the JCR officer in closest contact with Germans. Tirelessly, she traveled back and forth between occupation zones, holding discussions with state ministers for education and culture, directors of museums and libraries, staff of the American restitution agencies, and both members and leaders of reestablished Jewish congregations.[67] She searched meticulously for personnel who had held leading positions in research institutes, archives, and libraries during the Nazi era and who might be able to provide information on the whereabouts of looted items. Time and again she had to face high-ranking representatives of cultural institutions who refused to cooperate and strove to hang on to clearly identifiable looted collections of Jewish provenance, showing no awareness of the unjust nature of their actions. For example, she related a case in Hamburg in which the director of the city museum initially refused to allow deported Jews' confiscated household silver to pass to a Jewish trust organization, simply stating that the museum was keen to "establish with them a special division." The crime inherent in this collection—as Arendt concluded—was camouflaged by an invented story of rescue of the silver by the German authorities.[68] Outraged, she described to Fränkel the "animosity," "lack of understanding," and "malice" of many of the Germans with whom she interacted. In another letter, she spoke of the "denazified SS leaders, thick as thieves, who have access to a large quantity of money" and of whom "the entire German population believes they are the masters of tomorrow."[69] Despite the painful reverberations of the Nazi regime and its ideology, which were so apparent to Arendt time and again during her journey and provided her with empirical evidence for her great study of totalitarianism,[70] she showed a willingness to engage in dialogue. Whether she did so for pragmatic reasons or because she managed to preserve a remnant of trust is an open question. Unlike most other Jewish emissaries active in Germany on behalf of various international organizations, Arendt believed it necessary to enter into dialogue with the Germans. She explained this controversial stance to Scholem:

> God knows mistrust is certainly in order, but there is also a kind of mistrust that can be just as blind as blind trust. Or, to put it differently, you can take the position that everyone is lying, everyone is hiding something, that no one has any goodwill. But if you do this, you're not only closing off discussion, you're also preventing any possible action. As a matter of fact, in this context, I can say that many of the people at the top of public institutions in Germany are first-rate. (And Gerhard, don't hit the roof: this is a brute fact!) But in these very same offices I see the people—and I have names—trying their best to sabotage everything. Without question, the power of those who are trustworthy has never been great, and at the moment it is constantly dwindling as the de-Nazified people stream back.[71]

Overall, however, what Arendt felt most keenly was the loss of her former homeland: "Since I've been in Germany for the second time I've been overwhelmed by grief: the devastated cities with their lost façades, the devastated people. After all, there is still the German language and an incredibly beautiful, homelike landscape, a familiarity we have experienced nowhere else and never will again."[72]

Joshua Starr, Arendt's predecessor as executive secretary of the JCR, was equally ravaged by the confrontations with German reality that overwhelmed him during a number of trips on behalf of the JCR between 1946 and 1948. He committed suicide in New York just as Hannah Arendt was beginning her journey. In an obituary included in a commemorative anthology put together by the publishers and editors of *Jewish Social*

Studies, Abraham Duker reflected on the situation in postwar Germany as one reason for Starr's tragic step: "A sensitive person, Starr surely must have suffered extreme emotional strain and constant tension while living among the Germans and handling daily the visible testimonies to Nazi barbarism. [. . .] Indeed, he watched what he termed the re-nazification of Germany with a blend of anger and melancholy resignation."[73]

Salo Baron, who spent just a brief period in Germany in 1946, undertaking most of his activities for the salvage mission from Paris and London, related more hopeful moments than his colleagues Arendt and Starr. He was able to strengthen the cooperation with the JCR's future partners by meeting with representatives of the British Committee on Restoration and with Scholem in early summer in Paris. He coordinated with them the various interest groups' next steps toward establishing a Jewish trust organization and exchanged information on the situation in Germany and the former German-occupied areas. Scholem and Baron were particularly concerned that valuable books risked being displaced once again, this time to Eastern Europe, an anxiety that focused their attention on the incipient Cold War. Their meeting in Paris was a milestone in the cooperative endeavors of the Hebrew University and the Commission and, in the unique political initiative that resulted, a joint effort by Yishuv and Diaspora.[74]

For Baron, such experiences pointed the way ahead: after his trip, he led the Commission into the corporative framework of the JCR, thus laying the groundwork for practical cooperation among all those Jewish individuals with an interest in cultural restitution. Baron was long to remember another meeting in Paris, though this one was of more personal import. During a conversation with the local rabbi Maurice Liber of the École Rabbinique, with whom Baron met on several occasions to discuss looted French property, Baron asked him for his thoughts on the future of the Jews in Europe. He later remembered that in his reply, the rabbi made an analogy with the year 1349, a time of murderous pogroms of thousands of Jews all over Europe, who were blamed for the spread of the plague. No one, the rabbi told Baron, could have imagined that after a few years, Jewish life would thrive in Europe once again. Baron recalled that this comparison had given him hope and led him to look differently at the rebuilding of Jewish institutions in Europe—he himself, he noted, had joyfully welcomed the reopening of a Jewish school in Paris as an expression of a new beginning among the survivors.[75] The letters to his wife Jeanette in New York also confirm his positive impression of Paris: "I had the distinct feeling that things are picking up in France and that the French Jews are beginning to take care of themselves. They still need financial assistance, but are trying to do things on their own."[76] The anecdote about Maurice Liber and the letter demonstrate how Baron tried to maintain an optimistic perspective on Jewish life in Europe after 1945. Time and place allowed him to see the potential rather than the destruction that became increasingly apparent the further eastward one looked. Baron sought inspiration in the centuries-old history of Jewish survival, which had long preoccupied him. Yet his increasing focus on Jewish life in America was anchored in the same experiential nexus. Here, alongside Israel, he saw the new center of Jewish culture and community developing after the Second World War. Besides these tiny glimmers of hope in Europe, overall he understood and fully agreed that the focus of Jewish life was moving to new locations.

Ensuring Continuity and Justice

Right from the outset, the push for restitution was accompanied by debates on the future, survival, and security of Jewish life after catastrophe. For the protagonists, this was bound up with questions about the appropriate political framework for the Jews' ongoing existence, questions that foregrounded the ruptures and continuities of Jewish life as a whole. When it came to the salvage of books and other cultural property, all those involved tried to deal first and foremost with the preconditions for and limits to the preservation and revival of history, tradition, knowledge, and the Jewish cultural heritage. The second important field of debate centered on legal issues. For Arendt, Baron, Dawidowicz, and Scholem, negotiations on rightful jurisprudence were about more than securing formerly Jewish property: this was a battle for justice, recognition, the constitution of the Jewish collectivity, its security, and representation.

Reclaiming Historical Space

The debates on the postwar reconstruction of a Jewish cultural landscape were guided by a desire to reconstitute the past and by the idea that salvaging material remains would enable future generations to build on the traditions of Jewish knowledge. Time and again, in an attempt to imagine a post-Holocaust future, Salo Baron thus called for an appreciation of the Jewish people's strength, vitality, and indefatigable will to survive. He made it clear that while he saw the annihilation of European Jewry as historically unprecedented, he was still trying to promote Jewish strategies of continuance.[77] According to Barbara Kirshenblatt-Gimblett, Baron believed two elements of the Jewish quest for continuity to be central: a continued adherence to tradition and the pronounced Jewish sense of community.[78] He applied this vision to the situation prevailing in the 1940s. In 1945, before the war had ended, he was still expressing this belief in the form of a rather timid hope: "Religious history has given evidence of how deeply humanity may sink, and still rise again to high spiritual levels. [. . .] It is not unreasonable to hope that out of the depths of misery and despair some new saving forms of belief and observance may arise which will provide an answer to the perplexities of our Jewish experience."[79]

In his article "At the Turning Point," written just after the war, Baron already argued with more resolve, making an appeal of sorts to the Jews: "Without an inner determination to survive, without strong beliefs and a rich culture and powerful institutions, the Jewish people could not possibly have come down the ages."[80] His efforts to salvage cultural property fit with this notion in every respect, symbolizing the potential to secure and preserve past worlds, their knowledge, and traditions. His work also embodied the desire to strengthen Jewish community life outside Europe, particularly in the United States—communities he believed could in turn revitalize the Jewish world as a whole.[81] Baron underlined that the preservation of tradition, the fostering of community, and the securing of continuity were particularly potent motives for the JCR when he took stock of its work in 1955: "The Jewish people succeeded in salvaging some 500,000 volumes, 1,200 scrolls of law, 7,000 artistic and ceremonial objects. [. . .] Far beyond their monetary value, these collections symbolize the continuity of the heritage of the Jewish people."[82] The community-building function that Baron ascribed to the JCR is most clearly evident in his use of the term *Jewish people*, which he identified here as the subject of legal negotiations and the allocation of treasures. At the same time, he also emphasized the commemorative function of the JCR's work, which he believed facilitated the perpetuation of the Jews' historical legacy. The first official letter from the Commission to the State Department had already cited exactly the same arguments in an attempt to initiate negotiations on the JCR's eligibility for trustee status. Here too, emphasis was placed on books and ritual objects' special function for the Jewish collectivity and its ongoing existence. For generations, the letter stated, these objects had represented "the physical embodiment of this long, devoted, and often heroic spiritual and intellectual activity" in Europe and "constitute a priceless heritage and one of the proudest possessions of the Jewish people."[83]

In cultural restitution, then, Baron discerned the concrete manifestation of his notion of continuity—to him, the books represented the Jews' European legacy while also establishing identity and a sense of community. In emphatic terms, he claimed in 1945 that "books have always been the very life-blood of the 'people of the book,'" reiterating the imperative of salvaging them. In this sense, books symbolized the very existence of the Jewish people as a collectivity, their survival depending on this "life-blood."[84]

When it came to this function of salvaged objects and the enhancement of Jewish culture in the United States, Hannah Arendt had ideas resembling those of Baron even if she framed them differently. In her little-known 1947 article "Creating a Cultural Atmosphere," which appeared as an op-ed in *Commentary*'s series "Jewish Culture in This Time and Place," she called for a new consciousness of what Jewish culture might entail. There is no explicit reference to the JCR and its significance here, her focus being on the future of a secular Jewish culture in general. Nonetheless, Arendt's perspective demonstrates how close to her heart the initiatives of the JCR were.[85] Her remarks on the shattering of Jewish intellectual life and on the loss of ties to tradition as a result of secularization since the Renaissance and Enlightenment unquestionably speak to the situation in 1947: "The danger of losing historical continuity as such, along with the treasures of the past, was obvious; the fear of being robbed of the specifically human background of the past, of becoming an abstract ghost like the man without a shadow."[86] This account of losing stocks of knowledge and intellectual traditions, stripping people of their shadow—that is, leaving them devoid of history—reads like a description of her experiences in the postwar period. Arendt clearly advocated the redefining of modern cultural life in order to deal productively with these very experiences of loss. With a sense of urgency, she pleaded here for the recreation of a culture that, by means of a new consciousness and on its own terms, would draw on both the religious and folkloric traditions of the past.[87] She also shared Baron's conviction that the United States offered Jews the right environment for the development of a new cultural identity.[88] The link to Arendt's view of the JCR becomes even clearer if we consider a short text she wrote on its mission in 1950, where she stated, "Jewish scholarship everywhere in the world will have received that heritage of European Jewry to which it can rightly lay claim and many countries, especially Latin America and Israel, but also the United States, have received new and inspiring sources of learning."[89]

She was, in other words, concerned not just with preserving but also with productively developing Jewish scholarship and culture with the aid of holdings salvaged from Europe. Jews outside Europe ought to benefit from their ability to draw on the "remnants of many centuries of spiritual life of European Jewry" and take inspiration from them.[90] Her visible and profound dedication to Jewish culture at the time was also mirrored in Arendt's work as chief editor at Schocken Books in New York, headed by Salman Schocken. Between 1946 and 1948, she was responsible for the publication of Franz Kafka's diaries. With varying degrees of success, she also tried to persuade Schocken to publish English translations of the European Jewish intellectual canon, which she wished to introduce to an American Jewish readership. This included the work of such key figures as Spinoza, Heine, and Lazare but also lesser known Eastern European authors such as Bruno Schulz and Samuel Joseph Agnon.[91]

Unlike Baron, however, Arendt was not only concerned with the continuity of Jewish life after the Holocaust; in fact, we can discern a dual movement of thought here, as she appealed emphatically for an awareness of the rupture that had occurred as a result of National Socialism, a rupture that made it impossible to build seamlessly on the period "before" and its intellectual traditions. With respect to her epistemological approach to time—namely, the question of the ambivalent relationship between preservation, rupture, and renewal in conditions of modernity, Arendt articulated her thoughts most instructively in a 1968 essay on

Walter Benjamin.[92] Here she reflected on the potential for "new ways of dealing with the past" following the "irreparable" break with tradition engendered by the catastrophe of the twentieth century.[93] For Arendt, since "there was no such thing as a 'return' either to the German or the European or the Jewish tradition" and there was now no prospect of seamlessly passing on the Jewish cultural and intellectual canon, the only way to relate to what had gone before lay in wresting and gathering "the 'thought fragments'" from the past.[94] She related this to Benjamin's conception of time: "Like a pearl diver who descends to the bottom of the sea, [. . .] to pry loose the rich and the strange, the pearls and the coral in the depths, and to carry them to the surface, this thinking delves into the depths of the past—but not in order to resuscitate it the way it was and to contribute to the renewal of extinct ages."[95] This Benjamin-inspired trope casts a special light on Arendt's postwar experiences, as it can be applied metaphorically to the reality of salvaged books after the Holocaust. They too seemed like historical remnants, pearls from the depths of the past, and they too were no more than fragments in the present, but according to Arendt, they ought to contribute to renewal, to help people develop their culture while remaining aware of a destruction that persisted. In fact, this awareness could not be avoided in confrontation with the rescued books: the marks of theft and murder adhering to them remained and could not be denied.

Confronted with the Offenbach Depot, Lucy Dawidowicz penned a disturbing, impressive account of this state of affairs: "The orphaned books [. . .] inanimate remnants of the world the Germans had destroyed [. . .] had been dumb witnesses to mass murder. They were relics of six million murdered Jews."[96] As hinted at earlier, Dawidowicz's view of the potential to build a bridge to the past through the restitution of looted items changed over the course of her work in Europe. She had arrived hopeful that incorporating the books from Vilna into the holdings of its American successor institute would provide the devastated world of the Vilna YIVO with a new place in the present. In her vision, it was not only the continuity of personnel in New York, most prominently the institute's director Max Weinreich and YIVO's founding fathers, Elias Tscherikower and Jakob Lestschinsky, that would perpetuate a part of Vilna in New York; she also hoped to achieve continuity with the help of its material remains.[97] The high hopes that accompanied salvage initiatives during the war were bound up with this idea. Reminiscing about these years, Dawidowicz recalled, "If even a small portion of the YIVO library would be found among the ruins in Germany, it would be a sign that the Jerusalem of Vilna would yet rise phoenix-like from the ashes, that it would reestablish its earthly presence."[98] The advocates in New York viewed the search for these holdings and their transfer to the United States as a means of countering Nazi destruction. In addition, these activities were born of their desire for the continued existence of everything the institute in Vilna had stood for. Just as the language, spirit, folklore, and everyday life of Yiddish-speaking communities had been investigated and promoted at the YIVO in Vilna, they now wished to make use of the knowledge that had been acquired under new circumstances. Before the end of the war, Shlomo Noble, a member of staff at the YIVO in New York, had already described the institutionalized link between these two places and worlds: "From Vilna to New York—in this passage the Yivo symbolizes the timelessness and universality of Jewish life and Jewish learning. Vilna and New York! Vast is the distance separating these two cities, and the bond uniting them is Yivo."[99] By detaching YIVO's history from its specific time and place, and transcending its destruction, it seemed possible to imagine its future role in the United States and to build a seamless connection to the past. Max Weinreich confirmed this perception in 1947: "That a Vilna institution has put down roots in New York while remaining a Vilna institution is a miracle in itself. [. . .] That such a remnant of the world that was has made it over to the New World, that it is vibrant and creative, is one of the greatest miracles of the Jewish uprising amid mass murder."[100]

Yet the attempt by the New York activists to continue and build on YIVO's research on all fields of Yiddish life and learning inevitably tailed off, as did the idea that the Yiddish world could remain a vital part of Jewish life in the United States. Despite the many Yiddish-speaking immigrants, many of whom had already been living in the country for two generations, YIVO staff were compelled to reorient themselves, refocusing their work on the commemoration of the Yiddish heritage rather than its active perpetuation. They had to face up to new social realities: in the 1950s, more and more Jewish families were being integrated into the American middle class and thus were turning away from the language and traditional ways of life in general.[101] As she later remembered,

Dawidowicz became aware that there was little prospect of reenacting Vilna in New York, of conceptualizing its American branch as a geographical extension of its Lithuanian predecessor, partly as a result of her confrontation with the Vilna survivors whom she had met in Paris during her journey in 1946. This meeting prompted her to conclude, "Even if all of Vilna's survivors were to be assembled in one place, they would still be only fragments, from which no one could ever put Vilna together again."[102] Given what they had been through, including the experience of the Holocaust, the chasm between her and the survivors, and between present and past, was too wide to be bridged.[103]

In much the same way as her teacher Baron, whom she had studied under briefly at Columbia University, Dawidowicz tried to engage with the issues of the survival and endurance of Jewish life and culture. The salvage of cultural treasures could be integrated into this objective of continuity in a highly meaningful way. Similar to Arendt, however, as Dawidowicz grasped more and more of the reality on the ground, she too emphasized that Jewish life could only go on in full awareness of the catastrophe. Particularly with respect to Vilna, she thus shifted the focus of her scholarly work to historical reconstruction, documentation, and commemoration: "One of the last people to have seen Vilna, I have been haunted by the compelling Jewish obligation to remember. I wished [. . .] 'to make the silences of history speak,' to bestow on Vilna and its Jews a posthumous life. I felt it was my duty to resurrect it, if I could, by recreating the life in that world capital of the realm of Yiddish."[104] Precisely because she had seen that "Vilna had been reduced to fragments of paper" she felt the obligation to invest in its memory.[105] Ultimately, for her, ensuring continuity meant securing memory, saving the Yiddish culture from oblivion.

Gershom Scholem addressed the need for continuity or a new beginning, the notion of building on the past or acknowledging an existential rupture after 1945, from a different perspective. For him, the Holocaust marked a definitive end of the models of Jewish dwelling in Europe and proved them utopian. Consequently, the foundation of the state of Israel appeared to be the only consistent means of overcoming the flaws of earlier Jewish existence. This did not mean completely renouncing the thousands of years of Jewish history in Europe. As a historian aware of tradition, instead Scholem sought to maintain and breathe new life into certain intellectual and religious accomplishments of the European-Jewish canon—the transfer to Israel of as many collections of venerable Jewish provenance as possible seemed vital to this objective. He thus wrote to Leo Baeck in the aforementioned letter, "It is precisely the productive use of these collections, for the spiritual work within Judaism and in its most decisive centers, that has motivated us to take these steps."[106] The preservation of cultural treasures gave him a sense of returning to history, of preserving the Jewish tradition and thus laying the spiritual and cultural foundations for the Israeli polity. As a bibliophile textual scholar with a "passionate devotion to the sources,"[107] the salvage of books and manuscripts was close to his heart. In line with his specific approach to Jewish thought, his understanding of the restoration of lost and looted books differed from that of other scholars. Scholem devoted himself to very specific collections in Europe, his main interest being Judaica and Hebraica. First and foremost, this meant collections that had once been the property of the most famous and established Jewish communities, rabbinical seminaries, and yeshivot. Most important to him were their *pinkasim* (community records), collections of responsa and all sorts of rabbinical commentary, editions of the Talmud, and prayer books. Scholem's focus was evident in a number of ways: in the unauthorized transfer, which he initiated together with Rabbi Herbert Friedman, of religious documents and Hebrew manuscripts from the Offenbach Depot to Israel in the summer of 1946; in his meticulous search for such holdings throughout Germany, Czechoslovakia, and Austria; and in his unrelenting negotiations with representatives of Jewish communities and German librarians on the Hebrew manuscripts among their holdings, especially those in Frankfurt and Munich. His detailed knowledge of the Bavarian State Library's treasures stemmed from his own time as a student in the city from 1919 to 1922, where he had worked with the library's Hebraica collection and had become aware of the Talmud manuscript he later wished to transfer to Jerusalem. In his autobiographical text, *From Berlin to Jerusalem*, he recalled, "Most of my time, to be sure, I spent in the manuscript department of the Bavarian State Library, where my table was garnished with Hebrew codices and printed works."[108]

It was these same texts that Scholem wished to obtain for Israel after the war, though his wish was never to be granted. With steely determination, he negotiated with the heads of the Berlin community concerning the archival materials and *pinkasim* in their possession orig- inating from famous Jewish congregations throughout Europe, which in his assessment "no one in Berlin is even capable of reading."[109] His memoirs also show that he was familiar from his youth with the Ber- lin Congregational Library on Oranienburger Straße: "For years I was among the most zealous users of this library, which was later destroyed by the Nazis."[110] Resembling his own route from Berlin to Jerusalem, he strove to bring to Israel as much as possible of what little was left of this library. Scholem argued bitterly with the JCR leadership in New York over every fragment of rabbinical texts and rare books that was not to be sent to Jerusalem: he was outraged by the transfer to Switzerland of parts of the Breslau theological seminary collection and by what he perceived to be the favoritism shown to the JTS in New York when it came to the choice of manuscripts.[111]

His efforts to obtain the texts he longed for was part and parcel of the intellectual project he pursued throughout his life, one that threatened to end tragically with the total destruction of the European Jewish cul- tural landscape: the appropriation and renewal of the different strands of the Jewish religious and spiritual tradition. His early encounter, in Berlin as elsewhere, with the classical Jewish texts, was the foundation and point of departure for the development of his consciousness as a Jew and scholar of Jewish thought. Beginning in the 1920s, he ex- pressed opposition to modern assimilation—which intensified with the emancipation of Jews in the nineteenth century—as a model for Jewish life, advocating a return to a more Jewish self-awareness anchored in a profound knowledge of the traditional sources.[112] This connection to the written sources, according to Scholem, marked the continuous ex- istence of the Jewish people: "[That the Jews] were the ultimate people of the book there can be no doubt. For they not only *preserved* this book [the Torah] but *lived* with it. [. . .] It is fair to say that the book, in terms of its world-historical function, was the making of the Jews as a people."[113] He was convinced that even modern Jews' language, way of life, historical perspective, and spatial imaginations bore the traces of the Torah and religious exegeses, creating a sense of collectivity even in an age of increasing secularization.[114] The contemporary philoso- pher and writer George Steiner conveys this idea in similar terms when he emphasizes that the notion of "The People of the Book" "defines a lasting authenticity" and that an "addiction to textuality has character-ized, [and] continues to characterize Jewish practice and sentiment," thus also guaranteeing the "actual survival of the Jews."[115] But Scholem went beyond this focus, passed down over the centuries, on the "tex-tuality and bookishness" of the Jewish people.[116] As he saw it, if there was to be a future for "Jews as Jews," it was vital to maintain a histori-cal consciousness that refers dialectically to the traditional, fusing its conservation with its renewal.[117] Here his thinking was structurally con-sonant with that of Arendt and Benjamin, as he was to provide the renewed Jewish life (in Israel) with a new spiritual and cultural foun-dation: "The solution of questions regarding the Bible and the Talmud, the problems of living Jewish society and its physical and spiritual world—in short, everything about everything—demand a basic revi-sion, an intellectual stock-taking in light of our new understanding. A general change or orientation will not suffice. The new perception must penetrate into each and every detail: must examine it anew in light of the sources, each problem unto itself; reconsider it and plunge into its depths."[118]

As Scholem saw it, safeguarding the Jews' cultural and spiritual leg-acy was crucial if contemporary Jews were to critically engage with the realm of Jewish knowledge and thought. During the Second World War, his project was endangered by new forces and took on an unforeseen material aspect: the imperative was no longer merely to deal appropri-ately with the sources but to prevent them from disappearing altogether. After statehood, in some ways, Scholem echoed the mainstream Zionist reading of the 1950s and 1960s in Israel, linking the annihilation of the European Jews and the foundation of the state. This reading of events found expression in the widespread narrative of *Mi-Shoa Le'tkumah*, from the Holocaust to rebirth.[119] In the same vein, in light of a bibli-cal parable that held out hope for the future and the present, Scholem drew a parallel with the consequences of the destruction of the Second Temple in Jerusalem in 70 CE: "There is an old saying that is the basis for many a Jewish legend: on the day of the destruction of the Temple, the Messiah was born. This bold sentence [. . .] probably expresses in a paradoxical form the feeling—not to say the knowledge—that the great historical catastrophe of the Jewish people and redemption are inseparably connected, dialectically intermeshed. With the falling into ruin of the Temple, the main focus of a people [in other words,] the possibility of redemption is disclosed from another level and from a focal point that cannot as yet be determined."[120]

This implied that the emergence of the state of Israel equated to deliverance from the apocalypse that Nazism had brought upon the Jews of Europe, and Scholem integrated the Otzrot HaGolah committee's efforts to salvage books into this process of redemption. For its members, who rescued thousands of books and objects, their work was part of a greater historical interpretive framework—namely, national and cultural rebirth. One of the leading Israeli historians, Ben-Zion Dinur, himself a member of the Otzrot HaGolah and later a deputy in the Knesset and a government minister, described this framework in unambiguous terms: "This 'cultural heritage' [of exile], which is the bedrock of our existence, is also the foundation upon which the entire House of Israel rests; working diligently to preserve and strengthen it is one of the most important things the State of Israel must do."[121] Still, Scholem himself knew that such hopes could be no more than a utopian dream. The experience of the Holocaust and the awareness of millions of murdered victims was entrenched in Israel, where people "were deeply affected and transformed by the attempts to master this trauma." The "existential situation" of the Jews had changed after this experience, and "all were confronted by a fact with which they had not reckoned, a fact that boggled the mind, and the reaction to which involved a task for one's awareness that was as urgent as it was insoluble."[122] So while Scholem was deeply invested in the Jewish future, he was equally affected and disturbed by the past and the rupture it represented—a rupture that could never be overcome.

To varying degrees, Baron, Arendt, Dawidowicz, and Scholem felt a profound, almost existential desire to safeguard and preserve books and cultural objects. They saw it as a means of ensuring continuity and passing on centuries-old knowledge after the Nazi attempt to wipe it off the face of the earth. For these individuals, every saved volume provided an opportunity to extend fine, fragile threads into the past and preserve a fraction of the Jewish culture of Europe. In the course of their engagement, it became ever more apparent to them that the reconstruction of the old world, the revitalization of the past, was impossible. This left a strong albeit very individual mark on their efforts to come to terms with the Holocaust and engage with its commemoration.

Reclaiming the Legal Sphere

Efforts to ensure the continuity and security of Jewish life were closely linked to the spheres of law and justice. Legal issues were part and parcel of the salvage initiatives and impacted on them as significantly as did questions of continuity. Convinced that the reestablishment of a legitimate title of ownership—in other words, the return of looted items—would give Europe's Jews back their place within the legal order after the war, the Commission had dedicated itself to the cause of cultural restitution. Jewish lawyers who had formulated relevant plans came to believe that enforcing restitution and reparations was the only way to advance the political, social, and economic resurrection of Europe's devastated Jewish congregations and bring about justice and peace.[123] One of the specific consequences of the unprecedented, industrially organized mass murder of Jews was its profound challenge to all existing legal means of achieving restorative or retributive justice after armed conflict. Hannah Arendt captured the failure of the law in the face of the monstrousness of these crimes when she stated to Karl Jaspers, "The Nazi crimes, it seems to me, explode the limits of the law; and that is precisely what constitutes their monstrousness. For these crimes, no punishment is severe enough."[124] This was equally true of the prosecution of the Nazi theft of Jews' property. As part of the systematic war of annihilation, the crimes committed in connection with Aryanization, confiscation, dispossession, plunder, and theft undermined conventional principles of international criminal law after armed conflict. This aporia was a core element in the experience of those working for the JCR and YIVO. It brought in its wake political and legal negotiations into which general questions about Jewish life and its future in the face of the Holocaust forced their way.

During their work on cultural restitution, both Arendt and Scholem had always striven to move beyond the role of political adviser traditionally occupied by Jews within the international legal and political context; they aimed to play an active role and ensure that Jews helped shape international law to serve their own interests. Since the 1930s, Arendt had studied the historical circumstances of the European Jews' cumulative loss of rights, which extended from exclusionary developments within the nation states of interwar Eastern Europe, which left millions of Jews stateless, to the policies of Nazism, which stripped Jews of all their rights. The expulsion of Jews from the judicial arena as a precondition for murder is meticulously described in *The Origins of Totalitarianism*: "Even the Nazis started their extermination of Jews by first depriving them of all legal status (the status of second-class citizenship) and cutting them off from the world of the living by herding them into ghettos and concentration camps; and before they set the gas chambers into motion they had carefully tested the ground and found out to their satisfaction that no country would claim these people. The point is that a condition of complete rightlessness was created before the right to live was challenged."[125]

For Arendt, Jews' total rightlessness as experienced under Nazi domination was bound up with the process of depriving them of a place in the world in the most general sense. By creating this extralegal status for Jews, the Nazis were able to declare them "superfluous" and turn them into "living corpses," stripped of all capacity to act, think, and articulate their views, abilities that for Arendt defined the essence of humanity.[126] These insights into the logic of Nazi extermination policy formed the background to her demands in the postwar period, when she believed it crucial to reestablish the legal ground for Jews' political participation on a self-responsible basis. Her famous call for a "right to have rights," which envisaged a universal human right to participation in a political entity and hence a general right to citizenship also applied in its broadest sense to her political vision of Jewish reentry into the legal sphere. In the realm of restorative justice, she of course argued for the right to collective group rights—namely, the Jews' right to their cultural heritage.[127] Particularly when it came to the right to restitution, Arendt had recognized that traditional agreements, based on either private law or international law among nation states, would be ineffective. If the perpetrators or other states were to be prevented from benefiting from stolen property, the relevant legal entity must be the Jews as a nonstate collectivity. In 1945, Arendt pointed to the fact that the models that had been found to ensure this right needed advocates and further improvement: "And that leaves the restoration of Jewish property. The only remarkable thing in that regard is that thus far no Jewish body has found the courage to speak out against individual reparations—with which we have had the worst of experiences everywhere—and for a collective restitution, for which Jewish communities would appear as the plaintiffs and national states as the agents of restitution."[128]

Scholem put forward very similar arguments when he summed up his experiences in Europe in a 1947 article for *Haaretz*, the Hebrew daily: "These regulations on property and assets [the territorial principle in restitution law] [. . .] have [. . .] greatly damaged the interests of the Jewish people. There has been a failure to recognize its authority as an organized corporation that can lay claim to the treasures of which it has been robbed."[129] Partly through the tireless efforts of its protagonists, the JCR and JRSO did finally find the courage to take on such a role and advance the recognition of the Jewish collectivity as claimant. The success of both was in many ways linked with their integration of the various Jewish factions and of the Jews' different geographical centers after 1945.

Among those actively involved, however, JCR's diversity spawned tensions. There was a lack of clarity over the composition and location of the Jewish collectivity. Of the four activists, Scholem probably had the clearest solution to this problem. Notwithstanding pragmatic considerations, which made joint action with representatives outside Israel unavoidable, he regarded the Israeli polity as the Jews' most important representative. As he saw it, Israel would give the Jews of Europe what they had always lacked: sovereignty, their own entity, whose territory they could invoke as representative of their interests and guarantor of their survival and autonomy. Through the foundation of the state of Israel, he aimed to facilitate a new beginning for the entire Jewish collectivity: "It [the foundation of Israel] was none other than the decision to return to ourselves, to become fully and consciously involved with the flow of Jewish history and to take into our own hands the responsibility for our lives as participants in all areas—both the secular and the sacred or religious—as Jews, and as Jews alone."[130]

In Scholem's view, Israel should be recognized as the focal point of all Jews worldwide. This had less to do with nationalist politics than with his vision that there, in the "land of the fathers," the Jewish people could experience a "cultural and communal renaissance."[131] And just as he regarded Israel as a safe haven for Jews fleeing Europe, "books in search of refuge" should find a home there as well. In Scholem's thinking, law and justice for the Jewish collectivity chiefly meant ensuring the existence of an autonomous nation state that could develop into a scholarly and cultural center of Jewish life.

Arendt's, Baron's, and Dawidowicz's efforts were dedicated primarily to Jewries outside Israel. From their perspective, shaped by their diasporic experience, there was another way of looking at the constitution of the Jewish people, which they believed must still be seen as a transterritorial entity even after the disaster of the Holocaust. Arendt derived her convictions from her analysis of the Jews' political situation in modern Europe. She invoked the Jewish collectivity as an entity, and indeed a political one, as soon as this collectivity was attacked by the Nazis. And in 1942, when Jews failed to defend themselves collectively despite Germany's declaration of war, she predicted a dark future: "Those people who do not make history, but simply suffer it, [. . .] tend to lay their hands in their laps and wait for miracles that never happen. If in the course of this war we do not awaken from this apathy, there will be no place for us in tomorrow's world."[132] After the war, her hope for a Jewish Army was transformed into the demand for Jews' legal and political participation in the international arena. Her appeals for Jews' to take part in the war already contained the elements that were to become significant later in the context of the JCR. In 1941, Arendt had stated that it "must [. . .] become the living will of a majority of the Jewish people to join the battle against Hitler as Jews, in Jewish battle formations under a Jewish flag."[133] When the plan to create such an army resulted solely in the establishment of a Jewish brigade within the British armed forces, Arendt continued to believe that Jews across the world ought to regard themselves as a unified political entity and act as such. This was her key objective during the preparatory work on the "Frankfurt Agreement," which authorized the JCR to act as Jewish trustee and was signed in February 1949. Through her work at the JCR, she wished to help strengthen and safeguard this political entity, and it was within this entity and on its behalf that she sought to take political action. This perspective enabled her to discuss territorial and national questions on a universal level: ultimately, her aim was to rethink human coexistence and the Jews' place within this general framework after the caesura of the Holocaust.[134]

Baron too aspired to secure Jewish life in the diaspora through the establishment of binding legal structures. As the initiator of the Commission and JCR, he thus put all his efforts into negotiations with potential Jewish partners on the one hand and the American and Allied authorities on the other. In particular, he regarded it as incumbent upon the American Jewries to support survivors from Europe and thus help rebuild Jewish life: "Just as for the past three decades we have helped world Jewry with our economic and political efforts; just as we have attained new high marks in world Jewish philanthropy and world Jewish political action, so we must now assume the new role of guide and mentor for both the distressed Jewries of Europe and the perplexed Jewries of other lands."[135] Baron's objective of gaining the Commission a legal status was embedded in a far broader goal—namely, the security of Jewish life worldwide. Like Arendt, he highlighted that the survivors, and thus the remaining fragments of the Jewish congregations of Europe, required new political and legal foundations if they were to survive into the future. But as huge numbers of Jews fled from Eastern Europe toward the West and the new state was founded in Israel, Baron too was compelled to fully support both the Jewish nation state and the Jewish communities in the United States. When leading figures within the JCR realized that the hope of reestablishing Jewish life in Europe was essentially wishful thinking, detached from political and demographic realities, they changed their strategy. Baron himself now focused on the reconstruction and institutionalization of Jewish cultural institutions in Israel and the United States. His main concern, however, was with American Jewish communities. He advocated a certain degree of Jewish autonomy while highlighting that Jews in the United States enjoyed the full rights of citizenship. It was not assimilation that he saw as the most promising path for Jews, but a life balanced between Jewish self-determination and adaptation to the social and cultural premises of their environment.[136] Most importantly, he wished to establish the United States as the vibrant center of a visible and emancipated Jewish culture and thought—building on but also refining the traditions, institutions, visions, and ideas of the old center in Europe.

The panorama of perspectives described here demonstrates that the political and legal debate provided an initial means of coping with the reality of Nazi crimes. The political struggle over recognition and rights offered a way to respond to what had happened and translate the unfathomable into negotiable categories.[137] That the JCR, together with the JRSO, managed to ensure the transformation of property titles into administrative titles, facilitating a shift from individual to collective claims, implied in turn the official recognition of the Jewish people as a political and legal entity. In response to an international jurisprudence that had become hopelessly inadequate to coping with the monstrous crimes that had been committed, the Jewish collectivity now entered new legal territory. Ultimately, within the framework of the successor and trust organizations, its recognition in international law made a reality of what had previously been no more than a political dream. This was particularly significant partly because Jewish lawyers and activists were not as successful in other areas of post-Holocaust justice, especially the retributive field. The idea of ensuring official Jewish representation in the war crimes tribunals in Nuremberg, for example, failed—the Jews were not granted an amicus curiae or any other formal status in court.[138]

Cultural Restitution and Historical Consciousness

Alongside these historical and legal interpretive models so central to the four scholars' commitment to cultural restitution, which show intersections in their views on what it meant to reconstruct European Jewish culture, all four authors developed differing strategies for dealing with the Holocaust and its consequences. Arendt's unshakeable conviction that she had a duty to examine what had happened and try to confront it, which she perceived the moment she read the first reports on the catastrophe unfolding, inspired a historical assessment of the disaster that was, at the time, exceptionally incisive. Her many essays and her magnum opus, *The Origins of Totalitarianism*, are impressive testimony to this. She saw her political work for the JCR as bound up with a search for understanding, and by the late 1940s, both these ways of approaching events under Nazism were already shaping her historical judgment. During and after the war, Baron felt compelled to focus on forms of political organization aimed at "healing the wounds inflicted upon the Jewish community and culture by the Nazi barbarians."[139] While he considered the process of reflective confrontation with Nazism just as urgent as did Arendt, he stimulated other researchers to study Nazism and the Holocaust rather than subjecting the topic to historical analysis himself.[140] Instead, this catastrophic event reinforced his sense of obligation to strengthen Jewish community life in the United States.

One event that combined consideration of just what the JCR's field of action ought to be and the historical interpretations of Arendt and Baron was the conference "Problems of Research in the Study of the Jewish Catastrophe, 1939–1945," which took place in April 1949. This gathering was organized by the Conference on Jewish Relations in collaboration with YIVO and was held at the New School for Social Research to mark the ten-year anniversary of the *Jewish Social Studies* journal. As initiator and host of the conference, Salo Baron provided both introduction and moderation; Max Weinreich helped organize it; Philip Friedman, Joshua Starr, Hannah Arendt, Samuel Gringauz, Herbert Wechsler, and Solomon Bloom delivered the papers; Abraham Duker provided a commentary on them; and they were then discussed by Zosa Szajkowski, Mordecai Kosover, Paul Neurath, and Koppel Pinson.[141] It was the first conference in the United States to explicitly consider the general and methodological prerequisites for the investigation of the Holocaust in the English language. While it did not immediately achieve the goal of an academic institutionalization of Holocaust research, given its prominent attendees, profound insights, and detailed documentation, it can certainly be regarded as one of the first steps toward it. In a specific way it showed once again just how much the network established by Baron— within the orbit of the Conference on Jewish Relations, *Jewish Social Studies* and the JCR—became the engine, and hub, of a far-reaching attempt to respond and come to terms with Nazism and the Holocaust among Jewish intellectuals in New York.

It was the paper by Joshua Starr, still executive secretary of the JCR at the time, that most clearly addressed the link between the investigation of the Holocaust and efforts to salvage cultural treasures. While other speakers focused more on general problems involved in the scholarly confrontation with the topic, he provided an initial, detailed account of the history of Nazi cultural theft. Starr was the first to publicly present these events as an inherent feature of the Nazi plan of annihilation, highlighting the centrality of the topic during and after Hitler's rule.[142] Hannah Arendt's presentation operated on a different level. She reflected on the methodological and conceptual limits of traditional scholarship when facing an event compelling scholars in the humanities and social sciences to redefine their basic assumptions "regarding the course of the world and human behavior."[143] In many ways, she provided a preliminary glimpse of her later scholarly work on totalitarianism. Arendt analyzed the structure and character of the concentration and extermination camps established by the Germans, underlining the epistemological challenges thrown up by their investigation.[144] The main aim of her lecture was to create an awareness of the reality of the camps and their unprecedented modus operandi to show in what sense these camps had to be considered the "central institution of government" within totalitarianism, while their underlying structure challenged rationality, common sense, and utility.[145] Such a structure, Arendt asserted, was incompatible with the conventional logic of scholarly investigation and made it impossible to fit what had happened into the chronology and tropes of progress-oriented "human history."[146] No explanatory model could adequately grasp the "death factories"—"a human-made hell."[147] Neither war aims nor ideological, political, and economic goals— indeed, not even anti-Semitism—could fully explain this form of mass extermination. The "calculated establishment of a world of the dying in which nothing any longer made sense" and that aimed at the industrial "fabrication of corpses" defied imagination. And here she also reiterated publicly that this was a crime "which no punishment seems to fit."[148] Arendt was soon to capture these insights in the term *break with tradition*: "Totalitarian domination as an established fact, which in its unprecedentedness cannot be comprehended though the usual categories of political thought, and whose 'crimes' cannot be judged by traditional moral standards or punished within the legal framework of our civilization, has broken the continuity of Occidental history. The break in our tradition is now an accomplished fact."[149] Arendt managed to turn the experiences of her time into an epistemological analysis that sought to go beyond all established models of historical explanation and that led to a profound shift in her own thinking—a shift unusual at the time.

Baron had called for just such a revolution in thought in his brief opening address to the conference. This is one of the few sources to reveal his position on the necessity for a scholarly approach to the Holocaust and thus his own historical understanding. While his address remained sketchy, the fact that he agreed to organize this conference for the JSS anniversary in itself shows the centrality he ascribed to this topic and his desire to contribute to the emerging academic discourse about it. It was the duty of those present, he emphasized, "to subject the harrowing experiences of the great Catastrophe to rigorous scientific scrutiny." At the same time, he underlined his skepticism about such a project's chances of success. He felt that these historical events were still too recent for scholars to discern the great transformations resulting from them. Nonetheless, he called on his colleagues to not only focus on the preservation of the few remaining original sources on Nazism and the annihilation of the Jews but also take up the complex challenge involved in their investigation.[150] He explained this challenge on a number of levels. First, Baron underlined his reservations about attempts to fit the Holocaust into a historical series of anti-Jewish and anti-Semitic pogroms and massacres, thus declaring it the culmination of a centuries-long history of persecution, as was common at the time, especially among Zionist historians. In his account of the hallmarks of the German war of annihilation, which clearly distinguished it from earlier anti-Jewish and anti-Semitic events, he explicitly highlighted the singularity of this crime. Above all, he referred to its geographical scope: earlier "tragedies" had occurred within limited territories, but not the Holocaust, which had spanned most of Europe. Furthermore, no other form of persecution had entailed such a clear plan to annihilate all Jews everywhere, and never before had Jews been unable to save themselves through either conversion or other ways of renouncing their Judaism.[151] Second, like Arendt, Baron suggested that it was the Nazis' irrational motives, coupled with their totalistic intentions, that was truly novel. According to him, the Nazis' approach had contravened every military strategy, economic argument, and practical consideration, and its destructive impact had extended far beyond the national territory of Germany. It was thus misguided to compare Nazism with the Middle Ages, as many did at the time. Instead it was vital, according to Baron, to analyze *both* its historical roots and its unprecedented characteristics.[152]

This speech reveals a dualism typical of Baron's response to Nazi crimes at the time. Certainly he felt that action was necessary both to help the Jewish community and to advance a research agenda for coming generations dwelling in the United States. Yet while Baron gave crucial impetus to the nascent research on the Holocaust and Nazism, he did not see this as his own immediate scholarly priority. Overall it appears that he delegated this research to others, first and foremost his student Philip Friedman. The latter also spoke at the conference and presented an overview of the state of research, classifying and assessing all previously published documentary collections, first-hand accounts, and writings on the Second World War and the Holocaust.[153] Drawing on his experiences in Europe, where the different Jewish groups involved in early efforts to document the Holocaust tried to set up a transnational network inaugurating the field, he also called on the Conference on Jewish Relations to foster cooperative research and documentary projects between Israel, the United States, and Europe.[154] In this context, Friedman emphasized the urgent need to get trained scholars, chiefly historians, to work on this subject, which was still too dependent on the efforts of "amateurs."[155] He himself was quick to answer his own call, becoming with Baron's support a, if not the, pioneer of Holocaust research in the United States. Friedman is the author of several important publications in the field, covering case studies and methodological and bibliographical approaches, which were often introduced and brought to publication by Baron. In collaboration with the latter, he also developed seminars that integrated the Holocaust and Nazism into the history curriculum at Columbia University.[156]

In some ways, Gershom Scholem's approach resembled that of Baron. After returning from Germany, Scholem focused chiefly on his work for the Hebrew University with respect to restitution while stepping up his efforts to develop Israel's cultural and scholarly landscape. As late as 1967, he reflected on his commitment as follows: "I speak to you as one who has lived in Israel for the past forty-five years, and whose life has been bound up with the renaissance of the Jewish people in its old-new homeland in the Land of Israel."[157] At the same time, he distanced himself, in a way reminiscent of Baron, from the destructive realities of Europe, explaining this in light of his status as a contemporary witness. As a result, Scholem too composed virtually no essays and no scholarly texts on the Holocaust, either at the time of his direct confrontation with Nazi crimes or later.[158] He also avoided any extensive involvement in the Yad Vashem research and remembrance center in Jerusalem despite the offers made to him and his colleagues at the Hebrew University by Ben-Zion Dinur, one of the center's initiators. But Scholem had taken part in that institution's founding event, the "World Conference for the Study of the Shoah and Heroism," held in Jerusalem in July 1947 within the framework of the first "World Conference on Jewish Studies." The participants were asked to discuss the establishment of a national institution for research and commemoration of the Holocaust. At this conference, Scholem represented the group of historians, mostly of German Jewish background, who came to be known as the Jerusalem School, even though his main field of scholarship—Jewish mysticism and kabbalah—was generally distant from their research interests. These scholars pursued a historical-critical approach stemming from their education in Europe but were often committed to writing a unifying history of the Jewish people, a teleological narrative with Israel at its center.[159] Scholem's focus was different, yet he was part of this cohort, and he resembled these historians in his rejection of the impetus, generated by the conference, for systematic historical investigation of the Holocaust.[160] Similar to Baron, he explained, "I do not believe that we, the generation that experienced this event—which affected all that was dear to us—either directly ourselves or through our neighbors, can be in a position to draw the consequences as yet. However, the meaning of the holocaust must remain of overwhelming significance for the problematics of the Science of Judaism and, in my opinion, cannot be assessed too highly."[161]

A rather ambivalent stance—a personal reticence, coupled with a sense of the need to comprehensively investigate what had happened—seems to best describe Scholem's impulse to engage in a scholarly and public conversation about the Holocaust. Consonant with Arendt's thinking, he too underlined that "historical knowledge and conceptual clarity" about these events were the precondition for all thinking after the catastrophe,[162] but he was also convinced that the time for this had not yet come. In this vein, in 1952, he wrote to the German author Rudolf Hagelstange, "I am one of those who believes that a rationality that looks the events square in the face, that refuses to cover up or gloss over anything [. . .] must be rejected for now."[163] This diagnosis was clearly opposed to Arendt's project, as she articulated it later as the starting point for her study of totalitarianism: "This book is an attempt at understanding [. . .]. Comprehension however, does not mean denying the outrageous, deducing the unprecedented from precedents [. . .].

It means, rather, examining and bearing consciously the burden that events have placed upon us [. . .]. Comprehension, in short, means the unpremeditated, attentive facing up to, and resisting of, reality— whatever it may be or might have been."[164]

In this study, she set out her views on how best to deal with the destructive realities surrounding her. The book was a compilation of her political and historical analyses as they had developed from the early 1930s onward, shaped primarily by her experiential world in exile in France and, after her escape, the United States. Arendt's form of "facing up to and resisting of reality" was manifest in her writing, which expressed a spirit of shock and outrage. In 1948, she described this special approach and style as guided by sheer "fear of the concentration camp," which enabled her to avoid a paralyzed posture and led her to "keep thinking about horror" in order to achieve a mode of "perception of political contexts and the mobilization of political passions."[165] Arendt's engaged form of writing aroused opposition from the beginning. In her response to her critic Eric Voegelin, she defended her style by stating that an account of the concentration camps "*sine ira*" (without anger) would not result in objectivity but in the toleration of these camps' reality.[166] This political dimension of writing as an act of resistance is directly connected with Arendt's practical political work during this period. Like her writing, her activities too were geared toward facing the present as honestly as possible, understanding it as a warning, and shaping the future in light of it. Arendt discerned in action a crucial human mode that made it possible to participate in the world, to work out and advocate one's own views, and to enter into relationships with others— elements vital to ensuring human freedom.[167] These early postwar years cast an interesting light on Arendt's intellectual profile. The tense relationship between thought and action, one of Arendt's central concerns throughout her life, found its most specific expression during the period when she herself was most clearly challenged in this regard: in her work for the JCR and her concurrent quest to understand the rupture with tradition that had occurred.[168] More directly than all other protagonists of cultural restitution, we can discern the close connection between her thinking, writing, and political action during this period. She strove to advance the JCR agenda as head of the research group dedicated to drawing up lists of documents on European Jewish culture prior to 1939 and was JCR's executive secretary, which took her back to Germany for the first time after her forced flight. These activities were crucial to her search for historical understanding and judgment. She augmented her views on the structure and significance of Nazism and its consequences through intensive examination of the Nazis' systematic cultural theft, which she found to be a representative component of Nazi power and political practice. The negotiations on the JCR's status gave Arendt a new perspective on the legal situation of Jews and minorities within both national and international law—topics that had concerned her since her exile in France. In addition, she provided a comprehensive account of the principles at play in the extermination camps—namely, dehumanization and antirationality—thus demonstrating the historical singularity of the murder of the European Jews. She examined how one might portray and represent these crimes and cast light on the consequences of the disaster for the development of civilization in general, showing how Auschwitz had ruptured the parameters of conventional thought—ideas that are commonly associated with much later debates on the significance of the Holocaust. Arendt's writings after the war strive to relate the specific features of the Jews' situation under Nazism to human history as a whole. While acknowledging the particular position of the Jews, she was interested in the universal meaning of the events, eager to understand the structures, elements, and forms of political organization that had made politics "radically evil."[169]

Lucy Dawidowicz's desire to undertake historical research as a form of memorial work, an ambition she formulated, as discussed earlier in the chapter, while working for YIVO and during her trip to Germany, was rooted in motives similar to those underpinning Arendt's quest to understand. In the historical situation in which Dawidowicz found herself, she felt called upon to document and relate what had happened. Departing from her original plan, from the late 1930s, she dedicated herself entirely to the study of Jewish history: "Through the intervention of Jewish history, I became a Jewish Historian [. . .] at the time I was entering adulthood, Europe was rapidly overtaken by the darkness that was National Socialist Germany [. . .]. It was then that the unfolding events of Jewish history converted me into a devotee and eventually a practitioner of Jewish history."[170] Her "conversion" to history began following her research stay at the YIVO in Vilna. In the mid-1940s, in parallel to her work at that institution, Dawidowicz began her studies at Columbia University. It was during this period that events in Europe forced their way into her consciousness, molding Dawidowicz's subsequent endeavors: "We who lived in the safety of the United States, sheltered from the disasters that had overtaken the European Jews, were nevertheless beset by the turbulence of world events. Obsessively we followed the course of the war across the ocean. Our very existence hung on its outcome [. . .]. Consciousness of the war always intruded into our everyday existence, always persisted, even in moments of intense private joy."[171] Dawidowicz's description of the overwhelming psychological and emotional impact of the situation in Europe recalls Kazin's account of Hannah Arendt's life around the same time. From now on, Dawidowicz too devoted herself entirely to the fate of the European Jews. This is apparent among other things in her dedicated contribution to Max Weinreich's work on his 1946 monograph, *Hitler's Professors*, which he had started during the war.[172] Among other things, this study of scholarship and scholars under Nazism and their collusion in the systematic murder of Jews examines Alfred Rosenberg's Institute for Research on the Jewish Question in Frankfurt. Dawidowicz and Weinreich learned about the predatory raids carried out by Rosenberg's task force, the main profiteer of the library plunder of Vilna. The two scholars not only published one of the first comprehensive studies on Nazi policies; as they pursued their research, they also brought to light information of relevance to the search for the YIVO library.[173] And it was not just YIVO that benefited from the research undertaken for Weinreich's book. Arendt too cooperated with Weinreich while composing the Tentative Lists for the Commission, making use of the material and documents that Dawidowicz and Weinreich had available to them. In a review for the widely read Jewish journal *Commentary*, she called the book "the best guide to the nature of Nazi terror that I have read so far."[174] The collaborative work with Weinreich was Dawidowicz's first step into her new profession as a historian. When she realized during her later work in Offenbach that she herself would not be able to rebuild the Yiddish life of Vilna, she resolved to dedicate herself to its legacy and commemoration: "In the course of my melancholy work [. . .] I came to realize that all we can do is to remember and, [. . .] to create out of our memories lasting monuments of remembrance—poems and stories, memoirs and history. It is the only way through which the past, irrevocably destroyed, can survive."[175]

She devoted herself to this task after returning to the United States in December 1947. In contrast to Scholem and Baron, she viewed her personal status as witness as a kind of inescapable obligation.[176] Over the next few years, Dawidowicz developed the methodological toolkit and collated the empirical material needed to take the first steps toward writing an integrated history of the Holocaust. The special feature of her approach was her attempt to reconcile the criteria of historical objectivity and data-based facticity with an obligation to the dead and their remembrance—and thus to convey the specific vantage point from which she wrote. In his review of her later magnum opus, *The War against the Jews*, Irving Howe emphasized the outstanding effect of her form of writing:

> Mrs. Dawidowicz' "The War Against the Jews" comes to us as a major work of synthesis, providing for the first time a full account of the holocaust not merely as it completed the Nazi vision but as it affected the Jews of Eastern Europe. [. . .] It is a work committed to the sovereignty of fact [. . .] and emerging out of an awareness that no theory about the holocaust can be as important as a sustained confrontation with the holocaust itself. [. . .] This book comes to seem an exemplar of that Jewish belief—or human delusion—that somehow there may still be a moral use in telling what it meant to live or die in the 20th century.[177]

This book was Dawidowicz's most enduring contribution to the historiography of the Holocaust. In 1981, she added a comprehensive overview of the historiography: *The Holocaust and the Historians*. Always concerned that the history of the six million murdered Jews risked being forgotten, in her texts, she sought to underline that the Holocaust had been a key objective, a core feature, of Nazism, one planned and carried out by Adolf Hitler systematically and on a long-term basis.[178] This interpretation of the Holocaust, later categorized as intentionalist, is bound up with Dawidowicz's personal history during and after the war.[179] This history included the fact that, particularly when it came to Jewish Vilna, she herself was familiar with a steadily worsening history of persecution and annihilation during the German occupation, a history she found to be confirmed by her experience in postwar Europe. But in her collaboration with Max Weinreich, we already find an interpretation of the Holocaust as a plan of annihilation drawn up by the Nazis, and Hitler himself, from the very beginning of Nazi rule, and systematically carried out following the invasion of Poland in 1939. Dawidowicz considered the exclusion of Jews' perspective from the historical examination of Nazism until the late 1970s a grave failure, as she set out in *The Holocaust and the Historians*. This too prompted her, time and again, to place the Holocaust at the center of her historical appraisal of Nazism and the Second World War.

She took her lead from the traditions of Eastern European historiography taught at YIVO, particularly that of Simon Dubnow: she favored social scientific approaches that tried to honor the Jewish perspective and examine it in its social contexts. In her studies on Eastern European Jewry, she made use of material from YIVO that had been restituted via Offenbach or that belonged to survivors from Vilna.[180] At the same time, she was eager to use her scholarly work to create a place of commemoration for the Eastern European Jewish world in the United States. She herself described the historiography of the Holocaust as a "secular act of bearing witness to Auschwitz and to the mystery of Jewish survival."[181] With the help of anthologies such as *The Golden Tradition: Jewish Life and Thought in Eastern Europe* (1967), in which Dawidowicz published letters, autobiographical and literary texts, and essays by Eastern European Jews over several centuries, through the establishment of the Fund for the Translation of Jewish Literature, intended to make the world of Yiddish writing accessible to the American public, and through her work at YIVO, she sought to preserve the Jewish heritage of Vilna and Eastern Europe for future generations.

* * *

The experiences garnered by the four figures considered here—as they strove to salvage Jewish cultural property in Europe—continued to exercise an effect in their writings and subsequent activities. The two key studies by Arendt (*The Origins of Totalitarianism*) and Dawidowicz (*The War against the Jews*) reveal traces of these experiences. Because both of them were at the beginning of their scholarly careers during the Second World War, it is no surprise that the historical caesura they experienced and perceived had a more direct influence on their thinking and writing than in the case of the older and more established historians Scholem and Baron. Both women wrote virtually all their important studies against the background of the upheavals of the twentieth century and their experiences of it—they were, as Enzo Traverso aptly put it in reference to Arendt, "a product of the 'dark times' of [their] century, an age of extremes of which Germany was the epicenter. The stages of [their] intellectual and political formation are the same as those that marked the European collapse: Nazism, and the exile, persecution and genocide of the Jews."[182] Both acquired the material foundations and sources for their writings partly from salvaged holdings, and they tackled issues that molded their thinking and action in the postwar period. In Arendt's case, it was the functional principles and mechanisms of the Nazi form of rule, culminating in the superordinate attempt to determine what legal and political constellation might facilitate human coexistence under conditions of human diversity; hers was a distinctly universalistic approach. Dawidowicz, meanwhile, spoke from the perspective of the particular Jewish experience of the Holocaust while examining the potential for the continuity and preservation of Eastern European Jewish traditions in the new environment of the United States—subject areas, as in Arendt's case, that were linked with her working life in the 1940s and 1950s. Gershom Scholem and Salo Baron, meanwhile, half a generation older, were confronted with Auschwitz and its consequences having already taught and worked in established academic contexts outside Europe for a lengthy period. They felt a sense of historical rupture as they learned of the disaster that had befallen Europe's Jews and the losses they had suffered. But it was mainly on the charitable and political levels that they sought to respond, doing all they could to support different welfare and political initiatives and salvage the precious cultural property they considered vital to survival and intellectual development in the "shifting centers" of Jewish existence. In accordance with their interests and status as intellectuals, in a number of ways they strove to foster and safeguard Jewish scholarship and culture in the United States and Israel after 1945. That such different figures as Arendt, Baron, Dawidowicz, and Scholem all chose to dedicate themselves to salvaging the Jewish cultural heritage had much to do with their interests, education, personal experience, and political beliefs. Their engagement led to a direct and very early confrontation with the destruction of Jewish life in Europe during a period whose overwhelming, ungraspable reality raised questions about the meaningfulness of all forms of political activity. This in turn paved the way for their subsequent thinking and acting in the wake of the civilizational rupture that had occurred.

Conclusion

The trial of Adolf Eichmann in Jerusalem in 1961 is generally regarded as the turning point that ushered in an international public awareness of the Holocaust in the postwar period. Here, in contrast to the 1946 Nuremberg trials of major war criminals, the discussion of Nazi crimes foregrounded the Jewish experience and changed views of the Second World War. In its aftermath the systematic murder of the European Jews was increasingly considered its negative epicenter. In the 1960s, this boosted the scholarly investigation and documentation of the Holocaust, indirectly promoting the integration of victims' testimony into the corpus of sources. Through its broad coverage and manifold reverberations in the media, literature, and scholarship, the trial played a crucial part in shaping the Holocaust's role in the collective memory of Europe, Israel, and the United States. In later debate, this legitimate emphasis on the trial's significance to the historiography and public consciousness of the Holocaust led to a failure to acknowledge the many earlier efforts to document, publicize, and come to terms with Nazi crimes. A variety of scholars long persisted in claiming that after the war, victims, perpetrating societies, and Allied liberators had lapsed into a state of silence and withdrawal while throwing themselves into reconstruction and focusing on the future.[1] In the last few years, this narrative and periodization of Holocaust awareness and historiography has been challenged, while the "silence" of the postwar years has increasingly been revealed as "myth."[2] Researchers have uncovered widespread attempts, on many different levels, to respond to the catastrophe in the early aftermath of World War II. In particular, Jewish activists worldwide engaged in legal and political initiatives intended to deal with Nazi crimes and their consequences. They concurrently dedicated themselves to documentation and commemoration in an attempt to record the events and mourn the dead.

JCR's efforts to achieve restitution are a powerful and important expression of this will to engage politically with Nazi rule and confront its reality in the comparatively short period between 1945 and 1952. Eventually, the Cold War and the nuclear threat it launched into the foreground of public attention dimmed the urge to discuss the recent past so typical of the early postwar period, prompting a shift of focus to the present and future. In addition, the reluctance of majority societies in Europe and the United States to engage with past crimes and their meaning helped discourage Jewish groups and individuals from taking action. Many different factors contributed to the suppression and eventual forgetting of the many voices calling for, and trying to achieve, greater awareness of the Holocaust from the mid-1940s onward. Both the history and later marginalization of the JCR are an indication of these realities, providing new insights into the political and discursive character of the postwar period and the long-term development of Holocaust memory after 1945.

In an endeavor unique within Jewish diplomacy—one that united many different political and religious factions as well as individuals and organizations from Europe, the United States, and Israel—the JCR initiated far-reaching legal discussions with the goal of restituting and salvaging what was left of European Jewish culture. This was consonant with an overall tendency evident after Germany's capitulation: it was the prosecution of Nazi crimes—whether through trials or negotiations on restitution, indemnification, and compensation—that prompted sustained efforts by the various Jewish interest groups and attracted general public attention.[3] The Allies hoped to achieve the democratic reconsolidation of Germany by enforcing criminal prosecution and material restoration, thus avoiding the political mistakes inherent in the peace treaties signed after the First World War. For all parties involved, the law was both the only means available and the framework of choice for dealing with Nazi crimes. Inherent in this approach was the attempt to create a form of transitional justice that would convert the monstrous suffering and abuse of laws, which were ultimately incomprehensible, immeasurable, and unquantifiable, into nonequivalent forms of compensation, restitution, and judicial prosecution.[4] Many Jewish activists realized during the first few years after the war that the legal sphere was the aptest tool for confronting the ultimate genocide. The JCR's activities were significant in this context but were soon to be overshadowed by subsequent events, particularly the agreement between West Germany, Israel, and the Claims Conference in Luxembourg. The tendency to disregard the JCR's role prevailed despite the fact that its fight for representation and status for the Jewish collectivity helped bring about this agreement, a fact that is yet to be adequately acknowledged. The JCR's most significant success was the international recognition of this collectivity as a nonstate legal subject, as expressed in the organization's entrustment. As the official representatives of the Jewish collectivity, the JCR and its umbrella organization, the JRSO, were able to articulate its demands with respect to restitution and compensation vis-à-vis the initially responsible Allied occupation authorities and later the German states. This endowed the Jews with an equal voice within national and international legal frameworks, transcending the latter's intergovernmental structure and paving the way for the Claims Conference, which later operated on similar premises.[5] The number of eminent individuals involved in the JCR, the degree of its international networking, and the results of its activities into the 1950s are testimony to the range and wide impact of its political work. Its research committee provided a literal archive of Jewish collections and cultural institutions in Europe as they existed before 1939. These documents provide the very first basis for provenance research and remain valuable to this day. The same goes for the JCR's meticulous research on the agents of Nazi looting and plunder. The organization's executive organs gave the Jewish victims of Nazism a legal standing, ensuring that, rather than remaining in the possession of the perpetrating state, as provided for by the escheat principle of conventional jurisprudence, heirless Jewish property in Germany was instead returned to Jewish ownership. This entailed a widening of the concept of restitution, overcoming its initial equation with the return of items to their original location. The definition promoted by JCR instead entailed the return of items to the people. Since those entitled were expelled from Europe and had found refuge in and migrated to places all over the world, the material remains had to follow them.

From Europe, JCR staff initiated the transfer of well over five hundred thousand objects. In addition, they managed to ensure that relevant German institutions received official appeals to search through their holdings for stolen goods. They instigated crucial steps forward within the jurisprudence on restitution after the Second World War—despite failing to achieve some of their objectives. Just as relevant were the JCR's contributions to the construction and development of the community centers, research institutions, libraries, and archives established after 1945 in the new centers of Jewish cultural and scholarly activity, through which it actively helped shape the future of Jewish life after the Holocaust. Objects and books from Europe were transferred to more than thirty countries and placed at the service of community life, research, exhibitions, and commemorative work.

JCR members doubted that there was a viable future for Jewish life in Europe. Virtually none of them could envisage a revival of Jewish culture in the place of its total destruction. With respect to Eastern Europe, few believed there was any prospect of reconstructing a Jewish community life under the political conditions prevailing in the Soviet sphere of influence. This assessment seemed corroborated by the waves of Eastern European Jewish refugees who fled to DP camps in the western German occupation zones after the pogroms that had taken place in Poland against returnees from Nazi internment or temporary places of refuge in the Soviet Union. JCR members in the West also noted with alarm the failure of attempts to establish Jewish institutions, such as the Museum for Jewish Art and Culture planned by Abraham Sutzkever and Shmerke Kaczerginski in Vilna, which was rigorously supervised and finally closed down by the Soviet authorities. With almost no exceptions, then, the JCR leadership refrained from restituting cultural property to Eastern and Central Europe. Time and again, they highlighted the manifest disproportionality between the stolen and recovered Jewish treasures originating in Poland, the Ukraine, the Baltic Countries, and Russia and the number of Jews still living there. The history of the YIVO in Vilna reinforced their skepticism. The institute, once the focal point of the Eastern European tradition of Jewish scholarship, was never to be rebuilt after the Second World War. Vilna had forever lost its status as *Yerushalayim de Lite* (Jerusalem of Lithuania), while the many rare and valuable objects of Jewish provenance that had remained in the city did not end up serving the needs of Jewish congregations in Lithuania, Poland, or the Soviet Union; many of them disappeared into state libraries and archives. The work of the Vilna YIVO was continued in New York: to this day, the institute there views its mission as a continuation of its Vilna predecessor's work and as a reminder of its disastrous history. Books and materials from Vilna constitute a collection of great symbolic significance there.[6] All in all, the situation in Central and Eastern

Europe left Jews with little hope that it would ever again be home to a flourishing and autonomous Jewish cultural and intellectual life. As most saw it, the region had been transformed into a vast graveyard.

Due to strategic and practical considerations, there was a willingness to leave certain recovered holdings in Western Europe, Germany, and Austria chiefly to facilitate a community life for the Jews remaining there, but by the late 1940s, all those involved in the JCR mission agreed that they must focus on fostering Jewish cultural (re)construction outside continental Europe. Subsequent postwar history was to refute such negative assessments of Jews' future, particularly in Germany and Austria, often prompting retrospective criticism of the JCR's strict distribution policy.[7] From the perspective of those responsible, however, the situation immediately after the war looked very different. No one could predict how Germany as a state would develop, and the fear of Anti-Semitism persisted. Even more alarming was the fact that several hundred thousand *heirless* objects were at issue here. Amid the clash of Western Allied, Soviet, German, and Jewish interests, there was a danger that these items would be lost to state and private institutions, as had occurred with millions of other books, paintings, and art objects of Jewish origin that the JCR was unable to acquire. Until 1952, the Jewish congregations in western Germany were in no state to convince anyone of their likely growth. The decision to transfer as many recovered treasures as possible out of Europe to a new environment was also linked with the fact that the majority of JCR representatives had themselves fled from there. Given the situation at the time and their historical experience, they opted not to return from Israel or the United States to their former homeland.

Seen from a broader perspective, the JCR's activities were much more than a legal practice in response to war. The objects of which its staff took charge played a meaningful part in shaping collective processes of remembrance after the Holocaust. Like monuments, the books, documents, and ritual objects preserved elements of the culture and history of Jewish Europe, so brutally truncated by the Nazis, for the future. Having been amassed in various locations in an arbitrary way or in accordance with the Nazi strategy of plunder and scholarship, these remnants ended up at the Offenbach Depot as an undistinguishable mass. Not only did the JCR reconstitute their initial status as Jewish cultural property; the process of rescue it initiated assigned them the status of memory objects. Through a global pattern of distribution, JCR officials created an invisible net made up of these European material traces, thus building a transnational space of memory. By allocating the holdings to institutions such as the National Library of Israel, Yad Vashem, and the present-day Israel Museum in Jerusalem; the Leo Baeck Institutes in Jerusalem, London, and New York; YIVO, Yeshiva University, and JTS in New York; the Wiener Library in London; and the Centre de Documentation Juive Contemporaine in Paris, the JCR played a significant part in the development of new research and commemorative activities after the war.

Besides their preserving function as containers of the past, the books and objects in the care of the JCR entailed another layer of memory. The history of their home institutions' destruction and their owners' murder remained inscribed in them. Often the salvaged objects were the last material traces of the victims, whom they recalled either implicitly or explicitly through ex libris, dedications, and stamps. The process of their restitution often blurred the boundaries between object and former owner, with the books' rescue functioning as a metonym for the liberation of the murdered from their anonymity. In *The Origins of Totalitarianism*, Hannah Arendt explained the reality of anonymous deaths in the German extermination camps as one of the most disturbing hallmarks of Nazi rule: "Grief and remembrance are forbidden [. . .] The Western world has hitherto, even in its darkest periods, granted the slain enemy the right to be remembered as a self-evident acknowledgement of the fact that we are all men (and *only* men)." In the camps, however, "death itself [was made] anonymous" as a means to "take away the individual's own death, proving that henceforth nothing belonged to him and he belonged to no one."[8] To a degree, the preservation of books and other material remains helped avoid this outcome, preventing their former owners from vanishing without a trace. As contemporaries saw it, however, the rescue related not merely to individuals but to the entire collectivity of the Jews. This belief was reflected in the commemorative events, services, and ceremonies held when the treasures were received in their new homes. Similar to the processions organized in Tel Aviv and Jerusalem to mark the interment of urns containing ashes from the European death camps, official processions accompanied the burial of fragments of Torah scrolls, ritual objects, and liturgical textiles from Europe's ruined synagogues. Tens of thousands of people took part in funeral services arranged by the Israeli ministry of religious affairs, which were held on Mount Zion in Jerusalem. In August 1949, after the War of Independence, similar numbers turned up at the Jerusalem railroad station to greet the first incoming train from Tel Aviv, which was loaded with several dozen crates of books from Poland.[9] Communities and institutions in the United States also honored the collections entrusted to them with ceremonies and memorial exhibitions. The festive handling of the treasures highlighted the meaning attached to them; their rescue was seen as an expression of the survival and continuity of the "People of the Book."

The scholars involved in the JCR and YIVO operated in a field highly charged with symbolic meaning. Through their tireless efforts, Hannah Arendt, Salo Baron, Lucy Dawidowicz, and Gershom Scholem saved countless books and religious objects from Europe. They negotiated with the American military government, the State Department, German authorities, and the directors of museums and libraries over rights to the Jewish cultural heritage; scoured the holdings of German institutions for stolen property; and traveled throughout Europe to unearth Nazi caches. This chapter in the biography of these four scholars is little known. Yet for each of them, this work was what confronted them most directly with Nazi atrocities. And for all of them, this experience molded their conception of history and memory.

In the case of both Scholem and Baron, their work at the JCR became the starting point for their many years of cultural and academic engagement in the new centers of Jewish life after the Holocaust. They applied themselves with tremendous energy to the promotion of institutions of higher learning and the strengthening of the Jewish cultural infrastructure. In different ways, they sought to establish these institutions in the US and Israel as successors to their European forerunners and were deeply invested in securing and nurturing the intellectual, spiritual, and cultural legacy of the European past. Beyond this, both believed that the historical distance from the events of Nazism was still too short to engage with them on a scholarly, analytical level despite their disciplinary backgrounds. Neither Scholem nor Baron made explicit contributions to the nascent study of the Holocaust. Certainly, they were aware of the findings of this research and commented on it, while Baron also publicly promoted relevant research and aided its practitioners. But due to their experiences—and here their work for the JCR played an important role—they balked at involving themselves actively in the attempt to process these events through the discipline of history. As Scholem's travel journal and numerous letters attest, his confrontation with postwar Europe and the ubiquitous sense of emptiness he perceived there amounted to such a dramatic caesura in his life that he felt compelled to concentrate on the fate of Israel and delve into the worlds of Jewish mysticism, his life's work. We see the same kind of development in the case of Baron. His increasing dedication to the Jewish community and Jewish scholarly life in the United States from the 1950s onward seems to have been nurtured by his knowledge of the utter destruction of the former center of Jewish life. He was keen to invest in the future, to "help [the Jews] emerge from that nightmare of ages."[10] Baron had begun his engagement in Jewish politics in the 1930s with great dedication to supporting Jewish life in Europe, while later he sought to resurrect it, but his deepening personal confrontation with what had occurred convinced him that it had pulled the rug from under such visions. Instead, he devoted his energies to supporting those centers where, he believed, Jewish life could continue. This manifestly impacted on his scholarly work: he continued to approach the writing of Jewish history as he had done between the wars, with a focus on those elements connected with survival and development rather than destruction and annihilation.

Hannah Arendt and Lucy Dawidowicz present us with a quite different picture. They were younger than Scholem and Baron and less academically established at the time of their work for the JCR and YIVO, and they responded far more explicitly to the experience of the Holocaust, which was to forge their entire outlook and intellectual stature. It clearly prompted them to rethink the premises of their research. Departing from her prewar educational career, during the war and after, Dawidowicz decided to devote her future research entirely to the history of the Holocaust and use her writing and publications to commemorate the murdered Jews of Europe, particularly its eastern regions. Her career path was directly shaped by her experiences in the YIVO in Vilna, where she herself had carried out research between 1938 and 1939, and her years of collaboration with Max Weinreich at the YIVO in New York, while the impressions she gained during her trip to Germany in 1947 exercised a profound influence on her writing as well. Over time, she developed a specific approach to Jewish history. In one of her late methodological analyses entitled "What Is the Use of Jewish History?," she elaborated a concept that we might very well apply to her own work. Here she proclaimed the advantages of history writing driven by "ahavat yisrael, that distinctive Jewish concept of love of one's own people, which entails not only a sense of identity with the Jewish past and an involvement in its present, but also a commitment to a Jewish future."[11] Dawidowicz was convinced that "personal commitments do not distort, but instead they enrich, historical writing." Her work expresses this form of commitment, be it through her focus on making sources available and keeping traditions and narratives from the Yiddish realm alive or her dedication to the writing and interpretation of the Holocaust in Jewish history. This dual perspective on the preservation of sources, the material basis of thought and tradition, and on history writing from an explicitly Jewish standpoint is anchored in her experiences with YIVO during the 1930s and 1940s.

Hannah Arendt too moved away from her initial interest in philosophy toward political theory and history while living through the events of the Nazi period and its aftermath. Though she did not explicitly make the Holocaust her main field of research, it informed and deeply influenced her intellectual work. In their famous exchange of letters after Arendt's 1963 publication of her report *Eichmann in Jerusalem*, Gershom Scholem assailed her for the lack of "ahavat yisrael" in her writing. He felt that this very commitment to the people, which Dawidowicz called the engine of her thinking, was missing in Arendt's interpretation of the Holocaust and especially her tone in the book on the Eichmann trial.[12] As is widely known, it was not only Scholem who criticized Arendt's approach. Her report caused an international stir; Jewish critics mainly took offence at either her controversial perspective on Jews' behavior under Nazi repression or her universalizing reading of the Holocaust as "crimes against mankind committed on the body of the Jewish people," which seemed to blur the boundaries of Jewish victimhood.[13] Beyond the question of an adequate assessment of Arendt's report, the broader context of her reception history is interesting here: we can detect a development that resembles the structure and periodization of Holocaust awareness in general, as sketched at the beginning of these remarks, one that is paralleled in the history of the perception of the JCR itself. The copious research on Arendt has paid far too little attention to her far-sighted analyses of the significance and consequences of Nazi rule and the Holocaust, which appeared in essays written between 1943 and 1951 and in synthesized form in her pioneering study of totalitarianism. Like-wise, few scholars have written more than a few lines on her years of work for the JCR, though this was when she developed most of the ideas that would inform *The Origins of Totalitarianism*. The majority of re-searchers failed to acknowledge postwar initiatives of the kind pursued in the context of the JCR. In much the same way, Arendt's report on the Eichmann trial prompted many scholars (including Scholem) to forget what she had previously written and done. Upon publication, Arendt's *Eichmann in Jerusalem: A Report on the Banality of Evil* gained so much critical attention that it was to dominate how others viewed her his-torical assessment of the Holocaust. As a result, there was a tendency to diminish the validity of essays more explicit in this context, such as "Or-ganized Guilt," "The Concentration Camps," "The Rights of Man," and "Social Science Techniques," which were written much earlier, and ulti-mately, her book on totalitarianism as well.[14] The reception of her report on Eichmann tended to blot out these elements in Arendt's thought. We gain a different picture of her commitment to things Jewish and her in-sights into the devastating events of Jewish history in the twentieth cen-tury if we consider her early texts and her tremendous efforts to secure a viable legal framework for Jews and preserve their collective cultural heritage. It is only when we consider these experiential contexts and writings of the 1940s that we can fully grasp Arendt's contribution to the understanding of the disasters of twentieth-century European history.

Having recapitulated the history of the JCR and its protagonists, two elements relevant to our understanding of postwar Jewish existence stand out. First, this historical review shows the immense commit-ment to political activity among Jewish survivors, emigrants, refugees, politicians, and scholars resident in and outside Europe in response to war and the Holocaust. No silence prevailed here. On the contrary—particularly when it came to the legal sphere—we find a broad range of initiatives launched by Jewish organizations across the world to stimulate and help shape processes of appraisal and punishment.

The activities of the JCR, undertaken as a genuinely transnational endeavor, are a small but important element of these initiatives. Before the Cold War brought these activities to a standstill, within just under five years, Jewish organizations had chalked up significant successes when it came to recognition of the Jews' voice in international relations and international law. Second, the accomplishments of Otzrot HaGolah, the JCR, and YIVO highlight the close link between restitution and memory, which was due to the specific items in their charge and, in important part, to the efforts of key figures working for these organizations. They recognized that salvaging the material repositories of European Jewish culture paved the way for a rethinking of Jewish historical consciousness and memory after catastrophe, which in turn made them engaged promoters of memorialization, documentation, and Jewish scholarship. The rescue of books and manuscripts provided a material ground for Holocaust commemoration in the new worlds of postwar Jewry, and it facilitated a discussion on the future of Jewish existence in relation to its manifold European roots, a future understood as a countermovement against the cultural genocide inflicted by the Nazis. The herculean efforts to rescue the remnants of a European Jewish past that had faced ultimate destruction brought to the fore crucial aspects of postwar Jewish existence; here rupture and loss become just as visible as the dedicated efforts to ensure continuity and survival.

ACKNOWLEDGMENTS

This book is a translated and thoroughly revised version of a German-language book that was originally published with Vandenhoeck & Ruprecht in 2013. It owes more than can be described to the support, inspiration, critical questioning, and encouragement of numerous people at many different places.

Above all, I am obliged to Dan Diner, my academic adviser, who not only introduced me to the world of Jewish history but also inspired the topic of my research and was fully committed to patiently guiding me through the whole process of writing my first book. It has benefitted immensely from his astute critique and comments, and I am more than grateful to him for giving me the opportunity to pursue this work at the Dubnow Institute in Leipzig, Germany. It was due to its former deputy director Susanne Zepp's relentless encouragement that I embarked on the journey of composing and writing this book, and I thank her for her empathy and continuous help.

I owe special thanks to Atina Grossmann, Michael Brenner, Birgit Erdle, Raphael Gross, Eli Lederhendler, Paul Mendes-Flohr, Hannes Siegrist, and Nancy Sinkoff, who critically assessed my work at different stages and offered steady support. My sincere thanks for their suggestions and guidance as well as provisions of important material go to Irene Aue-Ben-David, Grace Cohen Grossman, Julie-Marthe Cohen, David Heredia, Frits J. Hoogewoud, Marie-Luise Knott, Jürgen Lillteicher, Katharina Rauschenberger, Gil Rubin, Dov Schidorsky, and Hansjakob Ziemer. Special thanks go to Natasha Gordinsky who is a devoted discussion partner and has helped me sharpen my perspective many times. I also want to especially thank Dana Herman for her exceptional collegiality. Our shared passion for the history of the JCR was the engine for a remarkably open discussion on relevant sources and contents—an experience I am truly grateful for.

I could not have written this book without the ongoing support, critical comments, and friendship provided by a great number of former and present colleagues at Dubnow Institute. Nicolas Berg and Laura Jockusch were the most committed readers and constructive critics of the German-language manuscript, who generously shared their insights into the complex political and intellectual configurations of the postwar period in Europe. Moreover, I express my profound thanks to David Jünger and Anna Pollmann, with whom I joined forces when we were in the process of writing, and to Judith Ciminski, Friederike Gremler, Marion Hammer, Klaus Kempter, Markus Kirchhoff, Ulrike Kramme, Thomas Meyer, Felix Pankonin, Grit N. Scheffer, and Charlotte Trottier. My warm thanks go to Petra Gamke-Breitschopf, who aided me, without tiring, in turning the German manuscript into a book and was extremely supportive when I was working to ensure that there would be an English-language translation.

I thank the staff of the many libraries and archives I worked at for their invaluable help and am most thankful to the Fritz Thyssen Foundation, who enabled me to pursue my research in those institutions in the United States, Israel, and different places in Europe.

After the publication of my German book, the time as a postdoc fellow at the Franz Rosenzweig Minerva Research Center, Hebrew University, Jerusalem, opened up new horizons to me. It introduced me to an extraordinary group of colleagues who also work in the field of Jewish material culture and who provided me with important insights and new material for the English edition. I want to thank, among others, Caroline Jessen, Anna Holzer-Kawałko, Enrico Lucca, and Bilha Shilo. The Rosenzweig Center's former director Yfaat Weiss was the driving force behind this collaborative and collegial exchange, and in her capacity as head of the Dubnow Institute, she continues to support my work and academic development with a dedication that I am deeply grateful for.

The translation of the German-language book was generously funded by the Börsenverein des Deutschen Buchhandels, the Fritz Thyssen Foundation, VG Wort, and the Federal Foreign Office, which awarded the book with the prize "Geisteswissenschaften international" and enabled me to take on the challenge of returning to and revising it. I am very thankful for this possibility.

It is a great honor for me that my monograph is included in the Goldstein-Goren Book Series in American Jewish History at New York University Press. I am indebted to Hasia Diner and her enthusiasm in supporting this project. Lisha Nadkarni from NYU Press helped me, with great devotion, to navigate the publication process, and I want to thank her for her patience and thoughtfulness in facilitating this transatlantic endeavor. I also want to thank Lauren Conkling and her team for their commitment to giving the manuscript its final edit and form.

My translator Alex Skinner did a tremendous job when turning the German version into English. He showed outstanding sensitivity for the topic, found the right tone for the manuscript, and was professional in every sense of the word. I want to express my appreciation for his outstanding patience and openness. I also want to dearly thank my student assistant Juliane Weiss, who was of invaluable help in the entire process of creating, revising, and polishing the final English manuscript.

Finally, I am deeply grateful to my family and friends. Without their encouragement, help, and belief in me, neither the German- nor the English-language edition of this book would have seen the light of the day. I thank with all my heart Friederike Ankele, Alexander Gallas, Verena Gallas, Gero Götschenberg, Tasja Langenbach, Christiane Lindstrot, Anke Lutze, Andrea Kirchner, Patricia Szilagyi, Alexandra Tyrolf, and especially my father Andreas Gallas. Last but not least, my warmest thanks go to my husband, sharpest critic, and greatest supporter, Lutz Fiedler.

This book is dedicated to the memory of my mother, Olivia Gallas, who did not live to witness the publication of either volume. It was she who taught me the curiosity, self-criticism, and perseverance that I needed to complete this project.

NOTES

INTRODUCTION

1. Reflecting the primary sources I draw on here, the historical place name of Vilna (German *Wilna*), present-day Vilnius, Lithuania, is used throughout.
2. Lengthy passages from the expressive diary Sutzkever wrote after delivering his testimony in Nuremberg are quoted in Leftwich, *Abraham Sutzkever*, 89–90. See also Jockusch, "Justice at Nuremberg?," 108.
3. See Abraham Sutzkever's testimony before the Nuremberg Military Tribunal on February 27, 1946, in International Military Tribunal, *Trial of the Major War Crimes, vol. 8*, 302–8, here 303–4.
4. Ibid., 303.
5. Lemkin, "Acts Constituting a General (Transnational) Danger," here "Acts of Vandalism."
6. Sutzkever, "Vilna Ghetto," 262.
7. Ibid., 263.
8. The Paper Brigade's work is meticulously described by Sutzkever in ibid., esp. 262–65; and by Herman Kruk, another Polish-Jewish political activist and librarian, who worked in the Ghetto library in Vilna. See Kruk, *Last Days of the Jerusalem*, 212–325. David Fishman recently devoted a book-length study to the intriguing history of the Paper Brigade: Fishman, *Book Smugglers*.
9. As Sutzkever noted on his arrival; quoted in Fishman, *Book Smugglers*, 139.
10. Dawidowicz, *From That Place and Time*, 316.
11. Jockusch, "Justice at Nuremberg?," 113.
12. See as examples of a thorough discussion of the status of books in Jewish life at the time Feierstein and Fuhrman, "Paper Bridge"; Feierstein, "Nor er redt nisht arois keyn vort"; Shavit, *Hunger for the Printed Word*; Borin, "Embers of the Soul."
13. On the history of the Claims Conference, see Zweig, *German Reparations*; and Henry, *Confronting the Perpetrators*. From a broader perspective, see Sagi, *German Reparations*.
14. See Morsink, "Cultural Genocide." For a detailed exploration of the link between cultural destruction and genocide, see Confino, *World without Jews*.
15. D. Diner, "Memory and Restitution," 15.
16. Representative of the many contributions made on this subject are Dean, Goschler, and Ther, *Robbery and Restitution*; Deak, Gross, and Judt, *Politics of Retribution*; Bazyler and Alford, *Holocaust Restitution*; Zweig, "Restitution,

Reparations and Indemnification"; Goda, *Rethinking Holocaust Justice*; Goschler, *Wiedergutmachung*; Goschler, *Schuld und Schulden*; and Lillteicher, *Raub, Recht und Restitution*.

17. See esp. Barkan, *Guilt of Nations*; Torpey, "Making Whole What Has Been Smashed"; Torpey, *Politics and the Past*; Goschler, *Schuld und Schulden*; and D. Diner and Wunberg, *Restitution and Memory*.

18. The eleven "Washington Principles," published in December 1998, were the outcome of a conference held in Washington, DC, featuring government representatives from forty-four countries and various nongovernmental organizations. They discussed the restitution of art stolen by the Nazis and proposed binding regulations compelling institutions to search for and restitute such items. These guidelines were set out in more detail at conferences in Vilnius (2000) and Prague (2009) and extended to include cultural goods, archival material, and Judaica. This culminated in the Theresienstadt Declaration, which built on the Washington principles, further extending the range of cultural property to be identified and restituted. The leading examples of research carried out at the behest of cultural institutions are Dehnel, *Jüdischer Buchbesitz als Raubgut*; Dehnel, *NS-Raubgut in Bibliotheken*; Bertz and Dorrmann, *Raub und Restitution*; Cohen and Heimann-Jelinek, *Neglected Witnesses*; and Heimann-Jelinek, *Was übrig blieb*. Austrian studies include Reininghaus, *Recollecting*; Hall, Köstner, and Werner, *Geraubte Bücher*; Brüggen, Schulze, and Müller, *Raubkunst?* For initial, comprehensive accounts instigating public debate and highlighting legal perspectives in this context, see Hoffmann, *Art and Cultural Heritage*. New directions in provenance research are discussed in Feigenbaum and Reist, *Provenance*. For the commitment of the Claims Conference in the field, see the webpage *Claims Conference/WRJO: Looted Art and Cultural Property* at http://art.claimscon.org. It provides an overview of their agenda, their work, resources for research on cultural property, and a news section.

19. See the pioneering studies on the theft of art and culture by Nicholas, *Rape of Europa*; Beker, *Plunder of Jewish Property*; Alford, *Nazi Plunder*; Heuss, *Kunst- und Kulturgutraub*; Volkert, "Der Kulturgutraub"; Lauterbach, *The Central Collecting Point in Munich*; Steinberg, *Orphaned Art*; and Huyssen, Rabinbach, and Shalem, *Nazi-Looted Art and Its Legacies*. For one of the first accounts of book destruction, see Rose, *Holocaust and the Book*. Two pathbreaking and comprehensive studies on theft and cultural restitution from a transnational and *longue durée* perspective are Greenfield, *Return of Cultural Treasures*; and Simpson, *Spoils of War*.

20. The most important publications in the field to be published after the first German version of this book are Amit, "Largest Jewish Library in the World"; Glickman, *Stolen Worlds*; Labendz, *Jewish Property after 1945*; Lustig, "Who Are to Be the Successors?"; Moses Leff, *Archive Thief*; Rydell, *Book Thieves*; Schidorsky, "Books as Mute Witnesses"; Shilo, "Funem Folk, Farn Folk, Mitn Folk"; and Weiss, "Von Prag nach Jerusalem."

21. Among them Aaroni and Buchman, "Europe's Jewish Cultural Material"; Cassou, *Le Pillage par les Allemands*; Farmer, *Safekeepers*; Friedman, "Fate of the Jewish Book"; Hall, "Recovery of Cultural Objects"; Hancock, "Experiences of a Monuments Officer"; Heller, "Operation Salvage"; Heller, "Homecoming"; Heller, "Recovery of Looted Sacred Objects"; Heller, "To the Victims Belong the Spoils"; Heller, "Invisible Spectators"; Heller, "Displaced Books and Displaced Persons"; Howe, *Salt Mines and Castles*; La Farge, *Lost Treasures of Europe*; Pomrenze, "Operation Offenbach"; Shunami, "Offenbach Jewish Book Collection"; Shunami, "Out of the Story of the Rescuing"; and Starr, "Jewish Cultural Property under Nazi Control."

22. Poste, "Development of U.S. Protection."

23. For initial studies of the Offenbach Depot, see Hoogewoud, "Nazi Looting of Books"; Peiss, "Cultural Policy"; Rothfeld, "Returning Looted European Library Collections"; and Waite, "Returning Jewish Cultural Property."

24. Kurtz, *America and the Return of Nazi Contraband*.

25. Ibid., ch. 8, and Kurtz, "Resolving a Dilemma."

26. See the early accounts by Raim, "Wem gehört das Erbe der Toten?"; and Heuberger, "Zur Rolle der 'Jewish Cultural Reconstruction' nach 1945"; and later, Albrink, "Von Büchern, Depots und Bibliotheken"; Herman, "Brand Plucked out of the Fire"; Nattermann, "Struggle for the Preservation of a German Jewish Legacy"; Rauschenberger, "Restitution of Jewish Cultural Objects"; Schreiber, "New Jewish Communities" Yavnai, "Jewish Cultural Property."

27. Adunka, *Der Raub der Bücher* (an English summary is provided by Evelyn Adunka, "The Nazi Looting of Books in Austria and Their Partial Restitution," Looted Art, 2002, https://www.lootedart.com); Adunka, "Die Zentralbibliothek der Hohen Schule"; Adunka, "Research on Looted Books in Austria"; Hoogewoudt, "Dutch Jewish Ex Libris"; Hoogewoudt, "Die Bibliotheca Rosenthaliana"; Hoogewoud, *Return of Looted Collections*; Grimsted, "Postwar Fate"; Grimsted, "Roads to Ratibor"; Grimsted, "Sudeten Crossroads"; Grimsted, "Silesian Crossroads"; Grimsted, "Road to Minsk"; Grimsted, Hoogewoud, and Ketelaar, *Returned from Russia*.

28. Schidorsky, "Salvaging of Jewish Books"; Schidorsky, "Library of the Reich Security Main Office"; Schidorsky, "Shunamis Suche nach Schätzen"; Schidorsky, *Burning Scrolls and Flying Letters*; Schidorsky, "Books as Mute Witnesses." New research findings from scholars of the Hebrew University are collected in Gallas, Holzer-Kawalko, Jessen, and Weiss, *Contested Heritage*.

29. Takei, "Jewish People as the Heir."

30. Herman, "Hashavat Avedah."

31. See esp. the approach promoted by D. Diner, "Memory and Restitution," 9–23; D. Diner, "Eigentum restituieren." See also Kirchhoff, "Looted Texts."

32. Representative of an ever-growing field of research are Bankier, *Jews are Coming Back*; H. Diner, *We Remember with Reverence and Love*; Grossmann, *Jews, Germans, and Allies*; Grossmann and Lewinsky, "Way Station, 1945–1949"; Jockusch, *Collect and Record!*; Mankowitz, *Life between Memory and Hope*; Myers Feinstein,

Holocaust Survivors in Postwar Germany; Patt and Berkowitz, *"We are here"*; Porat, *Israeli Society*; and Yablonka, *Survivors of the Holocaust.*

33. Tirosh-Samuelson and Dąbrowa, *Enduring Legacy of Salo W. Baron.*

34. See esp. Hertzberg, "Salo W. Baron"; and Schorsch, "Lachrymose Conception of Jewish History."

35. Liberles, *Salo Wittmayer Baron.*

36. The groundwork for further evaluation of Baron's work for the JCR has been laid chiefly by Grace Cohen Grossman. She interviewed Baron over a two-day period shortly before his death, thus obtaining indispensable material, particularly on his own evaluation of his political activities. Salo W. Baron, interview by Grace Cohen Grossman, July 3–4, 1988; Ms. Grossman was kind enough to provide me with the transcript. An initial summary is provided in Grossman, "Scholar as Political Activist."

37. See Brenner, "Secular Faith of Fallen Jews"; Brenner, *Prophets of the Past*, ch. 4, esp. 121–35; Engel, "Crisis and Lachrymosity"; Engel, "Holocaust Research"; and Engel, *Historians of the Jews*, ch. 2.

38. Dawidowicz, *From That Place and Time*; Sinkoff, "Introduction, Yidishkayt and the Making of Lucy S. Dawidowicz"; Sinkoff, "Polishness of Lucy S. Dawidowicz's Postwar Jewish Cold War"; Sinkoff, "From the Archives."

39. A start has been made by Kuznitz, "YIVO"; Kuznitz, *Yivo and the Making of Modern Jewish Culture*; Krah, *American Jewry*; Schwarz, "After the Destruction of Vilna"; Schwarz, *Survivors and Exiles*; and Shilo, "When YIVO was Defined by Territory." For differing portrayals of the salvage of YIVO with respect to Dawidowicz, see Lipphardt, *Vilne*, 179–86; Brenner, *Prophets of the Past*, 144; Farmer, *Safekeepers*, 102.

40. A detailed overview, including a bibliography of the research literature on Hannah Arendt from 2000 on, can be found at www.hannaharendt.net (accessed June 29, 2018).

41. Young-Bruehl, *Hannah Arendt*, esp. 187–88. I owe a lot to Althaus, *Erfahrung denken*, an important study about the link between experience and thinking in Arendt's biography.

42. Sznaider, "Die Rettung der Bücher"; Sznaider, *Jewish Memory*; and Sznaider, "Culture and Memory."

43. See esp. Schidorsky, "Hannah Arendt's Dedication." See also Dalby, "German-Jewish Female Intellectuals"; Rensmann, "Returning from Forced Exile"; and Ujma, "Nach der Katastrophe."

44. Zadoff, *Gershom Scholem*, 95–153.

45. *Correspondence of Arendt and Scholem.*

CHAPTER 1. CONFRONTING THE PRESENT

1. Staatsbibliothek zu Berlin (hereafter StaBi), Nachlass Nr. 266: Ernst Gottlieb Lowenthal (hereafter E. G. Lowenthal), folder 314, Severin Rochmann and Peter

Leinekugel, "Geschichte des Offenbach Archival Depot 1946–1948," unpublished sketch, August 1948, 16 and 19. (All translations by Alex Skinner unless otherwise indicated.)

2. The officers of the MFA&A were mostly American archivists, librarians, art historians, and curators. The MFA&A was established at the recommendation of the American Commission for the Protection and Salvage of Artistic and Historic Monuments in War Areas (also appointed by Franklin D. Roosevelt in 1943) as its operational arm and adhered to its guidelines on the protection of art and restitution. Better known simply as the Roberts Commission, after its chairman, Owen J. Roberts, this group was composed of members of the government and War Department along with scholars and art experts. For an introduction to the history of the MFA&A and the Roberts Commission, see Kurtz, *America and the Return of Nazi Contraband*, esp. ch. 3, 43–56; Edsel, *Monuments Men*; and Peiss, "Cultural Policy." An immediate impression of MFA&A operations is provided by the reports produced by those directly involved: Roberts Commission, *Report on the American Commission*; Rorimer and Rabin, *Survival*; Howe, *Salt Mines and Castles*; Hancock, "Experiences of a Monuments Officer"; Breitenbach, "Historical Survey"; Born, "Archives and Libraries"; Hall, "Recovery of Cultural Objects"; and Farmer, *Safekeepers*. Janet Flanner, a reporter for the *New Yorker* who had lived in Paris since 1944, wrote articles on the MFA&A as an accompanying journalist. These can be found in Flanner, *Paris, Germany*; further accounts of the MFA&A's work also appear in her later book *Men and Monuments*.

3. The Macmillan Committee on the Preservation and Restitution of Works of Art, Archives, and Other Material in Enemy Hands was the counterpart of the Roberts Commission in the United Kingdom. American and British art protection officers worked together under the auspices of the MFA&A during the war. The Commission de récupération artistique, responsible for the French zone and France itself, also deployed art protection officers.

4. Poste, "Books Go Home," 1704.

5. Volkert, "Der Kulturgutraub," 22.

6. The looting of significant works of art was carried out, for example, by the Nazis' Linz Special Taskforce (Einsatzgruppe Sonderauftrag Linz), made up of art dealers and curators who seized paintings and sculptures for the "Führermuseum" that Hitler planned to establish in that city.

7. Alon Confino describes the background to these processes meticulously in his study *World without Jews*.

8. Schroeder, "Beschlagnahme und Verbleib jüdischer Bibliotheken," 32.

9. Founding decree and citation quoted in Bollmus, *Amt Rosenberg*, 134. For a general account of Rosenberg, see Matthäus and Bajohr, *Political Diary of Alfred Rosenberg*; and Koop, *Alfred Rosenberg*.

10. On July 5, 1940, Rosenberg was authorized to deploy his units in France, Belgium, the Netherlands, and Luxembourg to search for and seize written and archival materials. On September 17, 1940, he was given leave to remove Jewish

property and valuable cultural assets, and on March 1, 1942, his mandate was extended to the whole of Eastern Europe. See Moll, *"Führer-Erlasse" 1939–1945.*

11. For an introduction to the history of the ERR and the Frankfurt Institute, see Collins and Rothfelder, "Einsatzstab Reichsleiter Rosenberg"; Manasse, *Verschleppte Archive*; Bollmus, "Einsatzstab Reichsleiter Rosenberg"; and Sutter, "Lost Jewish Libraries," esp. 219–23.

12. A comparative study of the looting campaigns in France and the Soviet Union is provided by Heuss, *Kunst- und Kulturgutraub.* A general overview is given in Rydell, *Book Thieves*; and Nicholas, *Rape of Europa.* On the individual parts of the collection, see the document "Library for Exploration of the Jewish Question" (a translation of the original document, 171-PS, produced by the ERR, namely, "Die Bibliothek des Institutes zur Erforschung der Judenfrage/Hohe Schule" of April 1943), which lists every item: Library of Congress, Washington, DC, Manuscript Division (hereafter LoC), the Records of the Library of Congress European Mission and Cooperative Acquisitions Project, 1942–1957 (hereafter LoC-Mission Papers), box 30, folder "Hohe Schule Reports."

13. Heuberger, *Bibliothek des Judentums*, esp. 100–109; Schidorsky, "Confiscation of Libraries," 347.

14. Adunka, "Die Zentralbibliothek der Hohen Schule"; Adunka, *Der Raub der Bücher*, ch. 1: "Die Bibliothek von Tanzenberg in Kärnten," 15–70. The Künsberg Unit was led by Eberhard von Künsberg that was integrated into the SS and Hitler's personal guard formation (Leibstandarte); it confiscated records and official documents in the occupied areas, often looting art as it did so. See Conze, Frei, Hayes, and Zimmermann, *Das Amt*, 214–20; for a general account of the role of the Ministry of Foreign Affairs in the history of plunder, see ibid., 221–94.

15. On the individual units, see Volkert, "Der Kulturgutraub," 21–48; and a number of articles in Dehnel, *Jüdischer Buchbesitz als Raubgut.* A general overview of the Nazi policy of spoliation is provided by Dean, *Robbing the Jews.* With respect to cultural assets, Simpson, *Spoils of War*; and Nicholas, *Rape of Europa.* On the looting of libraries and archives, see Glickman, *Stolen Words*; Rydell, *Book Thieves*; Kurtz, *America and the Return of Nazi Contraband*, ch. 2: "Nazi Looting," 12–42; and Schidorsky, "Das Schicksal jüdischer Bibliotheken." Three excellent examples of texts that demonstrate the solid documentation on this topic provided by Jewish scholars who were themselves involved in subsequent restitution are Lestschinsky, "Material Losses"; Starr, "Jewish Cultural Property"; and Friedman, "Fate of the Jewish Book."

16. Berg and Rupnow, "Einleitung," 307. See also Rupnow, "Annihilating—Preserving—Remembering"; Rupnow, "Racializing Historiography"; and Steinweis, *Studying the Jew.*

17. On the history of the RSHA library, see Rudolph, "Sämtliche Sendungen"; Friedman, "Fate of the Jewish Book," 121–22; and Schidorsky, "Jewish Libraries."

18. For an introduction, see Holzer-Kawałko, "Jewish Intellectuals"; and Schoor, *Vom literarischen Zentrum*, 408–14.

19. See Dr. Ernst Grumach, "Report on Confiscation and Treatment of the Former Jewish Libraries by the Gestapo from 1933 to 1945," in Schidorsky, "Confiscation of Libraries," 352–56. Grumach also composed another document for the MFA&A, in which he lists a selection of the private Jewish libraries seized by the RSHA: National Archives and Records Administration, College Park, Maryland (hereafter NA College Park), M1942, Ardelia Hall Collection (hereafter AHC), roll 2, folder Dr. Ernst Grumach, Ernst Grumach, Memorandum "Vom früheren Reichssicherheitshauptamt VII Berlin W 30, Eisenacherstr. 11–13, beschlagnahmte Privat-Bibliotheken," undated.

20. On the history of forced laborers at the RSHA library, see recently Holzer-Kawałko, "Jewish Intellectuals"; Rudolph, "Sämtliche Sendungen," 228–35; and the eyewitness report by Ernst Grumach and other survivors of the forced labor unit of February 23, 1954, in Schidorsky, "Confiscation of Libraries," 374–82. We can also reconstruct the forced labor experience with the help of a number of documents, reports, letters, and memos from Grumach's unpublished papers. These contain a detailed transcript of an interview with Grumach on March 3, 1960, conducted by A. J. van der Leeuw, research associate at the Netherlands State Institute for War Documentation, Central Archives for the History of the Jewish People, Jerusalem (hereafter CAHJP), P/205, Ernst Grumach Papers, folder 17a. A detailed catalog of the related papers is provided in Holzer-Kawałko, "Papers of Ernst Grumach." My sincere thanks go to Ernst Grumach's daughter, Dr. Irene Shirun-Grumach in Jerusalem, for allowing me access to his private papers and for the helpful information on her father's biography.

21. Apenszlak, *Black Book of Polish Jewry*, 300–301.

22. An overview is provided by Kurtz, *America and the Return of Nazi Contraband*, ch. 2; Heuss, *Kunst- und Kulturgutraub*.

23. Originally the Rothschild family's private mansion, this building was used for the Freiherrlich Carl von Rothschild Public Library from 1895 onward. In 1928, the city of Frankfurt took over the building, along with its library, installing part of the city library there, which continued to exist under the Nazis without reference to its founders. In late 1945, the Palais Rothschild initially remained a city library, later becoming part of the Frankfurt Historical Museum. In the 1980s, the building was restored and converted into the Jewish Museum Frankfurt, established in 1988.

24. The establishment of the collecting point in Frankfurt is described in a report compiled for the MFA&A and the American military government by Leslie Poste from November 2, 1945: NA College Park, M1942, AHC, roll 3, folder Administrative Records 1945–1949. See also NA College Park, M1949, MFA&A Records, roll 3, folder OAD 2, report "Rothschild Library Collecting Point," undated; and a lecture manuscript by Koppel S. Pinson, who describes the collecting point itself: "Commencement Address to Gratz College, 17. 6. 1947," Department of Special Collections, Stanford University Libraries, Stanford, CA (hereafter UL Stanford), M0670, Jewish Social Studies Papers, box 4, Correspondence M—S, folder Pinson Personal.

25. Weltsch, "Besuch in Frankfurt," 10.

26. See Poste, "Development of U.S. Protection," 334; Edsel, "Monuments Men," 291; and Nicholas, *Rape of Europa*, 337–38.

27. Report by Glenn Goodman on the collections found in Hungen: NA College Park, M1949, MFA&A records, roll 3, folder OAD 2, "Rosenberg Institut für Judenforschung. Repositories in Hungen, Oberhessen," undated; The National Library of Israel, Jerusalem (hereafter NLI), Library Papers, Arc 4°793/288/6, Herman Dicker, report "The Genizah of Hungen, Germany."

28. Flanner, *Men and Monuments*, 295–96. Janet Flanner was in close contact with the later head of the OAD, Theodore A. Heinrich, who provided her with materials and information on the theft of art and cultural assets, laying the foundations for her many essays on the topic. See Flanner, *Paris, Germany*.

29. These reports are quoted in Rochmann and Leinekugel, *Geschichte des Offenbach Archival Depot*, 5.

30. For a detailed account of the situation in Hungen, see ibid., 6–7.

31. We can reconstruct the tasks of the "Library of Congress European Mission and Cooperative Acquisitions Project, 1942–1957" (LoC-Mission) and the idea underlying it with the aid of the unpublished papers in the LoC. A number of staff members have also described its activities. See Peiss, "European Wartime Acquisitions"; Peiss, "Report on Europe"; and Downs, "Wartime Co-operative Acquisitions."

32. NA College Park, M1949, MFA&A Records, roll 3, folder OAD 2, OMGUS, "Establishment of the Offenbach Archival Depot," March 2, 1946.

33. Kurtz, *America and the Return of Nazi Contraband*, 92.

34. NA College Park, M1949, MFA&A Records, roll 3, folder OAD 2, MFA&A report, March 5, 1946.

35. Bundesarchiv Koblenz (hereafter BArch), Z 45 F, RG 260, OMGUS records, records of the Adjutant General, War Department (hereafter AG) 1945–46/9/6, G. H. Garde (adjutant general under military governor Lucius D. Clay) to the heads of the offices of the military governments of Bavaria, Württemberg-Baden and Hesse, report, "Removal to Central Archival Depot of Archives, Books and Other Library Material," May 1, 1946.

36. Pomrenze, "Restitution of Jewish Cultural Treasures."

37. See Hauschke-Wicklaus, Amborn-Morgenstern, and Jacobs, *Fast vergessen*, 66 and 70.

38. BArch, Z 45 F, RG 260, OMGUS Records, AHC, box 218, Offenbach Archival Depot (hereafter OAD), Office of Military Government Land Greater Hesse, Monthly Report, April 1946. On the recovered state library holdings, see BArch, Z 45 F, RG 260, OMGUS Records, AG 1945–46/9/6, William H. Draper (OMGUS/Economics Div.) to John H. Allen (OMGUS/Chief of the Restitution Branch), March 28, 1946, and the response on April, 16, 1946. For the complex history of loss and recovery of the Prussian State library's holdings and the 2.5 million books from the collections found dispersed across more than thirty

locations on German and former German territory, see Schochow, *Die Verlagerungsgeschichte der Preußischen Staatsbibliothek*.

39. Poste, "Development of U.S. Protection," esp. ch. 9: "Restitution. The Offenbach Archival Depot," 333–95.
40. Poste, "Books Go Home," 1704.
41. BArch, Z 45 F, RG 260, OMGUS Records, AHC, box 219, OAD Monthly Report, September 1946, 5.
42. YIVO Institute for Jewish Research, Archives, Center for Jewish History, New York (hereafter YIVO), 50433, OAD Collection, OAD/OMGUS Greater Hesse/ Economics Division, "Festschrift aus Anlass des einjährigen Bestehens, März 1946–März 1947," signed by Joseph Horne.
43. Dawidowicz, *From That Place and Time*, 322.
44. H. Chr. Schmolck, "Kultur und Anstand. Eine Betrachtung zur Wiedergutmachung des Bibliothekenraubes," *Frankfurter Rundschau*, October 12, 1946, BArch, Z 45 F, RG 260, OMGUS Records, AHC, box 219, OAD Monthly Report, October 1946.
45. A later account by a former German depot worker presents a different picture. In contrast to sources of the time, he foregrounds employees' sensitivity to the circumstances and challenges inherent in their work in Offenbach. But this was almost certainly a retrospective shift of perspective triggered by the increasing awareness of the destructive dimensions of National Socialism. See Hauschke-Wicklaus, Amborn-Morgenstern, and Jacobs, *Fast vergessen*, 84–86.
46. At the Paris Conference on Reparations in December 1945, the Allies agreed to enforce restitution of all property illegally removed during the German occupation. This included the return of all confiscated artworks and cultural treasures. The agreements made were based on Article 56 of the Hague Convention Respecting the Laws and Customs of War on Land (IV) of 1907, which referred explicitly to "works of art and science" and prohibited every form of deliberate destruction or seizure during armed conflict. The convention did not, however, include a specific clause on the restitution of cultural assets, just as it said nothing about cases of theft and confiscation within a state or outside the wartime context. A commitment to postwar restitution was officially incorporated into the "Inter-Allied Declaration against Acts of Dispossession Committed in Territories under Enemy Occupation and Control" (London Declaration) of January 5, 1943, which was signed by eighteen countries (among them the French National Committee, the Soviet Union, the UK, and US). This set out the victorious powers' responsibilities with respect to restitution and the restoration of prewar property relations. The declaration did not explicitly address cases of the systematic confiscation and destruction of Jewish property. The obligation to pursue restitution was reconfirmed by the United Nations in the final resolution of the Bretton Woods Conference of July 22, 1944, and eventually agreed upon in Paris. See Forrest, *International Law*, 63–75. For a general overview, cf. Dean, Goschler, and Ther, *Robbery and Restitution*.

47. On the definition of restitution by the Allied Control Council, see Jakubowski, *State Succession in Cultural Property*, 95–97.

48. Jürgen Lillteicher provides a detailed account of the problems the Allies faced after the war in the first restitution hearings on Jewish assets. Lillteicher, *Raub, Recht und Restitution*, 37–61.

49. Kurtz, *America and the Return of Nazi Contraband*, 141–43.

50. See BArch, Z 45 F, RG 260, OMGUS records, AHC, box 218, OAD Monthly Report, March 1946. Graswinckel's own assessment of these operations can be found in Graswinckel, *Mitteilungen über die Restitution*.

51. On the general situation of Jews in the Netherlands during the early postwar period, see Hondius, "Bitter Homecoming"; Kristel, "Revolution and Reconstruction"; and Gerstenfeld, "Postwar Renewal." On the fate of Jewish cultural property there, see Cohen, "Theft and Restitution."

52. Adunka, *Der Raub der Bücher*, 43–46.

53. See Manasse, *Verschleppte Archive und Bibliotheken*, ch. 4: "Rückerstattung des niederländischen Besitzes," 122–28; and Hoogewoud, "Nazi Looting of Books."

54. See Hoogewoud, "Nazi Looting of Books"; Hoogewoud, *Return of Looted Collections*; Hoogewoud, "Die Bibliotheca Rosenthaliana."

55. Quoted in Hoogewoud, "Reopening of the Bibliotheca Rosenthaliana," 106.

56. See OAD Monthly Report, April 1946. Those parts of the Alliance holdings that had been stored in the Central Library (Zentralbibliothek) of the RSHA in Berlin were either destroyed or transferred to Moscow immediately after the war. It was not until 1992 that they were restituted to the institution in Paris. For an introductory account of the French restitution process, in addition to the relevant monthly reports by the OAD, see Sutter, "Looting of Jewish Collections"; Andrieu, "Two Approaches to Restitution"; and Fogg, *Stealing Home*.

57. On Rose Valland, see her own memoir *Le Front de l'art* and Polack and Dagen, *Les carnets de Rose Valland*; Rorimer and Rabin, *Survival*, esp. 108–16; and Nicholas, *Rape of Europa*, esp. 126–36. On the French situation under German occupation, see also the contemporary collection of texts by Cassou, *Le Pillage par les Allemands*.

58. See BArch, Z 45 F, RG 260, OMGUS Records, AHC, box 220, OAD Monthly Report, December 1946.

59. OAD Monthly Report, April 1946.

60. See Poste, "Development of U.S. Protection," 356. The lists with their photographs of the stamps can be found in NA College Park, M1942, AHC, roll 11/12, Jewish Library Markings Found Among the Looted Books, Bencowitz; and roll 13, Ex-Libris Found Among the Looted Books, Bencowitz.

61. In addition to his official reports, such information is also provided by his personal remarks, as preserved in a Solemn Declaration on Claims for Compensation (Eidesstattliche Erklärung zur Entschädigungsforderung) and in a conversation between Grumach and van der Leeuw, CAHJP, P/205, Grumach Papers, folders 17a and 17b.

62. BArch, Z 45 F, RG 260, OMGUS Records, AHC, box 204, Ernst Grumach, Bemerkungen zum Ex-Libris-Album, OAD, February 20, 1947.

63. Poste, "Development of U.S. Protection," 371–72.

64. NA College Park, RG 260, OMGUS Records, AHC, box 66, folder Jewish Cultural Property, MFA&A memorandum, June 3, 1946.

65. See, for example, NA College Park, M1949, MFA&A records, roll 3, folder OAD 1, memorandum of a conversation between Isaac Bencowitz and Lester Born (Poste's successor as head of the archives and libraries division of the MFA&A), July 27, 1946.

66. This official adviser had been appointed as a consequence of the famous Harrison Report. This report by the American special envoy Earl G. Harrison of August 24, 1945, described the hardships faced by Jewish residents of the American-run DP camps and pushed for the alleviation of their suffering. He urged the American government to recognize the Jews' specific victimization under Nazi rule and opted to create special DP camps for the Jewish survivors in order to improve their living conditions. As advisers to the governor, the new appointees tasked with the coordination of activities relating to the Jewish DPs were selected by the leading American-Jewish relief organizations (AJC, AJConf, WJC, JA, and Joint). Besides Rifkind, Philip Bernstein, Judah Nadich, Louis Levinthal, William Haber, Harry Greenstein, and Abraham Hyman held the same position. Among the growing body of literature concerning the DPs in Germany, for a comprehensive description, see Grossmann, *Jews, Germans, and Allies*. On the repercussions of the Harrison Report, see Königseder and Wetzel, *Waiting for Hope*, 31–41.

67. NA College Park, M1942, AHC, roll 1, folder 1946–1949, correspondence, Simon Rifkind to Lucius Clay, January 7, 1946; NA College Park, M1949, MFA&A records, roll 3, folder OAD 2, Clay to Rifkind with consent to lend a maximum of twenty-five thousand volumes, January 12, 1946. For further MFA&A memorandums of February 7 and March 5, 1946, on personnel issues and the division of responsibility within this operation, see NA College Park, M1949, MFA&A records, roll 3, folder OAD 2.

68. UL Stanford, M0580, Salo W. Baron Papers (hereafter Baron Papers), box 39, folder 3, Koppel S. Pinson to Hannah Arendt, November 23, 1945.

69. On Pinson's activities in Offenbach and the DP camps, see the collection of photographs and texts in the Koppel S. Pinson Collection of the Magnes Museum in Berkeley: "On Hitler's Balcony. Koppel Pinson and the Rescue of Jewish Books in Post-War Germany," http://flickr.com (January 19, 2019).

70. NA College Park, M1942, AHC, roll 5, folder Cultural Object Restitution and Custody Records, 1946–1951, Koppel Pinson to Seymour Pomrenze, April 27, 1946.

71. Koppel Pinson describes the DPs' desperate desire to read in another essay as well: Pinson, "Jewish Life in Liberated Germany," esp. 121. See also Brenner, *After the Holocaust*, 19–22.

72. Dicker, *Of Learning and Libraries*, 57. On the history of the first printings of the Talmud in Germany after 1945, see Honigmann, "Talmuddrucke im Nachkriegsdeutschland"; and Brenner, *After the Holocaust*, 25.

73. NA College Park, M1949, MFA&A records, roll 2, folder 73, Joseph A. Horne to OMGUS/Economics Division, memorandum, "Loan of Books to the American Joint Distribution Committee," March 3, 1947.

74. American Jewish Historical Society, Archive, Center for Jewish History, New York (hereafter AJHS), P-675, Lucy S. Dawidowicz Papers (hereafter Dawidowicz Papers), box 55, folder 3, Lucy Schildkret (Dawidowicz) to Max Weinreich, February 16, 1947: "I personally would not care if they [OMGUS] refused the second application, despite the fact that there is a crying need for reading material in the camps. There are so many books missing from the original 20,000 and the possibility of ever returning those that were distributed is practically nil."

75. The Central Committee was the Jewish advocacy group created by survivors in all three Western occupation zones. On the Board of Education and Culture, see Königseder and Wetzel, *Waiting for Hope*, 72; on the Central Committee, see ibid., 83–90.

76. See various reports by OMGUS and MFA&A staff: NA College Park, M1949, MFA&A records, roll 2, folder 73; and YIVO, 15/6896 1947 (Per), OAD Collection, OAD Monthly Report, February 1948.

77. Weiser, "Coming to America,"; Weiser, "Saving Yiddish."

78. For a comprehensive history of YIVO in Vilna, see Kuznitz, *YIVO and the Making of Modern Jewish Culture*. See also Miron, "Between Science and Faith"; and Bramson-Alperniene, "YIVO in Wilna."

79. Quoted in Kuznitz, *YIVO and the Making of Modern Jewish Culture*, 131.

80. Weiser, "Coming to America," 235.

81. Abramowicz, "YIVO Library."

82. The original Russian version of his entreaty was written in 1891 and printed in the Russian-Jewish journal *Voskhod* ("Dawn"), no. 4–9 (1891): 1–91. The better-known Hebrew version of 1892 appeared under the title "Nachpesah venachkorah" in the Odessa-based literary anthology *Ha-Pardes Osef Sifruti* ("Orchard") 1 (1892); English translation: Dubnow, "Let Us Seek and Investigate"; Dawidowicz, "Toward a History of the Holocaust," 51. Dubnow's call as a harbinger of YIVO's work is also discussed by Kuznitz in *YIVO and the Making of Modern Jewish Culture*, 18. For an introduction to Dubnow's mission, see Hilbrenner, "Simon Dubnov's Master Narrative"; and Hilbrenner, "Nationalization in Odessa."

83. The connection between Dubnow's concerns and the establishment of YIVO is also underlined in Jockusch, "Introductory Remarks," 350; Fishman, "Embers Plucked from the Fire," 140; and Kuznitz, "YIVO's 'Old Friend and Teacher.'"

84. On the history of YIVO during and after the Nazi period, see Fishman, "Embers Plucked from the Fire"; and Kuznitz, *YIVO and the Making of Modern Jewish Culture*, 181–84.

85. On Pohl, see Kühn-Ludewig, *Johannes Pohl*.

86. Bramson-Alperniene, "Die YIVO-Bibliothek in Wilna," 9. On these events, see also Sutter, "Lost Jewish Libraries of Vilna."

87. The Strashun Library built on the private library of Matisyahu Strashun (1817–1885) and was opened to the Vilna public in 1892. It moved to the premises of the Great Synagogue of Vilna in 1902 and rose to become one of the largest Hebraic collections in Eastern Europe and the first public Jewish library in Eastern Europe. By 1940, it contained approximately forty thousand volumes, among them many rare books, imprints, manuscripts, and incunabula, some dating back to the sixteenth century. For its comprehensive history, see recently Rabinowitz, *Lost Library*.

88. See Sutzkever, "Vilna Ghetto," 262–65; Kruk's ghetto diary, *Last Days of the Jerusalem*, 212–325; and Schwarz, "After the Destruction of Vilna." For a recent, comprehensive account of the entire story of the brigade, see Fishman, *Book Smugglers*.

89. See the letters of Max Weinreich from 1944, which refer and respond to correspondence from 1942, including several letters to the State Department, Roberts Commission, and Library of Congress: AJHS New York, P-675, Dawidowicz Papers, box 51, folder 7. On Weinreich's role in the establishment of the American YIVO division, see Weiser, "Coming to America." Most recently, Bilha Shilo thoughtfully reconstructed the story of YIVO's restitution mission in the 1940s: Shilo, "'Funem Folk, Farn Folk, Mitn Folk.'"

90. For the relevant correspondence between YIVO, OMGUS, and the State Department, see NA College Park, RG 260, OMGUS Records, Records of the Executive Office/The Office of the Adjutant General, box 9, folder 2–007 (esp. the letter by Weinreich, May 7, 1945; confirmation from the reparation, deliveries, and restitution division, June 26, 1945; and Lucius Clay's response, July 4, 1945); and ibid., M1942, AHC, roll 1, folder Administrative Records, 1945–1949: Correspondence.

91. The relevant agreements between YIVO and the American authorities on recognition, delivery, and shipment of YIVO property can be found in BArch, Z 45, RG 260, OMGUS Records, AHC, MFA&A, box 206; ibid., AG 1945–46/9/6: YIVO Cases. Letters from Max Weinreich and Judah Nadich on behalf of YIVO to General Dwight D. Eisenhower, the State Department, and the MFA&A can be found in the AJHS, P-675, Dawidowicz Papers, box 55, folder 6, and box 51, folder 9.

92. AJHS, P-675, Dawidowicz Papers, box 55, folder 3, Lucy Schildkret (Dawidowicz) to Max Weinreich, February 16, 1947.

93. BArch, Z 45 F, RG 260, OMGUS Records, AHC, box 221, OAD Monthly Report, June 1947. On Pomrenze's contribution, see Pomrenze, "Restitution of Jewish Cultural Treasures."

94. NA College Park, M1942, AHC, roll 6, folder YIVO, Max Weinreich to Isaac Bencowitz, July 9, 1946, and ibid., YIVO Report "Yivo's Associates Libraries" to Pomrenze, June 5, 1947. A list of claimed Vilna libraries and collections can be found in an undated document signed by YIVO executive Mark Uveeler, AJHS, P-675, Dawidowicz Papers, box 51, folder 9. On the history of the various parts of

the collection and Dawidowicz's persuasive efforts, see Dawidowicz, *From That Place and Time*, 318. Dawidowicz's claims and supporting narratives are disputed today. Most prominently, Dan Rabinowitz argues that neither Strashun nor some of the private estates were ever entrusted to YIVO and should therefore have been handled differently. See Rabinowitz, *Lost Library*, ch. 5: "Lost and Found in a German Book Depot" and 6: "A Transatlantic Crossing," 87–127.

95. See AJHS, P-675, Dawidowicz Papers, box 55, folder 5: correspondence between Schildkret (Dawidowicz) and Weinreich (esp. letter of March 29, 1947); Dawidowicz's report on Prague of April 2, 1947; and correspondence between Max Weinreich and institutions in Czechoslovakia. For an introduction to the challenges of the Prague operation, see Shilo, "When YIVO was defined by Territory." For further details on the operation in Prague, see ch. 4, "Initiatives in Prague."

96. Dawidowicz, "History as Autobiography," 37.

97. For a comprehensive treatment of the material situation of Eastern Europe in comparison to Western Europe after the Second World War, see Judt, *Postwar*, 13–40. In his study *Burning Books*, Matthew Fishburn conveys the appalling destruction suffered by Eastern European libraries, which went far beyond anything in Western Europe. He refers to estimates of the number of books damaged by war or ideology in the Soviet Union as between one hundred and two hundred million. See Fishburn, *Burning Books*, 120–25. Information on looted cultural property, the Trophy Brigades, and restitution is provided by Grimsted, Hoogewoud, and Ketelaar, *Returned from Russia*; and Sargent, "New Jurisdictional Tools." For an introductory study of books subject to double confiscation, see Grimsted, "Road to Minsk"; Grimsted, "Nazi-Looted Art"; and Grimsted, "'Trophy' Archives in Moscow."

98. For the different perspectives on restitution issues in the east and west and among the Allies, see Kurtz, *America and the Return of Nazi Contraband*, ch. 9: "Conflict and Cooperation. The Politics of Restitution in the Cold War," esp. the section on "Russia and Restitution," 177–81; Kurtz, "Allied Struggle over Cultural Restitution"; Meng, *Shattered Spaces*, 29–59; and Akinsha, "Stalin's Decrees."

99. BArch, Z 45 F, RG 260, OMGUS Records, AHC, box 219, OAD Monthly Report, August 1946, 18–35.

100. According to the official reports of the OAD, a total of 6,522 objects were restituted to Czechoslovakia, 24,756 objects to the People's Republic of Poland, 232,100 objects to the Soviet Union (including Baltic, Belarusian and Ukrainian holdings), and 3,664 objects to the Federal People's Republic of Yugoslavia. Among these there were undoubtedly an unspecifiable number of books but virtually no complete library holdings of Jewish origin. See BArch, Z 45 F, RG 260, OMGUS Records, AHC, box 221, OAD Monthly Report, April 1947. The monthly report of October 1946 explicitly pointed out that the Soviet restitution officers had made a positive impression through their accommodating response to delayed restitution due to holdings' uncertain provenance. See ibid., box 219, OAD Monthly Report, October 1946.

101. Gershom Scholem to Leo Baeck, June 2, 1946, in Scholem, *Life in Letters*, 335.

102. Gershom Scholem to Leo Baeck, June 2, 1946, in Scholem, *Briefe*, vol. 1, 316 (the passage was not included in the English publication).

103. NLI, Arc 4°793/212, Otzrot HaGolah Papers, folder I: 1946, "Resúme [sic] der Besprechungen mit Capt. Benkowitz, Direktor des Archival Depot in Offenbach und Prof. Pinson vom 4.–7. Juli 1946," July 9, 1946.

104. UL Stanford, M0580, Baron Papers, box 58, folder 9, "Report of Prof. G. Scholem on His Mission to Europe (in the Summer of 1946) Concerning the Libraries of the Diaspora," undated.

105. Scholem to Baeck, June 2, 1946, in Scholem, *Life in Letters*, 335.

106. AJHS, P-675, Dawidowicz Papers, box 55, folder 3, Lucy Schildkret (Dawidowicz) to Joseph Horne, May 24, 1947 (it is uncertain whether the letter was in fact sent).

107. NA College Park, RG 260, OMGUS Records, Property Division/Property Control and External Assets Branch/Branch Chief, box 13, folder Jewish Displaced Persons and Property, OMGUS/Property Division to Richard F. Howard (MFA&A), July 2, 1948.

108. An official list of these crates' contents was drawn up by JNUL librarian Isaachar Joel for the American Consulate on June 22, 1947. NA College Park, RG 260, OMGUS Records, AHC, box 66, folder JCR, Inc.

109. Clay's help is emphasized, among others, by Hyman, "The Clay I Knew"; and in Grobman, *Rekindling the Flame*, 175–76. For the American reaction, see Haeger and Long, "Lost EC Treasures Found in Palestine." Documentation of the case can be found in NA College Park, M1949, Records of the MFA&A Section of the Reparations and Restitution Branch, OMGUS 1945–1951, roll 3, folder 456.

110. NLI, Arc 4°793/212, Otzrot HaGolah Papers, folder IV: 1948, Gershom Scholem to Judah Magnes, March 21, 1948.

111. Friedman, *Roots of the Future*, 110–11. On the history of transfer as a whole, see ibid., ch. 13: "The Stolen Books of Offenbach," 106–11.

112. For similar cases of "theft" of archival materials and books of Jewish provenance in the course of WWII and its aftermath and their complex evaluation, see Leff, *Archive Thief*.

113. For the official text of the law, see "Military Government, Law No. 59." On the negotiations in the Allied Control Council concerning restitution and art restitution, see Kurtz, *America and the Return of Nazi Contraband*, esp. ch. 6: "The Allies Agree on Restitution," 106–24. For a general account of the emerging legislation on restitution after 1945, see Lillteicher, "West Germany," esp. 101–4; and in a more detailed study, Lillteicher, *Raub, Recht und Restitution*, 37–84.

114. BArch, Z 45 F, RG 260, OMGUS Records, AHC, box 219, OAD Monthly Report, August 1946.

115. UL Stanford, M0580, Baron Papers, box 231, folder 18, Hannah Arendt, "Overall Report of the Activities of the Corporation from its Beginnings in October 1947,

until March 1952," 3: "JCR, Inc., World Distribution of Ceremonial Objects and Torah Scrolls, July 1, 1949 to January 31, 1952."

116. Feuchtwanger, *Jew Süss*, 126–27.

117. Yerushalmi, *Zakhor*, xxxiv. See also Halbertal, *People of the Book*, introduction: "Canonical Text and Text-Centered Community."

118. D. Diner, "Vorwort," 8.

119. On the function of books as the "symbolic gravestones" of those murdered in the Holocaust, see Feierstein, "Nor er redt nisht arois keyn vort," esp. 117; and Boyarin and Kugelmass, *From a Ruined Garden*.

120. Dawidowicz, *From That Place and Time*, 316.

121. Roth, "Jewish Love of Books," 179–80.

122. Friedman, "Fate of the Jewish Book," 3–4. See also H. Diner, *We Remember with Reverence*, 104.

123. Löwenthal, "Caliban's Legacy," 13.

124. Isaac Bencowitz, diary, quoted in Poste, "Development of U.S. Protection," 394.

125. Rochmann and Leinekugel, "Geschichte des Offenbach Archival Depot," 17.

126. Friedman, *Roots of the Future*, 112 (my emphasis).

127. Dawidowicz, *From That Place and Time*, 319.

128. Dawidowicz, *From That Place and Time*, 316.

129. "Die jüdischen Bücher in Offenbach," *Israelitisches Wochenblatt für die Schweiz/Journal Israélite Suisse* no. 39 (September 29, 1950): 33.

130. Poste, "Books Go Home," 1703.

131. For an overview of different perspectives on the links between archive and memory, see Blouin and Rosenberg, *Archives, Documentation, and Institutions*; Assmann, *Cultural Memory*; Raulff and Lepper, *Handbuch Archiv*, here esp. Berg, "Geschichte des Archivs im 20. Jahrhundert," 57–75; and Fritzsche, "Archive." On the relationship between archive, collection, and remembrance of the Holocaust, see, for example, Körte, "Flaschenpost"; and Bischoff, "Vom Überleben der Dinge."

132. Benjamin, "Unpacking My Library," 60.

133. On narrative structure and continuity, see D. Diner, "Gestaute Zeit."

134. Starr, "Jewish Cultural Property," 28.

135. Arendt, *Eichmann in Jerusalem*, 37. On the Nazi politics of memory and its consequences, see Rupnow, *Aporien des Gedenkens*.

136. For an instructive account of the form of the list and catalog in relation to literary narratives on the Holocaust, see Lachmann, "Zur Poetik der Kataloge."

137. This is attested by the numerous related articles in Jewish newspapers and journals worldwide. A number of them appeared in the *Palestine Post* (later the *Jerusalem Post*), the New York–based journal *Aufbau*, the *YIVO Bleter*, the *Mitteilungblatt des Irgun Oleij Merkas Europa*, *Haaretz*, and the Hebrew library journal *Yad La-Kore*.

CHAPTER 2. ENVISIONING A FUTURE

1. S. Baron, "What War Has Meant," 505–6.
2. The AJC, founded in 1906, was the oldest American institution for the defense of Jewish civil and religious rights, and it focused on mobilizing aid and support for persecuted Jews worldwide. On the history of the AJC, see Harris, "American Jewish Committee"; and Engel, "American Jewish Committee."
3. The key concerns of the Institute of Jewish Affairs were laying the groundwork for peace, international security policies, ensuring that Jewish representatives had a say in future peace conferences, the prohibition of war crimes, and collective claims for compensation and restitution against Germany. The demands formulated here—presented to the public at the "War Emergency Conference" of 1944 in Atlantic City—were to have far-reaching consequences. The writings of Nehemia Robinson, composed under the auspices of the institute on claims for reparations, compensation, and restitution, provided key elements in the preliminary work on the reparations agreement, known as the Luxembourg Agreement, between Israel and the Federal Republic of Germany of 1952. A brief overview of the institute's activities is provided by its anniversary publication: Institute of Jewish Affairs, *Twenty Years of the Institute of Jewish Affairs*; and Kaplan-Feuereisen, "Institute of Jewish Affairs," 130–36.
4. N. Robinson, *Ten Years of German Indemnification*; Institute of Jewish Affairs, "Reparations, Restitution, Compensation."
5. Moses, *Jewish Post-War Claims*; Roth, "Restoration of Jewish Libraries"; Adler-Rudel, "Aus der Vorzeit der kollektiven Wiedergutmachung." Chaim Weizmann's political role in the debate is highlighted in Jelinek, *Deutschland und Israel*, 49–50. An overview of worldwide Jewish efforts in this regard during the Second World War is provided by Sagi, *German Reparations*, part A, ch. 2: "Jewish Action during the War in the Matter of Securing Reparations from Germany"; Sagi, "Die Rolle der jüdischen Organisationen"; Goschler, *Wiedergutmachung*, esp. ch. 2: "Pläne von jüdischer Seite," 38–47; Zweig, *German Reparations*, esp. ch. 2: "Origins of the Claims Conference," 26–43. An overview of the various proposals, formulated at different times, is provided by Takei, "Gemeinde Problem," esp. 268–69.
6. A comprehensive, general account of the history of Jewish restitution claims and Jews' associated legal recognition after the Second World War is provided by Lillteicher, *Raub, Recht und Restitution*, esp. chs. 1 and 7.
7. On Nahum Goldmann's activities, see his autobiographical writings: Goldmann, *Autobiography*, here 250; Lillteicher, *Raub, Recht und Restitution*, 40; Goschler, *Wiedergutmachung*, 40.
8. Munz, "Restitution in Postwar Europe," 373. On the significance of this text, see Goschler, *Wiedergutmachung*, 41.
9. On the different meanings of the term *Jewish people* in this context, see D. Diner, "Ambiguous Semantics," 96.
10. Moses, *Jewish Post-War Claims*, 57.

11. Ibid., 23.
12. For a general introduction to the Israeli view of reparation and restitution during the Second World War and after, see Sagi, *German Reparations*; and D. Diner, *Rituelle Distanz*. on the specific initiatives of the Hebrew University, see esp. the studies by Dov Schidorsky, such as Schidorsky, "Salvaging of Jewish Books"; and Schidorsky, *Burning Scrolls and Flying Letters*.
13. Hannah Arendt to Fanja and Gershom Scholem, April 25, 1942, in *Correspondence of Arendt and Scholem*, 12–13, here 13.
14. Arendt, "All Israel Takes Care of Israel," 154–56, here 155.
15. Arendt, "Crisis of Zionism I," 178–80, here 178.
16. For an introduction to the idea of Gegenwartsarbeit, see Shumsky, "Gegenwartsarbeit."
17. S. Baron, "What War Has Meant," 497 and 504.
18. On Salo W. Baron's view of Jewish history and the Jewish self-image, see Engel, *Historians of the Jews*, 56–68.
19. N. Robinson, *Indemnification and Reparations*. For further insights into Robinson's views here, see his "Restitution of Jewish Property" and "Reparations and Restitution."
20. On the transformation of formerly private property into collective Jewish property after the Second World War, see D. Diner, "Eigentum restituieren."
21. For an introductory account of the different positions and their backgrounds, see the contemporary text: AJC, Reprint Series, no. 3: Duker, *Political and Cultural Aspects*, section, "Emigration vs. Adjustment on the Spot," 5–6.
22. AJC, "Annual Report 1941," 721.
23. AJC, "A Statement, 1943" 3.
24. Due to its political agenda, which was mainly shaped by Western European Jewish tradition, the AJC initially competed with the WJC, and this rivalry no doubt existed between their respective subsidiaries, the Research Institute of the AJC and the Institute of Jewish Affairs, as well. On the distinction between the Western and Eastern European traditions of Jewish politics, see Biale, *Power and Powerlessness*, 23–141; and Mendelsohn, *On Modern Jewish Politics*, ch. 2.
25. M. R. Cohen, "Jewish Studies of Peace and Post-war Problems," 112.
26. The institute's detailed research program can be found in the appendix of ibid., 123–25. On the shift of attention toward human rights, see J. Robinson, "From Protection of Minorities." A historical introduction is provided by Mazower, "Strange Triumph"; and Rubin "End of Minority Rights."
27. The range of different activities is evident in the University of Chicago Library, Special Collections Research Center, Papers of Morris Raphael Cohen (hereafter UChicago, Cohen Papers), esp. boxes 50 and 54.
28. The program of study comprised the following topics: (1) the necessity for postwar planning; (2) a comparison between the two world wars; (3) Jewish strategies to prepare for peace during the First World War; (4) Europe between the two world wars; (5) Jews' position in the postwar world; (6) Palestine and the New

World; (7) welfare, reconstruction, and migration; and (8) Jewish survival and the democracy of the future. The study by Gottschalk and Duker appeared under the title *Jews in the Post-War World*.

29. Ibid., 204.

30. First came a *Pamphlet Series* entitled *Jews in the Postwar World*, which was published between 1942 and 1945, followed by a *Reprint Series*, a new edition of writings by institute staff and associates with a focus on legal issues. In addition, two important studies on restitution and human rights were published: Goldschmidt, *Legal Claims against Germany*; and Lauterpacht, *International Bill*.

31. J. Robinson, "Preface," 8.

32. Moses, *Jewish Post-War Claims*. For a summary of the proposals, see ibid., 77–80. The English translation of Moses's text refers on a number of occasions to "reconstruction." The analogous arguments put forward by Robinson and Moses on issues of reconstruction are identified by Sagi, "Die Rolle der jüdischen Organisationen," 101.

33. New York Public Library, Dorot Jewish Division, *ZP–*PBM p.v. 478–85, microfilm: Jewish Life and Literature. A Collection of Pamphlets, 478, no. 5: American Jewish Conference, Program for Postwar Jewish Reconstruction, April 1945.

34. "Wenn ich verzweifelt bin," 37.

35. An exception here was the large-scale initiatives launched by the Joint, which did what it could to provision Jews in Europe and especially the Soviet Union. For an introduction to the history of the Joint during and after the Second World War, see Bauer, *American Jewry and the Holocaust*; Grossmann, Patt, Levi, and Maud, *JDC at 100*. Overall, the debate on US-based Jews' attentiveness to and mobilization and support for the European Jews during the Second World War is highly polarized. For an introduction, see Breitman and Lichtman, *FDR and the Jews*, introduction; Medoff, "New Perspectives"; and Medoff, "American Responses." In his book *Holocaust in American Life*, Peter Novick in particular produced a more radical version of the idea—previously put forward by Henry Feingold (*Bearing Witness*), Guile Ne'eman Arad (*America*), and David Wyman (*Abandonment of the Jews*)—that American Jews intervened in war and persecution in Europe in an essentially individual, even marginal, way. In his book *Ambiguous Relations*, particularly the first chapter, "American Jews and the German Problem until the End of the War" (21–39), Shlomo Shafir adopts an intermediate position and places emphasis on individual initiatives. Hasia Diner, by way of contrast, underlines the various attempts at intervention by American-Jewish organizations and individual activists, opening up a more complex perspective on the possibilities of, and limits to, American Jews' awareness of and influence on German politics. See H. Diner, *Jews of the United States*, ch. 6.

36. See Feingold, *Bearing Witness*, esp. ch. 10.

37. M. R. Cohen, "Jewish Studies of Peace and Post-war Problems," 121–22.

38. Karbach, "Max Gottschalk," 281.

39. S. Baron, "What War Has Meant," 506.

40. S. Baron, "Reflections on the Future," 357–56. On Baron's somewhat skewed perspective during the war, see Weiss, "Tricks of Memory."

41. For a synopsis, see Mazower, "Reconstruction," esp. 25–26.

42. Adorno, "Out of the Firing-Line."

43. On the contrast between the concepts of saving and preserving in the context of Jewish activism outside Europe during the Holocaust and their specific genesis and sacred implications, see D. Diner, "Ambiguous Semantics," 97–98.

44. S. Baron, "Reflections on the Future," 357 (my emphasis).

45. Ibid., 367.

46. Salo W. Baron, Memorandum, June 1941, UChicago, Cohen Papers, box 50, folder 2.

47. Lemkin, "Acts Constituting a General (Transnational) Danger."

48. Lemkin, Axis Rule, 84–85.

49. Ofer, "Linguistic Conceptualization," 578.

50. "Jewish Action Is Urged: Dr. Salo Baron Says World Agency Should Demand and Direct It," New York Times, April 24, 1933, 4.

51. UL Stanford, M0580, Baron Papers, box 5, folder 4, Morris Cohen to Salo Baron, June 3, 1933.

52. For an introduction to the German-Jewish Defense, see Barkai, Mendes-Flohr, and Lowenstein, German-Jewish History in Modern Times, section 1: "Initiatives for Active Defense"; and Paucker, Jewish Defense.

53. See Cohen's autobiography, Dreamer's Journey, ch. 27. A brief introduction to Cohen and his political stance in relation to Baron is provided by Liberles, Salo Wittmayer Baron, 222–38.

54. On the idea of the CJR and the history of its founding years, see the Descriptions, Annual Reports and President's Reports of the CJR published from 1937; and Liberles, Salo Wittmayer Baron, ch. 5, 221–42.

55. Cohen, Dreamer's Journey, 242.

56. UL Stanford, M0580, Baron Papers, box 5, folder 4, Morris Cohen to Salo Baron, February 16, 1934.

57. Pinson, Essays on Antisemitism; Gallas, "Theoriebildung und Abwehrkampf."

58. Saul Friedländer coined the concept of "redemptive" Nazi anti-Semitism. This, he contends, is derived from Christian Jew hatred but is taken to an extreme, fusing radical anti-Jewish measures and ideology with a vision or goal of a pure Aryan race—to be realized through the expulsion and ultimately annihilation of the Jews. See Friedländer, Nazi Germany and the Jews, vol. 1, introduction and ch. 3.

59. Salo W. Baron, interview by Grace Cohen Grossman, tape 3.

60. S. Baron, "Journal and the Conference."

61. Cohen, Dreamer's Journey, 243; "Notes of a Broadcast by Professor Salo W. Baron, President of the Conference on Jewish Relations, interviewed by Miss Estelle M. Sternberger on Jan. 1, 1954, Radio Station WLIB," UL Stanford, M0670, JSS Papers, box 2, folder: Baron, Professor Salo W., Correspondence.

62. Report "Present Status of Conference Projects," September 20, 1938, UChicago, Cohen Papers, box 49, folder 1.

63. Cohen, "Work of the Conference," 11.

64. Conference on Jewish Relations, *President's Report, 1940–1943*, 3.

65. Cohen, "Publisher's Foreword," 3.

66. Engel, "Jewish Social Studies."

67. Cohen, *Dreamer's Journey*, 251–52.

68. Arendt, "Paper and Reality," 152–54, here 153.

69. Arendt, "Days of Change," 214–17, here 214.

70. StaBi, Nachlass Nr. 266, E. G. Lowenthal, Ordner 255, Memorandum "Resolutions adopted on the Conference on Restoration of Continental Jewish Museums, Libraries and Archives," London, April 11, 1943.

71. Cecil Roth, "Opening Address," Conference on Restoration of Continental Jewish Museums, Libraries and Archives, London, April 11, 1943, published in Roth, "Restoration of Jewish Libraries," here 255; for a short introduction to the conference's aims and activities, see Dvorkin, "Jewish-English Debate."

72. Roth, "Opening Address," 256–57.

73. "Ihre Hauptsorge. Die Vermögenswerte der Juden," in *Der Stürmer* 37, September 9, 1943, StaBi, Nachlass Nr. 266, E. G. Lowenthal, Ordner 255.

74. UL Stanford, M0580, Baron Papers, box 19, folder 22, and box 23, folder 11, correspondence between Baron and Roth.

75. Ibid., box 40, folder 1, Theodor Gaster to Salo W. Baron, May 26, 1943.

76. StaBi, Nachlass Nr. 266, E. G. Lowenthal, Ordner 255, Memorandum "Conference on Jewish Relations: Project for Post-War Studies," undated. On the conference and Gaster's proposals, see also "Jüdisch-kulturelles Leben im Nachkriegs-Europa," *Aufbau*, December 24, 1943.

77. UChicago, Cohen Papers, box 48, folder 10, Minutes, "Meeting of Board of Directors" October 31, 1944.

78. UChicago, Cohen Papers, box 50, folder 4, Theodor Gaster, "Commission on European Jewish Cultural Reconstruction—Terms of Reference," CJR Report to Members, September 1944. See also the letter from Gaster to Baron of August 23, 1944, listing members recruited for the Commission in UL Stanford, M0580, Baron Papers, box 40, folder 4, Salo W. Baron.

79. An overview of the state of the debate on "Postwar Jewish Reconstruction" in early 1945 is provided by the *Journal of Educational Sociology* 18 (1945), issue 5: Katsh, "Jew in the Postwar World." On cultural reconstruction, see two articles of this special issue: Gaster, "Foundations of Jewish Cultural Reconstruction"; and Tartakower, "Problems of Jewish Cultural Reconstruction."

80. S. Baron, "Spiritual Reconstruction."

81. Ibid., 4.

82. Ibid., 6.

83. Ibid., 6–7.

84. See UL Stanford, M0580, Baron Papers, box 39, folder 2, statements on use of funds and relevant minutes.

85. Ibid., Theodor Gaster to Leo Jung (Joint), December 20, 1944.

86. Salo W. Baron, introduction, "Tentative List of Jewish Cultural Treasures," 5–11, here 5.

87. Ibid., 7.

88. See, for example, UL Stanford, M0580, Baron Papers, box 39, folder 3, reports by Rabbi Philip Bernstein and Chaplain Lev following their return from Europe, in "Minutes, Meeting of the Commission on European Jewish Cultural Reconstruction," July 16, 1945.

89. This was reported at the commission general assembly on June 13, 1945. The commission was already cooperating with the AJC, the AJCon, the National Refugee Service, the Federation of Central European Jews, and the International Refugee Organization, Geneva. UL Stanford, M0580, Baron Papers, box 39, folder 3, "Minutes, Meeting of the Commission on European Jewish Cultural Reconstruction," June 13, 1945. The preparation for and conceptualization of the Tentative Lists project can be traced through the material in UL Stanford, M0670, Jewish Social Studies Papers, boxes 13 and 16.

90. See model questionnaires in UL Stanford, M0670, Jewish Social Studies Papers, box 16/17.

91. NLI, Arc 4°793/212, Otzrot HaGolah Papers, folder I: 1946, Gershom Scholem and Daniel Goldschmidt, "The Jewish Cultural Property under the Nazi Regime," undated. Criticisms of the list were expressed at the general assembly of July 16, 1945; see UL Stanford, M0580, Baron Papers, box 39, folder 3, "Minutes, Meeting of the Commission on European Jewish Cultural Reconstruction," July 16, 1945.

92. Research Staff, "Tentative List of Jewish Cultural Treasures"; Research Staff, "Tentative List of Jewish Educational Institutions"; Research Staff, "Tentative List of Jewish Periodicals"; Research Staff, "Addenda and Corrigenda"; Research Staff, "Tentative List of Jewish Publishers."

93. S. Baron, Foreword, "Tentative List of Jewish Educational Institutions," 5–8, here 5.

94. S. Baron, Foreword, "Tentative List of Jewish Periodicals," 7–9, here 8.

95. NA College Park, M1942, AHC, roll 2, Herbert Strauss to Ernst Grumach, January 27, 1947.

96. UL Stanford, M0580, Baron Papers, box 39, folder 2, Hannah Arendt to Salo W. Baron, July 31, 1945.

97. See Research staff, "Addenda and Corrigenda."

98. S. Baron, Foreword, "Tentative List of Jewish Periodicals," 8.

99. UL Stanford, M0580, Baron Papers, box 39, folder 2, Herbert Strauss to Salo W. Baron, December 12, 1945, with a reference to the committee's "Card Index on the Present Situation in Europe." See also ibid., box 232, folder 2, Research Committee, "Tentative Report on the Present Jewish Educational Situation in Europe," September 6, 1946.

100. UL Stanford, M0580, Baron Papers, box 39, folder 2, Herbert Strauss to Salo W. Baron, February 11, 1947.

101. Ibid., folder 3, Commission on European Jewish Cultural Reconstruction, Press Release, January 1947.

102. On American-Jewish efforts to commemorate and document Nazi crimes in the postwar period in a variety of ways, see H. Diner, *We Remember with Reverence and Love*; L. Baron, "Holocaust and American Public Memory"; Bauer, *Out of the Ashes*; and Gallas, "Frühe Holocaustforschung in Amerika." On the activities of survivors and immigrants in Israel after the Holocaust, see, for example, Ofer, "Strength of Remembrance"; Cohen, "Birth Pangs of Holocaust Research"; and Bar, "Between the Chamber of the Holocaust." A general introduction is provided by Dawidowicz, *Holocaust and the Historians*, esp. ch. 6; and Stengel, *Opfer als Akteure*.

103. See Jockusch, "Collect and Record!"

104. UL Stanford, M0580, Baron Papers, box 39, folder 3, Koppel Pinson to Hannah Arendt, April 2, 1946.

105. Ibid., box 31, folder 6, Seymour Pomrenze to Salo W. Baron, May 15, 1946.

106. NA College Park, M1942, AHC, roll 1, Richard Howard (MFA&A officer), report, September 17, 1946.

107. Ibid., roll 6, Max Weinreich to Isaac Bencowitz, July 9, 1946.

108. UL Stanford, M0580, Baron Papers, box 39, folder 3, "Minutes, Meeting of the Commission on European Jewish Cultural Reconstruction," February 21, 1946.

109. See, for example, two articles published at the time that mention the impending publication of the tentative lists and the Commission's objectives: "Plan Is Evolved to Trace Books Looted by the Nazis," *Herald Tribune*, March 10, 1946; "Cultural Treasures in Nazi Loot Listed," *New York Times*, March 10, 1946.

110. S. Baron, Introduction, "Tentative List of Jewish Cultural Treasures," 5–11.

111. NA College Park, M1949, MFA&A Records, roll 3, folder 457, Louis B. LaFarge (MFA&A/Economics Division) to the commission, August 6, 1946. This missive is a request for further copies of the "excellent compilation" for the OMGUS Restitution Branch. See also UL Stanford, M0580, Baron Papers, box 392, folder 21, unpublished paper by the JCR, "A History of Jewish Cultural Reconstruction, Inc.," undated, with references to positive responses from the State Department.

112. S. Baron, "Spiritual Reconstruction," 5.

113. AJHS, P-675, Dawidowicz Papers, box 51, folder 6, Max Weinreich to John Walker (curator of the National Gallery of Art in Washington, DC, and leading member of the Roberts Commission), September 29, 1944. Subsequent correspondence, ibid., box 55, folder 3, also reinforces the impression that YIVO played an important role in laying the groundwork for cultural restitution after the war.

114. UL Stanford, M0580, Baron Papers, box 39, folder 2, Philip Bernstein to Salo W. Baron, July 18, 1945.

115. Ibid., Abraham Aaroni, Memorandum "Regarding Looted Jewish Books, Archives and Religious Articles now in the Vicinity of Frankfurt/M Germany," March 4, 1946, addendum to the letter from Simon Federbusch to the Commission, March 5, 1946.

116. UL Stanford, M0580, Baron Papers, box 58, folder 9, "Report of Prof. Gershom Scholem on his mission to Europe (in the summer of 1946) concerning the libraries of the Diaspora."

117. Two strategy papers by Otzrot HaGolah provide the clearest demonstration of its attitude: NLI, Arc 4°793/212, Otzrot HaGolah Papers, folder I: 1946, Memorandum "Taskir ha Vaada haMishpatit she-aljedei haVaada le Hatzalat Otzrot HaGolah" (Memorandum of the Otzrot HaGolah Legal Council), February 26, 1946; and a little later, UL Stanford, M0580, Baron Papers, box 42, folder 112, Memorandum "Jewish Books in Offenbach, Germany, and Other Localities of Germany, Austria, Czechoslovakia and Other Countries—the Policy of the Hebrew University," January 15, 1948. On the beginnings of the debate on the memory of the Holocaust in Israel, see Segev, *Seventh Million*; Yablonka, *Survivors of the Holocaust*; Kenan, *Between Memory and History*; and Ofer, "Strength of Remembrance."

118. Lynx, *Future of the Jews*, 10. Among the participants were Thomas Mann, Edvard Beneš, Salomon Adler Rudel, Edward Hulton, Hyman Levy, and Joseph Heller.

119. For an introductory account of the Jewish attitude toward Jewish life in Germany after the Second World War, see D. Diner, "Banished"; Brenner, "In the Shadow"; Kauders, *Unmögliche Heimat*, esp. chs. 1 and 2; Geis, *Übrig sein*; Brumlik, Kiesel, Kugelmann, and Schoeps, *Jüdisches Leben in Deutschland*.

120. Robert Weltsch, "Judenbetreuung in Bayern" (1946), quoted in Richarz, "Jews in Today's Germanies," 265.

121. Weltsch, "Besuch in Frankfurt," 10. Contrary to such statements, Weltsch mostly had a fairly ambivalent attitude toward Zionism. See Wiese, "Janus Face of Nationalism."

122. Weltsch, "Besuch in Frankfurt," 9.

123. AJHS, P-675, Dawidowicz Papers, box 55, folder 3, Lucy Schildkret (Dawidowicz) to Joseph Horne, May 24, 1947.

124. UL Stanford, M0580, Baron Papers, box 39, folder 2, Hannah Arendt to Salo W. Baron, July 31, 1945.

125. Ibid., folder 3, Commission, Memorandum "Survey of the Legal Situation," 1946.

126. Landauer, *Der Zionismus im Wandel*, 300.

127. On the history of the JRSO, see Kagan and Weismann, *Report on the Operations*; JRSO, *After Five Years*; Takei, "Jewish People as the Heir"; Schreiber, "New Jewish Communities"; Lillteicher, *Raub, Recht und Restitution*, esp. ch. 7; Goschler, *Wiedergutmachung*, 172–83; and more recently, Lustig, "Who Are to Be the Successors?"

128. JRSO, *Betrachtungen zum Rückerstattungsrecht*, 80–81. On JRSO's views, see also JRSO, *After Five Years*.

129. NA College Park, RG 260, OMGUS Records, Records of the Property Division/Property Control and External Assets, Records of Branch Chief, box 13, Fred Hartzsch (Chief of Property Div./OMGUS) to Richard Howard (Chief of MFA&A, Restitution Branch), July 2, 1948.

130. See Lustig, "Who Are to Be the Successors?"; Takei, "Gemeinde Problem"; Schreiber, "New Jewish Communities," esp. 177–82; Lillteicher, *Raub, Recht und Restitution*, 357–70; Goschler, *Wiedergutmachung*, esp. 172–74; and Geis, *Übrig sein*, esp. 387–92 and 409–23.

131. JRSO, *Betrachtungen zum Rückerstattungsrecht*, 78.

132. UL Stanford, M0580, Baron Papers, box 39, folder 3, Commission, Memorandum "Survey of the Legal Situation," 1946, 2.

133. JRSO, *Betrachtungen zum Rückerstattungsrecht*, 79.

134. On the Paris Reparation Agreement of January 14, 1946, and its article 8, which regulated allocations to the victims of National Socialism, see Zweig, *German Reparations*, 14; and Ludi, "Why Switzerland?," 182.

135. See the summary of the situation of Jewish cultural property in several European countries, which refers to a number of authors, among them Zorach Wahrhaftig and Léon Poliakov, in UL Stanford, M0580, Baron Papers, box 39, folder 3, Commission on European Jewish Cultural Reconstruction, "Survey of the Factual Situation," 1946.

136. UL Stanford, M0580, Baron Papers, box 209, folder 12, report by Pomrenze, in "Minutes, Meeting of the Commission on European Jewish Cultural Reconstruction," June 26, 1946; ibid., box 39, folder 2, Hannah Arendt to Jerome Michael, August 9, 1946. David Fishman writes about several cases of wrapping "herring and other food products in pages from the Vilna edition of the Talmud" at markets in early postwar Vilnius. See Fishman, *Book Smugglers*, 146.

137. UL Stanford, M0580, Baron Papers, box 209, folder 12, Salo W. Baron to Jerome Michael, June 4, 1946. For the context of the complex history of Jewish survival in the Asian parts of the Soviet Union and an account of Jewish settlements in Samarkand and Tashkent at the time, see Grossmann, "Remapping Survival."

138. On the problem of the confiscations, see Grimsted, "Road to Minsk"; and Grimsted, Hoogewoud, and Ketelaar, *Returned from Russia*. On the stance of the Soviet military government toward the Jewish interest groups, see Lillteicher, "West Germany," 103–4; and Henry, *Restitution of Jewish Property*, 11.

139. UL Stanford, M0580, Baron Papers, box 39, folder 3, Koppel Pinson to Jehuda Magnes, March 11, 1946, quoted in Commission, Memorandum "Survey of the Factual Situation," 1946.

140. Ibid., Koppel Pinson to Salo W. Baron, March 13, 1946, quoted in Commission, Memorandum "Survey of the Factual Situation."

141. Ibid., folder 2, Minutes of the meeting at the Hebrew University on the state of the Otzrot HaGolah operation on September 8, 1946, composed on September 17, 1946 by H. Rablasky (in Hebrew). The meeting was attended by Judah Magnes, Salo W. Baron, Simha Assaf, Martin Buber, David Zvi Beneth (Joshua [Yehoshua]) Gutman, Ben-Zion Dinur, Gotthold Weil, Werner Senator, and Gershom Scholem.

142. UL Stanford, M0580, Baron Papers, box 39, folder 3, Commission, Memorandum "Plan of Action" (1946).

143. Ibid., Jerome Michael, Memorandum submitted by the Commission on European Jewish Cultural Reconstruction to Assistant Secretary of State General J. H. Hilldring, June 5, 1946.

144. Ibid., 1.

145. Ibid.

146. NA College Park, M1949, MFA&A Records, roll 3, folder OAD 1, Philip Bernstein to Joseph T. McNarney, July 1, 1946.

147. NLI, Arc 4°793/212, Otzrot HaGolah Papers, folder I: 1946, Jerome Michael to John H. Hilldring, August 26, 1946.

148. NA College Park, RG 59, General Records of the Department of State, box 28, folder 1, Ralph Stinson (MFA&A), Ardelia Hall (MFA&A Adviser), and Noel Hemmerdinger (State Department), Memorandum "Jewish Cultural Treasures in Germany and Austria. Comments on one Phase of the Proposal for an International Jewish Trustee Corporation Submitted by the Commission on European Jewish Cultural Reconstruction," September 24, 1946.

149. BArch, Z 45 F, RG 260, OMGUS Records, AHC, box 108–2, War Department to OMGUS, September 22, 1946.

150. NA College Park, M1949, MFA&A Records, roll 3, folder 456, Lester Born, Notes, June 5, 1946.

151. BArch, Z 45 F, RG 260, OMGUS Records, AHC, box 108–2, OMGUS, "Statement Concerning the Proposal for an International Jewish Trustee Corporation Submitted by the Commission on European Jewish Cultural Reconstruction" (fall 1946); NA College Park, RG 260, OMGUS Records, AHC, box 66, folder Jewish Cultural Property, telegram from Lucius Clay to State and War Department, October 16, 1946. Michael summarized the American bodies' views, with comments from the Commission's perspective, in a strategy paper: NLI, Arc 4°793/212, Otzrot HaGolah Papers, folder II: 1946, Memorandum "Our Proposal/Objections," undated.

152. UL Stanford, M0580, Baron Papers, box 209, folder 12, "Minutes, Meeting of the Commission on European Jewish Cultural Reconstruction," June 26, 1946.

153. NLI, Arc 4°793/212, Otzrot HaGolah Papers, folder II: 1946, telegram from John H. Hilldring to Judah Magnes, September 19, 1946; ibid., reply from Magnes, September 20, 1946; ibid., Judah Magnes to Salo W. Baron, December 3, 1946. See also UL Stanford, M0580, Baron Papers, box 43, folder 5, Salo W. Baron to Cecil Roth, November 22, 1949.

154. UL Stanford, M0580, Baron Papers, box 39, folder 3, Koppel Pinson to Jehuda Magnes, March 11, 1946, quoted in Commission, Memorandum "Survey of the Factual Situation," 1946.

155. See Takei, "Jewish People as the Heir," 80; Armbruster, Rückerstattung der Nazi-Beute, esp. 476–77.

156. NLI, Arc 4°793/212, Otzrot HaGolah Papers, folder II: 1946, minutes of the meeting "Memorandum for Mr. Hemmendinger," undated. See also the account in Kurtz, America and the Return of Nazi Contraband, 159.

157. US military government law no. 59.

158. Clay, *Decision in Germany*, 311.

159. This is the argument made, for example, by Goschler, *Schuld und Schulden*, 58.

160. Kenan, *Between Memory and History*, xxi. On the construction of this narrative before and during the foundation of the state of Israel, see, for example, ibid., introduction and ch. 1: "The Jishuv"; and Don-Yehiya, "Memory and Political Culture."

161. Yablonka, *Survivors of the Holocaust*, 4.

162. Roth, "Jewish Culture," 331.

163. On Cecil Roth's self-image, see Brenner, *Prophets of the Past*, ch. 4, here 121–56; and the biography written by his wife: Irene Roth, *Cecil Roth*. Delving deeper into this issue, Yehuda Dvorkin argues that Cecil Roth's position is informed by an imperial perception of the mandate in Palestine as the main Jewish center within the British sphere of influence. This would explain his strong support for claims from Jerusalem and also his cautious efforts to pursue British claims after the end of the mandate. See Dvorkin, "A Jewish-English Debate."

164. S. Baron, introduction, "Tentative List of Jewish Cultural Treasures," 6.

165. UL Stanford, M0580, Baron Papers, box 39, folder 3, Jerome Michael, "Memorandum submitted by the Commission on European Jewish Cultural Reconstruction to General J. H. Hilldring," June 5, 1946.

166. For the history of the Danish initiative for a World Jewish Library, see Intrator, "Books across Borders," ch. 3, esp. 166–70, 189–204. My sincere thanks to Miriam Intrator for providing me with a copy of her important study.

167. UL Stanford, M0580, Baron Papers, box 39, folder 3, Jerome Michael to Raphael Edelmann, January 22, 1947.

168. Judah Magnes to Rafael Edelmann, January 22, 1947, quoted in Intrator, "Books across Borders," 196.

169. Gershom Scholem to Hugo and Escha Bergman, December 15, 1947, in Scholem, *Briefe*, vol. 1, 331–33, here 332–33. A translated, shortened version of this letter appears in Scholem, *Life in Letters*, 340–41. It does not include the quotation shown here.

170. LoC, LoC-Mission Papers, box 34, folder Restitution of "Unrestituted" Materials/Jewish Books, Theodor Gaster to Luther Evans, December 30, 1945.

171. NA College Park, M1949, MFA&A Records, roll 3, folder Jewish Archives and Libraries, Reuben Peiss to Lucius Clay, July 6, 1946.

172. NA College Park, RG 260, Property Division, box 8, folder 2: JRSO Charter, JRSO, Certificate of Incorporation, April 25, 1947 and Appointment of JRSO, June 23, 1948; details on the establishment of JRSO are provided by Takei, *Jewish People as the Heir*, esp. 77–85.

173. The Council for the Protection of the Rights and Interests of Jews from Germany had been founded in January 1945 on the initiative of Siegfried Moses in New York through the amalgamation of three existing German Jewish refugee organizations: the American Federation of Jews from Central Europe (which had emerged from the New York–based German Jewish Center that brought together

several clubs and federations of German Jewish immigrants in the US and was founded in New York in 1939—bearing its new name from December 1941), the Association of Jewish Refugees in Great Britain, and Irgun Olei Merkaz Europa in Palestine. In 1947, it was renamed the Council of Jews from Germany. When Leo Baeck arrived in London from Theresienstadt in June 1945, the council headquarters was moved to London, and Baeck became its president. On its history, see Nattermann, *Deutsch-jüdische Geschichtsschreibung*, esp. chs. 2 and 3; Nattermann, "Struggle for the Preservation of a German-Jewish Legacy"; Hoffmann, "Founding of the Leo Baeck Institute."

174. See Kubowitzki, *Unity in Dispersion*, 230, 359–60.

175. On the request for Baron's participation in the WJC, see UL Stanford, M0580, Baron Papers, box 39, folder 2, Hannah Arendt to Salo W. Baron, July 31, 1945; on the request made to Stephen Wise, ibid., Arendt to Baron, August 17, 1945.

176. See Leon Kubowitzki's (WJC) letter to Jerome Michael of June 14, 1946, in which he criticizes what he saw as the Commission's domineering behavior and attempts to outshine the WJC's own efforts; quoted in Herman, "Hashavat Avedah," 56.

177. For an account of the competition between the Commission and the WJC and how it was ultimately brought to an end, see ibid., 55–57 and 80.

178. UL Stanford, M0580, Baron Papers, box 231, folder 17, JCR, "Minutes of a Special Meeting of the Board of Directors," January 28, 1948.

179. UL Stanford, M0580, Baron Papers, box 232, folder 9, "Certificate of Incorporation of Jewish Cultural Reconstruction, Inc.," April 30, 1947.

180. JCR rules allowed for the incorporation of new members at the discretion of the board of directors. See UL Stanford, M0580, Baron Papers, box 231, folder 18, "By-Laws of Jewish Cultural Reconstruction, Inc." Evidence of the incorporation of these organizations comes from ibid., "Amendments to By-Laws" from October 17, 1949.

181. The Alliance's incorporation was first discussed in June 1947. See LBI, xMfW, WLD, doc. 1–42, reel 26, folder 561, JCR, "Minutes of a Special Meeting of the Board of Directors," December 19, 1949.

182. NLI, Arc 4°793/212, Otzrot HaGolah Papers, folder II: 1946, Salo W. Baron to Judah Magnes, December 26, 1946.

183. See Takei, "Jewish People as the Heir," 86–88.

184. UL Stanford, M0580, Baron Papers, box 39, folder 2, Salo W. Baron to Isaiah L. Kenen (American Jewish Conference), undated (before February 15, 1947).

185. Ibid., box 43, folder 5, draft of the agreement between JRSO and JCR, Inc., to be signed by Salo W. Baron and Edward M. Warburg (approved by the Joint and the JA), June 1947.

186. Ibid., Jewish Restitution Commission to JCR, Inc., August 21, 1947. At the request of the American military government, in spring 1948, the name Jewish Restitution Commission was changed to the Jewish Restitution Successor Organization to make it clear that it was not a state or military institution.

187. On the provision of funds for the JCR by the Joint and JA to the tune of $10,000 USD over its first six months, see UL Stanford, M0580, Baron Papers, box 231, folder 17, JCR, "Minutes of a Special Meeting of the Board of Directors," October 7, 1947.

CHAPTER 3. RECONSTRUCTING JEWISH CULTURE

1. The implementing regulation to the restitution law allowed for the appointment of a Jewish successor organization to file claims to heirless Jewish assets. This regulation came into force on June 23, 1948, and was based on § 13 of law 59. It set out, first, the prerequisites for a successor organization and its responsibilities and, second, identified the property assets under its jurisdiction. JRSO began to operate in the American zone on August 17, 1948.

2. NA College Park, RG 260, OMGUS Records, AHC, box 66, folder Jewish Cultural Property, telegram from Lucius Clay to the headquarters of the Department of the Army/Civil Affairs Division, September 4, 1948. Clay's outstanding role in facilitating the "Frankfurt Agreement" is also emphasized in a personal note of thanks telegraphed to him shortly after the authorization of the JCR/JRSO: "Undersigned organizations representing leading Jewish organizations in the world express their profound gratitude for your efforts in preserving many Jewish cultural and religious objects [. . .] and for recent agreement." BArch, Z 45 F, AG 1949/20/6, Salo W. Baron and Edward M. Warburg to General Lucius Clay, by telegram, March 14, 1949.

3. The US Department of War was renamed the Department of the Army on September 18, 1947. In 1949, it became a military division of the newly founded Department of Defense.

4. The Department of the Army replied to Clay's telegram on September 18, 1948: "State requests no arrangements be made with Jewish Cultural Reconstruction Incorporated redisposition Jewish Cultural material at Offenbach Depot prior receipt further communication from us. Question being studied and you will be advised soonest." NA College Park, RG 260, OMGUS Records, AHC, box 66, folder Jewish Cultural Property.

5. See Kurtz, *America and the Return of Nazi Contraband*, ch. 7: "Cultural Restitution in the American Zone, 1946–49," esp. 127.

6. BArch, Z 45 F, RG 260, OMGUS Records, shipment 17, box 314–1, "Regulation No. 3 under Military Government Law No. 59 and Appointment. Designation of Successor Organizations Pursuant to Military Law No. 59 and Appointment of a Successor Organization to Claim Jewish Property," June 23, 1948. Within this regulation, the appended "License No. 49" of August 17, 1949 authorized the JRSO to carry out all relevant activities within the American occupation zone. See ibid. On the JRSO's tasks and self-image, see Kagan and Weismann, *Report on the Operations*.

7. CAHJP, JRSO Papers, folder 923c, Hannah Arendt to Eli Rock (Joint/JRSO), September 1, 1950.

8. NA College Park, RG 260, OMGUS Records, AHC, box 66, folder Jewish Cultural Property, OMGUS/Property Division, "Memorandum of Agreement, Subject 'Jewish Cultural Property,'" February 15, 1949.

9. The memorandum literally states, "These properties are transferred to JCR, Inc. with the proviso that they are to be utilized for the maintenance of the cultural heritage of the Jewish people." Ibid.

10. Ibid.

11. Brunner, Frei, and Goschler, "Komplizierte Lernprozesse. Zur Geschichte und Aktualität der Wiedergutmachung," in Brunner, Frei, and Goschler, *Die Praxis der Wiedergutmachung*, 9–47, here 12.

12. On the successor organizations' contribution to implementing the Luxembourg Agreement, see Zweig, *German Reparations*, ch. 2; Goschler, *Wiedergutmachung*, esp. 257–77; and Henry, *Confronting the Perpetrators*, 108–20.

13. UL Stanford, M0580, Baron Papers, box 231, folder 17, report "Excerpts from Dr. Joshua Starr's Report Dated Frankfurt, June 2, 1948."

14. YIVO, 15/6896 1947 (Per), OAD Collection, "Report on Jewish Materials in the Depot by Mr. Joshua Starr," in OAD Monthly Report, September 1948. Information on Starr's contribution to the sorting and identifying of Hebrew-language books in the depot is also provided by the monthly depot reports of October and November 1948. Ibid.

15. On Philipp Auerbach's prominent and tragic role in postwar restitution and indemnification negotiations, see Goschler, "Der Fall Philipp Auerbach"; Goschler, "Attitude toward Jews"; Geller, *Jews in Post-War Germany*, 47–85 and 208–11; and Brenner, *After the Holocaust*, ch. 3.1. For more detail on the tensions between Auerbach and the JCR, see various letters sent from Europe by Hannah Arendt, UL Stanford, M0580, Baron Papers, box 232, folder 5, such as Arendt, Memorandum to Dr. [George] Weis (JRSO) on the meeting of the Bavarian Association of Jewish Communities (Bayrischer Landesverband jüdischer Gemeinden) under Auerbach's chairmanship on January 22, 1950.

16. UL Stanford, M0580, Baron Papers, box 231, folder 17, Joshua Starr, Field Report No. 3, "Visit to Vienna," September 4, 1948.

17. Alexander Marx (Jewish Theological Seminary) acted as chair of the committee; further members as of January 1949 were Samuel Belkin (Yeshiva University), Joshua Bloch (Jewish Division of the New York Public Library), Oscar Fasman (Hebrew Theological College, IL), Louis Finkelstein (Jewish Theological Seminary), Nelson Glueck (Hebrew Union College), Isaac Edward Kiev (Jewish Institute for Religion), Abraham Neuman (Dropsie College, Joint), David de Sola Pool (Union of Sephardic Congregations), and Max Weinreich (YIVO).

18. NA College Park, M1949, MFA&A Records, AHC, roll 3, folder 456, Joseph Horne, report "Transfer of OAD-Property to Wiesbaden," May 7, 1948.

19. UL Stanford, M0580, Baron Papers, box 43, folder 5, Bernard Heller to Joshua Starr, July 27, 1949. This letter includes Heller's entire speech, while the official report, following its abbreviation, includes just a few quotations from it. See LBI,

xMfW, WLD, doc. 1–42, reel 26, folder 561, Bernard Heller, Field Report No. 8, July 25, 1949.

20. The Mapu Library in the Lithuanian city of Kaunas, founded by Zionists in 1908, was named after author Abraham Mapu (1808–1867), who wrote in Hebrew and was a representative of the Haskalah. On the arrangements made for the Baltic Collection, see documents in NA College Park, RG 260, OMGUS Records, AHC, Wiesbaden Central Collecting Point, General Records, 1945–1952, box 28, folder Jewish Cultural Property and folder Jewish Cultural Reconstruction, Inc.

21. On the discussion of the State Department's proposal to the JCR to take care of the collection, see Baron Papers, M0750, box 231, folder 17, "Minutes, Board of Directors Meeting," May 5, 1949 and "Minutes, Board of Directors Meeting," June 7, 1949; for the final agreement, see NA College Park, RG 260, OMGUS Records, AHC, box 66, folder JCR, "Addendum II to Memorandum of Agreement of 15 February 1949, Subject 'Jewish Cultural Property,'" July 22, 1949, signed on behalf of the JCR by Bernard Heller.

22. NA College Park, RG 260, OMGUS Records, AHC, box 66, folder JCR, Chief of Staff US Army/Chief Civil Affairs Division to HQ European Command and OMGUS, November 17, 1948.

23. Kurtz, *America and the Return of Nazi Contraband*, 166.

24. LBI, xMfW, WLD, doc. 1–42, reel 26, folder 561, JCR, "Minutes, Annual Meeting of the Corporation JCR," October 17, 1949. See also Kurtz, *America and the Return of Nazi Contraband*, 167.

25. See Hannah Arendt's open remarks to Gershom Scholem on the subject: "We are now preparing the procedure for claimants of individually owned books of six or more per owner. In the roster which shows the names of the people found in the books, we included the names of the owners of the Baltic collection on the same principle: we shall publicize only private owners of six or more books and we shall not publicize, at least for the time being, the names of the institutions in the Baltic countries, to which the majority of the Baltic books belonged. I don't believe that you will have any trouble in getting the bulk of the unclaimed Baltic collection allocated to Israel, even though the demand for books of this kind is also quite considerably strong not only in the United States but in all of the Western hemisphere (Latin American countries)," Arendt to Scholem, March 6, 1951, in *Correspondence of Arendt and Scholem*, 158.

26. UL Stanford, M0580, Baron Papers, box 58, folder 9, JCR, "Minutes Board of Directors Meeting," June 4, 1951; call to vote and result: NLI, Arc 4°793/288, Otzrot HaGolah Papers, folder 334/335, Hannah Arendt to all corporation members, June 12, 1951/July 11, 1951. In September 1952, Arendt then reported that even the few objects that had been surrendered to the Joint could not be allocated, as a result of which further sections were shipped to Israel. UL Stanford, M0580, Baron Papers, box 59, folder 1, Hannah Arendt to Salo W. Baron, September 2, 1952.

27. For detailed discussions of different aspects of the American policy towards Germany after 1945, see Junker, *United States and Germany*. On the topic of the

transfer of responsibility for restitution to German authorities, see Lillteicher, *Raub, Recht und Restitution*, 312–25; and in a more general context, Rickman, *Conquest and Redemption*, 143–75.

28. LBI, xMfW, WLD, doc. 1–42, reel 26, folder 561, Bernard Heller, Field Report No. 9, September 1949.

29. On Narkiss's background and his mission to salvage artworks in Europe after the war, see Berger, *Jewish Museum*, 488–510; Kochavi, "Value of Objects."

30. UL Stanford, M0580, Baron Papers, box 231, folder 17, JCR, "Minutes Meeting Advisory Committee JCR, Inc.," February 6, 1949.

31. Arendt, "Jewish Cultural Reconstruction, Inc.," 792.

32. On the history of Jewish ceremonial objects during World War II, see Cohen and Heimann-Jelinek, *Neglected Witnesses*. For the various ways in which the Nazis sought to extinguish the Jewish memory, see Rupnow, "Annihilating— Preserving—Remembering"; and Confino, *World without Jews*.

33. "Burying Jewish Religious Objects in Jersey," *New York Times*, January 14, 1952.

34. UL Stanford, M0580, Baron Papers, box 231, folder 17, JCR, "Minutes Annual Meeting Board of Directors," October 17, 1949; and ibid., Cecil Roth to Salo W. Baron, December 7, 1949. Roth complained that the public reaction to this operation had been one of incomprehension, with criticisms being directed at his group because of its presence in England.

35. LBI, xMfW, WLD, doc. 1–42, reel 26, folder 561, Bernard Heller, "Field Report No. 8," July 25, 1949.

36. "JCR, Inc. World Distribution of Ceremonial Objects and Torah Scrolls, July 1, 1949–January 31, 1952," facsimile in Heuberger, "Zur Rolle der 'Jewish Cultural Reconstruction,'" 101a. On the distribution of ritual objects, see also Herman, "Brand Plucked out of the Fire."

37. A number of lists from the *Jewish Chronicle* and *Aufbau* can be found in StaBi, Nachlass Nr. 266, E. G. Lowenthal, Ordner 314. f. ex."Bücher suchen ihre Eigentümer: In Deutschland gefundene Bücher werden zurückerstattet," *Aufbau*, March 30, 1951. Subsequent to Arendt's proposal to Curt Wormann in Israel, these lists were distributed and also broadcast in *The Voice of Israel*, see NLI, Arc 4°793/288, Otzrot HaGolah Papers, folder 254, Curt Wormann to Hannah Arendt, August 1, 1951.

38. LBI, xMfW, WLD, doc. 1–42, reel 26, folder 561, Ernst G. Lowenthal, "Field Report No. 17," February 1950; NLI, Arc 4°793/288, Otzrot HaGolah Papers, folder 337, Hannah Arendt, "Minutes, Annual Meeting of the Corporation," December 10, 1951.

39. On the JCR's decision, see NLI, Arc 4°793/228, Otzrot HaGolah Papers, folder 332, "Minutes, Board of Directors Meeting," June 4, 1951. It was not possible to reconstruct with complete certainty how this decision was put into effect. For an introduction to the historical context of the Agathe Lasch case, see Vaughn, *Interim Solution*. On other parts of the confiscated library of Agathe Lasch, see Harbeck and Kobold, "Spurensicherung."

40. UL Stanford, Mo580, Baron Papers, box 58, folder 9, JCR, "Minutes, Board of Directors Meeting," December 21, 1950.

41. On the process of distribution, see ibid., box 231, folder 18, Hannah Arendt, "Overall Report of the Activities of the Corporation from its Beginnings in October 1947, until March 1952," sheet no. 1: "World Distribution of Books, July 1, 1949–January 31, 1952," July 1952. On the debate on the distribution of archival materials, see ibid., folder 15, JCR, "Minutes, Meeting of Board of Directors," December 21, 1950.

42. LBI, xMfW, WLD, doc. 1–42, reel 26, folder 561, JCR, "Minutes, Board of Directors Meeting," June 5, 1950.

43. Hannah Arendt to Heinrich Blücher, February 5, 1950, in *Within Four Walls*, 127.

44. Karl Jaspers, in a note attached to a letter from Hannah Arendt to Heinrich Blücher from Basel, December 28, 1949, in ibid., 112–13.

45. Estimates of the number of Jewish DPs in Germany between 1945 and 1952 vary. Atina Grossmann and Tamar Lewinsky give a figure of a quarter of a million. See Grossmann and Lewinsky, "Way Station," 59; Michael Brenner estimates 182,000 in Brenner, *After the Holocaust*, 16; Zeev Mankowitz suggests that there were around 300,000 DPs in Germany, Austria, and Italy in Mankowitz, *Life between Memory and Hope*, 2; Margarete Myers Feinstein estimates 300,000 DPs for Germany alone; see Myers Feinstein, *Holocaust Survivors in Postwar Germany*, 1. In a "Resolution on Germany," World Jewish Congress members at the first postwar conference in Montreux, Switzerland, in June 1948 reaffirmed "the previous resolutions adopted by the World Jewish Congress in regard to Germany and particularly the determination of the Jewish people never again to settle on the bloodstained soil of Germany," World Jewish Congress, Second Plenary Assembly, Montreux 1948, Political Commission, Resolution on Germany, 1, accessible online at the site of the Berman Jewish Policy Archive, Stanford University: https://www.bjpa.org.

46. See Kauders, *Unmögliche Heimat*, esp. 45–49, here 48.

47. For a more detailed account of Jews in Germany in the postwar period and their relationship with Jewish organizations and Jews worldwide, see D. Diner, "Banished"; Geis, *Übrig sein*; Gay, *Safe among the Germans*; Mankowitz, *Life between Memory and Hope*; Grossmann, *Jews, Germans, and Allies*; Geller, *Jews in Post-Holocaust Germany*; and Brenner, "In the Shadow."

48. Hannah Arendt to Gertrud Jaspers, May 30, 1946, in *Correspondence 1926–1969*, 41.

49. Hannah Arendt to Heinrich Blücher, December 14, 1949, in *Within Four Walls*, 103.

50. Hannah Arendt to Heinrich Blücher, July 25, 1952, in ibid., 208–9. On Arendt's attitude toward Germany in the postwar period, see Gallas, "Rückkehr im Schreiben."

51. UL Stanford, Mo580, Baron Papers, box 232, folder 5, Hannah Arendt, "Memorandum to Dr. [Georg] Weis (JRSO) concerning the meeting of the Bavarian State Association on January 22, 1950" (original in spaced letters).

52. Ibid., box 43, folder 6, Hannah Arendt to Salo W. Baron, December 30, 1949. Against the background of this and other incidents, Arendt urged the JCR to make a public statement underlining that it was not selling objects. Hannah

Arendt, "Field Report No. 18," February 15–March 10, 1950, in *Correspondence of Arendt and Scholem*, 247–54, here 248.

53. UL Stanford, M0580, Baron Papers, box 232, folder 5, Meir Ben-Horin, "Field Report No. 21," October 1950.

54. Ibid., box 231, folder 17, JCR, "Minutes, Board of Directors Meeting," May 5, 1949.

55. BArch, MFA&A, Box 219, OAD Monthly Report, August 1946; Pinson reports here that half the material found by the MFA&A in Nuremberg from the Stürmer Collection (looted books held by the Nazi Stürmer publishing house and Julius Streicher's private collection) was passed on to him by the Nuremberg community, whose members planned to emigrate. The other half remained in the possession of the Nuremberg Municipal Library because it had received it from the MFA&A as a form of compensation for war-destroyed collections.

56. CAHJP, JRSO Papers, folder 923b, Mordechai Narkiss, "Ceremonial Objects in German Museums, Preliminary Findings," probably August/September 1949 (not clearly dated). The items involved were Torah scrolls, fabrics, and the congregational library.

57. The clearest account of the JRSO's situation is provided by Takei, "Gemeinde Problem"; see also Steinberg, "Road to Recovery"; Meng, *Shattered Spaces*, 31–36; Lillteicher, *Raub, Recht und Restitution*, 357–70.

58. On Grumach's biography, his involvement in cultural restitution, and his life in Berlin after 1945, see Holzer-Kawałko, "Jewish Intellectuals"; and Holzer-Kawałko, "Lost on the Island."

59. UL Stanford, M0580, Baron Papers, box 231, folder 17, Joshua Starr, "Field Report No. 6," April 8, 1949; and Hannah Arendt, "Field Report No. 16: Report on Berlin," February 11–18, 1950, in *Correspondence of Arendt and Scholem*, 241–46.

60. On the 7,761 volumes from the Berlin Congregational Libraries in the OAD or in Wiesbaden, see LBI, xMfW, WLD, doc. 1–42, reel 26, folder 561, Bernard Heller, "Field Report No. 9," September 1949.

61. Hannah Arendt, "Field Report No. 16, Report on Berlin, February 11–18, 1950," in *Correspondence of Arendt and Scholem*, 241–46, here 242.

62. Ibid., 245.

63. Grossmann, "Rabbi Steven Schwarzschild's Reports," 239. For a general introduction, see Grossmann and Lewinsky, "Way Station," 72–73; and Gay, *Safe among the Germans*, 144–201.

64. Schwarzschild, "Note on Steven Schwarzschild," 244.

65. The official note from Heinz Galinski on behalf of the Jewish community of Berlin was enclosed with the letter from Hannah Arendt to Gershom Scholem of August 8, 1950. The English translation of the correspondence does not include Galinski's letter; therefore, see *Arendt-Scholem Briefwechsel*, 298–99. Arendt laconically commented to Scholem, "For your planned trip to Berlin, please find enclosed a lovely note from the community gentlemen [Galinski]. For your information, the books are now in the Oranienburger Strasse in the attic, and when and if you are there don't forget to climb a little stairway which leads from one attic to the one above." *Correspondence of Arendt and Scholem*, 135.

66. BArch, Z 45 F, RG 260, OMGUS Records, AHC, box 204, Berthold Breslauer to Commanding Officer, Offenbach Archival Depot, December 5, 1946.
67. Ernst Grumach, "Bericht über die Beschlagnahme und Behandlung der früheren jüdischen Bibliotheksbestände durch die Stapo-Dienststellen in den Jahren 33–45," translated in Schidorsky, "Confiscation of Libraries," 356.
68. On Grumach's position in postwar Berlin, see Holzer-Kawałko, "Lost on the Island."
69. Galinski, "New Beginning of Jewish Life," 101. On Galinski himself, see Nachama and Schoeps, *Aufbau nach dem Untergang*; and Nachama, "Heinz Galinski." For an English account of his commitment to rebuilding Jewish life in Germany, see Holmgren, "Heinz Galinski."
70. A memorandum penned by Arendt and minutes of a meeting of the JCR board of directors describe these difficulties. The situation in Berlin was not discussed at subsequent meetings. NLI, Arc 4°793/288, Otzrot HaGolah Papers, folder 328, Hannah Arendt, "Memorandum to the Members of the Board of Directors," November 28, 1950; UL Stanford, M0580, Baron Papers, box 231, folder 15, JCR, "Meeting of the Board of Directors," December 21, 1950. On the recurring doubts felt about the collection and its composition, see a number of letters between Hannah Arendt and Gershom Scholem in *Correspondence of Arendt and Scholem*, esp. letter no. 52, 93–94 and 292n3; letter no. 57, 97n2 (which lacks some information on the community library given in the published German version of the letters); letter no. 65, 109–11; and letter no. 83, 144–46, here esp. 144–45.
71. UL Stanford, M0580, Baron Papers, box 231, folder 18, Hannah Arendt, "Overall Report of the Activities of the Corporation from its Beginnings in October 1947, until March 1952," sheet no. 1: "World Distribution of Books July 1, 1949–January 31, 1952," July 1952. On the Berlin Torah scrolls: NLI, Arc 4°793/288, Otzrot HaGolah Papers, folder 337, Hannah Arendt, "Minutes of the Annual Meeting of the Corporation," December 10, 1951. The remark about the tussle over the scrolls appears in a letter from Hannah Arendt to Gershom Scholem, January 1, 1952, in *Correspondence of Arendt and Scholem*, 167.
72. Hannah Arendt to Heinrich Blücher, February 14, 1950, in *Within Four Walls*, 133–34.
73. NA College Park, RG 260, OMGUS Records, Records of the Property Division, box 15, "Appointment of Successor Organization," Berlin, October 1, 1949.
74. On the rich Jewish library culture in Berlin before 1933, see Kirchhoff, "Urbane Lesewelten. Berlin," in Kirchhoff, *Häuser des Buches*, 83–98.
75. The Museum Jüdischer Altertümer (Museum of Jewish Antiquities) was established in 1922 on the premises of the Frankfurt Jewish Community and held a large and rare collection of Judaica. In the *Novemberpogrom* of 1938, the building was plundered and destroyed, with a significant number of items subsequently being transferred to the Frankfurt Historical Museum (Historisches Museum Frankfurt). The Museum of Jewish Antiquities was not rebuilt or reopened after the war. See Heimann-Jelinek, *Was übrig blieb*.
76. The Frankfurt Historical Museum, opened in 1878, was renamed the Stadtgeschichtliches Museum in 1934 and placed under Nazi leadership. It regained its

original name in 1954. During the war, its staff stashed twenty-three crates of ritual objects from the Jewish Museum and synagogues in a bunker for safekeeping. See Tauber, *Zwischen Kontinuität und Neuanfang*, 133. A large portion of Schönberger's correspondence and negotiations with the city of Frankfurt am Main can be found in the museum's archive under Auslagerungsakten 1032/Altkorrespondenz Schönberger. I would like to thank Katharina Rauschenberger for kindly granting me access to these files.

77. For an introduction to the postwar history of the Frankfurt Jewish Community, see Kolinsky, *After the Holocaust*, 157–86; Freimüller, "Mehr als eine Religionsgemeinschaft"; and Tauber, *Zwischen Kontinuität und Neuanfang*.

78. On the dispute over the allocation of the holdings, see UL Stanford, M0580, Baron Papers, box 231, folder 15, JCR, "Minutes, Board of Directors Meeting," December 21, 1950. The result of the vote was announced in July the same year: NLI, Arc 4°793/288, Otzrot HaGolah Papers, folder 335, Hannah Arendt to all members of the JCR, July 11, 1951.

79. See his correspondence and the account by Rauschenberger, "Restitution of Jewish Cultural Objects," here esp.: "Guido Schönberger's Work for the JCR," 205–10.

80. Tauber, *Zwischen Kontinuität und Neuanfang*, 133.

81. CAHJP, JRSO Papers, box 923c, "Special Report by Prof. G. Scholem on 'Non-Jewish Books in Frankfurt,' which had been handed to the Land Hessen by Military Authorities in Offenbach and about which the JCR has successfully negotiated with the German Authorities," September 14, 1950; Gershom Scholem to Hannah Arendt, September 14, 1950, in *Correspondence of Arendt and Scholem*, 141–44.

82. NLI, Arc 4°793/288, Otzrot HaGolah Papers, folder 326, JCR, "Minutes, Board of Directors Meeting," October 9, 1950.

83. Despite the formal establishment of the Federal Republic of Germany in May 1949, in line with the occupation statute of April 10, 1949 (signed by the three Allied military governors Pierre Koenig, Lucius Clay, and Brian Robertson), until May 5, 1955, restitution policy was regulated by the occupying powers. It was thus with the Allies, represented by the Allied High Commission in West Germany, that the JRSO and JCR still had to negotiate. On the positions of France, the United Kingdom, and the Soviet Union with respect to laws on compensation and restitution, see esp. Lillteicher, *Raub, Recht und Restitution*, esp. 56–81.

84. Hannah Arendt mentions this when reporting to Baron: "The feeling of the British as well as the French authorities is that cultural objects should not be removed from their place of origin." See Baron Papers, M0580, box 59, folder 1, Hannah Arendt to Salo W. Baron, September 2,1952.

85. For an overview of the course of events in the British zone, see Lillteicher, *Raub, Recht und Restitution*, esp. chs. 1.5 and 7; Goschler, *Wiedergutmachung*, ch. 5.1.; and Lavsky, *New Beginnings*, 26 and 53–55. On the history of the URO, see Bentwich, *United Restitution Organisation*. On the establishment and work of the

JTC, see the texts composed by its general secretary, Charles Kapralik: Kapralik, *Reclaiming the Nazi Loot*; Kapralik, *History of the Work*.

86. Hannah Arendt gives a detailed account of the situation in the British zone in her "Field Report No. 18" in *Correspondence of Arendt and Scholem*, 247–54. The objection raised by the Allied High Commissioners related to the case of North Rhine-Westphalia, where a decree issued by the state government after consultation with the British authorities had recognized the Jewish communities as legal successors to their prewar equivalents, thus making them heirs to all recoverable Jewish material and property. The High Commissioners subsequently pointed out that the German authorities had exceeded their mandate and declared the decree null and void.

87. CAHJP, JRSO Papers, folder 923c, memorandum "Work in British Zone of Germany," Committee on Restoration to JTC, July 6, 1950; UL Stanford, Baron Papers, M0580, box 232, folder 5, Jewish Trust Corporation for Germany LTD, Note on Conversation between Mr. Meir Ben-Horin, Field Director for Western Europe of the Jewish Cultural Reconstruction Inc. and Dr. Kapralik and Dr. Lachs on the 11th August 1950.

88. See esp. StaBi, Nachlass Nr. 266, E. G. Lowenthal, file 315, Oscar Rabinowicz to Ernst G. Lowenthal, November 2, 1949. Correspondence between Lowenthal, Starr and Arendt, between Rabinowicz and Lowenthal, and between Roth and Baron attest to the tremendous tensions; see the same file. The competition between Baron and Roth is discussed in Weiss, "Tricks of Memory."

89. Ben-Horin was the first to support this idea. In a memorandum of August 1950, he stated, "If Lowenthal is employed by JTC for cultural property, a considerable portion of JCR experience in collecting and handling these materials is ipso facto and unconditionally at the disposal of JTC. All that JCR is and can be interested in, [. . .] is that its experience in research, search, and distribution be utilized." UL Stanford, Baron Papers, M0580, box 232, folder 5, Meir Ben-Horin, Memorandum to Salo W. Baron and Hannah Arendt, August 17, 1950. This position was adopted by Baron and the board of directors. See NLI, Arc 4°793/288, Otzrot HaGolah Papers, folder 326, JCR, "Minutes, Board of Directors Meeting," October 9, 1950.

90. NLI, Arc 4°1599, Scholem Papers, folder Correspondence Lowenthal, Ernst G. Lowenthal to Gershom Scholem, May 7, 1951.

91. Frank Bajohr describes the systematic Nazi confiscation of silverware in Hamburg: Bajohr, *"Aryanisation,"* 247. For a more detailed account of spoliation and restitution efforts, see Lillteicher, *Raub, Recht und Restitution*, 285–94. On the specific situation in Hamburg with respect to cultural property, see Gallas, "Jewish Cultural Assets." Provenance research in the context of museums and exhibitions in Hamburg also led to a reappraisal of the history of the theft of art and silver from Jews during the 1930s. See two exhibition catalogs: Brüggen, Schulze, and Müller, *Raubkunst?*; and Schulze, *Raubkunst?* A short summary of

these activities is provided by the following newspaper article: von Münchhausen, "Hamburg Exhibition Delves into Murky History."

92. NLI, Arc 4°1599, Scholem Papers, folder Correspondence Lowenthal, E. G. Lowenthal to Gershom Scholem, July 15, 1952.

93. Armbruster, *Rückerstattung der Nazi-Beute*, 504.

94. Kagan and Weismann, *Report on the Operations of the JRSO*. See also UL Stanford, M0580, Baron Papers, box 231, folder 17, memorandum "Meeting in Nürnberg," May 12, 1952, attended by Hannah Arendt, Curt Wormann, Benjamin Ferencz, Ernst Katzenstein, and Samuel Dallob.

95. Hannah Arendt, "Field Report (No. 15)," in *Correspondence of Arendt and Scholem*, 233–41, here 234 and 238–39. On the significance of "Jewish Worms" in the postwar period, see Roemer, *German City*, ch. 3, esp. 146–50.

96. On the assessment of the situation in the British and French zones, see Arendt, *"Field Report (No. 15),"* *Correspondence of Arendt and Scholem*, 233–41.

97. Goschler, *Wiedergutmachung*, 188. Armbruster, *Rückerstattung der Nazi-Beute*, 511–19.

98. UL Stanford, Baron Papers, M0580, box 43, folder 6, Hannah Arendt to Salo W. Baron, December 3, 1949; Hannah Arendt, "Field Report (No.15)," in *Correspondence of Arendt and Scholem*, 233–41; Hannah Arendt to Gershom Scholem, February 5, 1950, in *ibid.*, 104–7, here 106.

99. Hannah Arendt, "Field Report (No.15)," in *ibid.*, 233–41. An indication of the difficulties involved in the restitution of Jewish property in France is provided by Ludi, *Reparations for Nazi-Victims*, ch. 3, "France"; Fogg, *Stealing Home*; and Goschler, "German Compensation," here 379.

100. Armbruster, *Rückerstattung der Nazi-Beute*, 517.

101. Among the organizations represented here were the JA, the Alliance, the AJC, the Joint, the Association pour la Défense des Droits Inserts des Victimes de l'Axe, the Conseil Représentatif des Institutions Juives de France, the Fonds Social Juif Unifié, and the WJC. See Armbruster, *Rückerstattung der Nazi-Beute*, 518n2110.

102. UL Stanford, M0580, Baron Papers, box 232, folder 5, Meir Ben-Horin to Hannah Arendt, September 5, 1950.

103. Albrink, "Von Büchern, Depots und Bibliotheken," 124–25.

104. Hoppe, *Jüdische Geschichte*, 206–7; Bönnen, "Beschlagnahmt, geborgen, ausgeliefert." It should be noted here that in a pilot project that ran from April to July 1951, the JCR had already had the congregational records in Worms microfilmed before passing them to the American Jewish Archives in Cincinnati. See Hannah Arendt to Gershom Scholem, September 27, 1950, and January 8, 1952, in *Correspondence of Arendt and Scholem*, 148–50, here 149 and 167.

105. UL Stanford, M0580, Baron Papers, box 43, folder 5, Jerome Michael from France to Hannah Arendt, August 20, 1949. On the wording of the law, see article 73, "Duty to Report and Penalties," US military government law no. 59, 38–39. Jens Hoppe, meanwhile, underlines that a number of institutions and museums distinguished themselves by voluntarily returning materials to Jewish communities

or to former community members who moved to Israel after the war, citing examples from Altona, Alsfeld, Celle, and Munich. See Hoppe, *Jüdische Geschichte*, 201–5.

106. UL Stanford, M0580, Baron Papers, box 232, folder 5, memorandum from Hannah Arendt to Salo W. Baron and Werner Senator, October 17, 1949.

107. Narkiss worked at the Munich collecting point until shortly before its closure in 1949 and sorted the—sometimes highly valuable—Jewish art collections, furniture, rare items, and ritual objects or organized their transfer to New York, Israel, and the JRSO in Nuremberg. Thirty-five paintings, for example, went to the Bezalel Museum, several hundred pictures were entrusted to the care of the Jewish Museum New York, while other heirless images were sold despite Narkiss's opposition and the proceeds transferred to the JRSO to support the DPs and the reconstruction in Israel. See UL Stanford, M0580, Baron Papers, box 43, folder 5, Bernard Heller to Joshua Starr, June 1, 1949; and Heller to Salo W. Baron, August 24, 1949. On the transactions involving these images, see JRSO, *Report on the Operations*; Augustin, "Nazi Looted Art." On the investigations carried out by Narkiss in collaboration with Lowenthal in museums and communities, see CAHJP, JRSO Papers, folder 923b, Mordechai Narkiss, "Ceremonial Objects in German Museums, Preliminary Findings," probably August/September 1949 (not clearly dated); and Berger, *Jewish Museum*, 507–19. On Bernstein's activities, see Honigmann, "Die Akten des Galuts."

108. Hannah Arendt, final report: "Report of My Mission to Germany Respectfully Submitted to the Board of Directors for the Meeting on April 12, 1950," in *Correspondence of Arendt and Scholem*, 255–61.

109. An initial version written by Arendt, which is almost identical to the published text, can be found in UL Stanford, M0580, Baron Papers, box 232, folder 5, "Appeal to German Librarians through the Bulletin of the German Librarians' Association, Submitted by Dr. Hannah Arendt to Dr. Gustav Hofmann, President on December 23, 1949." The appeal was first printed in "Meldung von Eigentum jüdischer Herkunft in deutschen Bibliotheken," *Nachrichten für wissenschaftliche Bibliotheken* 3, no. 4 (1950): 4, 62.

110. See UL Stanford, M0580, Baron Papers, box 232, folder 5, Hannah Arendt, "Memorandum Concerning Restitution of Jewish Cultural Property, Submitted to Herrn Minister Dr. A. Hundhammer, Munich, on January 18, 1950" (English translation of the letter to Hundhammer in German). Arendt describes the backstory to this memorandum in "Report of My Mission to Germany." An overview of Arendt's negotiations and initiatives during her first trip back to Germany from 1949 to 1950 is also provided by Sznaider, "Die Rettung der Bücher."

111. UL Stanford, M0580, Baron Papers, box 43, folder 6, Meir Ben-Horin to Salo W. Baron, July 20, 1950.

112. NLI, Arc 4°793/288, Otzrot HaGolah Papers, folder 326, JCR, "Minutes, Board of Directors Meeting," October 9, 1950. See also UL Stanford, M0580, Baron Papers, box 232, folder 5, Hannah Arendt to Benjamin Ferencz, June 19, 1950.

113. UL Stanford, M0580, Baron Papers, box 232, folder 5, Meir Ben-Horin, "Field Report No. 21," 6.

114. On the decree issued by the state of Hesse, see UL Stanford, M0580, Baron Papers, box 59, folder 8, JCR, "Minutes, Board of Directors Meeting," June 4, 1951.

115. NLI, Arc 4°793/288, Otzrot HaGolah Papers, folder 337, Minutes, "Annual Meeting of the Corporation," December 10, 1951.

116. UL Stanford, M0580, Baron Papers, box 59, folder 1, Hannah Arendt to Salo W. Baron, September 2, 1952, 2.

117. Gershom Scholem to Hannah Arendt, October 10, 1952, in *Correspondence of Arendt and Scholem*, 173–74, here 174; and Hannah Arendt to Gershom Scholem, August 15, 1953, in ibid., 177–79, here 179.

118. UL Stanford, M0580, Baron Papers, box 59, folder 1, Hannah Arendt to Salo W. Baron, April 24, 1952. Here Arendt quotes in detail from Scholem's letter to the Israeli delegation in the Hague.

119. Ibid., box 231, folder 17, memorandum "Meeting in Nürnberg," May 12, 1952. The JCR followed the example of the JRSO's negotiations with individual German states, in which the latter organization sought to achieve a so-called global agreement specifying the compensation due for failures to restitute former Jewish property. An agreement of this kind was ratified with Hesse in February 1951, in Baden-Württemberg in November 1951, and in Bavaria in July 1952. See Goschler, *Wiedergutmachung*, 177–78.

120. UL Stanford, M0580, Baron Papers, box 59, folder 1, Hannah Arendt to Salo W. Baron, September 2, 1952.

121. Ibid., Salo W. Baron to Nahum Goldman, March 21, 1952.

122. Ibid., Salo W. Baron from Bonn to Carl Gussone, August 21, 1952 (following a meeting with the latter).

123. Ibid., Hannah Arendt to Salo W. Baron, June 12, 1952.

124. After the suspension of its official activities, finds were shipped to Israel or allocated to European Jewish communities. See NLI, Arc 4°1599, Scholem Papers, folder Correspondence Hannah Arendt, JCR, "Minutes of Meeting of Board of Directors," April 5, 1954.

125. This project had been discussed for some time: NLI, Otzrot Hagolah Papers, Arc 4°793/288/313, JCR, "Memorandum on Microfilming in Germany Submitted to the Board of Directors Meeting," April 12, 1950.

126. NLI, Arc 4°1599, Scholem Papers, folder Correspondence Arendt, JCR, "Minutes, Board of Directors Meeting," April 5, 1954. The minutes list projects by the Israel Ministry of Education (represented by Nehemiah Aloni), Yad Vashem, YIVO, and the National Archives in Jerusalem (represented by Alexander Bein and Georg Herlitz) to microfilm manuscripts and documents of relevance all over Europe. See also Herman, *Hashavat Avedah*, 213–14, who shows that the Israeli Institute for Hebrew Manuscripts under the supervision of Aloni and Moshe Catane was able to process more than fifteen thousand manuscripts by 1963.

127. Zweig, *German Reparations*, 106–11.

128. Schidorsky, "Shunamis Suche."

129. The last meeting of its members and representatives took place on February 24, 1977, and was chaired by Baron, with Max Gruenewald as secretary. Remaining funds were transferred to the Conference on Jewish Social Studies. See the records of the JCR's final meetings: UL Stanford, M0580, Baron Papers, box 233, folder 1.

130. For the exact figures and details of the financing of the JCR, see Hannah Arendt's final report on its work: UL Stanford, M0580, Baron Papers, box 231, folder 18, Hannah Arendt, "Overall Report on the Activities of the Corporation from Its Beginnings in October 1947, until March 1952."

131. UL Stanford, M0580, Baron Papers, box 232, folder 5, Meir Ben-Horin to Hannah Arendt, September 5, 1950.

132. On the distributive priorities, see ibid., box 231, folder 17, JCR, "Minutes, Board of Directors Meeting," January 11, 1949 and March 14, 1949. Allocation according to the 40/40/20 formula is also described in LBI, xMfW, WLD, doc. 1–42, reel 26, folder 561, JCR, "Minutes of the Annual Meeting of the Board of Directors," October 17, 1949.

133. At a meeting of the JCR board of directors in January 1949, the following members of the allocations committee were announced in a move intended to strengthen the Advisory Committee: Alexander Marx (JTS), Samuel Belkin (Yeshiva University New York), Joshua Bloch (New York Public Library), Oscar Z. Fasman (HUC), Louis Finkelstein (JTS), Nelson Glueck (HUC), Isaac E. Kiev (Jewish Institute of Religion), Abraham Neuman (Dropsie College), David de Sola Pool (Union of Sephardic Congregations), and Max Weinreich (YIVO). For reasons of practicability, Baron had proposed the selection of a purely American body and managed to get his way despite a number of objections: UL Stanford, M0580, Baron Papers, box 231, folder 17, JCR, "Minutes of a Special Meeting of the Board of Directors," January 11, 1949.

134. Ibid., box 43, folder 6, Hannah Arendt to Salo W. Baron, December 3, 1949.

135. The allocation of holdings in Western Europe is listed in partial form in NLI, Arc 4°793/288, Otzrot HaGolah Papers, folder 301, Meir Ben-Horin, memorandum "Total Distribution of Books Received by JDC Paris," December 14, 1949. Information on the volumes taken to France can also be found in Hannah Arendt's final report. On the decision by the board of directors on non-Jewish beneficiaries, see UL Stanford, M0580, Baron Papers, box 231, folder 17, JCR, "Minutes, Board of Directors Meeting," March 14, 1949.

136. A Hebrew-language school in Casablanca established by the Alliance—the only one of its kind in North Africa—received special attention here. See NLI, Arc 4°793/288, Otzrot HaGolah Papers, Hannah Arendt, "Memorandum to Members of the Board of Directors/Advisory Committee," April 24, 1950.

137. On the decision, reached by vote, to send five thousand of the eleven thousand books from Breslau in the care of the JCR to Israel and the rest in equal parts to Switzerland and South America, see LBI, xMfW, WLD, doc. 1–42, reel 26, folder

561, JCR, "Special Meeting of the Board of Directors," December 19, 1949. For the context, see Kawałko, "From Breslau to Wrocław"; and Larralde, "Stolen Past."

138. The letter to Baron is quoted by Keller, "Jüdische Bücher," 28. See also UL Stanford, M0580, Baron Papers, box 43, folder 5, Bernard Heller to Hannah Arendt, August 11, 1949.

139. Shlomo Shunami to Hannah Arendt, November 2, 1949, quoted in *Arendt–Scholem Briefwechsel*, 216n1 (this quote and Hannah Arendt's response can only be found in the German version of the correspondence). Many letters between Gershom Scholem and Hannah Arendt throughout 1950 address the problem of the Breslau collection and Scholem's wish to allocate every fragment of it to Jerusalem. See, for example, Arendt to Scholem, November 7, 1949, in *Correspondence of Arendt and Scholem*, 96–97; Scholem to Arendt, September 20, 1950, ibid., 144–46; Scholem to Arendt, December 7, 1950, ibid., 153–55.

140. See the summary of these events in Keller, "Jüdische Bücher"; and Domhardt, "Von Breslau nach Genf." For a general overview of the fate of the library, see Cieślińska-Lobkowicz, "Raub und Rückführung."

141. For an introduction to the situation in postwar Poland, see Gross, *Fear*; and Aleksiun, "Vicious Circle." Concerning property issues and Jewish activities in the aftermath of World War II, see, among others, Engel, "Reconstruction of Jewish Communal Institutions"; Sroka, "Forsaken and Abandoned"; Cieślińska-Lobkowicz, "Judaika in Polen"; Meng, *Shattered Spaces*; Fishman, *Book Smugglers*; Cichopek, *Beyond Violence*; and Friedla, "A Naye Yiddishe Heym."

142. On its history, see Jockusch, *Collect and Record*, ch. 3; Bergman, "Jewish Historical Institute"; and Bergman, "Jewish Historical Institute in Warsaw."

143. Trunk, "Research Library of the Jewish Historical Institute."

144. Sylberberg, "Saving Jewish Treasures," 10–11.

145. Ibid., 11.

146. Kupfer, "Manuscript Treasures."

147. See also Adunka, *Der Raub der Bücher*, 80–81.

148. On the history of the Jewish Historical Institute in Warsaw, see Stach, "Geschichtsschreibung und politische Vereinnahmungen."

149. For an introductory account, see Polonsky, *Jews in Poland and Russia*, esp. part 3: "From the End of the Second World War to the Collapse of the Communist System."

150. Stabi, Nachlass Nr. 266, E. G. Lowenthal, Ordner 314, E. G. Lowenthal, "Schedule of Shipments and Distribution of Books and Jewish Cultural Objects from U.S. Zone of Germany to European Countries and Countries Overseas, March 1949–January 1951," January 31, 1951. On Edelmann's efforts, see the section in chapter 2, "Creating Networks," in this book.

151. UL Stanford, M0580, Baron Papers, box 43, folder 6, Leo Baeck to Salo W. Baron, April 12, 1949.

152. Ibid., box 231, folder 17, JCR, "Minutes of a Special Meeting of the Board of Directors," October 7, 1947. The request made by Gruenewald and Täubler was

discussed again in June 1949. See ibid., JCR, "Minutes, Board of Directors Meeting," June 7, 1949.

153. Quoted in Nattermann, *Deutsch-Jüdische Geschichtsschreibung*, 93; see esp. ch. 2, which describes initiatives to establish research institutes made up of German Jewish emigrants after the Holocaust, and Nattermann, "Struggle for the Preservation."

154. On the transfers to the United Kingdom, see UL Stanford, M0580, Baron Papers, box 58, folder 9, Roth Committee to Jewish Trust Corporation, memorandum, July 1950.

155. Memorandum "Canadian Jewish Congress Puts Labels in Books Recovered from Germany," October 23, 1952, quoted in Presidential Advisory Commission, *Plunder and Restitution*, here *Staff Report*, ch. 4: "Heirless Assets and the Role of Jewish Cultural Reconstruction, Inc.," 194.

156. Quoted in Belling, "From Cemetery to Cyberspace," 2.

157. Ibid., 3.

158. Ibid., 1.

159. Wolf Blattberg, memorandum "Present Activities of the Department of Culture and Education," November 14, 1949, quoted in Presidential Advisory Commission, *Plunder and Restitution*, *Staff Report*, 194.

160. Wilke, "Von Breslau nach Mexiko," 321–22.

161. The community center, along with its library, was the victim of a bomb attack in 1994, after which it was slowly rebuilt. A substantial part of the large Yiddish-language collection was, however, destroyed. For an illuminating description of the Yiddish-speaking world and its post-Holocaust commitment to culture, books, and commemoration of the Eastern European realm in Argentina, especially Buenos Aires, see Schwarz, *Survivors and Exile*, 92–117.

162. Arendt, "Jewish Cultural Reconstruction, Inc.," 792.

163. Ibid.

164. LBI, xMfW, WLD, doc. 1–42, reel 26, folder 561, JCR, "Minutes, Board of Directors Meeting," April 12, 1950. This decision was justified in light of the fact that American citizens, through their taxes, had done much to support the military government in Germany, and thus also the work of the JCR, and should receive something in return.

165. See Herman, "Hashavat Avedah," 254.

166. NLI, Arc 4°793/288, Otzrot HaGolah Papers, folder 326, JCR, "Minutes, Board of Directors Meeting," October 9, 1950.

167. Friedman, "Fate of the Jewish Book," 122.

168. On the German population's extensive participation in the robbing of Jews, see the introductory account by Wojak and Hayes, *"Arisierung."* Martin Dean underlines the "widespread participation of the local population as beneficiaries from Jewish property" but also shows how the "bulk of the profit thus remained with the state." See Dean, *Robbing the Jews*, 15. On the history of the collection of the Stürmer publishing house in Nuremberg, see Tobias, "Die 'Stürmer-Bibliothek.'" The Israelite Community (Israelitische Kultusgemeinde) has lent the

roughly nine thousand volumes that remained in Germany to the Nuremberg City Library, where they can still be found. After the launch of a comprehensive program of research to determine their provenance in 1999, certain volumes were individually restituted.

169. UL Stanford, M0580, Baron Papers, box 231, folder 15, JCR, "Minutes, Board of Directors Meeting," December 21, 1950.

170. Ibid., folder 18, Hannah Arendt, "Overall Report of the Activities of the Corporation from its Beginnings in October 1947, until March 1952," sheet no. 2: "JCR, Inc., Distribution of Books to Libraries in the United States," July 1952.

171. See Landau, "Jüdische Kulturschätze wandern aus."

172. Steven S. Kayser to Michel Oppenheim (who helped mediate the restitution of the Judaica from Mainz and Worms), July 24, 1951, quoted in Hoppe, *Jüdische Geschichte*, 202. For the context, see Herman, "'Brand Plucked out of the Fire.'"

173. Ibid., box 231, folder 18, Hannah Arendt, "Overall Report of the Activities of the Corporation from its Beginnings in October 1947, until March 1952," sheets no. 1 and 3, July 1952.

CHAPTER 4. BUILDING THE NEW STATE

1. The many library transfers from Germany to the prestate Jewish community in Palestine, as long as the German Foreign Exchange Law (Devisengesetz) still permitted this, are discussed in Jütte, *Die Emigration*; Jessen, "Das problematische Bild"; and Jessen, "Alte Bücher in Haifa," esp. 467–68. A comprehensive picture of the books' significance in Israel is provided in Jessen's study *Kanon im Exil*.

2. See the foreword in Schidorsky, *Burning Scrolls and Flying Letters*, 1–10, here 3.

3. Josef Ben Aharon Chasanowicz in his foreword to the anniversary publication *Die jüdische Nationalbibliothek in Jerusalem* (in Yiddish) published in 1912, translated and quoted in Weldler, *Die Jüdische National- und Universitätsbibliothek*, 7.

4. For an introduction to the library's history, see Joel, "Jewish National and University Library"; Kirchhoff, *Häuser des Buches*, here ch. 3: "Im Lande Israel," 67–81; Stanciu, "Jewish National and University Library of Jerusalem"; and Weldler, *Die Jüdische National- und Universitätsbibliothek*. The yearbook of the Hebrew University (*The Hebrew University of Jerusalem 1960*, Jerusalem 1960) includes a chapter on JNUL staff, holdings, and history. Ibid., 172–86. On the German Jewish tradition uniting the JNUL directors, see Schidorsky, "Germany in the Holy Land." The extraordinary situation of the university in the Mt. Scopus enclave is described in Weiss, "Nicht durch Macht." She also cites the memorandum on the "Library in Exile," ibid., 76.

5. Bergman, "Jubilee of the Library." I thank Enrico Lucca for providing me with the article; see also Schidorsky, "Salvaging of Jewish Books," 197.

6. "Hebrew University Seeks to Recover Jewish Cultural Treasures Plundered by the Nazis," *Jewish Telegraphic Agency*, October 8, 1944, http://archive.jta.org.

7. For a reading of the term *golah* as a description of exile with negative connotations in this period, see, for example, Gorny, "Negation of the Galut," here 76. David Engel argues that the terms were essentially used as synonyms. See his lecture "On Studying Jewish History." The latter sees both terms as entailing Zionist connotations and a rejection of the Diaspora. In his book *Return of Zionism* (95), meanwhile, Gabriel Piterberg asserts that the term *golah* is a neutral way of referring to the Jewish Diaspora.

8. On the Zionist outlook of many academics at the Hebrew University, particularly with respect to the experience of the Holocaust, see Kenan, *Between Memory and History*, esp. xvi; and Myers, "Between Diaspora and Zion."

9. Zertal, *Israel's Holocaust*, 61.

10. An account of official Zionist rhetoric after the Second World War and the opposing views put forward by several scholars is provided by Porat, *Israeli Society*, 337–50.

11. See Myers, *Von Berlin nach Jerusalem*; and Aschheim, *Beyond the Border*, 6–44.

12. Hugo Bergman to Robert Weltsch, July 17, 1928, quoted in Myers, *Von Berlin nach Jerusalem*, 339.

13. For another introduction to this topic, see the multiauthored volume by Zimmermann and Hotam, *Zweimal Heimat*.

14. Myers, *Von Berlin nach Jerusalem*, 346. On the ambivalent position of German Zionists, see also Gelber, "Deutsch-jüdische Identität"; and Du-Nour, "Cultural Identity."

15. NLI Jerusalem, 4°793/212, Otzrot HaGolah Papers, folder I: 1946, Judah Magnes to the High Commissioner for Palestine in Jerusalem, May 15, 1945.

16. NA College Park, M1949, MFA&A Records, AHC, roll 3, folder OAD2, Chaim Weizmann and Judah Magnes to MFA&A, US State Department and Colonial Office London, July 8, 1945.

17. In his journal, Hugo Bergman wrote about Rifkind's visit to Palestine in January 1946 and the meeting between him, Magnes, Scholem, and Senator. See Bergman, *Tagebücher*, 680–81.

18. This and the following quotes are from NLI, Arc 4°793/212, Otzrot HaGolah Papers, folder I: 1946, "Tazkir hava'adah hamishpatit she'al yad hava'adah lehatzalat otzrot hagolah" (Memorandum of the Otzrot HaGolah Committee's Legal Board), February 26, 1946.

19. On Feinberg's position with reference to the Treaty of Sèvres, see Sagi, "Wiedergutmachung für Israel," 25. On Feinberg's distinguished status within the field of international law, see Graf, *Die Bernheim-Petition 1933*, esp. 148–50 and 298–99.

20. Dov Schidorsky and recently Noam Zadoff also discuss this report in detail. See Schidorsky, "Salvaging of Jewish Books"; Zadoff, *From Berlin to Jerusalem*, 95–101, esp. 99–100.

21. NLI, 4°793/212, Otzrot HaGolah Papers, folder I: 1946, Judah Magnes to Koppel Pinson, May 3, 1946.

22. NA College Park, RG 260, OMGUS Records, AHC, Box 66, folder Jewish Cultural Property, Jewish Agency for Palestine Head Office, US Zone, Germany (Munich) to OMGUS and MFA&A Berlin, August 26, 1946.

23. UL Stanford, M0580, Baron Papers, box 42, folder 11, "Jewish Books in Offenbach, Germany, and Other Localities of Germany, Austria, Czechoslovakia and Other Countries—the Policy of the Hebrew University," January 15, 1948.

24. Gershom Scholem to Leo Baeck, June 2, 1946, in Scholem, *Life in Letters*, 334–35.

25. Between 1946 and 1948, 56,467 Jews went to Palestine—for the most part illegally—followed by another 648,201 between 1948 and 1951. For the figures, see Mendes-Flohr and Reinharz, *Jew in the Modern World*, tables 16 and 17, 716–17.

26. NLI, Arc 4°793/212, Otzrot HaGolah Papers, folder IV: 1948; Haeger and Long, "Lost EC Treasures."

27. Scholem set out his position and arguments in his defense in a letter: ibid., Scholem to Judah Magnes, March 21, 1948.

28. NA College Park, RG 260, OMGUS Records, AHC, box 66, folder JCR, Inc., "Addendum I to Memorandum of Agreement of 15 February 1949, Subject: 'Jewish Cultural Property,'" Berlin, April 5, 1949. This addendum states, "There are transferred hereby to the JCR, Inc., approximately 366 manuscripts, as listed on the attached inventory [. . .], American Consul General Jerusalem, Palestine, comprising all cultural properties moved in one single shipment from Offenbach Archival Depot, Germany, to Jerusalem and placed into custody of Dr. I. Joel, acting Librarian, Hebrew University, 22 June 1947." For JCR's deliberations, see UL Stanford, M0580, Baron Papers, box 231, folder 17, "Special Meeting of the Board of Directors," May 5, 1949; and ibid., "Special Meeting of the Board of Directors," June 7, 1949.

29. On the history of this transfer and related restitution efforts, see Grimsted, "Sudeten Crossroads"; Weiss, "Von Prag nach Jerusalem"; and the forthcoming research project of Anna Holzer-Kawałko, "Dissonant Heritage. German-Jewish Book Collections and Nation-Building in Czechoslovakia, 1918–1948."

30. The history and fate of the Prague Jewish Museum during the Nazi period is reconsidered in Rupnow, *Täter—Gedächtnis—Opfer*; Rupnow, "From Final Depository to Memorial"; and Potthast, *Das jüdische Zentralmuseum der SS*. More detailed information on the museum library and the looting processes can be found in an account by a contemporary: Adler, "Die Geschichte des Prager Jüdischen Museums"; and in Braunová, "Origins of the Book Collection," as well as in a publication produced by the museum itself: Bušek, *"Hope Is on the Next Page."*

31. On the camp library and liberation, see Adler, *Theresienstadt 1941–1945*, esp. ch. 19: "Cultural Life," 517–54; and Intrator, "Theresienstadt Ghetto Central Library."

32. Schidorsky, "Jewish Libraries."

33. NLI, Arc 4°793/212, Otzrot HaGolah Papers, folder II: 1946, Zeev Scheck and Robert Weinberger to Judah Magnes, January 28, 1946.

34. Both, H. G. Adler and Gershom Scholem reported that from 1945 to 1946, tens of thousands of the museum's books, originally Jews' private property, had been sold

to buyers in the United States or to antiquarian bookstores in Switzerland and Israel. See Strzolka, "Vernichtung jüdischer Identität," here 7n13. Gershom Scholem to Hannah Arendt, March 6, 1950, in *Correspondence of Arendt and Scholem*, 109–11. See also Albrink, "Von Büchern, Depots und Bibliotheken," 120–22.

35. Scheck and Weinberger to Magnes, January 28, 1946.

36. Hugo Bergman reported the arrival of Zeev Scheck and the box to Luise Herrmann, July 14, 1946, in Bergman, *Tagebücher*, 663.

37. NLI, Arc 4°793/212, Otzrot HaGolah Papers, folder I: 1946, Gershom Scholem in Paris to Judah Magnes in New York, May 22, 1946.

38. UL Stanford, M0580, Baron Papers, box 58, folder 9, "Report of Prof. Gershom Scholem on his Mission to Europe (in the Summer of 1946) Concerning the Libraries of the Diaspora," undated; also NLI, Arc 4°793/212, Otzrot HaGolah Papers, folder I: 1946, report by Gershom Scholem from Prague to the Hebrew University, undated (June 1946).

39. Gershom Scholem to Siegmund Hurwitz, June 8, 1946, in Scholem, *Life in Letters*, 336–37.

40. NLI, Arc 4°793/212, Otzrot HaGolah Papers, folder II: 1946, Paul März to Gershom Scholem, July 17, 1946.

41. Gershom Scholem to Leo Baeck, June 2, 1946, in Scholem, *Life in Letters*, 334–36. Here Scholem states, "I would be extraordinarily grateful if you would support the university's trusteeship of the remains of Jewish collections from Germany now in Czechoslovakia," 336. In the original German version of the letter, he continues, "Any approach you might make to Dr. Stein, president of the Jewish congregation in Prague, would be of tremendous value in this regard." See Scholem, *Briefe*, vol. 1, 316.

42. NLI, Arc 4°793/212, Otzrot HaGolah Papers, folder I: 1946, Protocol by Gershom Scholem in Prague [captioned in Hebrew script: A protocol of my conversations in Prague], undated (June 1946).

43. NLI, Arc 4°793/212, Otzrot HaGolah Papers, folder II: 1946, Gershom Scholem to the Council of the Jewish Communities of Bohemia and Moravia-Silesia (Rat der Jüdischen Kultusgemeinden Böhmen und Mähren), June 17, 1946.

44. Ibid., folder I: 1946, Gershom Scholem, "Report on My Activities in Prague, Bratislava and Vienna," June 23, 1946 (in Hebrew). Whether the books from Bratislava did in fact make it to Jerusalem could not be ascertained.

45. UL Stanford, M0580, Baron Papers, box 58, folder 9, "Report of Prof. Gershom Scholem on His Mission to Europe (in the Summer of 1946) Concerning the Libraries of the Diaspora," undated. Gershom Scholem called for investigations to be carried out in Niemes in a letter to Sam Sharp of August 4, 1946 (partly) in Scholem, *Life in Letters*, 338. For Grumach's report, which reached MFA&A officers and Jewish representatives in 1946 and revealed the history of the RSHA library, see Grumach, "Report on the Confiscation and Treatment of the Former Jewish Libraries by the Gestapo from 1933–1945," in Schidorsky, "Confiscation of Libraries," 352–56.

46. For an account of Bergman's journey and mission, see Lucca, "A Safe Home for German-Jewry."

47. In 1943, in addition to individual consignments to Theresienstadt, the RSHA had divided large parts of its valuable looted collection between four castles: Niemes (Mimoň), Hauska (Houska), Neu-Pürstein (Nový Berštejn), and Neufalkenburg (Nový Falkenburk).

48. NLI, Arc 4°793/212, Otzrot HaGolah Papers, folder II: 1946, Jerome Michael to John H. Hilldring, August 26, 1946; UL Stanford, M0580, Baron Papers, box 43, folder 5, J. H. Hilldring to Jerome Michael, July 8, 1947; NA College Park, RG 260, OMGUS Records, AHC, box 66, folder Jewish Cultural Property, Office of Political Affairs/State Department to W. H. Draper (OMGUS, Economics Department) and John Allen (Chief of Restitution Branch, OMGUS), September 3, 1946, and replying telegram from Allen, September 14, 1946.

49. Yavnai, "Jewish Cultural Property," 131. References to this also in AJHS, P-675, Dawidowicz Papers, box 55, folder 5, Lucy Schildkret (Dawidowicz) to Joseph Horne, April 19, 1947.

50. UL Stanford, M0580, Baron Papers, box 39, folder 2, "Prof. Bergman's Report on His Trip to Prague, 6.–15. November 1946," composed in December 1946. A Hebrew equivalent can be found in NLI, Arc 4°793/212, Otzrot HaGolah Papers, folder II: 1946.

51. Hugo Bergman to Escha Bergman, November 7, 1946 from Prague, in Bergman, *Tagebücher*, 701.

52. AJHS, P-675, Dawidowicz Papers, box 55, folder 5, Lucy Schildkret (Dawidowicz) to Joseph Horne, April 19, 1947.

53. Ibid., Seymour Pomrenze, memorandum "YIVO Property in Czechoslovakia," July 8, 1947. Bilha Shilo has recently argued that the newspaper collection almost certainly stayed in Prague among the now "nationalized" Jewish property, while parts of Yiddish book collections may have ended up in Jerusalem without notice to YIVO New York. See Shilo, "When YIVO was Defined by Territory."

54. This and the following quotations in NLI, Arc 4°793/212, Otzrot HaGolah Papers, folder III: 1947, Arthur Bergman, "Streng vertraulicher Bericht von Dr. Arthur Bergman über seine Tätigkeiten in Prag," September 25, 1947. In a later passage of the report, Bergman indicates that books from the Breslau Seminary had been found but not placed in the boxes described.

55. Ibid., folder IV: 1948, Gershom Scholem to Werner Senator, September 17, 1948, and Gershom Scholem to Joshua Starr, November 25, 1948. On Schneurson's work, see Schidorsky, "Salvaging of Jewish Books," 204–5.

56. The figures vary in the reports and secondary literature. Announcement of the first delivery: NLI, Arc 4°793/212, Otzrot HaGolah Papers, folder IV: 1948, JCR, "Minutes of a Special Meeting of the Boards of Directors," January 28, 1948. The previously cited letter from Scholem to Starr of November 25, 1948, refers to the dispatch of a second consignment. For an introductory account of all these events, see Yavnai, "Jewish Cultural Property."

57. See the museum's website, http://www.jewishmuseum.cz (accessed November 26, 2018).

58. Scholem presented these proposals to Magnes and asked him for his assessment of possible Jewish reactions to such a transfer. NLI, Arc 4°793/212, Otzrot HaGolah Papers, folder I: 1946, Gershom Scholem to Judah Magnes, July 29, 1946.

59. Freimann, *Die hebraeischen Inkunabeln*; Freimann, *Katalog der Judaica*.

60. The remaining Hebraica were probably discovered in 1963 by Ernst Loewy, then working in the library's Judaica department. They still form part of its holdings. On the history of this collection as well as that of Aron Freimann, see Heuberger, *Bibliothek des Judentums*. Nehemiah Aloni was director of the Institute until 1963 and made eight trips to Europe to obtain microfilm of as many surviving Hebrew manuscripts as possible. Around fifteen thousand texts were microfilmed under his supervision and made available to researchers at the Institute for Hebrew Manuscripts, then part of the JNUL.

61. UL Stanford, M0580, Baron Papers, box 43, folder 7, Gershom Scholem to Joshua Starr, August 30, 1948.

62. Ibid., box 58, folder 9, Fritz Moser to Josef Knecht, May 3, 1952. Senate Director Erich Lüth was head of the public press office of Hamburg City Hall and, in mid-1951, together with journalist Rudolf Küstermeier, had initiated the peace initiative "Die Friedensbitte an Israel" (Appeal to Israel for Peace), which later merged with the Society for Christian-Jewish Cooperation (Gesellschaft für Christlich-Jüdische Zusammenarbeit). His appeal for olive tree donations to Israel was made in 1952, initially in Hamburg and later throughout West Germany. It was cosigned mainly by high-level church representatives and politicians. See Lüth, "Aufruf zur Ölbaumspende."

63. NLI, Arc 4°1599, Scholem Papers, folder correspondence "Senator, Werner," Werner Senator to Gershom Scholem, September 18, 1952.

64. On the details of the book donation, see the correspondence between Gershom Scholem and Curt Wormann in the summer and fall of 1952 (above all, Scholem to Wormann, September 26, 1952 from Berlin): ibid., folder correspondence "Wormann, Kurt." A letter dealing with this subject from Scholem to Wormann of September 3, 1952, has been published in Scholem, *Briefe*, vol. 2, 32–34. The book donations are also mentioned in Jelinek, *Deutschland und Israel*, 379.

65. NLI, Arc 4°1599, Scholem Papers, folder correspondence "Senator, Werner," Gershom Scholem to Werner Senator, undated (September or October 1952).

66. On the context of the complex relations between Israel and Germany in the postwar period, see Jelinek, *Deutschland und Israel*; and D. Diner, *Rituelle Distanz*. On the public debate on this topic in Israel, see Segev, *Seventh Million*, 189–252.

67. UL Stanford, M0580, Baron Papers, box 44, folder 1, Chaim Yahil, "Anmerkungen zur Denkschrift des Herrn Oberbürgermeisters der Stadt Worms über die jüdischen Altertümer dort selbst," June 1954.

68. Jelinek states that Konrad Adenauer himself intervened in Worms to expedite the transfer of archival materials to Israel. See Jelinek, *Deutschland und Israel*, 380;

and recently Lustig, "Who Are to Be the Successors?," who discusses the Worms case in detail.

69. Lustig explores the ideological motifs and practical struggles involved in the vast Israeli operation of "collecting archives" in his article "Who Are to Be the Successors?"

70. Gershom Scholem to Hannah Arendt, April 6, 1950, in *Correspondence of Arendt and Scholem*, 112–14, here 113.

71. The microfilms found after the war were distributed to congregations in Germany. Jacob Jacobson described these as highly important in communication with Hannah Arendt. In a letter of July 19, 1950, he wrote, "[They] represent a most valuable contribution to the history of German Jewry, their communities, families, and individual personalities. It would be worth while to save them for the future by developing the microfilms [. . .]. One should remember how much of our knowledge about the past generations is lost by destruction and desecration of our cemeteries." LBI, AR 7002, Jacobson Collection, microfilm: reel 23, no. vi.6. For the history of the holdings after 1945, see Honigmann, "Central Archives for Research"; and several papers in Honigmann and Bischoff, *Jüdisches Archivwesen*. On their postwar fate, see Rein, "Die Bestände der ehemaligen jüdischen Gemeinden."

72. For an introductory account of GDR policy toward Israel, see Timm, "Burdened Relationship"; Timm, "Ideology and Realpolitik." The shift in perspective is also discussed by Tompkins, "Israel as Friend and Foe." On the restitution negotiations, see Timm, *Jewish Claims against East Germany*. An assessment of the situation is given in correspondence between Gershom Scholem, Alexander Bein, and Georg Herlitz, director of the Zionist Archives in Jerusalem until 1955. See esp. NLI, Arc 4°793/288, Otzrot HaGolah Papers, folder 185, Gershom Scholem to Alexander Bein, September 20, 1950; ibid., folder 260, Bein from Berlin to Georg Herlitz, May 12, 1951.

73. Quoted in Lustig, "Who Are to Be the Successors?" 542.

74. The restitution of the congregational archival materials is discussed in Rein, "Die Bestände der ehemaligen jüdischen Gemeinden." On the Munich negotiations, see UL Stanford, M0580, Baron Papers, box 231, folder 15, JCR, "Minutes, Board of Directors Meeting," December 21, 1950, and Hannah Arendt's final report on her second trip to Germany in 1952: ibid., box 59, folder 1, Hannah Arendt to Salo W. Baron, September 2, 1952.

75. Goldberg, *Lady of the Castle*.

76. On the various actors, see Schidorsky, "Salvaging of Jewish Books."

77. Schidorsky, "Shunamis Suche," 331. Shunami was not only involved in obtaining European books; as the historian Gish Amit has shown, he was also involved in JNUL's acquisitions policy with respect to Palestinian libraries and private collections. During the 1948 War of Independence, this led to around thirty thousand books belonging to Palestinians who had fled Jerusalem to come into the library's possession. See Amit, "Ownerless Objects?" and Amit, "Salvage or Plunder?"

78. See Adunka, *Der Raub der Bücher*, 164–77. A short English summary of her book also mentioning Shunami is given in Adunka, "Nazi Looting of Books." See also Schidorsky, *Burning Scrolls and Flying Letters*, 263–74.

79. An overview of the library of the Vienna Jewish community is provided by Hacken, "Jewish Community Library." For a general account of the situation of looted books in Austria after the war, see Adunka, *Der Raub der Bücher*; Adunka, "Bücherraub"; and Adunka, "Research on Looted Books."

80. NLI, Arc 4°793/212, Otzrot HaGolah Papers, folder I: 1946, Gershom Scholem, Report on My Activities in Prague, Bratislava, and Vienna, June 23, 1946 (in Hebrew).

81. UL Stanford, M0580, Baron Papers, box 59, folder 1, Shlomo Shunami, Europe Travel Report, April 14, 1954 (in Hebrew). This report also deals with Shunami's trip to Vienna in 1952. See also Schidorsky, *Burning Scrolls and Flying Letters*, 263–74. On the arrival of the first twenty thousand volumes in Israel, see "H.U. Gets Plundered Books from Austria," *Jerusalem Post*, August 11, 1958.

82. The books from the community library not transferred to Israel are now in the library of the Jewish Museum Vienna (Jüdisches Museum Wien). The dispute between the Israelite Community and the Central Archives in Israel concerning the return of the archival holdings reached the Israeli Supreme Court in 2015, which ruled against reallocating the documents and classified them as part of the national cultural heritage. For the details of the different legal proceedings, see https://www.ikg-wien.at (accessed May 12, 2018).

83. Shunami, "Elusive Treasure."

84. On specific countries, see Shunami's travel report of 1954. His search for books and the negotiations in Germany, including those with former Nazi functionaries, are described in detail in Schidorsky, "Shunamis Suche"; and Schidorsky, *Burning Scrolls and Flying Letters*, ch. 7, see esp. the subchapter "Shlomo Shunami Following the Footsteps of Rare and Precious Books. Investigations and Disappointments," 280–84.

85. Oz, *Tale of Love and Darkness*, 22.

86. Berger, *Jewish Museum*, 525.

87. "Ausstellung geretteten Kulturgeräts im Jerusalemer Bezalel Museum," *Der Weg*, August 4, 1950.

88. This evident devotion to material from Europe would diminish considerably in subsequent years at the Bezalel Museum and its successor, the Israel Museum. See Steinberg, *Orphaned Art*.

89. See "Introduction: The Glas Box," in Segev, *Wiesenthal*, 1–11; Don-Yehiya, "Memory and Political Culture," 140–41; Stauber, *Holocaust in Israeli Public Debate*, 98; and Kenan, *Between Memory and History*, 48–50.

90. On the commemorative events and rituals that took place in the Chamber of the Holocaust on Mount Zion in connection with the arriving ritual objects and Torah scrolls, see Bar, "Holocaust Commemoration in Israel." I thank Dana Herman for alerting me to this text.

91. Salo W. Baron, interview with Grace Cohen Grossman, tape 7. There are photographs of such festivities among the Otzrot Hagolah collection in the Hebrew University Historical Archive.
92. StaBi, Nachlass Nr. 266, E. G. Lowenthal, Ordner 314, Curt Wormann, Vom Scopus nach Terra Sancta. In der größten jüdischen Bibliothek—Umzug von isolierter Stellung ins jüdische Jerusalem, December 15, 1950.
93. CAHJP, JRSO Papers, folder 923b, Werner Senator to Salo W. Baron, August 4, 1949.
94. UL Stanford, M0580, Baron Papers, box 231, folder 18, Hannah Arendt, "Overall Report of the Activities of the Corporation from Its Beginnings in October 1947, until March 1952," sheet no. 1, July 1952.
95. Israel's distribution problems were for example discussed at a meeting of the JCR board of directors: UL Stanford, M0580, Baron Papers, box 231, folder 17, JCR, "Minutes, Board of Directors Meeting," October 17, 1949.
96. NLI, Arc 4°793/288, Otzrot HaGolah Papers, folder 88, Shlomo Shunami to Hannah Arendt, February 3, 1950.
97. D. Diner, "Kumulative Kontingenz," 204.

CHAPTER 5. TAKING ACTION IN DARK TIMES

1. H. Diner, "Salo Baron," 248.
2. On Baron's role and impact in the United States, see Liberles, *Salo Wittmayer Baron*, chs. 5–7. Peter Steinfels's obituary also provides information on Baron's special importance in the United States: Steinfels, "Salo W. Baron." In addition to H. Diner's text, the recently published volume by Hava Tirosh-Samuelson and Edward Dąbrowa on *Enduring Legacy of Salo W. Baron* provides several illuminating articles on Baron's American life, context, and work.
3. Baron talked about this in his interview with Grace Cohen Grossman, tape 1.
4. Liberles, *Salo Wittmayer Baron*, ch. 5. On Baron's initiatives between 1933 and 1944, see section 1, "Negotiations during World War II" of ch. 2 in the present book.
5. Evelyn Adunka highlights his support for Austrian refugees: Adunka, "Salo W. Baron's Efforts."
6. On October 28, 1941, Hannah Arendt wrote a letter of introduction to Salo W. Baron in which she mentioned her academic teacher, Elbogen, outlined her career, and asked for a meeting. UL Stanford, M0580, Baron Papers, box 11, folder 14. This folder also contains letters concerning the publication of Arendt's essay "From the Dreyfus Affair to France Today," which appeared in *Jewish Social Studies* in 1942 and on several job applications, which Baron supported. On Arendt's agreement to work for the Commission, see UL Stanford, M0580, Baron Papers, box 40, folder 4, Theodor Gaster to Salo W. Baron, August 23, 1944. On the relationship between Arendt and Baron, see also Rubin, "Salo Baron and Hannah Arendt."

7. In addition to what is still the only monograph on Baron's life and oeuvre by Robert Liberles, numerous authors have dealt with aspects of his work and historical thinking. See, for example, Engel, *Historians of the Jews*, 29–84; Engel, "Crisis and Lachrymosity"; Brenner, *Prophets of the Past*, 123–30; Schorsch, "Last Jewish Generalist"; Schorsch, "Lachrymose Conception"; Stanislawski, "Salo W. Baron"; Chazan, "New Vision of Jewish History"; and Hertzberg, "Salo W. Baron."

8. S. Baron, "Reflections on the Future"; S. Baron, "What War Has Meant"; S. Baron, "Spiritual Reconstruction"; and S. Baron, "At the Turning-Point."

9. Salo W. Baron to Alexander Marx, September 16, 1940, quoted in Liberles, *Salo Wittmayer Baron*, 281. Baron's enduringly hopeful stance is also underlined by Engel, *Historians of the Jews*, 47–49.

10. Liberles, *Salo Wittmayer Baron*, 270–74. Liberles states that Baron learned of his family's murder from the foreman of the family estate in Tarnów. His papers also include correspondence between Baron and his student, Philip Friedman, whom he contacted in summer 1945 in Poland with a request to make inquiries about his family. UL Stanford, M0580, Baron Papers, box 28, folder 5, Salo Baron to Philip Friedman, August 2, 1945, and his response of October 2, 1945, with news of the history of his family's deportation.

11. Liberles, *Salo Wittmayer Baron*, 216.

12. Hannah Arendt to Gershom Scholem, October 21, 1940, in *Correspondence of Arendt and Scholem*, 4.

13. On January 8, 1941, Scholem wrote to his friend Shalom Spiegel, a scholar of Jewish studies and literature: "The most important event in recent times has been the death of my friend Walter Benjamin, who committed suicide while fleeing from France to Spain. This is a terrible blow and there is no getting over it. [. . .] He had an entry visa for the United States, money and everything [. . .] and yet he still fell victim to these criminals." In Scholem, *Briefe*, vol. 1, 283–84. The significance of Benjamin to Arendt and Scholem is evident in many passages of their writings and in their correspondence. This can be seen most clearly in Arendt, "Walter Benjamin"; Scholem, *Walter Benjamin*; and Scholem, "Walter Benjamin." On the significance of Benjamin's death for Arendt, see Young-Bruehl, *Hannah Arendt*, 160. For an introductory account of Benjamin's role in the relationship between Scholem and Arendt, see Knott, "Why Have We Been Spared?," xiv–xvi.

14. In his book *Seventh Million*, Tom Segev describes unambiguously just how threatening Rommel's campaign was felt to be in Palestine and the extent to which Jews, particularly those from Central and Eastern Europe in the Yishuv, followed the Holocaust in Europe with sorrow and fear. This was reflected only to a limited degree in the official political rhetoric surrounding the Zionist project in Palestine during this period. See Segev, *Seventh Million*, 67–81. On the general situation of the approximately five hundred thousand Jews in Palestine from 1939 onward and their awareness of what was happening in Europe, see ibid., part 2, chs. 3–5, 67–110: "Holocaust: It Was in the Papers." In his latest book, *David Ben Gurion*, ch. 14, "Holocaust und Spaltung," Segev provides another comprehensive account of politics

and mentalities in the Yishuv during the Holocaust. Two books by Dina Porat provide a comprehensive introduction to this topic: Porat, *Blue and the Yellow Stars of David*; and Porat, *Israeli Society*. In her study *Israel's Holocaust*, Idith Zertal suggests a more critical reading of the situation than Porat, emphasizing the conscious effort to ignore European realities on the part of the Zionist leadership in Palestine.

15. Gershom Scholem to Hannah Arendt, November 12, 1942, in *Correspondence of Arendt and Scholem*, 15–16, here 15; the second sentence is missing in the English translation but is included in the German *Arendt–Scholem Briefwechsel*, 34.

16. Gershom Scholem to Hannah Arendt, December 21, 1943, in *Correspondence of Arendt and Scholem*, 18–21, here 21.

17. Noam Zadoff provides a new and convincing elaboration of Scholem's state of mind and personal crisis during the war years in his book *Gershom Scholem*, ch. 4: "Responses to the Holocaust."

18. Gershom Scholem to Hannah Arendt, February 6, 1942, in *Correspondence of Arendt and Scholem*, 10–12, here 10–11 and 12.

19. On Scholem's shifting Zionist perspective, see Biale, "Scholem und der moderne Nationalismus"; Rotenstreich, "Gershom Scholem's Conception"; and Raz-Krakotzkin, "Geschichte, Nationalismus, Eingedenken."

20. On the development of the Hebrew University's profile, see the articles by David N. Myers. He stresses that in its founding years, Scholem took on the "role of custodian of scholarly standards." Myers, "Von Berlin nach Jerusalem," 340; Myers, "Gershom Scholem"; Myers, "Between Diaspora and Zion." See also "Patricide: Scholem's Metaphorics of Death" in Brenner, *Prophets of the Past*, 163–70.

21. On Scholem's activities at the JNUL and his private library, see Dan, "Gershom Scholem"; and Jütte, *Die Emigration*, 102–3.

22. For an instructive take on this, see Pilling, *Denken und Handeln*.

23. On Arendt's first few years in the United States, see Young-Bruehl, *Hannah Arendt*, 164–88; and Vowinckel, *Hannah Arendt*, 40–45. Her articles for *Aufbau* have been collected in Arendt, *Jewish Writings*. She expresses her increasing distance from political Zionism in her 1945 essay "Zionism Reconsidered."

24. Hannah Arendt, interview with Günther Gaus, 1964, in Arendt, *Portable Hannah Arendt*, 3–22, here 13–14.

25. Kazin, *New York Jew*, 299–300 (original emphasis).

26. Hannah Arendt to Kurt Blumenfeld, July 19, 1947, in "*. . . in keinem Besitz verwurzelt*," 43.

27. The most important essays were Arendt, "Concerning Minorities"; Arendt, "Jew as Pariah"; Arendt, "Race-Thinking before Racism"; Arendt, "Approaches to the 'German Problem'"; Arendt, "Imperialism, Nationalism, Chauvinism"; Arendt, "Organized Guilt"; Arendt, "Stateless People"; Arendt, "Parties, Movements and Classes"; Arendt, "Imperialism: Road to Suicide"; and Arendt, "Concentration Camps." All these texts also contained ideas and arguments relating to Arendt's later study of totalitarianism. Ursula Ludz shows this in her comprehensive Arendt bibliography: Arendt, *Ich will verstehen*, 257–342.

28. Arendt, *Origins of Totalitarianism*, xiv (first ed.: 1951 without the preface quoted here).

29. Arendt, "Understanding and Politics," 307–8. An interesting approach to this method is provided by Luban, "Explaining Dark Times."

30. Hannah Arendt to Gershom Scholem, September 22, 1945, in *Correspondence of Arendt and Scholem*, 35–37, here 37.

31. On the specific synergy of action and thought in Arendt's life, see Gallas, "In der Lücke der Zeit." More recently, Dov Schidorsky has also discussed the meaning of Arendt's work for JCR within the broader scope of her activities and thinking. See Schidorsky, "Hannah Arendt's Dedication."

32. Kazin, *New York Jew*, 300.

33. This is also emphasized by Young-Bruehl, *Hannah Arendt*, 187–88; Kirchhoff, "Looted Texts," 186; and Kristeva, *Hannah Arendt*, 110. The most important examples in *Origins of Totalitarianism* are to be found on pages 339, 345, and 402.

34. Hannah Arendt, "On Hannah Arendt," in Melvyn, *Hannah Arendt*, 301–39, here 308.

35. Arendt, "Organized Guilt," 326. Most accounts discussing Hannah Arendt's confrontation with the Holocaust focus on her work on the Eichmann Trial. Far fewer authors examine her early attempts to come to terms with the significance and consequences of the catastrophe. Representative of these are Dietz, "Arendt and the Holocaust"; Stone, "Ontology or Bureaucracy?"; and Traverso, "Das Bild der Hölle." A brief summary of his thoughts in English is provided in Traverso, *End of Jewish Modernity*, 71–75; Aharony, "Hannah Arendt"; Vowinckel, *Geschichtsbegriff und Historisches Denken*, here esp. 86–98; Aschheim, "Nazism, Culture"; Villa, "Genealogies of Total Domination"; and Lang, "Explaining Genocide."

36. For the vividest account of Lucy Dawidowicz's life, see her autobiography *From That Place and Time*. See also several works by her biographer Nancy Sinkoff: her introduction, "Yidishkayt," to the autobiography's new 2008 edition and her articles "The Polishness" and "From the Archives."

37. Dawidowicz, *From That Place and Time*, 227 and 237–38. Kuznitz and Lipphardt too underline that the YIVO in New York, as one of the first organizations in the United States, had already publicized the events in Europe during the war. See Kuznitz, "YIVO," 1094–95; and Lipphardt, *Vilne*, 181–82. Lipphardt, however, bases her comments here on the work of Dawidowicz.

38. Dawidowicz, *From That Place and Time*, 229 and 238.

39. Ibid., 261 and 267.

40. Fishman, *Book Smugglers*.

41. Dawidowicz, *From That Place and Time*, 267.

42. Ibid., 290. References to the use of this publishing house can also be found in Brenner, *After the Holocaust*, 20.

43. Dawidowicz, *From That Place and Time*, 295–96.

44. In a circular of February 22, 1947, to the YIVO in New York and Weinreich, Dawidowicz made some highly critical and at times malicious remarks on her work

for the Joint and on the DPs, underlining that the Offenbach Depot provided her with a far more interesting challenge. AJHS, P-675, Dawidowicz Papers, box 55, folder 4. Dawidowicz, *From That Place and Time*, 315.

45. Dawidowicz, *From That Place and Time*, 315.

46. For the actual lists of items found and identified in the Offenbach Archival Depot, see BArch, Z 45 F, RG 260, OMGUS Records, AHC, Box 221, OAD Monthly Report, May 1947 and June 1947.

47. Dawidowicz, *From That Place and Time*, 316. The biblical term *Amalek* for Germany was commonly used by survivors in the postwar period. This was a reference to the biblical King Amalek, archenemy of the people of Israel and conceptualized Germany as one of his descendants. See Michman, *Holocaust Historiography*, 316; and Grossmann, *Jews, Germans, and Allies*, 218n134.

48. The Jewish survivors in the DP camps chose to refer to themselves in this way. The term *Sherit HaPletah* comes from the Books of Chronicles, where it is applied to the Jews remaining in the land of Israel following the Exile and the Babylonian Captivity.

49. Dawidowicz, *From That Place and Time*, 321.

50. Fania Scholem quoted in Zadoff, *Gershom Scholem*, 144.

51. NLI, Arc 4°1599, Scholem Papers, file 265, folder 24 Gershom Scholem, Diary of 1946, 4, 24, and 33 (in Hebrew).

52. On the results of his investigations in libraries and archives, see UL Stanford, M0580, Baron Papers, box 58, folder 9, "Report of Prof. Gershom Scholem on his Mission to Europe (in the Summer of 1946) Concerning the Libraries of the Diaspora," undated; and a German-language report by Gershom Scholem from Prague for the Hebrew University: NLI, Arc 4°793/212, Otzrot HaGolah Papers, folder I: 1946, June 1946.

53. The different phases of his journey are also discernible in his travel journal. The details and meaning of his postwar experience and his journey have recently been reconstructed in Zadoff, *Gershom Scholem*, 95–151.

54. For this and the following quotations, see Scholem, "Besuch bei den Juden."

55. Gershom Scholem to Siegmund Hurwitz, November 1, 1946, in Scholem, *Briefe*, vol. 1, 324–25. (A shortened version of this letter in Scholem, *Life in Letters*, 338–39, does not contain the quoted passage.)

56. Gershom Scholem to Ernst Grumach, April 24, 1947, ibid., 326.

57. This and the following quotes are taken from Gershom Scholem to Hannah Arendt, November 6, 1946, in *Correspondence of Arendt and Scholem*, 59–62 (original emphasis).

58. Gershom Scholem to Rudolf Hagelstange, June 22, 1952, in Scholem, *Briefe*, vol. 2, 32.

59. Writing to him from Germany, she asked her husband Heinrich Blücher the question that "follows me wherever I go": *"Does Germany still exist?"* Hannah Arendt to Heinrich Blücher, December 28, 1949, in *Within Four Walls*, 113. On the issue of Arendt's nonreturn to Germany, see Gallas, "Hannah Arendt."

60. Hannah Arendt to Gershom Scholem, November 27, 1946, in *Correspondence of Arendt and Scholem*, 63–65, here 64.
61. Arendt, "Aftermath of Nazi Rule," 342.
62. Ibid., 349.
63. Gershom Scholem to Hans-Joachim Schoeps, November 6, 1949, in Scholem, *Briefe*, vol. 2, 14; and to Morton Smith, December 30, 1950, in Scholem, *Life in Letters*, 361.
64. Hannah Arendt to Gershom Scholem, December 10, 1949, in *Correspondence of Arendt and Scholem*, 101.
65. UL Stanford, M0580, Baron Papers, box 43, folder 6, Hannah Arendt to Salo Baron, December 30, 1949.
66. Hannah Arendt to Hilde Fränkel, February 4, 1950, in Arendt, *Briefwechsel mit den Freundinnen*, 291.
67. A detailed overview of Arendt's work for the JCR in Germany is provided by the field reports she composed for the board of directors, all of which are included in *Correspondence of Arendt and Scholem*, 225–61.
68. Arendt, "Field Report No. 18," in ibid., 247–54, here 250.
69. Hannah Arendt to Hilde Fränkel, December 3 and 20, 1949, in Arendt, *Briefwechsel mit den Freundinnen*, 257 and 268.
70. This is also implied in her report "Aftermath of Nazi Rule." It concludes with a diagnosis that reads like the point of departure for the study of totalitarianism that was soon to follow: "What could one reasonably expect from a people after twelve years of totalitarian rule? [. . .] Totalitarianism kills the roots." Arendt, "Aftermath of Nazi Rule," 353.
71. Hannah Arendt to Gershom Scholem, February 5, 1950, in *Correspondence of Arendt and Scholem*, 104–7, here 105.
72. Hannah Arendt to Hilde Fränkel, December 20, 1949, in Arendt, *Briefwechsel mit den Freundinnen*, 269. In his essay "Returning from Forced Exile," Lars Rensmann discusses the relationship between Arendt's critical intervention and her personal connection with Germany. For an instructive analysis, see also Barnouw, *Visible Spaces*, ch. 4: "The Quality of Guilt," 135–76.
73. Duker, "Joshua Starr," 5.
74. UL Stanford, M0580, Baron Papers, box 39, folder 2, letter from Salo Baron to Jerome Michael, June 4, 1946.
75. Baron told this story of his journey to Paris in 1946 in his address to the fifth plenary assembly of the World Jewish Congress of 1966 in Brussels: Baron, "Deutsche und Juden," 89–90; and in an interview with Grace Cohen Grossman, tape 6.
76. UL Stanford, M0580, Baron Papers, box 73, folder 4, Salo W. Baron to Janette Baron, June 3, 1946, quoted in Rubin, "Final Stages." I thank Gil Rubin for providing me with this letter.
77. Engel, *Historians of the Jews*, 64–66; Hertzberg, "Salo W. Baron."
78. Kirshenblatt-Gimblett, "Introduction," 2.
79. S. Baron, "Spiritual Reconstruction," 4–5.

80. S. Baron, "At the Turning Point," 8.
81. Ibid., 2 and 10. Baron's focus on the United States as the center of Jewish life did not mean that he did not support the foundation of a state in Israel; it was in fact a way of underlining his commitment to the notion of a diverse Jewish diaspora—as a complement to the Jewish life in Israel organized within the framework of the nation state. He put forward very similar arguments with respect to South Africa: Baron, "How S. A. [South African] Jewry Should Plan its Future." On Baron's general view of the relationship between the Diaspora and Israel, see Engel, *Historians of the Jews*, 56–57; and Brenner, *Prophets of the Past*, 44.
82. S. Baron, "Communal Responsibility," 73.
83. UL Stanford, M0580, Baron Papers, box 39, folder 3, Jerome Michael, "Memorandum submitted by the Commission on European Jewish Cultural Reconstruction to General J. H. Hilldring," June 5, 1946.
84. S. Baron, "Spiritual Reconstruction," 6.
85. Arendt, "Creating a Cultural Atmosphere." Marie Luise Knott interprets Hannah Arendt's article in a similar way: Knott, "Why Have We Been Spared?," xvi–xviii.
86. Arendt, "Creating a Cultural Atmosphere," 298. Ibid., 300–301.
87. Ibid., 300–301.
88. Ibid., 302.
89. Arendt, "Jewish Cultural Reconstruction," 793.
90. Arendt, "New Homes for Hitler's Jewish Library," 5. See also Arendt, "New Homes for Jewish Books."
91. See Knott, "Bei Schocken Books"; Hahn, "'Wesentlich ein Übersetzungsverlag'?"; and Young-Bruehl, *Hannah Arendt*, 189–99. The efforts made by Arendt and Scholem from 1941 onward to arrange for the publication of the writings of Walter Benjamin also belong in the context of their initiatives to preserve the intellectual traditions buried by National Socialism. See esp. the letters between Arendt and Scholem from 1941 to 1950, in *Correspondence of Arendt and Scholem*. In 1950, Scholem decided to cooperate with Theodor W. Adorno to ensure the publication of Benjamin's writings.
92. Arendt, "Walter Benjamin," here esp. part 3: "The Pearl Diver." For an inspiring discussion of these issues, see: Benhabib, *Reluctant Modernism of Hannah Arendt*, 91–95; Benhabib, "Hannah Arendt."
93. Arendt, "Walter Benjamin," 38.
94. Ibid., 40 and 50.
95. Ibid., 51.
96. Dawidowicz, *From That Place and Time*, 322.
97. On the construction of continuity in the context of YIVO, see Lipphardt, "Forgotten Memory," 194–95; Lipphardt, "Post-Holocaust Reconstruction," Lipphardt, *Vilne*, 179–86; and Miron, "Between Science and Faith." On the general role and outlook of the YIVO in New York and its function in preserving the Yiddish world of the past and adapting it to conditions in the US during and shortly after the war, see Krah, *American Jewry*, 47–70.

98. Dawidowicz, *From That Place and Time*, 261.

99. Noble, "The Yivo," 391. In her study *Vilne*, Lipphardt too underlines that YIVO already occupied a key position in the "transatlantic cultural nexus" in the interwar period, which served as a foundation for postwar activities. See Lipphardt, *Vilne*, 97.

100. Max Weinreich, "Ovnt tsum yortsayt fun Vilner geto" [annual evening of commemoration of the Vilna ghetto], September 22, 1947, speech quoted in Lipphardt, *Vilne*, 364.

101. See Kuznitz, "YIVO," 2095; Lipphardt, *Vilne*, 505–12; Krah, *American Jewry*, 67–70.

102. Dawidowicz, *From That Place and Time*, 311.

103. Dawidowicz discusses the shift in her perception triggered by the search for and salvage of the "YIVO property" in "History as Autobiography," 37. Her reference to the "distance which the Holocaust created between the past and present" appears in ibid., 30.

104. Ibid., 24.

105. Dawidowicz, *From That Place and Time*, 324.

106. Gershom Scholem to Leo Baeck, June 2, 1946, in Scholem, *Life in Letters*, 336.

107. Scholem, *From Berlin to Jerusalem*, 93. On Scholem's bibliophilia: Myers, "Gershom Scholem"; Beit-Arié, "Gershom Scholem as Bibliophile."

108. Scholem, *From Berlin to Jerusalem*, 121.

109. Gershom Scholem to Hannah Arendt, March 6, 1950, in *Correspondence of Arendt and Scholem*, 109–11, here 110.

110. Scholem, *From Berlin to Jerusalem*, 37.

111. The most instructive material on all disputes of this kind is Scholem's correspondence with Hannah Arendt. See their exchange between September 1949 and October 1952 in *Correspondence of Arendt and Scholem*, 91–175.

112. In addition to Scholem's autobiographical text, mentioned earlier, see also Weidner, *Gershom Scholem*, esp. 152–62. For a general introduction to Scholem's Zionism and world of thought, see Biale, "Gershom Scholem"; and Zadoff, *From Berlin to Jerusalem*.

113. Scholem, "Volk des Buches," 95 (original emphasis).

114. Ibid., 96–99.

115. Steiner, *My Unwritten Books*, 103.

116. Ibid.

117. See Scholem, "Reflections on the Possibility."

118. Scholem, "Reflections on Modern Jewish Studies" (1944), 66–67.

119. See, for example, the remarks in Kenan, *Between Memory and History*, xvi–xxi; Ezrahi, "Considering the Apocalypse," 145–50.

120. Scholem, "Israel and the Diaspora," 245.

121. Ben-Zion Dinur (1975), quoted in Engel, *Historians of the Jews*, 121.

122. Scholem, "Israel and the Diaspora," 250.

123. For a representative example of the arguments being made by many lawyers at the time, see Jacob Robinson's introduction in N. Robinson, *Indemnification and Reparations*, 7–9.

124. Hannah Arendt to Karl Jaspers, August 17, 1946, *Correspondence*, 51–56, here 54.
125. Arendt, *Origins of Totalitarianism*, 296. Key legal issues discussed here had already been raised in an article of 1949: Arendt, "Rights of Man."
126. Arendt, *Origins of Totalitarianism*, 455–59.
127. The dictum of the "right to have rights" is formulated in ibid., 296. On Arendt's political engagement and self-image during this period, see Pilling, *Denken und Handeln als Jüdin*, here ch. 4: "Theoretische Grundlagen einer erneuerten Politik"; Canovan, *Hannah Arendt*, esp. "Introduction" and ch. 2; also Kohn, "Freedom."
128. Hannah Arendt, "Jewish Chances," *Aufbau*, April 20, 1945, in Arendt, *Jewish Writings*, 238–40, here 240. It is striking that at this point in time Arendt was not yet calling for a trust organization, instead referring in her article to communities and states that should act as representatives of the Jewish collectivity.
129. Scholem, "Zur Frage," 476.
130. Scholem, "A Lecture about Israel," 36.
131. Biale, "Gershom Scholem," 61.
132. Hannah Arendt, "Jewish Politics" (1942), in Arendt, *Jewish Writings*, 241–43, here 241.
133. Hannah Arendt, "Jewish Army" *Aufbau*, November 14, 1941, in Arendt, *Jewish Writings*, 136–39, here 137.
134. Benhabib, "Hannah Arendt's Political Engagements"; Bernstein, "Hannah Arendt and the Jewish Question," here esp. "Introduction" and ch. 1; Canovan, *Hannah Arendt*; D. Diner, "Marranische Einschreibungen." On the issue of Universalism in Arendt's work, see Sznaider, *Jewish Memory and the Cosmopolitan Order*; D. Diner, "Hannah Arendt Reconsidered"; and Benhabib and Eddon, "From Anti-Semitism."
135. UL Stanford, M0580, Baron Papers, box 382, folder 18, Salo W. Baron, "The Cultural Reconstruction of European Jewry," undated manuscript from around 1946.
136. He was already rejecting overzealous efforts to assimilate in the 1920s. See Baron, "Ghetto and Emancipation," 526. For more on this, see Engel, *Historians of the Jews*, 56. On Baron's perception of the United States, see H. Diner, "Salo Baron"; and Wenger, "Salo Baron."
137. See Maier, "Overcoming the Past?," 297.
138. Jockusch, "Justice at Nuremberg?"
139. S. Baron, "Journal and the Conference," 8.
140. On the role of the Holocaust in Baron's scholarly view of history, see Engel, *Historians of the Jews*, ch. 1, esp. 42–51 and 59–71; Engel, "Holocaust Research"; Engel, "On Studying Jewish History." Baron's otherwise comprehensive accounts of modern and contemporary Jewish history address the topic of the Holocaust barely or not at all. See S. Baron, *Modern Nationalism and Religion*; S. Baron, "Modern and Contemporary Periods"; S. Baron, "Modern Age." Baron's history of the Jews in three volumes, *Social and Religious History*, touches on the topics of fascism and nationalism. In his masterly eighteen-volume revised edition of

Social and Religious History, he did not get beyond 1650. Even his testimony at the 1961 trial of Adolf Eichmann in Jerusalem, published under the title "European Jewry before and after Hitler," is no exception: he avoids an in-depth discussion of the Holocaust itself, instead focusing on the history preceding it and general Jewish responses to persecution across the ages.

141. With the exception of the contribution by Herbert Wechsler on the Nuremberg trials, all the papers appeared in *Jewish Social Studies* 12 (January 1950).

142. Starr, "Jewish Cultural Property."

143. Arendt, "Social Science Techniques", 49. See also Arendt, "Understanding and Politics," 310.

144. Arendt, "Social Science Techniques."

145. Ibid., 55.

146. Ibid., 51.

147. Ibid., 53 and 60.

148. Ibid., 63–64.

149. Arendt, *Between Past and Future*, 26.

150. S. Baron, "Opening Remarks," 14.

151. Ibid., 15.

152. Ibid., 16. The fact that Baron rejected comparison with the Middle Ages has to do with his own research on the position of Jews in premodern contexts. Contrary to the usual reading, which foregrounded the persecution and pogroms of Jews, Baron's work underscored Jews' specific social position and their associated room for maneuver within the medieval and early modern social order. See esp. S. Baron, "Ghetto and Emancipation."

153. The term *Holocaust* was not yet being used in the context of the conference. The participants referred to *khurbn*, the Yiddish word for total destruction, or to catastrophe, annihilation, extermination and the war against the Jews.

154. In December 1947, members of the Jewish Historical Commissions from thirteen European countries met in Paris to discuss the future of their research and "join forces to comprehend the Jewish catastrophe." Friedman took part and was a driving force in the attempt to build a transnational "collective of scholars" to approach the issue. After his immigration to the US, he remained one of the motors of this early, highly transnational scholarship. See Jockusch, *Collect and Record*, 160–85, quotes on 160.

155. Friedman, "Research and Literature," 26. This sideswipe at supposed "amateurs" was chiefly directed against certain members of the historical commissions active in Europe and survivors in Israel. See Jockusch, *Collect and Record*, 194–98.

156. The close cooperation between Friedman and Baron is reflected in their correspondence and two important publications: Friedman, *Roads to Extinction*; and Friedman and Robinson, *Guide to Jewish History*. Their collaboration is corroborated by researchers who have studied Baron and Friedman. See Stauber, "Philip Friedman"; Stauber, *Laying the Foundations*; Engel, *Historians of the Jews*, 67–70; and Aleksiun, "Philip Friedman."

157. Scholem, "Lecture about Israel," 35.
158. The only scholarly debate initiated by Scholem on the question of the impact of the Holocaust explored the definition, ambivalent development, and quality of the relationship between Germans and Jews. Scholem, "Against the Myth"; Scholem, "Once More"; Scholem, "Jews and Germans." For a detailed contextualization of Scholem's position here, see Zadoff, *From Berlin to Jerusalem*, 201–14.
159. On the conference and its relevance to early Holocaust research, see Friedman, "Problems of Research"; and Cohen, *Israeli Holocaust Research*, 57–78. On the role of the Jerusalem School in the first debates on the foundation and character of Yad Vashem and Holocaust research in Israel in general, see Michman, "Is There an 'Israeli School'?"; Cohen, "Birth Pangs"; Engel, *Historians of the Jews*, 110–11.
160. Engel, *Historians of the Jews*, 111. Regardless of Scholem's personal decision, this reticence can also be explained in light of the polarization typical of the period during which Yad Vashem was founded, as established historians found themselves confronted with the views of survivors from Eastern Europe. See Stauber, "Confronting the Jewish Response."
161. Scholem, "Science of Judaism," 311.
162. Scholem, "Jews and Germans," 73.
163. Gershom Scholem to Rudolf Hagelstange, June 22, 1952, in Scholem, *Briefe*, vol. 2, 32.
164. Arendt, *Origins of Totalitarianism* (1973), xiv. (This introduction was not part of the first edition.)
165. Arendt, *Origins of Totalitarianism*, 746–47. These thoughts were first published in her 1948 article, "The Concentration Camps," which was then integrated into her book as part of chapter 12, "Totalitarianism in Power." See Arendt, *Origins of Totalitarianism*, 437–59. On the centrality of this chapter in Arendt's thought, see Berg, *Der Holocaust*, 469–86; and Gallas, "In der Lücke der Zeit."
166. Arendt, "A Reply," 79, emphasis in original.
167. Arendt, "Freedom and Politics." For an instructive take on her concept of action and its political implications, see Heuer, *Citizen*, esp. ch. 8, here esp. 274–93; Kohn, "Hannah Arendt's Jewish Experience."
168. Kohn too underlines that the experience of the Holocaust helped shape the specific theoretical model of action in Arendt's work. See ibid., 181. Her concepts of action and thought and their interrelatedness are developed in Arendt, *Human Condition*; and Arendt, *Life of the Mind*.
169. Arendt, *Origins of Totalitarianism*, 459.
170. AJHS, P-675, Dawidowicz Papers, box 70, folder 7, Lucy S. Dawidowicz, lecture at Ramah Academy, March 7, 1986.
171. Dawidowicz, "History as Autobiography," 31.
172. Weinreich, *Hitler's Professors*.
173. Dawidowicz, *From That Place and Time*, 262. Chs. 19 and 20 in Weinreich's study are devoted to the Frankfurt Institute.

174. Arendt, "Image of Hell," 200. Reference is also made to Weinreich's book in *Origins of Totalitarianism*. See ibid., 339.

175. Dawidowicz, "History as Autobiography," 36–37. In his introduction to Dawidowicz's essay collection, *What Is the Use of Jewish History?*, Neal Kozodoy too emphasizes her strong sense of responsibility with respect to both history and commemoration. See ibid., x–xiv.

176. AJHS, P-675, Dawidowicz Papers, box 70, folder 7, Lucy S. Dawidowicz, Selig Adler Memorial Lecture, Jewish Community Bookfair, Amherst Jewish Community Center, Buffalo, November 16, 1989. However, her arguments reveal some inconsistencies concerning the position of the witness. On the one hand, she criticized the "subjectivity" of the historians working in Yad Vashem and their problematic attempts to "divorce [themselves] from the painful recollection" due to the mere fact that they were survivors (Dawidowicz, "Toward a History of the Holocaust," 52–53.) At the same time, she contended that only Jews were truly in a position to examine Jewish history, especially when it came to the Holocaust (Dawidowicz, *Holocaust and the Historians*, 2), and highlighted her own experience as the engine of her history writing.

177. Howe, *War against the Jews*.

178. She articulates this fear in the introduction to *Holocaust and the Historians*, 1.

179. On Dawidowicz's intentionalist interpretation of the Holocaust in Nazism, see, for example, Marrus, *Holocaust in History*, 35–36.

180. An initial methodological approach to the subject is provided by Dawidowicz, "Toward a History of the Holocaust." Later writings by Dawidowicz that cast light on her methodological procedures are Dawidowicz, "Holocaust as Historical Record"; Dawidowicz, *Holocaust and the Historians*; and Dawidowicz, "What Is the Use of Jewish History?" One foundational text on which numerous YIVO scholars drew as they developed the tradition of Eastern European-Jewish historiography was Dubnow's essay "Let Us Seek and Investigate."

181. Dawidowicz, "Toward a History of the Holocaust," 56.

182. Traverso, *End of Jewish Modernity*, 62.

CONCLUSION

1. An instructive overview of the development of Holocaust awareness and its reading is provided in Wachsmann, *KL*, 10–17; and in Cesarani, "Introduction," in *After Eichmann*, 1–17. For early analyses of the numerous historical, literary, and theological attempts to get to grips with the Holocaust undertaken prior to the Eichmann trial, see L. Baron, "Holocaust and American Public Memory"; and Korman, "Holocaust in American Historical Writing."

2. Wasserstein, "Myth of 'Jewish Silence'"; H. Diner, *We Remember with Reverence and Love*; Cesarani and Sundquist, *After the Holocaust*; Jockusch, *Collect and Record*; Magilow and Silverman, *Holocaust Representations in History*, 34–41. Important examples of studies focused on a specific national context in an attempt

to counter this myth are Azouvi, *Le Mythe du grand Silence*; and Laczó, *Hungarian Jews*.

3. For an introduction, see Bankier and Michman, *Holocaust and Justice*; and Déak, Gross, and Judt, *Politics of Retribution*. An intriguing example of Jewish activity in the legal realm is provided in Jockusch, "Justice at Nuremberg?"

4. On such processes of conversion, see Weigel, "Entgeltung durch Geld"; and Weigel, "Shylocks Wiederkehr." On the processing of historical injustice through legal procedures, see Barkan, *Guilt of Nations*; Torpey, *Politics and the Past*; and here esp. Maier, "Overcoming the Past?"

5. See S. Baron, "Journal and the Conference," 9; and S. Baron, "Personal Notes," 189.

6. Today, YIVO is pursuing an ambitious project to reunite YIVO's prewar library by digitalizing holdings in New York and those found in Vilnius and creating a web portal to access them.

7. An interesting debate on the possible "return" to Europe of the objects distributed by the JCR can be found in Lipman, "Jewish Cultural Reconstruction Reconsidered."

8. Arendt, *Origins of Totalitarianism*, 452.

9. Holzer-Kawałko, "Double Dynamics."

10. UL Stanford, M0580, box 382, folder 18, Salo W. Baron, "The Cultural Reconstruction of European Jewry," 3 (undated manuscript).

11. Dawidowicz, "What Is the Use of Jewish History?" 16.

12. Gershom Scholem to Hannah Arendt, June 23, 1963, in *Correspondence of Arendt and Scholem*, 201–5, here 202. Their exchange was published in German and English at the time: "Ein Briefwechsel über Hannah Arendts Buch zwischen Prof. Gershom Gerhard Scholem und Hannah Arendt" in *Mittelungsblatt des Irgun Olej Merkas Europa 33, August 16, 1963*, 2–4; and in *Neue Zürcher Zeitung*, October 20, 1963; "'Eichmann in Jerusalem': An Exchange of Letters between Gershom Scholem and Hannah Arendt" in *Encounter* 22 (January 1964): 51–56.

13. Arendt, *Eichmann in Jerusalem*, 7. For contemporary critiques of Arendt's report on Eichmann, see Krummacher, *Die Kontroverse*; Council of Jews from Germany, *In the Wake of the Eichmann Trial*. During this period, through critiques and readers' letters, the New York journal *Commentary* became a central forum of the debate; see the issues from 1963 and 1964. For an overview of the contentious reception of Arendt's report, see, for example, Rabinbach, "Eichmann in New York"; Cohen, "A Generation's Response"; and Ezra, "Eichmann Polemics."

14. Arendt, "Organized Guilt"; Arendt, "Concentration Camps"; Arendt, "Rights of Man"; Arendt, "Social Science Techniques."

BIBLIOGRAPHY

ARCHIVAL COLLECTIONS

American Jewish Historical Society, Archive, Center for Jewish History, New York (AJHS)
P-675: Lucy S. Dawidowicz Papers

Bundesarchiv (German Federal Archive) Koblenz (BArch)
Abteilung B—Bundesrepublik Deutschland mit westlichen Besatzungszonen 1945ff.
   Z 45 F: Records of the United States Occupation Headquarters, World War II, Office of Military Government for Germany, United States (OMGUS), RG 260
   Records of the Adjutant General, War Department (AG)
   Ardelia Hall Collection (AHC), Property Division, MFA&A: Box 1–448
   Z 46: Records of the Allied Control Authority, Office of Records and Archives

Central Archives for the History of the Jewish People, Jerusalem (CAHJP)
Jewish Restitution Successor Organization, New York, Administration Files
P-205: Ernst Grumach Papers

Hannah Arendt-Zentrum, Carl von Ossietzky Universität Oldenburg (HAZ)
Hannah Arendt Papers (copies from her papers held at the Library of Congress, Washington, DC)

Historisches Museum Frankfurt (Historical Museum), Frankfurt am Main
Auslagerungsakten 1032: Altkorrespondenz Guido Schönberger

Leo Baeck Institute, Archives, Center for Jewish History, New York (LBI)
xMfW: The Wiener Library—Document Archives
AR 65: Conference on Jewish Material Claims against Germany Collection
AR 5890: Council of Jews from Germany Collection
AR 7002: Jacob Jacobson Collection

Library of Congress, Manuscript Division, Washington, DC (LoC)
The Records of the Library of Congress European Mission and Cooperative Acquisitions Project, 1942–1957

National Archives and Records Administration, College Park, MD (NA College Park)

MICROFILM COLLECTIONS

M1941: Records Concerning the Central Collection Points (Ardelia Hall Collection): OMGUS Headquarters Records, 1938–1951, Records of the United States Occupation Headquarters, World War II, Record Group 260

M1942: Records Concerning the Central Collecting Points (Ardelia Hall Collection): Offenbach Archival Depot, 1946–1951, Records of the United States Occupation Headquarters, World War II, Record Group 260

M1947: Records Concerning the Central Collection Points (Ardelia Hall Collection): Wiesbaden Collecting Point, 1945–1952, Records of the United States Occupation Headquarters, World War II, Record Group 260

M1949: Records of the Monuments, Fine Arts, and Archives (MFA&A) Section of the Reparations and Restitution Branch, OMGUS, 1945–1951, Records of the United States Occupation Headquarters, World War II, Record Group 260

COLLECTION OF DOCUMENTS

RG 59: General Records of the Department of State

RG 260: Records of the United States Occupation Headquarters, World War II, Office of Military Government for Germany (OMGUS)
Records of the Property Division
Records of the Executive Office
Records Maintained by the Fine Arts & Monuments Adviser (Ardelia Hall Collection), 1945–1961

RG 466: Records of the United States High Commission for Germany
Records of the Property Office

The National Library of Israel, Archives Department (NLI)

Arc 4°793: Library Papers
Arc 4°793/212 and Arc 4 793/288–89: Otzrot HaGolah Papers
Arc 4°1599: Gershom Scholem Papers

New York Public Library, Stephen A. Schwarzman Building, New York

MANUSCRIPTS AND ARCHIVES DIVISION

MssCol 2429: Koppel S. Pinson Papers

DOROT JEWISH DIVISION

ZP-1190, P: Offenbach Archival Depot, Isaac Bencowitz (microfilm)
ZP-*PBM p. v. 478–85: Jewish Life and Literature. A Collection of Pamphlets (microfilm)

Staatsbibliothek zu Berlin (Berlin State Library), Manuscript Department (StaBi)
Nachlass Nr. 266: Ernst Gottlieb Lowenthal

Stanford University Libraries, Stanford, CA, Department of Special Collections (UL Stanford)
M0580: Salo W. Baron Papers
M0670: Jewish Social Studies Papers

University of Chicago Library, Special Collections Research Center (UChicago)
Morris Raphael Cohen Papers, 1898–1981

YIVO Institute for Jewish Research, Archives, Center for Jewish History, New York (YIVO)
15/6896 (Per): Monthly Reports, United States, Office of the Military Government, Offenbach Archival Depot

PRIMARY SOURCES

Aaroni, Abraham, and Julius H. Buchman. "Europe's Jewish Cultural Material." *National Jewish Monthly* (May 1947): 309–11.

Adler, H. G. "Die Geschichte des Prager Jüdischen Museums (1947)." *Monatshefte* 103, no. 2 (2011): 161–72.

———. *Theresienstadt 1941–1945: The Face of a Coerced Community*. Translated by Belinda Cooper. New York: Cambridge University Press, 2017.

Adler-Rudel, Salomon. "Aus der Vorzeit der kollektiven Wiedergutmachung." In *In zwei Welten: Siegfried Moses zum fünfundsiebzigsten Geburtstag*, edited by Hans Tramer, 200–217. Tel Aviv: Bitaon, 1962.

Adorno, Theodor W. "Out of the Firing-Line." In *Minima Moralia: Reflections on a Damaged Life*, translated from the German by E. F. N. Jephcott, 53–56. New York: Verso, 2005.

American Jewish Committee. "Annual Report 1941." *American Jewish Yearbook* 43 (1941/42): 699–762.

———. "A Statement." *Contemporary Jewish Record* 6, no. 1 (1943): 3–4.

Apenszlak, Jacob, ed. *The Black Book of Polish Jewry: An Account of the Martyrdom of Polish Jewry under Nazi Occupation*. New York: Roy Publication, 1943.

Arendt, Hannah. "The Aftermath of Nazi Rule: Report from Germany." *Commentary* 10 (1950): 342–53.

———. "All Israel Takes Care of Israel." *Aufbau*, April 24, 1942. Reprinted in *The Jewish Writings*, 154–56.

———. "Approaches to the 'German Problem.'" *Partisan Review* 12, no. 1 (1945): 93–106.

———. *Between Past and Future: Six Exercises in Political Thought*. New York: Viking, 1961.

——. "The Concentration Camps." *Partisan Review* 15, no. 2 (1948): 304–12.

——. "Concerning Minorities." *Contemporary Jewish Record* 7, no. 4 (1944): 353–68.

——. "Creating a Cultural Atmosphere." *Commentary* 4, no. 5 (1947): 424–26. Reprinted in *The Jewish Writings*, 298–302.

——. "The Crisis of Zionism I." *Aufbau*, October 22, 1942. Reprinted in *The Jewish Writings*, 178–80.

——. "Days of Change." *Aufbau*, July 28, 1944. Reprinted in *The Jewish Writings*, 214–17.

——. *Eichmann in Jerusalem: A Report on the Banality of Evil*. Revised and enlarged edition. New York: Penguin, 1994.

——. *Essays in Understanding, 1930–1954: Formation, Exile, and Totalitarianism*. Edited by Jerome Kohn. New York: Harcourt Brace, 1994.

——. "Freedom and Politics: A Lecture." *Chicago Review* 14, no. 1 (1960): 28–46.

——. "From the Dreyfus Affair to France Today." *Jewish Social Studies* 4, no. 3 (1942): 195–240.

——. *The Human Condition: A Study of the Central Dilemmas Facing Modern Man*. New York: Doubleday, 1959.

——. *Ich will verstehen: Selbstauskünfte zu Leben und Werk*. 2nd ed. Edited by Ursula Ludz. Munich: Piper, 2006.

——. "The Image of Hell." *Commentary* 2, no. 3 (1946): 291–95. Reprinted in *Essays in Understanding*, 197–205.

——. "Imperialism: Road to Suicide: The Political Origins and Use of Racism." *Commentary* 1, no. 4 (1945/46): 27–35.

——. "Imperialism, Nationalism, Chauvinism." *Review of Politics* 7, no. 4 (1945): 441–63.

——. "JCR Field Report No. 12, 15, 16, 18 and Final Report to the JCR Commission 'Report of My Mission to Germany Respectfully Submitted to the Board of Directors for the Meeting on April 12, 1950.'" In *The Correspondence of Hannah Arendt and Gershom Scholem*, edited by Marie Luise Knott and translated by Anthony David, 225–61. Chicago: University of Chicago Press, 2017.

——. "The Jew as Pariah: A Hidden Tradition." *Jewish Social Studies* 6, no. 2 (1944): 99–122.

——. "The Jewish Army—the Beginning of Jewish Politics?" *Aufbau*, November 14, 1941. Reprinted in *The Jewish Writings*, 136–39.

——. "Jewish Chances: Sparse Prospects, Divided Representation." *Aufbau*, April 20, 1945. Reprinted in *The Jewish Writings*, 238–40.

——. "Jewish Cultural Reconstruction, Inc." (1950). In *The Jew in the Modern World: A Documentary History*, edited by Paul Mendes-Flohr and Jehuda Reinharz, 790–94. New York: Oxford University Press, 2011.

——. "Jewish Politics" (1942). In *The Jewish Writings*, 241–43.

——. *The Jewish Writings*. Edited by Jerome Kohn and Ron H. Feldman. New York: Schocken Books, 2007.

——. *The Life of the Mind.* One-volume edition. San Diego: Harcourt, 1981.

——. "New Homes for Hitler's Jewish Library." *Canadian Jewish Chronicle*, October 28, 1949.

——. "New Homes for Jewish Books." *American Hebrew* 159, no. 30 (November 18, 1949): 14.

——. "On Hannah Arendt." In *Hannah Arendt: The Recovery of the Public World*, edited by Melvyn A. Hill, 301–39. New York: St. Martin's, 1979.

——. "Organized Guilt and Universal Responsibility." *Jewish Frontier* 12, no. 1 (1945): 19–23. Reprinted in *Essays in Understanding*, 121–32.

——. *The Origins of Totalitarianism.* New York: Harcourt Brace, 1951. New edition with added prefaces. San Diego: Harcourt Brace, 1973.

——. "Paper and Reality." *Aufbau*, April 10, 1942. Reprinted in *The Jewish Writings*, 152–54.

——. "Parties, Movements and Classes." *Partisan Review* 12, no. 4 (1945): 504–13.

——. "Race-Thinking before Racism." *Review of Politics* 6, no. 1 (1944): 36–73.

——. "A Reply [to Eric Voegelin]." *Review of Politics* 15, no. 1 (1953): 76–84.

——. "'The Rights of Man': What Are They?" *Modern Review* 3, no. 1 (1949): 24–37.

——. "Social Science Techniques and the Study of Concentration Camps." *Jewish Social Studies* 12, no. 1 (1950): 49–64.

——. "The Stateless People." *Contemporary Jewish Record* 8, no. 2 (1945): 137–53.

——. "Understanding and Politics." *Partisan Review* 20, no. 4 (1953): 377–92. An extended version is reprinted in *Essays in Understanding*, 307–27.

——. "Walter Benjamin." In *Illuminations*, by Walter Benjamin, edited and with an introduction by Hannah Arendt and translated by Harry Zohn, 7–58. London: Bodley Head, 2015.

——. "What Remains? The Language Remains: A Conversation with Günther Gaus." In *The Portable Hannah Arendt*, edited and with an introduction by Peter Baehr, 3–22. New York: Penguin, 2000.

——. *Wie ich einmal ohne dich leben soll, mag ich mir nicht vorstellen: Briefwechsel mit den Freundinnen Charlotte Beradt, Rose Feitelson, Hilde Fränkel, Anne Weil und Helen Wolff.* Edited by Ursula Ludz and Ingeborg Nordmann. Munich: Piper, 2017.

——. "Zionism Reconsidered." *Menorah Journal* 33, no. 2 (1945): 162–96.

——, and Heinrich Blücher. *Within Four Walls: The Correspondence between Hannah Arendt and Heinrich Blücher, 1936–1968.* Edited and with and introduction by Lotte Köhler. Translated from the German by Peter Constantine. New York: Harcourt, 2000.

——, and Kurt Blumenfeld. *". . . in keinem Besitz verwurzelt": Die Korrespondenz.* Edited by Ingeborg Nordmann and Iris Pilling. Hamburg: Rotbuch-Verlag, 1995.

——, and Karl Jaspers. *Correspondence 1926–1969.* Edited by Lotte Köhler. New York: Harcourt Brace Jovanovich, 1992.

——, and Mary McCarthy. *Between Friends: The Correspondence of Hannah Arendt and Mary McCarthy, 1949–1975.* Edited and with an introduction by Carol Brightman. New York: Harcourt Brace, 1995.

——, and Gershom Scholem. *The Correspondence of Hannah Arendt and Gershom Scholem*. Edited by Marie Luise Knott and translated by Anthony David. Chicago: University of Chicago Press, 2017. Original German version: *Hannah Arendt, Gershom Scholem: Der Briefwechsel*, edited by Marie Luise Knott in cooperation with David Heredia. Berlin: Jüdischer Verlag, 2010.

Baron, Salo W. "At the Turning Point." *Menorah Journal* 33, no. 1 (1945): 1–10.

——. "Communal Responsibility for Jewish Social Research." *Jewish Social Studies* 18, no. 3 (1955): 72–75.

——. "Deutsche und Juden, Rede vor der 5. Plenarversammlung des Jüdischen Weltkongresses 1966 in Brüssel." In *Deutsche und Juden: Beiträge von Nahum Goldmann, Gershom Scholem, Golo Mann, Salo W. Baron, Eugen Gerstenmaier und Karl Jaspers*, 70–95. Frankfurt am Main: Suhrkamp, 1967.

——. "European Jewry before and after Hitler." *American Jewish Yearbook* 63 (1962): 3–49.

——. Foreword to "Tentative List of Jewish Educational Institutions," 5–8.

——. Foreword to "Tentative List of Jewish Periodicals," 7–9.

——. "Ghetto and Emancipation: Shall We Revise the Traditional View." *Menorah Journal* 14 (1928): 515–26.

——. "How S. A. [South African] Jewry Should Plan Its Future." *Jewish Affairs* 2, no. 4 (1947): 4–9.

——. Interview with Grace Cohen Grossman Canaan, CT, July 3/4, 1988, transcript version of 7 tapes (tape 1–7).

——. Introduction to "Tentative List of Jewish Cultural Treasures," 5–10.

——. "The Journal and the Conference of Jewish Social Studies." In *Emancipation and Counter-emancipation: Selected Essays from Jewish Social Studies*, edited by Abraham Duker and Meir Ben-Horin, 1–11. New York: KTAV, 1974.

——. "The Modern Age." In *Great Ages and Ideas of the Jewish People*, edited and with an introduction by Leo Schwarz, 315–484. New York: Modern Library, 1956.

——. "The Modern and Contemporary Periods: Review of the History." In *Violence and Defense in the Jewish Experience*, edited by Salo W. Baron and George S. Wise, 163–90. Philadelphia: Jewish Publication Society of America, 1977.

——. *Modern Nationalism and Religion*. New York: Harper, 1947.

——. "Opening Remarks (Conference: 'Problems of Research in the Study of the Jewish Catastrophe 1939–1945,' April 3, 1949, New York)." *Jewish Social Studies* 12, no. 1 (1950): 13–16.

——. "Personal Notes: Hannah Arendt 1906–1975." *Jewish Social Studies* 38, no. 2 (1976): 187–89.

——. "Reflections on the Future of the Jews of Europe." *Contemporary Jewish Record* 3, no. 4 (1940): 355–69.

——. *A Social and Religious History of the Jews*. 3 vols. New York: Columbia University Press, 1937–1939.

——. *A Social and Religious History of the Jews*. 18 vols. New York: Columbia University Press, 1952–1983.

———. "The Spiritual Reconstruction of European Jewry." *Commentary* 1, no. 1 (1945): 4–12.

———. "What War Has Meant to Community Life." *Contemporary Jewish Record* 5, no. 5 (1942): 493–507.

Benjamin, Walter. "Unpacking My Library." In *Illuminations*, by Walter Benjamin, edited and with an introduction by Hannah Arendt and translated by Harry Zohn, 61–69. London: Bodley Head, 2015.

Bentwich, Norman. *The United Restitution Organisation, 1948–1968: The Work of Restitution and Compensation for Victims of Nazi Oppression*. London: Vallentine Mitchell, 1968.

Bergman, Hugo. "Jubilee of the Library." *Davar*, August 7, 1942 (hebr.).

———. *Tagebücher und Briefe: Bd. 1: 1901–1948*. Edited by Miriam Sambursky. König-stein in Taunus: Jüdischer Verlag, Athenäum, 1985.

Born, Lester K. "The Archives and Libraries in Postwar Germany." *American Historical Review* 56, no. 1 (1950): 34–57.

Breitenbach, Edgar. "Historical Survey of the Activities of the Intelligence Department, MFA&A Section, OMGB, 1946–1949." *College Art Journal* 2 (1949/50): 192–98.

Cassou, Jean, ed. *Le Pillage par les Allemands des oeuvres d'art et des bibliothèques appartenant à des Juifs en France*. Paris: Éd. du Centre, 1947.

Clay, Lucius D. *Decision in Germany*. Garden City, NY: Doubleday, 1950.

Cohen, Morris Raphael. *A Dreamer's Journey*. Boston: Beacon, 1949. Reprint edition. New York: Arno Press, 1975.

———. "Jewish Studies of Peace and Post-war Problems." *Contemporary Jewish Record* 4, no. 2 (1941): 110–25.

———. "Publisher's Foreword." *Jewish Social Studies* 1, no. 1 (1939): 3–4.

———. *The Work of the Conference on Jewish Relations: An Address Made before a Dinner Meeting of the Conference Held on February 7, 1937, at the Hotel Delmonico, New York City*. Edited by the Conference on Jewish Relations. New York: Conference on Jewish Relations, 1937.

Conference on Jewish Relations. *President's Report, 1940–1943*. New York: Conference on Jewish Relations, 1943.

Council of Jews from Germany, eds. *In the Wake of the Eichmann Trial*. London: Council of Jews from Germany, 1964.

Dawidowicz, Lucy S. *From That Place and Time: A Memoir, 1938–1947*. Edited by Nancy Sinkoff. New Brunswick, NJ: Rutgers University Press, 2008.

———. *The Golden Tradition: Jewish Life and Thought in Eastern Europe*. Boston: Beacon, 1967.

———. "History as Autobiography: Telling a Life." In *What Is the Use of Jewish History? Essays*, 20–37.

———. *The Holocaust and the Historians*. Cambridge, MA: Harvard University Press, 1981.

———. "The Holocaust as Historical Record." In *Dimensions of the Holocaust: Lectures at Northwestern University, Lectures by Elie Wiesel, Lucy Dawidowicz, Dorothy*

Rabinowitz und Robert McAfee Brown, 76–81. Evanston, IL: Northwestern University Press, 1977.

———. "Toward a History of the Holocaust." *Commentary* 47, no. 4 (1969): 51–56.

———. *The War against the Jews: 1933–1945*. New York: Holt, Rinehart and Winston, 1975.

———. *What Is the Use of Jewish History? Essays*. Edited and with an introduction by Neal Kozodoy. New York: Schocken Books, 1992.

———. "What Is the Use of Jewish History?" In *What Is the Use of Jewish History? Essays*, 3–19.

Downs, Robert B. "Wartime Co-operative Acquisitions." *Library Quarterly* 19, no. 3 (1949): 157–65.

Dubnow, Simon. "Let Us Seek and Investigate (1891)." *Simon Dubnow Institute Yearbook* 7 (2008): 353–82.

Duker, Abraham G., ed. *The Joshua Starr Memorial Volume: Studies in History and Philology*. New York: Conference on Jewish Relations, 1953.

———. "Joshua Starr." In *The Joshua Starr Memorial Volume*, 1–8.

———, and Meir Ben-Horin, eds. *Emancipation and Counter-emancipation: Selected Essays from Jewish Social Studies*. New York: KTAV, 1974.

———, and Max Gottschalk. *Jews in the Post-war World*. New York: Dryden, 1945.

Farmer, Walter I. *The Safekeepers: A Memoir of the Arts of the End of World War II*. Berlin: De Gruyter, 2015.

Feuchtwanger, Lion. *Jew Süss: A Historical Romance*. Translated from the German by Willa Muir and Edwin Muir. London: Hutchinson's International Authors, 1945.

Flanner, Janet. *Men and Monuments*. London: Hamilton, 1957.

———. *Paris, Germany . . . : Reportagen aus Europa 1931–1950*. Compiled by Klaus Blanc. Munich: Kunstmann, 1992.

Freimann, Aron. *Die hebraeischen Inkunabeln der Stadtbibliothek zu Frankfurt am Main*. Frankfurt am Main: Stadtbibliothek, 1920.

———. *Katalog der Judaica und Hebraica: Stadtbibliothek Frankfurt am Main*. Frankfurt am Main: Stadtbibliothek, 1932.

Friedman, Herbert A. *Roots of the Future*. Jerusalem: Gefen, 1999.

Friedman, Philip. "The Fate of the Jewish Book during the Nazi Era (1957)." In *Essays on Jewish Booklore*, articles selected by Philip Goodman, 112–22. New York: KTAV, 1972.

———. "Problems of Research on the European Jewish Catastrophe." *Yad Vashem Studies* 3 (1959): 25–39.

———. "Research and Literature on the Recent Jewish Tragedy." *Jewish Social Studies* 12, no. 1 (1950): 17–26.

———. *Roads to Extinction: Essays on the Holocaust*. Edited by Ada June Friedman, with an introduction by Salo W. Baron. New York: Conference on Jewish Social Studies, Jewish Publication Society of America, 1980.

———, and Jacob Robinson. *Guide to Jewish History under Nazi Impact*. Jerusalem: Yad Vashem Martyrs' and Heroes' Memorial Authority, 1960.

Galinski, Heinz. "New Beginning of Jewish Life in Berlin." In *After the Holocaust: Rebuilding Jewish Lives in Postwar Germany*, by Michael Brenner, translated from the German by Barbara Harshav, 100–102. Princeton, NJ: Princeton University Press, 1997.

Gaster, Theodor H. "Foundations of Jewish Cultural Reconstruction in Europe." *Journal of Educational Sociology* 18, no. 5 (January 1945): 267–70.

Goldberg, Lea. "Lady of the Castle, (Hebrew first ed. 1955)." In *Selected Poetry and Drama*, poetry translated from Hebrew by Rachel Tzvia Back and drama translated from Hebrew by T. Carmi. New Milford, CT: Toby Press, 2005.

Goldmann, Nahum. *The Autobiography of Nahum Goldmann: Sixty Years of Jewish Life.* New York: Holt, Rinehart and Winston, 1969.

Goldschmidt, Siegfried. *Legal Claims against Germany: Compensation for Losses Resulting from Anti-Racial Measures* (Publication of the AJC Research Institute on Peace and Post-War Problems). New York: Dryden, 1945.

Graswinckel, Dirk Petrus M. *Mitteilungen über die Restitution der nach Deutschland verbrachten niederländischen Bibliotheken und Archive 1946.* Giessen: 1991.

Hall, Ardelia R. "The Recovery of Cultural Objects Dispersed during World War II." *Department of State Bulletin* 25, no. 635 (1951): 337–45.

Hancock, Walker. "Experiences of a Monuments Officer in Germany." *College Art Journal* 5, no. 4 (1946): 271–311.

Heller, Bernard. "Displaced Books and Displaced Persons." *Liberal Judaism*, March 1951, 18–22.

———. "The Homecoming." *Liberal Judaism*, September 1950, 24–28.

———. "Invisible Spectators." *Liberal Judaism*, June 1951, 34–37.

———. "Operation Salvage." *Jewish Horizon* 6 (February 1950): 12–14.

———. "Recovery of Looted Sacred Objects." *Liberal Judaism*, March 1950, 9–12.

———. "To the Victims Belong the Spoils." *Liberal Judaism*, June 1950, 21–24.

Howe, Thomas Carr. *Salt Mines and Castles: The Discovery and Restitution of Looted European Art.* Indianapolis: Bobbs-Merrill, 1946.

Institute of Jewish Affairs. "Reparations, Restitution, Compensation: The Jewish Aspects." In *Institute's Annual*, edited by the Institute of Jewish Affairs, 1–54. New York: Institute of Jewish Affairs, 1956.

———. *Twenty Years of the Institute of Jewish Affairs, 1941–1961: A Record of Activities and Achievements.* New York: Institute of Jewish Affairs / World Jewish Congress, 1961.

Institute on Jewish Peace and Post-War Problems, Publications, ed. by the American Jewish Committee, New York.

Pamphlet Series (Jews in the Postwar World):

No. 1: Mahler, Raphael. Jewish Emancipation, A Selection of Documents 1 (1941), 2 (1942) und 3 (1944).

No. 2: Weinryb, Bernard. Jewish Emancipation under Attack: Its Legal Recession until the Present War, 1942.

No. 3: Duker, Abraham. Governments-in-Exile on Jewish Rights, 1943.

No. 4: Kulischer, Eugene Michael. Jewish Migrations: Past Experiences and Post-War Prospects, 1943.

No. 5: Zeeland, Paul van: Post War Migrations: Proposals for an International Agency, 1943.

No. 6: Vishniak, Mark. The Legal Status of Stateless Persons, 1945.

Reprint Series:

No. 1: Hevesi, Eugene. Hitler's Plan for Madagascar, 1941.

No. 2: Moskowitz, Moses. The Jewish Situation in the Protectorate of Bohemia-Moravia, 1942.

No. 3: Duker, Abraham. Political and Cultural Aspects of Jewish Post-War Problems, 1943.

No. 4: Munz, Ernest. Restitution in Post-War Europe, 1943.

No. 5: Sinder, Henri. Lights and Shades of Jewish Life in France 1940–42, 1943.

No. 6: Stillschweig, Kurt. Nationalism and Autonomy among Eastern European Jewry, 1944.

No. 7: Mahler, Raphael. Jews in Public Service and the Liberal Professions in Poland, 1918–39, 1944.

No. 8: Segal, Simon. Problems of Minorities Regarding an International Bill of Rights, 1945.

International Military Tribunal. *Trial of the Major War Crimes before the International Military Tribunal.* Vol. 8, *Proceedings, February 20, 1946–March 7, 1946.* Nuremberg: International Military Tribunal, 1947.

Jewish Restitution Successor Organization. *After Five Years, 1948–1953.* Nuremberg: JRSO, 1953.

———. *Betrachtungen zum Rückerstattungsrecht.* Coblenz: Humanitas-Verlag, 1951.

Kagan, Saul, and Ernest H. Weismann. *Report on the Operations of the Jewish Restitution Successor Organization, 1947–1972.* New York: The Organization, 1973.

Kapralik, Charles I. *The History of the Work of the Jewish Trust Corporation: Volume II.* London: Jewish Trust Corporation, 1971.

———. *Reclaiming the Nazi Loot: The History of the Work of the Jewish Trust Corporation for Germany, a Report.* London: Jewish Trust Corporation, 1962.

Karbach, Oscar. "Max Gottschalk/Abraham Duker, Jews in the Post-War World (Review)." *Jewish Social Studies* 7, no. 3 (1945): 281–83.

Katsh, Abraham I., ed. *The Jew in the Postwar World,* special issue of *Journal of Educational Sociology* 18, no. 5 (1945).

Kruk, Herman. *The Last Days of the Jerusalem in Lithuania: Chronicles from the Vilna Ghetto and the Camps, 1939–1944.* With an introduction by Benjamin Harshav and translated by Barbara Harshav. New Haven, CT: Yale University Press, 2002.

Kupfer, Ephraim. "Manuscript Treasures." *Yedies: Byuletin fun Yidishn Historishn Institut in Polyn* (November 1949, yidd.). An English translation was prepared by Meir Ben-Horin: UL Stanford, M0580, Baron Papers, box 232, folder 5, Meir Ben-Horin to Salo Baron, March 13, 1950.

La Farge, Henry. *Lost Treasures of Europe: 427 Photographs.* New York: Pantheon, 1946.

Landau, Ernest. "Jüdische Kulturschätze wandern aus." *Die Neue Zeitung*, February 9, 1951.

Landauer, Georg. *Der Zionismus im Wandel dreier Jahrzehnte*. Edited by Max Kreutzberger. Tel Aviv: Bitaon, 1957.

Lemkin, Raphael. "Acts Constituting a General (Transnational) Danger Considered as Offences against the Law of Nations: Additional Explications to the Special Report Presented to the 5th Conference for the Unification of Penal Law in Madrid (October 14–20, 1933)." Translated from the French by Jim Fussell. http://www.preventgenocide.org.

———. "Akte der Barbarei und des Vandalismus als delicta juris gentium." *Internationales Anwaltsblatt* 19, no. 6 (November 1933): 117–19.

———. *Axis Rule in Occupied Europe: Laws of Occupation, Analysis of Government, Proposals for Redress*. Washington, DC: Carnegie Endowment for International Peace, Division of International Law, 1944.

Lestschinsky, Jakob. "The Material Losses: The Cultural Destruction of European Jewry." In *Crisis, Catastrophe and Survival: A Jewish Balance Sheet, 1914–1945*, 62–73. New York: Institute of Jewish Affairs of the World Jewish Congress, 1948.

Löwenthal, Leo. "Caliban's Legacy." *Cultural Critique* 8 (Winter 1987–1988): 5–17.

Lüth, Erich. "'Aufruf zur Ölbaumspende' durch Senatsdirektor Lüth: Aktion 'Friede mit Israel.'" *Rundbrief zur Förderung der Freundschaft zwischen dem Alten und dem Neuen Gottesvolk* 16 (April 1952): 21–22.

Lynx, Joachim Joe, ed. *The Future of the Jews: A Symposium*. London: Drummond, 1945.

Moses, Siegfried. *Jewish Post-War Claims (Tel Aviv 1944)*. Münster: Lit, 2001.

Munz, Ernest. "Restitution in Postwar Europe." *Contemporary Jewish Record* 6, no. 4 (1943): 371–80.

Noble, Shlomo. "The Yivo." *Contemporary Jewish Record* 7, no. 4 (1944): 385–91.

Peiss, Reuben. "European Wartime Acquisitions and the Library of Congress Mission." *Library Journal*, June 15, 1946, 863–76.

———. "Report on Europe." *College and Research Libraries* 8, no. 2 (1947): 114–19.

Pinson, Koppel S. *Essays on Antisemitism*. New York: Conference on Jewish Relations, 1942. Second revised and enlarged edition, 1946.

———. "Jewish Life in Liberated Germany: A Study of the Jewish DP's." *Jewish Social Studies* 9, no. 2 (1947): 101–26.

Pomrenze, Seymour J. "'Operation Offenbach': The Salvaging of Jewish Cultural Treasures in Germany." *YIVO Bleter* 29, no. 2 (1947): 282–85 (yidd.).

———. "The Restitution of Jewish Cultural Treasures after the Holocaust: The Offenbach Archival Depot's Role in the Fulfillment of U. S. International and Moral Obligations (A First Hand Account)." *Rosaline and Meyer Feinstein Lecture in Judaic Bibliography*, 37th Annual Convention of the Association of Jewish Libraries (Denver, Co., June 23–26, 2002). http://www.jewishlibraries.org.

Poste, Leslie I. "Books go Home from the Wars." *Library Journal* 73, no. 21 (1948): 1699–1704.

———. "The Development of U. S. Protection of Libraries and Archives in Europe during World War II." PhD diss., University of Chicago, 1958.

Research Staff of the Commission on European Jewish Cultural Reconstruction. "Addenda and Corrigenda to Tentative List of Jewish Cultural Treasures in Axis-Occupied Countries." *Jewish Social Studies* 10, no. 1 (1948): supplement.

———. "Tentative List of Jewish Cultural Treasures in Axis-Occupied Countries, Edited by Commission on European Jewish Cultural Reconstruction." *Jewish Social Studies* 8, no. 1 (1946): supplement.

———. "Tentative List of Jewish Educational Institutions in Axis-Occupied Countries." *Jewish Social Studies* 8, no. 3 (1946): supplement.

———. "Tentative List of Jewish Periodicals in Axis-Occupied Countries." *Jewish Social Studies* 9, no. 3 (1947): supplement.

———. "Tentative List of Jewish Publishers of Judaica and Hebraica in Axis-Occupied Countries." *Jewish Social Studies* 10, no. 2 (1948): supplement.

Roberts Commission. *Report on the American Commission for the Protection of Artistic and Historic Monuments in War Areas.* Washington, DC: US Gov. Printing Office, 1946.

Robinson, Jacob. "From Protection of Minorities to Promotion of Human Rights." *Jewish Yearbook of International Law* 1 (1948): 115–51.

———. "Preface." In *Indemnifications and Reparations: Jewish Aspects*, by Nehemia Robinson, 7–9. New York: Institute of Jewish Affairs of the American Jewish Congress and World Jewish Congress, 1944.

Robinson, Nehemia. *Indemnification and Reparations: Jewish Aspects.* New York: Institute of Jewish Affairs of the American Jewish Congress and World Jewish Congress, 1944.

———. "Reparations and Restitution in International Law as Affecting Jews." *Jewish Yearbook of International Law* 1 (1948): 186–205.

———. "Restitution of Jewish Property." *Congress Weekly* 10 (March 12, 1948): 11–12.

———. *Ten Years of German Indemnification (Memorial Edition).* New York: Conference on Jewish Material Claims against Germany, 1964.

Rorimer, James, and Gilbert Rabin. *Survival: The Salvage and Protection of Art in War.* New York: Abeland, 1950.

Roth, Cecil. "Jewish Culture: Renaissance or Ice Age? A Scholar Discusses the Creative Outlook." *Commentary* 4 (1947): 329–33.

———. "The Jewish Love of Books (1944)." In *Essays on Jewish Booklore*, edited by Philip Goodman, 179–84. New York: KTAV, 1971.

———. "The Restoration of Jewish Libraries, Archives, and Museums." *Contemporary Jewish Record* 7, no. 3 (1944): 253–57.

Scholem, Gershom. "Against the Myth of the German-Jewish Dialogue." In *On Jews and Judaism in Crisis: Selected Essays*, 61–70.

———. "Besuch bei den Juden in Deutschland." *Yediot Chadashot* [Latest News], November 22, 1946.

———. *Briefe*. 3 vols. Vol. 1: 1914–1947, edited by Itta Shedletzky. Munich: Beck, 1994. Vol. 2: 1948–1970, edited by Itta Shedletzky and Thomas Sparr. Munich: Beck, 1995. Vol. 3: 1971–1982, edited by Itta Shedletzky. Munich: Beck, 1999.

———. *From Berlin to Jerusalem: Memories of My Youth*. Translated by Harry Zohn. New York: Schocken Books, 1980.

———. "Israel and the Diaspora." In *On Jews and Judaism in Crisis: Selected Essays*, 244–60.

———. "Jews and Germans." In *On Jews and Judaism in Crisis: Selected Essays*, 71–92.

———. *Judaica*. 6 vols. Frankfurt am Main: Suhrkamp, 1963–1997.

———. "A Lecture about Israel." In *On the Possibility of Jewish Mysticism on our Time and Other Essays*, 35–39.

———. *A Life in Letters, 1914–1982*. Edited and translated by Anthony D. Skinner. Cambridge, MA: Harvard University Press, 2002.

———. "Once More: The German-Jewish Dialogue." In *On Jews and Judaism in Crisis: Selected Essays*, 65–70.

———. *On Jews and Judaism in Crisis: Selected Essays*. New York: Schocken Books, 1976.

———. *On the Possibility of Jewish Mysticism in Our Time*. Edited by Avraham Shapira and translated by Jonathan Chipman. Philadelphia: Jewish Publication Society, 1997.

———. "Reflections on Modern Jewish Studies." In *On the Possibility of Jewish Mysticism in Our Time*, 51–71.

———. "Reflections on the Possibility of Jewish Mysticism in Our Time." In *On the Possibility of Jewish Mysticism in Our Time*, 6–19.

———. "The Science of Judaism—Then and Now." In *The Messianic Idea in Judaism: And Other Essays on Jewish Spirituality*, 304–13. New York: Schocken Books, 1974.

———. "Volk des Buches." In *Sie werden lachen, die Bibel: Überraschungen mit dem Buch*, edited by Hans Jürgen Schultz, 93–101. Stuttgart: Kreuz-Verlag, 1975.

———. "Walter Benjamin (1965)." In *Judaica*, vol. 2, 193–227.

———. *Walter Benjamin. The Story of a Friendship*. Philadelphia: Jewish Publication Society of America, 1981.

———. "Zur Frage der geplünderten jüdischen Bibliotheken" (translated from the Hebrew typescript of the *Haaretz* article, October 5, 1947). In *Scholem: Briefe*, vol. 1, 472–78.

Shunami, Shlomo. "The Elusive Treasure." *Jerusalem Post*, April 1, 1983.

———. "The Offenbach Jewish Book Collection." *Yad La-Kore* 2, no. 1 (1950): 73–74 (hebr.).

———. "Out of the Story of the Rescuing of Jewish Books from Europe." *Yad La-Kore* 5, no. 2 (1958): 113–18 (hebr.).

Starr, Joshua. "Jewish Cultural Property under Nazi Control." *Jewish Social Studies* 12, no. 1 (1950): 27–48.

Sutzkever, Abraham. "Vilna Ghetto." In *The Complete Black Book of Russian Jewry*, by Ilya Ehrenburg and Vasily Grossman, translated and edited by David Patterson, 241–93. New Brunswick, NJ: Transaction, 2002.

Sylberberg, Michael. "Saving Jewish Treasures in Poland." *Jewish Chronicle*, July 15, 1949.

Tartakower, Ariel. "Problems of Jewish Cultural Reconstruction in Europe." *Journal of Educational Sociology* 18, no. 5 (1945): 271–77.

Trunk, Isaiah. "The Research Library of the Jewish Historical Institute." *Yedies: Byuletin fun Yidishn Historishn Institut in Polyn* (November 1949, yidd.). An English translation was prepared by Meir Ben-Horin: UL Stanford, M0580, Baron Papers, box 232, folder 5, Meir Ben-Horin to Salo Baron, March 13, 1950.

United States Military Government. "United States Area of Control, Germany, Law No. 59, Restitution of Identifiable Property." *American Journal of International Law* 42, no. 1 (Jan. 1948): supplement: Official Documents, 11–45.

Valland, Rose. *Le front de l'art: Défense des collections françaises, 1939–1945*. Paris: Plon, 1961.

Voegelin, Eric. "The Origins of Totalitarianism (Review)." *Review of Politics* 15, no. 1 (1953): 68–85.

Weinreich, Max. *Hitler's Professors: The Part of Scholarship in Germany's Crimes against the Jewish People*. New York: Yiddish Scientific Institute—YIVO, 1946.

Weltsch, Robert. "Besuch in Frankfurt." *Mitteilungsblatt des Irgun Olej Merkaz Europa*, January 11, 1946.

"'Wenn ich verzweifelt bin, was geht's mich an?' Gespräch mit Günther Anders." In *Die Zerstörung einer Zukunft: Gespräche mit emigrierten Sozialwissenschaftlern*, edited by Matthias Greffrath, 19–57. Frankfurt am Main: Campus Verlag, 1989.

World Jewish Congress, Second Plenary Assembly, Montreux 1948, Political Commission, Resolution on Germany. https://www.bjpa.org.

SECONDARY SOURCES

Abramowicz, Dina. "The YIVO Library." *Jewish Book Annual* 25 (1967/68): 87–102.

Adunka, Evelyn. "Bücherraub in und aus Österreich während der NS-Zeit und die Restitutionen nach 1945." *Exilforschung* 22 (2004): 180–200.

———. *Der Raub der Bücher: Über Verschwinden und Vernichten von Bibliotheken in der NS-Zeit und ihre Restitution nach 1945*. Vienna: Czernin, 2002.

———. "Research on Looted Books in Austria." In *The Future of the Lost Cultural Heritage: The Documentation, Identification and Restitution of the Cultural Assets of WWII Victims*, edited by Mečislav Borák, 113–17. Prague: Tilia, 2006.

———. "Salo W. Baron's Efforts to Rescue Austrian Colleagues and Students." In *The Enduring Legacy of Salo W. Baron*, edited by Hava Tirosh-Samuelson and Edward Dąbrowa, 301–20. Kraków: Jagiellonian University Press, 2017.

———. "Die Zentralbibliothek der Hohen Schule in Tanzenberg." In *Geraubte Bücher: Die Österreichische Nationalbibliothek stellt sich ihrer NS-Vergangenheit*, edited by Murray G. Hall, Christina Köstner, and Margot Werner, 71–81. Vienna: Österreichische Nationalbibliothek, 2004.

Aharony Michal. "Hannah Arendt and the Idea of Total Domination." *Holocaust and Genocide Studies* 24, no. 2 (2010): 193–224.

Akinsha, Konstantin. "Stalin's Decrees and Soviet Trophy Brigades: Compensation, Restitution in Kind, or 'Trophies' of War?" *International Journal of Cultural Property* 17, no. 2 (2010): 195–216.

Albrink, Veronica. "Von Büchern, Depots und Bibliotheken: Zur Restitutionsgeschichte nach 1945." In *Die Suche nach NS-Raubgut in Bibliotheken: Recherchestand, Probleme, Lösungswege*, edited by Bernd Reifenberg, 110–49. Marburg: Universitätsbibliothek, 2006.

Aleksiun, Natalia. "Philip Friedman and the Emergence of Holocaust Scholarship: A Reappraisal." *Simon Dubnow Institute Yearbook* 11 (2012): 333–46.

———. "The Vicious Circle: Jews in Communist Poland, 1944–1956." *Studies in Contemporary Jewry* 19 (2003): 157–80.

Alford, Kenneth D. *Nazi Plunder: Great Treasure Stories of World War II.* Cambridge, MA: Da Capo, 2001.

Alker, Stefan, Christina Köstner, and Markus Stumpf, eds. *Bibliotheken in der NS-Zeit: Provenienzforschung und Bibliotheksgeschichte.* Vienna: Universitätsbibliothek, 2008.

Althaus, Claudia. *Erfahrung denken: Hannah Arendts Weg von der Zeitgeschichte zur politischen Theorie.* Göttingen: Vandenhoeck and Ruprecht, 2000.

Amit, Gish. "'The Largest Jewish Library in the World': The Books of Holocaust Victims and Their Redistribution following World War II." *Dapim* 27, no. 2 (2013): 107–28.

———. "Ownerless Objects? The Story of the Books Palestinians Left Behind in 1948." *Jerusalem Quarterly* (Institute of Jerusalem Studies) 33 (2008): 7–20.

———. "Salvage or Plunder? Israel's 'Collection' of Private Palestinian Libraries in West Jerusalem." *Journal of Palestine Studies* 40, no. 4 (2011): 6–23.

Andrieu, Claire. "Two Approaches to Restitution in France: Restitution and Reparation." In *Robbery and Restitution: The Conflict over Jewish Property in Europe*, edited by Martin Dean, Constantin Goschler, and Philipp Ther, 134–54. New York: Berghahn Books, 2007.

Armbruster, Thomas. *Rückerstattung der Nazi-Beute: Die Suche, Bergung und Restitution von Kulturgütern durch die westlichen Alliierten nach dem Zweiten Weltkrieg.* Berlin: De Gruyter, 2008.

Aschheim, Steven E. *Beyond the Border: The German-Jewish Legacy Abroad.* Princeton, NJ: Princeton University Press, 2007.

———. "Nazism, Culture, and 'The Origins of Totalitarianism': Hannah Arendt and the Discourse of Evil." In *In Times of Crisis: Essays on European Culture, Germans and Jews*, 122–36. Madison, WI: University of Wisconsin Press, 2001.

Assmann, Aleida. *Cultural Memory and Western Civilization: Functions, Media, Archives.* Cambridge, UK: Cambridge University Press, 2011.

Augustin, Anna-Carolin. "'Nazi Looted Art in Israel': Kulturguttransfer nach 1945 und Restitution heute." *Medaon: Magazin für jüdisches Leben in Forschung und Bildung* 9 (2011). http://medaon.de.

Azouvi, François. *Le Mythe du grand Silence: Auschwitz, les Français, la mémoire.* Paris: Fayard, 2012.

Bajohr, Frank. *"Aryanisation" in Hamburg: The Economic Exclusion of Jews and the Confiscation of Their Property in Nazi Germany*. New York: Berghahn Books, 2002.

Bankier, David, ed. *The Jews Are Coming Back: The Return of the Jews to Their Countries of Origin after World War II*. New York: Berghahn Books, 2005.

———, and Dan Michman, eds. *Holocaust and Justice: Representation and Historiography of the Holocaust in Post-War Trials*. Jerusalem: Yad Vashem, 2010.

———, and Dan Michman, eds. *Holocaust Historiography in Context: Emergence, Challenges, Polemics and Achievements*. Jerusalem: Yad Vashem, 2008.

Bar, Doron. "Between the Chamber of the Holocaust and Yad Vashem: Martyrs' Ashes as a Focus of Sanctity." *Yad Vashem Studies* 38, no. 1 (2010): 195–227.

———. "Holocaust Commemoration in Israel during the 1950s: The Holocaust Cellar on Mount Zion." *Jewish Social Studies* 12, no. 1 (2005): 16–38.

Barkai, Avraham, Paul Mendes-Flohr, and Steven M Lowenstein. *German-Jewish History in Modern Times*. Vol. 4, *Renewal and Destruction, 1918–1945*. New York: Columbia University Press, 1998.

Barkan, Elazar. *Guilt of Nations—Restitution and Negotiating Historical Injustices*. New York: W. W. Norton, 2014.

Barnouw, Dagmar. *Visible Spaces: Hannah Arendt and the German-Jewish Experience*. Baltimore: Johns Hopkins University Press, 1990.

Baron, Lawrence. "The Holocaust and American Public Memory, 1945–1960." *Holocaust and Genocide Studies* 17, no. 1 (2003): 62–88.

Bauer, Yehuda. *American Jewry and the Holocaust: The American Jewish Joint Distribution Committee, 1939–1945*. Detroit: Wayne State University Press, 1981.

———. *Out of the Ashes: The Impact of American Jews on Post-Holocaust European Jewry*. Oxford: Pergamon, 1989.

Bazyler, Michael J., and Roger P. Alford, eds. *Holocaust Restitution: Perspectives on the Litigation and Its Legacy*. New York: New York University Press, 2006.

Beit-Arié, Malachi. "Gershom Scholem as Bibliophile." In *Gershom Scholem: The Man and His Work*, edited by Paul Mendes-Flohr, 120–27. Albany: State University of New York Press, 1994.

Beker, Avi, ed. *The Plunder of Jewish Property during the Holocaust: Confronting European History*. Basingstoke: Palgrave Macmillan, 2001.

Belling, Veronica. "From Cemetery to Cyberspace: The Riddle of the Holocaust Era Collection at the University of Capetown." Proceedings of the 38th Annual Convention of the Association of Jewish Libraries, June 15–18, 2003, Toronto. http://www.jewishlibraries.org.

Benhabib, Seyla. "Hannah Arendt's Political Engagements." In *Thinking in Dark Times: Hannah Arendt on Ethics and Politics*, edited by Roger Berkowitz, Jeffrey Katz, and Thomas Keenan, 55–61. New York: Fordham University Press, 2010.

———. "Hannah Arendt und die erlösende Kraft des Erzählens." In *Zivilisationsbruch: Denken nach Auschwitz*, edited by Dan Diner, 150–74. Frankfurt am Main: Fischer-Taschenbuch-Verlag, 1988.

———. *The Reluctant Modernism of Hannah Arendt*. Lanham, MD: Rowman and Littlefield, 2000.

———, and Raluca Eddon. "From Anti-Semitism to 'the Right to Have Rights': The Jewish Roots of Hannah Arendt's Cosmopolitanism." *Babylon: Beiträge zur jüdischen Gegenwart* 22 (2007): 44–61.

Berg, Nicolas. "Geschichte des Archivs im 20. Jahrhundert." In *Handbuch Archiv: Geschichte, Aufgaben, Perspektiven*, edited by Ulrich Raulff and Marcel Lepper, 57–75. Stuttgart: J. B. Metzler, 2016.

———. *Der Holocaust und die westdeutschen Historiker: Erforschung und Erinnerung*. Göttingen: Wallstein-Verlag, 2003.

———, and Dirk Rupnow. "Einleitung zum Schwerpunkt 'Judenforschung': Wissenschaft und Ideologie von der Jahrhundertwende bis zum Nationalsozialismus." *Simon Dubnow Institute Yearbook* 5 (2006): 301–12.

Berger, Natalia. *The Jewish Museum: History and Memory, Identity and Art from Vienna to the Bezalel National Museum, Jerusalem*. Boston: Brill, 2017.

Bergman, Eleonora. "The Jewish Historical Institute: History of Its Building and Collections." In *Neglected Witnesses: The Fate of Jewish Ceremonial Objects during the Second World War and After*, edited by Julie-Marthe Cohen and Felicitas Heimann-Jelinek, 183–98. Crickadarn: Institute of Art and Law, 2011.

———. "The Jewish Historical Institute in Warsaw and Its Treasures." *Cuadernos Judaicos* 25 (2008): 283–95.

Bernstein, Richard. *Hannah Arendt and the Jewish Question*. Cambridge, UK: Polity Press, 1996.

Bertz, Inka, and Michael Dorrmann, eds. *Raub und Restitution: Kulturgut aus jüdischem Besitz von 1933 bis heute: Eine Ausstellung der Jüdischen Museen Berlin und Frankfurt am Main*. Göttingen: Wallstein-Verlag, 2008.

Biale, David. "Gershom Scholem: 'Einst und Jetzt' Zionist Politics and Kabbalistic Historiography." In *Against the Grain: Jewish Intellectuals in Hard Times*, edited by Ezra Mendelsohn, Stefani Hoffman, and Richard I. Cohen, 51–63. New York: Berghahn Books, 2014.

———. *Power and Powerlessness in Jewish History*. New York: Schocken Books, 1987.

———. "Scholem und der moderne Nationalismus." In *Gershom Scholem: Zwischen den Disziplinen*, edited by Peter Schäfer and Gary Smith, 257–74. Frankfurt am Main: Suhrkamp, 1995.

Bischoff, Doerthe. "Vom Überleben der Dinge: Sammlung und Exil in Edmund de Waals Der Hase mit den Bernsteinaugen und Nicole Krauss' Das große Haus." In *Sprachen des Sammelns: Literatur als Medium und Reflexionsform des Sammelns*, edited by Sarah Schmidt, 59–80. Paderborn: Wilhelm Fink Verlag, 2016.

Blouin, Francis X., Jr., and William G. Rosenberg, eds. *Archives, Documentation, and Institutions of Social Memory: Essays from the Sawyer Seminar*. Ann Arbor: Michigan University Press, 2007.

Bollmus, Reinhard. *Das Amt Rosenberg und seine Gegner: Studien zum Machtkampf im nationalsozialistischen Herrschaftssystem.* Munich: Oldenbourg, 2006. First published 1970.

———. "Einsatzstab Reichsleiter Rosenberg." In *Enzyklopädie des Nationalsozialismus,* edited by Wolfgang Benz, Hermann Graml, and Hermann Weiss. 3rd and corrected edition, 441–43. Munich: Klett-Cotta, 1998.

Bönnen, Gerold. "Beschlagnahmt, geborgen, ausgeliefert: Zum Schicksal des Wormser jüdischen Gemeindearchivs 1938–1957." In *Das deutsche Archivwesen und der Nationalsozialismus: 75. Deutscher Archivtag 2005 in Stuttgart,* edited by Robert Kretzschmar, 101–15. Essen: Klartext-Verlag, 2007.

Borin, Jacqueline. "Embers of the Soul: The Destruction of Jewish Books and Libraries in Poland during World War II." *Libraries and Culture* 28, no. 4 (1993): 445–60.

Bramson-Alperniene, Esfir. "Die YIVO-Bibliothek in Wilna: Ein Sammelpunkt der jiddischen Kultur." In *Jüdische Kultur(en) im Neuen Europa,* edited by Marina Dmitrieva and Heidemarie Petersen, 5–10. Wiesbaden: Harrassowitz, 2004.

———. "YIVO in Wilna: Zur Geschichte des 'Jüdischen Wissenschaftlichen Instituts.'" In *Annäherungen: Beiträge zur jüdischen Geschichte in Mittel- und Osteuropa,* edited by Stefi Jersch-Wenzel, 31–49. Leipzig: Leipziger Universitäts-Verlag, 2002.

Braunová, Andrea. "Origins of the Book Collection of the Library of the Jewish Museum in Prague." *Judaica Bohemiae* 36 (2000): 160–72.

Breitman, Richard, and Lichtman, Allen J. *FDR and the Jews.* Harvard, MA: Harvard University Press, 2013.

Brenner, Michael. *After the Holocaust: Rebuilding Jewish Lives in Postwar Germany.* Translated by Barbara Harshav. Princeton, NJ: Princeton University Press, 1997.

———. *In the Shadow of the Holocaust: The Changing Image of German Jewry after 1945.* Washington, DC: United States Holocaust Memorial Museum, 2010. https://www.ushmm.org.

———. *Prophets of the Past: Interpreters of Jewish History.* Translated by Steven Rendall. Princeton, NJ: Princeton University Press, 2010.

———. "Secular Faith of Fallen Jews: Rewriting Jewish History without Tears." *Simon Dubnow Institute Yearbook* 3 (2004): 315–24.

Brüggen, Maike, Sabine Schulze, and Wiebke Müller, et al., eds. *Raubkunst? Provenienzforschung zu den Sammlungen des Museum für Kunst und Gewerbe Hamburg.* Hamburg: MKG, 2014.

Brumlik, Micha, Doron Kiesel, Cilly Kugelmann, and Julius H. Schoeps, eds. *Jüdisches Leben in Deutschland seit 1945.* Frankfurt am Main: Athenäum, 1988.

Brunner, José; Norbert Frei, and Constantin Goschler, eds. *Die Praxis der Wiedergutmachung: Geschichte, Erfahrung und Wirkung in Deutschland und Israel.* Göttingen: Wallstein-Verlag, 2009.

Bušek, Michal, et al. *"Hope Is on the Next Page": 100 Years of the Library of the Jewish Museum in Prague.* Prague: Jewish Museum, 2007.

Canovan, Margaret. *Hannah Arendt: A Reinterpretation of Her Political Thought.* Cambridge, UK: Cambridge University Press, 1992.

Cesarani, David, ed. *After Eichmann: Collective Memory and the Holocaust since 1961.* London: Routledge, 2005.

———, and Eric J. Sundquist, eds. *After the Holocaust: Challenging the Myth of Silence.* London: Routledge, 2012.

Chazan, Robert. "A New Vision of Jewish History: The Early Historical Writings of Salo Baron." *AJS Review* 39, no. 1 (2015): 27–47.

Cichopek, Anna. *Beyond Violence: Jewish Survivors in Poland and Slovakia, 1944–48.* Cambridge, UK: Cambridge University Press, 2014.

Cieślińska-Lobkowicz, Nawojka. "Judaika in Polen: Herkunft, Schicksal, Status." *Osteuropa* 4 (2011): 85–183.

———. "Raub und Rückführung der Leon Vita Saraval Sammlung der Bibliothek des Jüdisch-Theologischen Seminars in Breslau." In *Jüdischer Buchbesitz als Raubgut: Zweites Hannoversches Symposium*, edited by Regine Dehnel, 366–78. Frankfurt am Main: Klostermann, 2006.

Cohen, Boaz. "The Birth Pangs of Holocaust Research in Israel." *Yad Vashem Studies* 33 (2005): 203–43.

———. *Israeli Holocaust Research: Birth and Evolution.* London: Routledge, 2012.

Cohen, Julie-Marthe, and Felicitas Heimann-Jelinek, eds. *Neglected Witnesses: The Fate of Jewish Ceremonial Objects during the Second World War and After.* Crickadarn: Institute of Art and Law, 2011.

———. "Theft and Restitution of Judaica in the Netherlands during and after the Second World War." In *Neglected Witnesses: The Fate of Jewish Ceremonial Objects during the Second World War and After*, 199–252.

Cohen, Richard I. "A Generation's Response to Eichmann in Jerusalem." In *Arendt in Jerusalem*, edited by Steven Aschheim, 253–77. Berkeley: University of California Press, 2001.

Collins, Donald E., and Herbert P. Rothfelder. "The Einsatzstab Reichsleiter Rosenberg and the Looting of Jewish and Masonic Libraries during World War II." *Journal of Library History* 18 (1983): 21–36.

Confino, Alon. *A World without Jews: The Nazi Imagination from Persecution to Genocide.* New Haven, CT: Yale University Press, 2014.

Conze, Eckart, Norbert Frei, Peter Hayes, and Moshe Zimmermann. *Das Amt und die Vergangenheit: Deutsche Diplomaten im Dritten Reich und in der Bundesrepublik.* Munich: Blessing, 2010.

Dalby, Hannah-Villette. "German-Jewish Female Intellectuals and the Recovery of German-Jewish Heritage in the 1940s and 1950s." *Leo Baeck Institute Year Book* 52 (2007): 111–29.

Dan, Joseph. "Gershom Scholem (1897–1982): 'Jeder kann viele Bücher zusammentragen, aber eine Bibliothek zu schaffen, ist eine andere Sache.'" In *"Wie würde ich ohne Bücher leben und arbeiten können?" Privatbibliotheken jüdischer Intellektueller im 20. Jahrhundert*, edited by Ines Sonder, Karin Bürger, and Ursula Wallmeier, 289–307. Berlin: Verlag für Berlin-Brandenburg, 2008.

Deák, István, Jan T. Gross, and Tony Judt, eds. *The Politics of Retribution in Europe: World War II and Its Aftermath.* Princeton, NJ: Princeton University Press, 2000.

Dean, Martin. *Robbing the Jews: The Confiscation of Jewish Property in the Holocaust, 1933–1945.* Cambridge, UK: Cambridge University Press, 2008.

———, Constantin Goschler, and Philipp Ther, eds. *Robbery and Restitution: The Conflict over Jewish Property in Europe.* New York: Berghahn Books, 2007.

Dehnel, Regine, ed. *Jüdischer Buchbesitz als Raubgut: Zweites Hannoversches Symposium.* Frankfurt am Main: Klostermann, 2006.

———. *NS-Raubgut in Bibliotheken: Suche, Ergebnisse, Perspektiven, Drittes Hannoversches Symposium.* Frankfurt am Main: Klostermann, 2008.

Dicker, Herman. *Of Learning and Libraries: The Seminary Library at One Hundred.* New York: Jewish Theological Seminary of America, 1988.

Dietz, Mary. "Arendt and the Holocaust." In *The Cambridge Companion to Hannah Arendt,* edited by Dana Villa, 86–109. Cambridge, UK: Cambridge University Press, 2000.

Diner, Dan. "Ambiguous Semantics. Reflections on Jewish Political Concepts." *Jewish Quarterly Review* 98, no. 1 (2008): 89–102.

———. "Banished: Jews in Germany after the Holocaust." In *A History of Jews in Germany since 1945: Politics, Culture, and Society,* edited by Michael Brenner and translated by Kenneth Kronenberg, 7–54. Bloomington: Indiana University Press, 2018.

———. "Eigentum restituieren." In *Zeitenschwelle: Gegenwartsfragen an die Geschichte,* 207–21. Munich: Pantheon, 2010.

———. "Gestaute Zeit: Massenvernichtung und Erzählstruktur." In *Fünfzig Jahre danach: Zur Nachgeschichte des Nationalsozialismus,* edited by Sigrid Weigel and Birgit Erdle, 3–15. Zurich: vdf, Hochschulverlag an der ETH Zürich, 1996.

———. "Hannah Arendt Reconsidered: On the Banal and the Evil in Her Holocaust Narrative." *New German Critique* 24, no. 71 (1997): 177–90.

———. "Kumulative Kontingenz: Jüdische Erfahrung und israelische Legitimität." In *Gedächtniszeiten: Über jüdische und andere Geschichten,* 201–27. Munich: Beck, 2003.

———. "Marranische Einschreibungen: Erwägungen zu verborgenen Traditionen bei Hannah Arendt." *Babylon: Beiträge zur jüdischen Gegenwart* 22 (2007): 62–71.

———. "Memory and Restitution: World War II as a Foundational Event in a Uniting Europe." In *Restitution and Memory: Material Restoration in Europe,* 9–23.

———. *Rituelle Distanz: Israels Deutsche Frage.* Munich: Deutsche Verlags-Anstalt, 2015.

———. "Vorwort." In *Häuser des Buches: Bilder jüdischer Bibliotheken,* by Markus Kirchhoff, 7–9. Leipzig: Reclam, 2002.

———. "Den Zivilisationsbruch erinnern: Über Entstehung und Geltung eines Begriffs." In *Zivilisationsbruch und Gedächtniskultur: Das 20. Jahrhundert in der Erinnerung des beginnenden 21. Jahrhunderts,* edited by Heidemarie Uhl, 17–34. Innsbruck: Studien-Verlag, 2003.

———, and Gotthard Wunberg, eds. *Restitution and Memory: Material Restoration in Europe.* New York: Berghahn Books, 2007.

Diner, Hasia R. *The Jews of the United States, 1654 to 2000.* Berkeley: University of California Press, 2006.

———. "Salo Baron: An American." In *The Enduring Legacy of Salo W. Baron,* edited by Hava Tirosh-Samuelson and Edward Dąbrowa, 245–58. Kraków: Jagiellonian University Press, 2017.

———. *We Remember with Reverence and Love: American Jews and the Myth of Silence after the Holocaust, 1945–1962.* New York: New York University Press, 2009.

Dmitrieva, Marina, and Heidemarie Petersen, eds. *Jüdische Kultur(en) im neuen Europa—Wilna 1918–1939.* Wiesbaden: Harrassowitz, 2004.

Domhardt, Yvonne. "Von Breslau nach Genf: Hannah Arendt als Vermittlerin bei der Überführung von Teilen der Bibliothek des Breslauer Rabbinerseminars in die Schweiz." In *Bibliotheken und Sammlungen im Exil,* edited by Claus-Dieter Krohn and Lutz Winckler, 154–65. Exilforschung, vol. 29. Munich: Edition text + kritik, 2011.

Don-Yehiya, Eliezer. "Memory and Political Culture: Israeli Society and the Holocaust." *Studies in Contemporary Jewry* 9 (1993): 139–62.

Du-Nour, Miryam. "The Cultural Identity of Former German-Jewish Immigrants in Israel." In *The German-Jewish Dilemma: From the Enlightenment to the Shoah,* edited by Edward Timms and Andrea Hammel, 305–16. Lewiston, NY: Edwin Mellen, 1999.

Dvorkin, Yehuda. "A Jewish-English Debate on Restitution: Patriotism, Zionism and Continentalism." In *Contested Heritage: Jewish Cultural Property after 1945,* edited by Elisabeth Gallas, Anna Holzer-Kawałko, Caroline Jessen, and Yfaat Weiss. Göttingen: Vandenhoeck and Ruprecht, 2019 (forthcoming).

Edsel, Robert M. *The Monuments Men: Allied Heroes, Nazi Thieves, and the Greatest Treasure Hunt in History,* edited by Bret Witter. New York: Center Street, 2009.

Engel, David. "American Jewish Committee." In *Enzyklopädie jüdischer Geschichte und Kultur,* vol. 1, edited by Dan Diner, 67–72. Stuttgart: J. B. Metzler, 2011.

———. "Crisis and Lachrymosity: On Salo Baron, Neobaronianism, and the Study of Modern European Jewish History." *Jewish History* 20, no. 3/4 (2006): 243–64.

———. *Historians of the Jews and the Holocaust.* Stanford, CA: Stanford University Press, 2010.

———. "Holocaust Research and Jewish Historiography: Mutual Influences." In *Holocaust Historiography in Context: Emergence, Challenges, Polemics and Achievements,* edited by David Bankier and Dan Michman, 67–79. Jerusalem: Yad Vashem, 2008.

———. "Jewish Social Studies." In *Enzyklopädie jüdischer Geschichte und Kultur,* vol. 3, edited by Dan Diner, 192–95. Stuttgart: J. B. Metzler, 2012.

———. "On Studying Jewish History in Light of the Holocaust." Maurice R. and Corinne P. Greenberg Inaugural Lecture, Washington, DC, April 16, 2002. http://www.ushmm.org.

———. "The Reconstruction of Jewish Communal Institutions in Postwar Poland: The Origins of the Central Committee of Polish Jews, 1944–1945." *East European Politics and Societies* 10, no. 1 (1996): 85–107.

Ezra, Michael. "The Eichmann Polemics: Hannah Arendt and Her Critics." *Democratyia* 9 (2007): 141–65.

Ezrahi, Sidra DeKoven. "Considering the Apocalypse: Is the Writing on the Wall only Graffiti?" In *Writing and the Holocaust*, edited by Berel Lang, 137–53. New York: Holmes and Meier, 1988.

Feierstein, Liliana Ruth. "'Nor er redt nisht arois keyn vort': Name, Memory, Silence: Darkness of the Shoah." *Jewish Studies Quarterly* 9, no. 2 (2002): 109–20.

———, and Liliana Fuhrman. "The Paper Bridge: Jewish Responses to Destruction." *European Judaism* 40 (2007): 38–55.

Feigenbaum, Gail, and Inge Reist, eds. *Provenance: An Alternate History of Art*. Los Angeles: Getty, 2013.

Feingold, Henry L. *Bearing Witness: How America and Its Jews Responded to the Holocaust*. Syracuse, NY: Syracuse University Press, 1995.

Fishburn, Matthew. *Burning Books*. Basingstoke: Palgrave Macmillan, 2008.

Fishman, David. *The Book Smugglers: Partisans, Poets, and the Race to Save Jewish Treasures from the Nazis*. Lebanon, NH: ForeEdge, 2017.

———. "Embers Plucked from the Fire: The Rescue of Jewish Cultural Treasures in Vilna." In *The Rise of Modern Yiddish Culture*, 139–53. Pittsburgh, PA: University of Pittsburgh Press, 2005.

Fogg, Shannon Lee. *Stealing Home: Looting, Restitution, and Reconstructing Jewish Lives in France, 1942–1947*. Oxford: Oxford University Press, 2017.

Forrest, Craig. *International Law and the Protection of Cultural Heritage*. London: Routledge, 2010.

Freimüller, Tobias. "Mehr als eine Religionsgemeinschaft: Jüdisches Leben in Frankfurt am Main nach 1945." *Studies in Contemporary History* 7, no. 3 (2010): 386–407.

Friedla, Katharina. "'A Naye Yiddishe Heym in Nidershlezye' Polnische Shoah-Überlebende in Wrocław (1945–1949): Eine Fallstudie." *SIMON* 1, no. 1 (2014): 32–42.

Friedländer, Saul. *The Years of Extermination: Nazi Germany and the Jews, 1939–1945*. New York: HarperCollins, 2007.

———. *The Years of Persecution: Nazi Germany and the Jews, 1933–1939*. New York: HarperCollins, 1997.

Fritz Bauer Institut, ed. *"Beseitigung des jüdischen Einflusses . . . ": Antisemitische Forschung, Eliten und Karrieren im Nationalsozialismus*, Fritz Bauer Institute Yearbook 3. Frankfurt am Main: Campus-Verlag, 1999.

Fritzsche, Peter. "The Archive." *History and Memory* 17, no. 1/2 (2005): 15–44.

Gallas, Elisabeth. "Frühe Holocaustforschung in Amerika: Dokumentation, Zeugenschaft und Begriffbildung." *Simon Dubnow Institute Yearbook* 15 (2016): 535–69.

———. "Hannah Arendt: Rückkehr im Schreiben." In *"Ich staune, dass Sie in dieser Luft atmen können": Jüdische Intellektuelle in Deutschland nach 1945*, edited by Monika Boll and Raphael Gross, 233–63. Frankfurt am Main: Fischer-Taschenbuch-Verlag, 2013.

———. "In der Lücke der Zeit: Über Hannah Arendts 'Elemente und Ursprünge totaler Herrschaft.'" In *Konstellationen: Über Geschichte, Erfahrung und Erkenntnis:*

Festschrift für Dan Diner zum 65. Geburtstag, edited by Nicolas Berg, Omar Kamil, Markus Kirchhoff, and Susanne Zepp, 261–82. Göttingen: Vandenhoeck and Ruprecht, 2011.

———. "Jewish Cultural Assets in the Postwar Period: Hannah Arendt's Report on the Situation in Hamburg." *Key Documents of German-Jewish History: A Digital Source Edition*. January 30, 2017. http://jewish-history-online.net.

———. "Theoriebildung und Abwehrkampf vor der Katastrophe—Essays on Antisemitism, New York 1942." In *Beschreibungsversuche der Judenfeindschaft—Zur Geschichte der Antisemitismusforschung vor 1944*, edited by Hans-Joachim Hahn and Olaf Kistenmacher, 403–25. Berlin: De Gruyter, 2014.

———, Anna Holzer-Kawałko, Caroline Jessen, and Yfaat Weiss, eds. *Contested Heritage: Jewish Cultural Property after 1945*. Göttingen: Vandenhoeck and Ruprecht, 2019 (forthcoming).

Gay, Ruth. *Safe among the Germans: Liberated Jews after World War II*. New Haven, CT: Yale University Press, 2002.

Geis, Jael. *Übrig sein—Leben "danach": Juden deutscher Herkunft in der britischen und amerikanischen Zone Deutschlands 1945–1949*. Berlin: Philo-Verlag, 2000.

Gelber, Yoav. "Deutsch-jüdische Identität in der 'Heimstätte': Deutsche Zionisten in Palästina zwischen Distanz, Eigensinn und Integration." In *Janusfiguren: "Jüdische Heimstätte," Exil und Nation im deutschen Zionismus*, edited by Andrea Schatz and Christian Wiese, 263–76. Berlin: Metropol, 2006.

Geller, Jay Howard. *Jews in Post-Holocaust Germany, 1945–1953*. Cambridge, UK: Cambridge University Press, 2005.

Gerstenfeld, Manfred. "The Postwar Renewal of Jewish Communities in the Netherlands." In *Postwar Jewish Displacement and Rebirth, 1945–1967*, edited by Françoise S. Ouzan and Manfred Gerstenfeld, 150–69. Leiden: Brill, 2014.

Glickman, Marc. *Stolen Words: The Nazi Plunder of Jewish Books*. Philadelphia: Jewish Publication Society, 2016.

Goda, Norman J. W., ed. *Rethinking Holocaust Justice: Essays across Disciplines*. New York: Berghahn Books, 2018.

Gorny, Yosef. "Negation of the Galut and the Centrality of Israel: Nahum Goldmann and Ben-Gurion." In *Nahum Goldmann: Statesman without a State*, edited by Maik A. Raider, 75–92. Albany: State University of New York Press, 2009.

Goschler, Constantin. "The Attitude toward Jews in Bavaria after the Second World War." *Leo Baeck Institute Year Book* 36 (1991): 443–58.

———. "Der Fall Philipp Auerbach: Wiedergutmachung in Bayern." In *Wiedergutmachung in der Bundesrepublik Deutschland*, edited by Ludolf Herbst and Constantin Goschler, 77–98. Munich: Oldenbourg, 1989.

———. "German Compensation to Jewish Nazi Victims." In *Lessons and Legacies: New Currents in Holocaust Research VI*, edited by Peter Hayes and Jeffrey M. Diefendorf, 373–412. Evanston, IL: Northwestern University Press, 2004.

———. *Schuld und Schulden: Die Politik der Wiedergutmachung für NS-Verfolgte seit 1945*. Göttingen: Wallstein-Verlag, 2005.

——. *Wiedergutmachung: Westdeutschland und die Verfolgten des Nationalsozialismus.* Munich: Oldenbourg, 1992.

——, and Jürgen Lillteicher, eds. *"Arisierung" und Restitution: Die Rückerstattung jüdischen Eigentums in Deutschland und Österreich nach 1945 und 1989.* Göttingen: Wallstein-Verlag, 2002.

——, and Philipp Ther. "A History without Boundaries: The Robbery and Restitution of Jewish Property in Europa." In *Robbery and Restitution: The Conflict over Jewish Property in Europe,* edited by Dean Martin, Constantin Goschler, and Philipp Ther, 3–20. New York: Berghahn Books, 2007.

Graf, Philipp. *Die Bernheim-Petition 1933: Jüdische Politik in der Zwischenkriegszeit.* Göttingen: Vandenhoeck and Ruprecht, 2008.

Greenfield, Jeannette. *The Return of Cultural Treasures,* 3rd ed. Cambridge, UK: Cambridge University Press, 2007.

Grimsted, Patricia Kennedy. "The Postwar Fate of Einsatzstab Reichsleiter Rosenberg: Archival and Library Plunder, and the Dispersal of ERR Records." *Holocaust and Genocide Studies* 20, no. 2 (2006): 278–308.

——. "The Road to Minsk for Western 'Trophy' Books. Twice Plundered and Not yet 'Home from the War.'" *Libraries and Culture* 39, no. 4 (2004): 351–404.

——. "Roads to Ratibor: Library and Archival Plunder by the Einsatzstab Reichsleiter Rosenberg." *Holocaust and Genocide Studies* 19, no. 3 (2005): 390–458.

——. "Silesian Crossroads for Europe's Displaced Books: Compensation or Prisoners of War?" In *The Future of the Lost Cultural Heritage: Proceedings of the International Academic Conference held in Prag 2005,* edited by Mečislav Borák, 133–69. Prague: Tilia, 2005.

——. "Sudeten Crossroads for Europe's Displaced Books: The 'Mysterious Twilight' of the RSHA Amt VII Library and the Fate of a Million Victims of War." In *Restitution of Confiscated Art Works: Wish or Reality? Documentation, Identification and Restitution of Cultural Property of the Victims of World War II: Proceedings of the International Academic Conference held in Liberec 2007,* edited by Mečislav Borák, 123–80. Prague: Tilia, 2008.

——. "'Trophy' Archives in Moscow and the Art Scene in France and Germany under the National Socialist Regime, 1933–1945: A Brief Orientation." In *Echoes in Exile: Moscow Archives and the Arts in Paris 1933–1945,* edited by Ines Rotermund-Reynard, 45–65. Berlin: De Gruyter, 2015.

——, Frits Hoogewoud, and Eric Ketelaar, eds. *Returned from Russia: Nazi Archival Plunder in Western Europe and Recent Restitution Issues.* Builth Wells: Institute of Art and Law, 2007.

Grobman, Alex. *Rekindling the Flame: American Jewish Chaplains and the Survivors of European Jewry, 1944–1948.* Detroit: Wayne State University Press, 1993.

Gross, Jan T. *Fear: Antisemitism in Poland after Auschwitz: An Essay in Historical Interpretation.* New York: Random House, 2006.

Grossman, Grace Cohen. "Scholar as Political Activist: Salo W. Baron and the Founding of the Jewish Cultural Reconstruction." In *For Every Thing a Season: Proceedings of the Symposium on Jewish Ritual Art, September 13, 2000,* edited by Joseph Gutmann, 146–57. Cleveland, OH: Cleveland State University, 2002.

Grossmann, Atina. *Jews, Germans, and Allies: Close Encounters in Occupied Germany.* Princeton, NJ: Princeton University Press, 2007.

———. "Rabbi Steven Schwarzschild's Reports from Berlin, 1948–1950." *Leo Baeck Institute Year Book* 60 (2015): 237–42.

———. "Remapping Survival: Jewish Refugees and Lost Memories of Displacement, Trauma, and Rescue in Soviet Central Asia, Iran, and India." *Simon Dubnow Institute Yearbook* 15 (2016): 71–97.

———, and Tamar Lewinsky. "Way Station, 1945–1949." In *A History of Jews in Germany since 1945: Politics, Culture, and Society,* edited by Michael Brenner and translated by Kenneth Kronenberg, 55–144. Bloomington: Indiana University Press, 2018.

———, and Avinoam Patt, et al., eds. *The JDC at 100. A Century of Humanitarianism.* Detroit: Wayne State University Press, 2019 (forthcoming).

Hacken, Richard. "The Jewish Community Library in Vienna: From Dispersion and Destruction to Partial Restoration." *Leo Baeck Institute Year Book* 47 (2002): 151–72.

Haeger, Robert, and Bill Long. "Lost EC Treasures Found in Palestine." *Stars and Stripes,* February 13, 1948.

Hahn, Barbara. "'Wesentlich ein Übersetzungsverlag'? Hannah Arendt als Lektorin bei Schocken Books in New York." In *Konsum und Gestalt: Leben und Werk von Salman Schocken und Erich Mendelsohn vor 1933 und im Exil,* edited by Antje Borrmann, Doreen Mölders, and Sabine Wolfram, 259–70. Berlin: Hentrich and Hentrich Verlag, 2016.

Halbertal, Moshe. *People of the Book: Canon, Meaning, and Authority.* Cambridge, MA: Harvard University Press, 1997.

Hall, Murray G., Christina Köstner, and Margot Werner, eds. *Geraubte Bücher: Die Österreichische Nationalbibliothek stellt sich ihrer NS-Vergangenheit.* Vienna: Österreichische Nationalbibliothek, 2004.

Harbeck, Matthias, and Sonja Kobold. "Spurensicherung: Provenienzforschung zur Bibliothek von Agathe Lasch: Ein Projekt an der Universitätsbibliothek der Humboldt-Universität zu Berlin." In *Bibliotheken in der NS-Zeit: Provenienzforschung und Bibliotheksgeschichte,* edited by Stefan Alker, Christina Köstner, and Markus Stumpf, 89–101. Göttingen: V & R Unipress, 2008.

Harris, David A. "The American Jewish Committee at 100." *American Jewish Yearbook* 106 (2006): 2–30.

Hartmann, Uwe. *Kulturgüter im Zweiten Weltkrieg: Verlagerung—Auffindung—Rückführung,* edited by the Koordinierungsstelle Magdeburg. Magdeburg: Koordinierungsstelle für Kulturgutverluste, 2007.

Hartung, Hannes. *Kunstraub in Krieg und Verfolgung: Die Restitution der Beute- und Raubkunst im Kollisions- und Völkerrecht.* Berlin: De Gruyter, 2005.

Hauschke-Wicklaus, Gabriele, Angelika Amborn-Morgenstern, and Erika Jacobs, eds. *Fast vergessen: Das amerikanische Bücherdepot in Offenbach am Main von 1945 bis 1949,* edited by the Geschichtswerkstatt Offenbach. Offenbach am Main: OE, Offenbacher Ed., 2011.

Heimann-Jelinek, Felicitas, ed. *Was übrig blieb: Das Museum jüdischer Altertümer in Frankfurt 1922–1938*, edited for the Dezernat für Kultur und Freizeit vom Jüdischen Museum Frankfurt. Frankfurt am Main: Jüdisches Museum, 1988.

Henry, Marilyn. *Confronting the Perpetrators: A History of the Claims Conference*. London: Vallentine Mitchell, 2007.

———. *The Restitution of Jewish Property in Central and Eastern Europe*. New York: American Jewish Committee, 1997.

Herbst, Ludolf, and Constantin Goschler. *Wiedergutmachung in der Bundesrepublik Deutschland*. Munich: Oldenbourg, 1989.

Herman, Dana. "'A Brand Plucked Out of the Fire': The Distribution of Heirless Jewish Cultural Property by Jewish Cultural Reconstruction, Inc., 1947–1952." In *Neglected Witnesses: The Fate of Jewish Ceremonial Objects during the Second World War and After*, edited by Julie-Marthe Cohen and Felicitas Heimann-Jelinek, 29–61. Crickadarn: Institute of Art and Law, 2011.

———. "'Hashavat Avedah': A History of Jewish Cultural Reconstruction, Inc." PhD diss., McGill University, Montreal, 2008.

Hertzberg, Arthur. "Salo W. Baron and the Writing of Modern Jewish History: Speculations in Honor of His Centennial." In *Writing a Modern Jewish History: Essays in Honor of Salo W. Baron*, edited by Barbara Kirshenblatt-Gimblett, 10–24. New York: Jewish Museum, 2006.

Heuberger, Georg. "Zur Rolle der Jewish Cultural Reconstruction nach 1945." In *Was übrig blieb: Das Museum jüdischer Altertümer in Frankfurt 1922–1938*, edited by Felicitas Heimann-Jelinek for the Dezernat für Kultur und Freizeit vom Jüdischen Museum Frankfurt, 97–103. Frankfurt am Main: Jüdisches Museum, 1988.

Heuberger, Rachel. *Bibliothek des Judentums: Die Hebraica- und Judaica-Sammlung der Stadt- und Universitätsbibliothek Frankfurt am Main; Entstehung, Geschichte und heutige Aufgaben*. Frankfurt am Main: Klostermann, 1996.

Heuer, Wolfgang. *Citizen: Persönliche Integrität und politisches Handeln: Eine Rekonstruktion des politischen Humanismus Hannah Arendts*. Berlin: Akad.-Verlag, 1992.

Heuss, Anja. *Kunst- und Kulturgutraub: Eine vergleichende Studie zur Besatzungspolitik der Nationalsozialisten in Frankreich und in der Sowjetunion*. Heidelberg: Winter, 2000.

Hilbrenner, Anke. "Nationalization in Odessa—Simon Dubnow and the Society for the Dissemination of Enlightenment among the Jews in Russia." *Simon Dubnow Institute Yearbook* 2 (2003): 223–39.

———. "Simon Dubnov's Master Narrative and the Construction of Jewish Collective Memory in the Russian Empire." *Ab Imperio* 4 (2003): 143–64.

Hoffmann, Barbara T. *Art and Cultural Heritage: Law, Policy, and Practice*. Cambridge, UK: Cambridge University Press, 2006.

Hoffmann, Christhard, ed. "The Founding of the Leo Baeck Institute, 1945–1955." In *Preserving the Legacy of German Jewry: A History of the Leo Baeck Institute 1955–2005*, 15–57.

———. *Preserving the Legacy of German Jewry: A History of the Leo Baeck Institute 1955–2005*. Tübingen: Mohr Siebeck, 2005.

Holmgren, Fredrick Carlson. "Heinz Galinski: The Driving Force of the Postwar Jewish Community in Germany." *Journal of Ecumenical Studies* 44, no. 4 (2009): 599–616.

Holzer-Kawałko, Anna. "Double Dynamics of the Postwar Cultural Restoration: On the Salvage and Destruction of the Breslau Rabbinical Library." In *Contested Heritage: Jewish Cultural Property after 1945*, edited by Elisabeth Gallas, Anna Holzer-Kawałko, Caroline Jessen, and Yfaat Weiss. Göttingen: Vandenhoeck and Ruprecht, 2019 (forthcoming).

———. "From Breslau to Wroclaw: Transfer of the Saraval Collection to Poland and the Restitution of Jewish Cultural Property after WW II." *Naharaim: Zeitschrift Für Deutsch-Jüdische Literatur und Kulturgeschichte* 9, no. 1–2 (November 2015): 48–72.

———. "Jewish Intellectuals between Robbery and Restitution: Ernst Grumach in Berlin, 1941–1946." *Leo Baeck Institute Year Book* 63 (2018): 273–95.

———. "Lost on the Island: Mapping an Alternative Path of Exile in the Life and Work of Ernst Grumach." *Simon Dubnow Institute Yearbook* 16 (forthcoming).

———. "The Papers of Ernst Grumach (1902–1967): Records Related to the Salvage and Restitution of Looted Jewish Cultural Property," August 2015. www.daat-hamakom .com.

Hondius, Dienke. "Bitter Homecoming: The Return and the Reception of Dutch and Stateless Jews in the Netherlands." In *The Jews Are Coming Back: The Return of the Jews to Their Countries of Origin after World War II*, edited by David Bankier, 108–35. New York: Berghahn Books, 2005.

Honigmann, Peter. "Die Akten des Galuts: Betrachtungen zu den mehr als hundertjährigen Bemühungen um die Inventarisierung von Quellen zur Geschichte der Juden in Deutschland." Universität Heidelberg, 2008. https://zentralarchiv-juden.de.

———. "Central Archives for Research on the History of the Jews in Germany." In *Preserving Jewish Archives as Part of the European Cultural Heritage: Proceedings of the Conference on Judaica Archives in Europe, for Archivists and Librarians, Potsdam, 1999, 11–13 July*, edited by Jean-Claude Kuperminc and Rafaële Arditti, 104–6. Paris: Les éditions du Nadir de l'Alliance israélite universelle, 2001. https://zentralarchiv -juden.de.

———. "Talmuddrucke im Nachkriegsdeutschland." In *Überlebt und Unterwegs: Jüdische Displaced Persons im Nachkriegsdeutschland*, edited by Fritz Bauer Institut, 249–66. Frankfurt am Main: Campus-Verlag, 1997.

———, and Frank M. Bischoff, eds. *Jüdisches Archivwesen: Beiträge zum Kolloquium aus Anlass des 100. Jahrestages der Gründung des Gesamtarchivs der deutschen Juden*. Marburg: Archivschule Marburg, 2007.

Hoogewoud, Frits J. "Die Bibliotheca Rosenthaliana: Von Amsterdam nach Hungen und über Offenbach zurück (1940–1946)." In *Raub und Restitution: Kulturgut aus jüdischem Besitz von 1933 bis heute; Eine Ausstellung der Jüdischen Museen Berlin und Frankfurt am Main*, edited by Inka Bertz and Michael Dorrmann, 253–58. Göttingen: Wallstein-Verlag, 2008.

———. "Dutch Jewish Ex Libris Found among Looted Books in the Offenbach Archival Depot." In *Dutch Jews as Perceived by Themselves and by Others: Proceedings of the Eights International Symposium on the History of the Jews in the Netherlands*, edited by Chaya Brasz and Yosef Kaplan, 247–61. Leiden: Brill, 2000.

———. "The Nazi Looting of Books and Its American Antithesis: Selected Pictures from the Offenbach Archival Depot's Photographic History and Its Supplement." *Studia Rosenthalia* 26 (1992): 158–92.

———. "The Reopening of the Bibliotheca Rosenthaliana in 1946." In *The Return of Looted Collections (1946–1996): An Unfinished Chapter*, 104–6.

———, ed. *The Return of Looted Collections (1946–1996): An Unfinished Chapter; Proceedings of the International Symposium to Mark the 50th Anniversary of the Return of Dutch Book Collections from Germany in 1946 (April 1996, Amsterdam)*. Amsterdam: Stichting Beheer IISG, 1997.

Hoppe, Jens. *Jüdische Geschichte und Kultur in Museen: Zur nichtjüdischen Museologie des Jüdischen in Deutschland*. Münster: Waxmann, 2002.

Howe, Irving. "Review of Lucy Dawidowicz: The War against the Jews 1933–1945." *New York Times*, April 20, 1975.

Huyssen, Andreas, Anson Rabinbach, and Avinoam Shalem, eds. "Nazi-Looted Art and Its Legacies." Special issue of *New German Critique* 44, no. 1 (2017): 130.

Hyman, Abraham. "The Clay I Knew." *Jerusalem Post*, June 13, 1978.

Intrator, Miriam. "Books across Borders and between Libraries: UNESCO and the Politics of Postwar Cultural Reconstruction, 1945–1951." PhD diss., City University of New York, 2013.

———. "'People Were Literally Starving for Any Kind of Reading': The Theresienstadt Ghetto Central Library, 1942–1945." *Library Trends* 55, no. 3 (2007): 513–22.

———. "The Theresienstadt Ghetto Central Library, Books and Reading: Intellectual Resistance and Escape during the Holocaust." *Leo Baeck Institute Year Book* 50 (2005): 3–28.

Jakubowski, Andrzej. *State Succession in Cultural Property*. Oxford: Oxford University Press, 2015.

Jelinek, Yeshayahu A. *Deutschland und Israel 1945–1965: Ein neurotisches Verhältnis*. Munich: Oldenbourg, 2004.

Jessen, Caroline. "'Alte Bücher in Haifa': Materielle Zeugnisse und Erinnerungsrhetorik." In *Deutsche und zentraleuropäische Juden in Palästina und Israel: Kulturtransfers, Lebenswelten, Identitäten—Beispiele aus Haifa*, edited by Anja Siegemund, 461–82. Berlin: Neofelis-Verlag, 2016.

———. *Kanon im Exil: Lektüren deutsch-jüdischer Emigranten in Palästina/Israel*. Göttingen: Wallstein Verlag, 2019 (forthcoming).

———. "Das problematische Bild der geretteten Kultur: Büchersammlungen deutschjüdischer Einwanderer in Israel." In *Deutsche(s) in Palästina und Israel: Alltag, Kultur, Politik*, edited by José Brunner, 179–94. Göttingen: Wallstein-Verlag, 2013.

Jockusch, Laura. *Collect and Record!: Jewish Holocaust Documentation in Early Postwar Europe*. Oxford: Oxford University Press, 2012.

———. "Historiography in Transit: Survivor Historians and the Writing of Holocaust History in the late 1940s." *Leo Baeck Institute Year Book* 58 (2014): 75–94.

———. "Introductory Remarks on Simon Dubnow's 'Let Us Seek and Investigate.'" *Simon Dubnow Institute Yearbook* 7 (2008): 343–52.

———. "Justice at Nuremberg? Jewish Responses to Nazi War-Crime Trials in Allied-Occupied Germany." *Jewish Social Studies* 19, no. 1 (2013): 107–47.

Judt, Tony. *A History of Europe since 1945*. New York: Penguin, 2005.

Junker, Detlef, ed. *The United States and Germany in the Era of the Cold War, 1945–1990. A Handbook*. Vol. 1: 1945–1968. Cambridge, UK: Cambridge University Press, 2004.

Jütte, Robert. *Die Emigration der deutschsprachigen "Wissenschaft des Judentums": Die Auswanderung jüdischer Historiker nach Palästina*. Stuttgart: Steiner, 1991.

Kaplan-Feuereisen, Omry. "Institute of Jewish Affairs." In *Enzyklopädie jüdischer Geschichte und Kultur*, vol. 3, edited by Dan Diner, 130–36. Stuttgart: J. B. Metzler, 2012.

Kauders, Anthony. *Unmögliche Heimat: Eine deutsch-jüdische Geschichte der Bundesrepublik*. Munich: Deutsche Verlags-Anstalt, 2007.

Kazin, Alfred. *New York Jew*. New York: A. Knopf, 1978.

Keller, Zsolt. "Jüdische Bücher und der Schweizer Israelitische Gemeindebund (1930–1950)." *Bulletin der schweizerischen Gesellschaft für Judaistische Forschung* 14 (2005): 20–34.

Kenan, Orna. *Between Memory and History: The Evolution of Israeli Historiography of the Holocaust, 1945–1961*. New York: Lang, 2003.

Kilcher, Andreas B. "'Volk des Buches': Zur kulturpolitischen Aktualisierung eines alten Topos in der jüdischen Moderne." *Münchner Beiträge zur jüdischen Geschichte und Kultur*, no. 2 (2009): 43–58.

Kirchhoff, Markus. *Häuser des Buches: Bilder jüdischer Bibliotheken*. Leipzig: Reclam, 2002.

———. "Looted Texts: Restituting Jewish Libraries." In *Restitution and Memory: Material Restoration in Europe*, edited by Dan Diner and Gotthard Wunberg, 161–88. New York: Berghahn Books, 2007.

Kirshenblatt-Gimblett, Barbara, ed. "Introduction." In *Writing a Modern Jewish History: Essays in Honor of Salo W. Baron*, 1–8.

———. *Writing a Modern Jewish History: Essays in Honor of Salo W. Baron*. New York: Jewish Museum, 2006.

Knott, Marie Luise. "Bei Schocken Books." In *Hannah Arendt—Von den Dichtern erwarten wir Wahrheit: Ausstellung Literaturhaus Berlin*, edited by Marie Luise Knott and Barbara Hahn, 19–27. Berlin: Matthes und Seitz, 2007.

———. "Introduction: 'Why Have We Been Spared?'" In *The Correspondence of Hannah Arendt and Gershom Scholem*, vii–xxvi. Chicago: University of Chicago Press, 2017.

Kochavi, Shir. "The Value of Objects: A Case Study in Material Culture." *International Journal of Art and Art History* 3, no. 1 (June 2015): 83–97.

Kohn, Jerome. "Freedom: The Priority of the Political." In *The Cambridge Companion to Hannah Arendt*, edited by Dana Villa, 113–29. Cambridge, UK: Cambridge University Press, 2000.

———. "Hannah Arendt's Jewish Experience: Thinking, Acting, Judging." In *Thinking in Dark Times: Hannah Arendt on Ethics and Politics*, edited by Roger Berkowitz, Jeffrey Katz, and Thomas Keenan, 179–94. New York: Fordham University Press, 2010.

Kolinsky, Eva. *After the Holocaust: Jewish Survivors in Germany after 1945*. London: Pimlico, 2004.

Königseder, Angelika, and Juliane Wetzel. *Waiting for Hope: Jewish Displaced Persons in Post-World War II Germany*. Evanston, IL: Northwestern University Press, 2001.

Koop, Volker. *Alfred Rosenberg: Der Wegbereiter des Holocaust—Eine Biographie*. Cologne: Böhlau Verlag, 2016.

Korman, Gerd. "The Holocaust in America Historical Writing." *Societas* 2 (1972): 251–70.

Körte, Mona. "Flaschenpost: Vom 'Eigenleben' jüdischer Erinnerungsarchive." In *Jüdische Intellektuelle im 20. Jahrhundert*, edited by Ariane Huml and Monika Rappenecker, 275–96. Würzburg: Königshausen und Neumann, 2003.

Krah, Markus. *American Jewry and the Re-Invention of the East European Jewish Past*. Berlin: De Gruyter Oldenbourg, 2018.

Kristel, Conny. "Revolution and Reconstruction: Dutch Jewry after the Holocaust." In *The Jews Are Coming Back*, edited by David Bankier, 136–47. Jerusalem: Yad Vashem, 2005.

Kristeva, Julia. *Hannah Arendt: Life Is a Narrative*. Toronto: University of Toronto Press, 2001.

Krummacher, Friedrich A., ed. *Die Kontroverse: Hannah Arendt, Eichmann und die Juden*. Munich: Nymphenburger Verl.-Handl., 1964.

Kubowitzki, A. Leon. *Unity in Dispersion: A History of the World Jewish Congress*. New York: World Jewish Congress, 1948.

Kugelmass, Jack, and Jonathan Boyarin, eds. *From a Ruined Garden: The Memorial Books of Polish Jewry*. 2nd and expanded edition. Bloomington: Indiana University Press, 1998.

Kühn-Ludewig, Maria. *Johannes Pohl (1904–1960): Judaist und Bibliothekar im Dienste Rosenbergs; Eine biographische Dokumentation*. Hannover: Laurentius-Verl. Dehmlow, 2000.

Kurtz, Michael J. "The Allied Struggle over Cultural Restitution, 1942–1947." *International Journal of Cultural Property* 17, no. 2 (2010): 177–94.

———. *America and the Return of Nazi Contraband: The Recovery of Europe's Cultural Treasures*. Cambridge, UK: Cambridge University Press, 2006.

———. "Resolving a Dilemma: The Inheritance of Jewish Property." *Cardozo Law Review* 20, no. 2 (1998): 625–55.

Kuznitz, Cecile Esther. "YIVO." In *YIVO Encyclopedia of Jews in Eastern Europe*, edited by Gershon Hundert, vol. 2, 2090–96. New Haven, CT: Yale University Press, 2008.

———. *YIVO and the Making of Modern Jewish Culture: Scholarship for the Yiddish Nation*. Cambridge, UK: Cambridge University Press, 2014.

———. "YIVO's 'Old Friend and Teacher': Simon Dubnow and his Relationship to the Yiddish Scientific Institute." *Simon Dubnow Institute Yearbook* 15 (2016): 477–507.

Labendz, Jacob Ari, ed. *Jewish Property after 1945: Cultures and Economies of Ownership, Loss, Recovery, and Transfer*, special issue of *Jewish Culture and History* 18 (2017).

Lachmann, Renate. "Zur Poetik der Kataloge bei Danilo Kiš." In *Wortkunst, Erzählkunst, Bildkunst: Festschrift für Aage Hansen-Löve*, edited by Rainer Grübel and Wolf Schmid, 297–309. Munich: Sagner, 2008.

Laczó, Ferenc. *Hungarian Jews in the Age of Genocide: An Intellectual History, 1929–1948*. Leiden: Brill, 2016.

Lang, Johannes. "Explaining Genocide: Hannah Arendt and the Social-Scientific Concept of De-humanization." In *The Anthem Companion to Hannah Arendt*, edited by Peter Baehr and Philip Walsh, 175–95. London: Anthem Press, 2017.

Larralde, Carlos M. "The Stolen Past: Looting and Death of a Sacred Library." *Journal of Spanish, Portuguese, and Italian Crypto Jews* 7 (2015): 61–88.

Lauterbach, Iris. *The Central Collecting Point in Munich: A New Beginning for the Restitution and Protection of Art*. Los Angeles: Getty Research Institute, 2018.

Lavsky, Hagit. *New Beginnings: Holocaust Survivors in Bergen-Belsen and the British Zone in Germany, 1945–1950*. Detroit: Wayne State University Press, 2002.

Lawson, Tom. "'The Theory and Practice of Hell:' Postwar Interpretations of the Genocide of the Jews." In *Debates on the Holocaust*, 17–51. Manchester: Manchester University Press, 2010.

Leftwich, Joseph. *Abraham Sutzkever: Partisan Poet*. New York: Thomas Yosseloff, 1971.

Lepper, Marcel, and Ulrich Raulff, eds. *Handbuch Archiv: Geschichte, Aufgaben, Perspektiven*. Stuttgart: J. B. Metzler, 2016.

Liberles, Robert. *Salo Wittmayer Baron: Architect of Jewish History*. New York: New York University Press, 1995.

Lillteicher, Jürgen. *Raub, Recht und Restitution: Die Rückerstattung jüdischen Eigentums in der frühen Bundesrepublik*. Göttingen: Wallstein-Verlag, 2007.

———. "West Germany and the Restitution of Jewish Property in Europe." In *Robbery and Restitution: The Conflict over Jewish Property in Europe*, edited by Martin Dean, Constantin Goschler, and Philipp Ther, 99–112. New York: Berghahn Books, 2007.

Lipman, Rena. "Jewish Cultural Reconstruction Reconsidered: Should the Jewish Religious Objects Distributed around the World after WW II Be Returned to Europe?" *KUR: Kunst und Recht, Journal für Kunstrecht, Urheberrecht und Kulturpolitik* 4 (2006): 89–93.

Lipphardt, Anna. "Forgotten Memory: The Jews of Vilne in the Diaspora." *Osteuropa*, special issue: Impulses for Europe (2008): 187–98.

———. "The Post-Holocaust Reconstruction of Vilne, 'the Most Yiddish City in the World' in New York, Israel and Vilnius." *Ab Imperio* 4 (2004): 167–92.

———. *Vilne: Die Juden aus Vilnius nach dem Holocaust: Eine transnationale Beziehungsgeschichte*. Paderborn: Schöningh, 2010.

Luban, David. "Explaining Dark Times: Hannah Arendt's Theory of Theory." *Social Research* 50, no. 1 (Spring 1983): 215–48.

Lucca, Enrico. "A Safe Home for German-Jewry: Hugo Bergman, Ozrot Ha-Golah, and his Return to Europe (1946–1948)." In *Contested Heritage: Jewish Cultural Property after 1945*, edited by Elisabeth Gallas, Anna Holzer-Kawałko, Caroline Jessen, and Yfaat Weiss. Göttingen: Vandenhoeck and Ruprecht, 2019 (forthcoming).

Ludi, Regula. *Reparations for Nazi Victims in Postwar Europe*. Cambridge, UK: Cambridge University Press, 2012.

———. "'Why Switzerland?' Remarks on a Neutral's Role in the Nazi Program of Robbery and Allied Postwar Restitution Policy." In *Robbery and Restitution: The Conflict over Jewish Property in Europe*, edited by Martin Dean, Constantin Goschler, and Philipp Ther, 182–210. New York: Berghahn Books, 2007.

Lustig, Jason. "Who Are to Be the Successors of European Jewry? The Restitution of German Jewish Communal and Cultural Property." *Journal of Contemporary History* 52 (2017): 519–45.

Magilow, Daniel H., and Lisa Silverman. *Holocaust Representations in History: An Introduction*. London: Bloomsbury, 2015.

Maier, Charles M. "Overcoming the Past? Narrative and Negotiation, Remembering and Reparation: Issues at the Interface of History and the Law." In *Politics and the Past: On Repairing Historical Injustices*, edited by John Torpey, 295–304. Oxford: Rowman and Littlefield, 2003.

Manasse, Peter M. *Verschleppte Archive und Bibliotheken: Die Tätigkeit des Einsatzstabes Rosenberg während des Zweiten Weltkrieges*. St. Ingbert: Röhrig, 1997.

Mankowitz, Zeev. *Life between Memory and Hope: The Survivors of the Holocaust in Occupied Germany*. Cambridge, UK: Cambridge University Press, 2007.

Marrus, Michael. *The Holocaust in History*. New York: Meridian, 1989.

Matthäus, Jürgen, and Frank Bajohr. *The Political Diary of Alfred Rosenberg and the Onset of the Holocaust*. Lanham, MD: Rowman and Littlefield, 2015.

Mazower, Mark. "Reconstruction: The Historiographical Issues." *Past and Present* 210 (2011): Supplement 6: Post-War Reconstruction in Europe: International Perspectives, 1945–1949, 17–28.

———. "The Strange Triumph of Human Rights, 1933–1950." *Historical Journal* 47, no. 2 (2004): 379–98.

Medoff, Rafael. "American Responses to the Holocaust: New Research, New Controversies." *American Jewish History* 100, no. 3 (July 2016): 379–409.

———. "New Perspectives on How America, and American Jewry, Responded to the Holocaust." *American Jewish History* 84, no. 3 (September 1996): 253–66.

Mendelsohn, Ezra. *On Modern Jewish Politics*. New York: Oxford University Press, 1993.

Mendes-Flohr, Paul, and Jehuda Reinharz, eds. *Gershom Scholem: The Man and His Work*. Albany: State University of New York Press, 1994.

————. *The Jew in the Modern World: A Documentary History.* 2nd ed. New York: Oxford University Press, 1995.

Meng, Michael. *Shattered Spaces: Encountering Jewish Ruins in Postwar Germany and Poland.* Cambridge, MA: Harvard University Press, 2011.

Michman, Dan. *Holocaust Historiography: A Jewish Perspective; Conceptualizations, Terminology, Approaches, and Fundamental Issues.* London: Vallentine Mitchell, 2003.

————. "Is There an 'Israeli School' of Holocaust Research?" In *Holocaust Historiography in Context,* edited by David Bankier and Dan Michman, 37–65. Jerusalem: Yad Vashem, 2008.

Miron, Dan. "Between Science and Faith: Sixty Years of the YIVO-Institute." *YIVO Annual* 19 (1990): 1–15.

Moll, Martin. *"Führer-Erlasse" 1939–1945: Edition sämtlicher überlieferter, nicht im Reichsgesetzblatt abgedruckter, von Hitler während des Zweiten Weltkrieges schriftlich erteilter Direktiven aus den Bereichen Staat, Partei, Wirtschaft, Besatzungspolitik und Militärverwaltung.* Stuttgart: Steiner, 1997.

Morsink, Johannes. "Cultural Genocide, the Universal Declaration, and Minority Rights." *Human Rights Quarterly* 21, no. 4 (1999): 1009–60.

Moses Leff, Lisa. *The Archive Thief: The Man Who Salvaged French Jewish History in the Wake of the Holocaust.* New York: Oxford University Press, 2015.

Münchhausen, Anna von. "Hamburg Exhibition Delves into Murky History of Art Items Taken from Jews." *Handelsblatt Global Edition,* September 15, 2014. https://global.handelsblatt.com.

Myers, David N. "Between Diaspora and Zion: History, Memory, and the Jerusalem Scholars." In *The Jewish Past Revisited: Reflections on Modern Jewish Historians,* edited by David M. Myers and David R. Ruderman, 88–103. New Haven, CT: Yale University Press, 1998.

————. "Gershom Scholem: Between 'Pure Science' and 'Religious Anarchy.'" In *Re-Inventing the Jewish Past: European Jewish Intellectuals and the Zionist Return to History,* 151–76. New York: Oxford University Press, 1995.

————. "Von Berlin nach Jerusalem: Zionismus, jüdische Wissenschaft und die Mühsal kultureller Dissonanz." In *Janusfiguren: "Jüdische Heimstätte," Exil und Nation im deutschen Zionismus,* edited by Andrea Schatz and Christian Wiese, 331–47. Berlin: Metropol, 2006.

Myers Feinstein, Margarete. *Holocaust Survivors in Postwar Germany, 1945–1957.* Cambridge, UK: Cambridge University Press, 2009.

Nachama, Andreas. "Heinz Galinski: Wir wollten, dass die Geschichte des Judentums in Deutschland nicht zu Ende ist." In *Engagierte Demokraten: Vergangenheitspolitik in kritischer Absicht,* edited by Claudia Fröhlich, 95–105. Münster: Westfälisches Dampfboot, 1999.

————, and Julius H. Schoeps, eds. *Aufbau nach dem Untergang: Deutsch-Jüdische Geschichte nach 1945.* Berlin: Argon, 1992.

Nattermann, Ruth. *Deutsch-jüdische Geschichtsschreibung nach der Shoah: Die Gründungs- und Frühgeschichte des Leo Baeck Institute.* Essen: Klartext, 2004.

————. "A Struggle for the Preservation of a German-Jewish Legacy: The Foundation of the Leo Baeck Institute in New York." *European Judaism* 45, no. 2 (2012): 90–102.

Ne'eman Arad, Gulie. *America, Its Jews, and the Rise of Nazism*. Bloomington: Indiana University Press, 2000.

Nicholas, Lynn H. *The Rape of Europa: The Fate of Europe's Treasures in the Third Reich and the Second World War*. New York: Knopf, 1995.

Novick, Peter. *The Holocaust in American Life*. Boston: Houghton Mifflin, 1999.

Ofer, Dalia. "Linguistic Conceptualization of the Holocaust in Palestine and Israel, 1942–53." *Journal of Contemporary History* 31 (1996): 567–95.

————. "The Strength of Remembrance: Commemorating the Holocaust during the First Decade of Israel." *Jewish Social Studies* 6, no. 2 (2000): 24–55.

Oz, Amoz. *A Tale of Love and Darkness*. London: Vintage Books, 2005.

Patt, Avinoam J., and Michael Berkowitz, eds. *"We Are Here": New Approaches to Jewish Displaced Persons in Postwar Germany*. Detroit: Wayne State University Press, 2010.

Paucker, Arnold. *Der jüdische Abwehrkampf gegen Antisemitismus und Nationalsozialismus in den letzten Jahren der Weimarer Republik*. 2nd and revised edition. Hamburg: Leibniz-Verlag, 1969.

Peiss, Kathy. "Cultural Policy in a Time of War: The American Response to Endangered Books in World War II." *Library Trends* 55, no. 3 (2007): 370–86.

Pilling, Iris. *Denken und Handeln als Jüdin: Hannah Arendts politische Theorie vor 1950*. Frankfurt am Main: Lang, 1996.

Piterberg, Gabriel. *The Return of Zionism: Myths, Politics and Scholarship in Israel*. London: Verso, 2008.

Polack, Emmanuelle, and Philippe Dagen, eds. *Les carnets de Rose Valland: Le pillage des collections privées d'uvres d'art en France durant la seconde guerre mondiale*. Lyon: Fage, 2011.

Polonsky, Antony. *The Jews in Poland and Russia, vol 3: 1914 to 2008*. Oxford: Littman Library of Jewish Civilization, 2012.

Porat, Dina. *The Blue and the Yellow Stars of David: The Zionist Leadership in Palestine and the Holocaust, 1939–1945*. Cambridge, MA: Harvard University Press, 1990.

————. *Israeli Society, the Holocaust and Its Survivors*. London: Vallentine Mitchell, 2008.

Potthast, Jan Björn. *Das jüdische Zentralmuseum der SS in Prag: Gegnerforschung und Völkermord im Nationalsozialismus*. Frankfurt am Main: Campus-Verlag, 2002.

Presidential Advisory Commission on Holocaust Assets in the United States. *Plunder and Restitution: The U.S. and Holocaust Victims' Assets: Findings and Recommendations of the Presidential Advisory Commission on Holocaust Assets in the United States and Executive Summary of the Staff Report*. Washington, DC: US Gov. Printing Office, 2000.

Rabinbach, Anson G. "Eichmann in New York: The New York Intellectuals and the Hannah Arendt Controversy." *Princeton University Library Chronicle* 63, no. 1–2 (2001/2002): 261–81.

Rabinowitz, Dan. *The Lost Library: The Legacy of Vilna's Strashun Library in the Aftermath of the Holocaust.* Waltham, MA: Brandeis University Press, 2018.

Raim, Edith. "Wem gehört das Erbe der Toten? Die Jewish Cultural Reconstruction." *Tribüne. Zeitschrift zum Verständnis des Judentums* 34, no. 135 (1995): 168–73.

Rauschenberger, Katharina. "The Judaica Collection of Frankfurt's Museum Jüdischer Altertümer and Its Worldwide Dispersion after 1945." In *Neglected Witnesses: The Fate of Jewish Ceremonial Objects during the Second World War and After,* edited by Julie-Marthe Cohen and Felicitas Heimann-Jelinek, 81–102. Crickadarn: Institute of Art and Law, 2011.

———. "The Restitution of Jewish Cultural Objects and the Activities of Jewish Cultural Reconstruction, Inc." *Leo Baeck Institute Year Book* 53 (2008): 193–211.

Raz-Krakotzkin, Amnon. "Geschichte, Nationalismus, Eingedenken." In *Jüdische Geschichtsschreibung heute: Themen, Positionen, Kontroversen,* edited by Michael Brenner and David N. Myers, 181–206. Munich: Beck, 2002.

Rein, Denise. "Die Bestände der ehemaligen jüdischen Gemeinden Deutschlands in den 'Central Archives for the History of the Jewish People' in Jerusalem: Ein Überblick über das Schicksal der verschiedenen Gemeindearchive." *Der Archivar* 55, no. 4 (2002): 318–27.

Reininghaus, Alexandra, ed. *Recollecting: Raub und Restitution.* Vienna: Passagenverlag, 2009.

Rensmann, Lars. "Returning from Forced Exile: Some Observations on Theodor W. Adorno's and Hannah Arendt's Experience of Postwar Germany and Their Political Theories of Totalitarianism." *Leo Baeck Institute Year Book* 49 (2004): 171–93.

Richarz, Monika. "Jews in Today's Germanies." *Leo Baeck Institute Year Book* 30 (1985): 265–74.

Rickman, Gregg J. *Conquest and Redemption: A History of Jewish Assets from the Holocaust.* New Brunswick, NJ: Transaction, 2011.

Roemer, Nils H. *German City, Jewish Memory: The Story of Worms.* Waltham, MA: Brandeis University Press, 2010.

Rose, Jonathan, ed. *The Holocaust and the Book: Destruction and Preservation.* Amherst: University of Massachusetts Press, 2001.

Rotenstreich, Nathan. "Gershom Scholem's Conception of Jewish Nationalism." In *Gershom Scholem: The Man and His Work,* edited by Paul Mendes-Flohr, 104–19. Albany: State University of New York Press, 1994.

Roth, Irene. *Cecil Roth: Historian without Tears.* New York: Sepher-Hermon, 1982.

Rothfeld, Anne. "Returning Looted European Library Collections: A Historical Analysis of the Offenbach Archival Depot, 1945–1948." *RBM: A Journal of Rare Books, Manuscripts, and Cultural Heritage* 6, no. 1 (2005): 14–24.

Rubin, Gil. "The End of Minority Rights: Jacob Robinson and the 'Jewish Question' in World War II." *Simon Dubnow Institute Yearbook* 11 (2012): 55–71.

———. "Final Stage of Jewish Emancipation. Salo W. Baron in the Postwar Jewish World." In *Contested Heritage: Jewish Cultural Property after 1945,* edited by

Elisabeth Gallas, Anna Holzer-Kawałko, Caroline Jessen, and Yfaat Weiss. Göttingen: Vandenhoeck and Ruprecht, 2019 (forthcoming).

———. "Salo Baron and Hannah Arendt: An Intellectual Friendship." *Naharaim: Zeitschrift für Deutsch-Jüdische Literatur und Kulturgeschichte* 9, no. 1–2 (2015): 73–88.

Rudolph, Jörg. "'Sämtliche Sendungen sind zu richten an . . .': Das RSHA-Amt VII 'Weltanschauliche Forschung und Auswertung' als Sammelstelle erbeuteter Archive und Bibliotheken." In *Nachrichtendienst, politische Elite und Mordeinheit: Der Sicherheitsdienst des Reichsführers SS*, edited by Michael Wildt, 204–40. Hamburg: Hamburger Ed., 2003.

Rupnow, Dirk. "Annihilating—Preserving—Remembering: The 'Aryanization' of Jewish History and Memory during the Holocaust." In *Cultural Memories: The Geographical Point of View*, edited by Peter Meusburger, Michael Heffernan, and Edgar Wunder, 189–200. Dordrecht: Springer, 2011.

———. *Aporien des Gedenkens: Reflexionen über "Holocaust" und Erinnerung.* Freiburg im Breisgau: Rombach, 2006.

———. "From Final Depository to Memorial: The History and Significance of the Jewish Museum in Prague." *European Judaism* 37, no. 1 (2004): 142–59.

———. "Racializing Historiography: Anti-Jewish Scholarship in the Third Reich." *Patterns of Prejudice* 42, no. 1 (2008): 27–59.

———. *Täter—Gedächtnis—Opfer: Das "Jüdische Zentralmuseum" in Prag.* Vienna: Picus-Verlag, 2000.

Rydell, Anders. *The Book Thieves: The Nazi Looting of Europe's Libraries and the Race to Return a Literary Inheritance.* New York: Viking, 2017.

Sagi, Nana. *German Reparations: A History of the Negotiations.* Jerusalem: Magnes, Hebrew University, 1980.

———. "Die Rolle der jüdischen Organisationen in den USA und die Claims Conference." In *Wiedergutmachung in der Bundesrepublik Deutschland*, edited by Ludolf Herbst and Constantin Goschler, 99–118. Munich: Oldenbourg, 1989.

Sargent, Amelia L. B. "New Jurisdictional Tools for Displaced Cultural Property in Russia: From 'Twice Saved' to 'Twice Taken.'" *Yearbook of Cultural Property Law* 10 (2010): 167–212.

Schatz, Andrea, and Christian Wiese, eds. *Janusfiguren: "Jüdische Heimstätte," Exil und Nation im deutschen Zionismus.* Berlin: Metropol, 2006.

Schidorsky, Dov. "Books as Mute Witnesses to Mass Murder: The Archival Depot in Offenbach as an Agent of Memory and a Testimony to Persecution, Migration, and Genocide." *Moreshet* 13 (2016): 44–83.

———. *Burning Scrolls and Flying Letters: A History of Book Collections and Libraries in Mandatory Palestine and of Book Salvaging Efforts in Europe after the Holocaust [Gevilim nisrafim ve-otiot porhot: le-toldoteihem shel osafei sefarim ve-sifriot be-erez yisra'el ve-nisionot le-hazalat srideihem be-eiropa leahar ha-shoah].* Jerusalem: Magnes, 2008 (hebr.).

———. "Confiscation of Libraries and Assignments to Forced Labor: Two Documents of the Holocaust." *Libraries and Culture* 33, no. 4 (1998): 347–88.

——. "Germany in the Holy Land: Its Involvement and Impact on Library Development in Palestine and Israel." *Libri* 49 (1999): 26–42.

——. "Hannah Arendt's Dedication to Salvaging Jewish Culture." *Leo Baeck Institute Year Book* 59 (2014): 181–95.

——. "Jewish Libraries under German Occupation: The Reich Security Main Office as an Agent of Nazi looting." *Moreshet* 11 (2014): 34–62.

——. "The Library of the Reich Security Main Office and Its Looted Jewish Book Collections." *Libraries and the Cultural Record* 42, no. 1 (2007): 21–47.

——. "The Salvaging of Jewish Books in Europe after the Holocaust: The Efforts of the Hebrew University and the Jewish National and University Library." In *Jüdischer Buchbesitz als Raubgut: Zweites Hannoversches Symposium*, 197–212. Frankfurt am Main: Klostermann, 2006.

——. "Das Schicksal jüdischer Bibliotheken im Dritten Reich." In *Bibliotheken während des Nationalsozialismus*, vol. 2, edited by Peter Vodosek and Manfred Komorowski, 189–222. Wiesbaden: Harrassowitz, 1992.

——. "Shunamis Suche nach Schätzen im europäischen Exil und die Problematik der Restitution im Staat Israel." In *Bibliotheken in der NS-Zeit: Provenienzforschung und Bibliotheksgeschichte*, edited by Stefan Alker, Christina Köstner, and Markus Stumpf, 329–40. Vienna: Vienna University Press, 2008.

Schochow, Werner. *Die Verlagerungsgeschichte der Preußischen Staatsbibliothek: Auslagerung, Zerstörung, Entfremdung, Rückführung: Dargestellt aus den Quellen.* Berlin: Walter de Gruyter, 2003.

Schoor, Kerstin. *Vom literarischen Zentrum zum literarischen Ghetto: Deutsch-jüdische Literatur in Berlin zwischen 1933 und 1945.* Göttingen: Wallstein-Verlag, 2010.

Schorsch, Ismar. "The Lachrymose Conception of Jewish History." In *From Text to Context: The Turn to History in Modern Judaism*, 376–88. Hanover, NH: Brandeis University Press, 1994.

——. "The Last Jewish Generalist." *AJS Review* 18, no. 1 (1993): 39–50.

Schreiber, Ruth. "New Jewish Communities in Germany after World War II and the Successor Organizations in the Western Zones." *Journal of Israeli History* 18, no. 2/3 (1997): 167–90.

Schroeder, Werner. "Beschlagnahme und Verbleib jüdischer Bibliotheken." In *Jüdischer Buchbesitz als Raubgut: Zweites Hannoversches Symposium*, 27–36. Frankfurt am Main: Klostermann, 2006.

Schulze, Sabine, and Silke Reuther, eds. *Raubkunst? Silber aus ehemals jüdischem Besitz—wie gehen Museen damit um? Symposium anlässlich der Ausstellung "Raubkunst? Provenienzforschung zu den Sammlungen des Museums für Kunst und Gewerbe Hamburg."* Hamburg: Museum für Kunst und Gewerbe, 2016.

Schwarz, Jan. "After the Destruction of Vilna: Abraham Sutzkever's Poetry, Testimony and Cultural Rescue Work, 1944–46." *East European Jewish Affairs* 35, no. 2 (2005): 209–24.

——. *Survivors and Exiles: Yiddish Culture after the Holocaust.* Detroit: Wayne State University Press, 2015.

Schwarzschild, Maimon. "A Note on Steven Schwarzschild and the Letters from Berlin." *Leo Baeck Institute Year Book* 60 (2015): 243–47.

Segev, Tom. *David Ben Gurion: Ein Staat um jeden Preis*. Munich: Siedler Verlag, 2018.

———. *The Seventh Million: Israelis and the Holocaust*. New York: Hill and Wang, 1993.

———. *Simon Wiesenthal: The Life and Legends*. New York: Doubleday, 2010.

Shafir, Shlomo. *Ambiguous Relations: The American Jewish Community and Germany since 1945*. Detroit: Wayne State University Press, 1999.

Shavit, David. *Hunger for the Printed Word: Books and Libraries in the Jewish Ghettos of Nazi-Occupied Europe*. Jefferson, NC: McFarland, 1997.

Shilo, Bilha. "'Funem Folk, Farn Folk, Mitn Folk': The Restitution of the YIVO Collection from Offenbach to New York." *Moreshet* 14 (2017): 362–412.

———. "When YIVO was defined by Territory: Two Perspectives on the Restitution of YIVO's Collections." In *Contested Heritage: Jewish Cultural Property after 1945*, edited by Elisabeth Gallas, Anna Holzer-Kawałko, Caroline Jessen, and Yfaat Weiss. Göttingen: Vandenhoeck and Ruprecht, 2019 (forthcoming).

Shumsky, Dimitry. "Gegenwartsarbeit." In *Enzyklopädie jüdischer Geschichte und Kultur*, vol. 2, edited by Dan Diner, 402–6. Stuttgart: J. B. Metzler, 2012.

Simpson, Elizabeth, ed. *The Spoils of War: World War II and Its Aftermath: The Loss, Reappearance, and Recovery of Cultural Property*. New York: Harry N. Abrams, 1997.

Sinkoff, Nancy. "From the Archives: Lucy S. Dawidowicz and the Restitution of Jewish Cultural Property." *American Jewish History* 100, no. 1 (2016): 117–47.

———. "Introduction, Yidishkayt and the Making of Lucy S. Dawidowicz." In *From That Place and Time: A Memoir, 1938–1947*, xiii–xxxix. New Brunswick, NJ: Rutgers University Press, 2008.

———. "The Polishness of Lucy S. Dawidowicz's Postwar Jewish Cold War." In *A Jewish Feminine Mystique? Jewish Women in Postwar America*, edited by Hasia R. Diner, Shira Kohn, and Rahel Kranson, 31–47. New Brunswick, NJ: Rutgers University Press, 2010.

Sroka, Marek. "'Forsaken and Abandoned': The Nationalization and Salvage of Deserted, Displaced, and Private Library Collections in Poland, 1945–1948." *Library and Information History* 28, no. 4 (2012): 272–88.

Stach, Stephan. "Geschichtsschreibung und politische Vereinnahmungen: Das Jüdische Historische Institut in Warschau 1947–1968." *Simon Dubnow Institute Yearbook* 7 (2008): 401–31.

Stanciu, Măriuca. "Jewish National and University Library of Jerusalem—an Accomplished Mission." *Studia Judaica* 8 (1999): 267–77.

Stanislawski, Michael. "Salo Wittmayer Baron: Demystifying Jewish History." In *Living Legacies at Columbia*, edited by William Theodore De Bary with Jerry Kisslinger and Tom Mathewson, 397–403. New York: Columbia University Press, 2006.

Stauber, Roni. "Confronting the Jewish Response during the Holocaust: Yad Vashem: A Commemorative and a Research Institute in the 1950s." *Modern Judaism* 20 (2000): 277–98.

———. *The Holocaust in Israeli Public Debate in the 1950s: Ideology and Memory*. London: Vallentine Mitchell, 2007.

———. *Laying the Foundations for Holocaust Research: The Impact of Philip Friedman*. Jerusalem: Yad Vashem, 2009.

———. "Philip Friedman and the Beginning of Holocaust Studies." In *Holocaust Historiography in Context*, edited by David Bankier and Dan Michman, 83–102. Jerusalem: Yad Vashem, 2008.

Steinberg, Shlomit. *Orphaned Art: Looted Art from the Holocaust in the Israel Museum*. Jerusalem: Israel Museum, 2008.

———, ed. "The Road to Recovery: From the Central Collecting Points to a Safe Haven—the JRSO Dossier." In *Kunst sammeln, Kunst handeln: Beiträge des Internationalen Symposiums in Wien*, edited by Eva Bliminger and Monika Mayer, 119–31. Vienna: Böhlau Verlag, 2012.

Steiner, George. *My Unwritten Books*. New York: New Directions Books, 2008.

Steinfels, Peter. "Salo W. Baron, 94, Scholar of Jewish History, Dies." *New York Times*, November 26, 1989.

Steinweis, Alan E. *Studying the Jew: Scholarly Antisemitism in Nazi Germany*. Cambridge, MA: Harvard University Press, 2006.

Stengel, Katharina, ed. *Opfer als Akteure: Interventionen ehemaliger NS-Verfolgter in der Nachkriegszeit*. Frankfurt am Main: Campus-Verlag, 2008.

Stone, Dan. "Ontology or Bureaucracy? Hannah Arendt's Early Interpretations of the Holocaust." *European Judaism: A Journal for the New Europe* 32, no. 2 (Autumn 1999): 11–25.

Strzolka, Rainer. "Vernichtung jüdischer Identität durch den nationalsozialistischen Raub von Wort und Schrift." *AKMB News* 1 (2003): 3–7.

Sutter, Sem C. "Looting of Jewish Collections in France by the Einsatzstab Reichsleiter Rosenberg." In *Jüdischer Buchbesitz als Raubgut: Zweites Hannoversches Symposium*, 120–34. Frankfurt am Main: Klostermann, 2006.

———. "The Lost Jewish Libraries of Vilna and the Frankfurt Institut zur Erforschung der Judenfrage." In *Lost Libraries: The Destruction of Great Book Collections since Antiquity*, edited by James Raven, 219–35. Basingstoke: Palgrave Macmillan, 2004.

Sznaider, Natan. "Culture and Memory: The Role of Jewish Cultural Property." *Kwartalnik Historii Żydów (Jewish History Quarterly)* 2 (2013): 227–35.

———. *Jewish Memory and the Cosmopolitan Order*. Cambridge, UK: Polity Press, 2011.

———. "Die Rettung der Bücher: Hannah Arendt in München (1949/50)." *Mittelweg 36*, no. 2 (2009): 61–76.

Takei, Ayaka. "The 'Gemeinde Problem': The Jewish Restitution Successor Organization and the Postwar Jewish Communities 1947–1951." *Holocaust and Genocide Studies* 16 (2002): 266–88.

Tauber, Alon. *Zwischen Kontinuität und Neuanfang: Die Entstehung der jüdischen Nachkriegsgemeinde in Frankfurt am Main 1945–1949*. Wiesbaden: Komm. für die Geschichte der Juden in Hessen, 2008.

———. "The Jewish People as the Heir: The Jewish Successor Organizations (JRSO, JTC, French Branch) and the Postwar Jewish Communities in Germany." PhD diss., Waseda University, Tokyo, 2004.

Timm, Angelika. "The Burdened Relationship between the GDR and the State of Israel." *Israel Studies* 2, no. 1 (1997): 22–49.

———. "Ideology and Realpolitik: East German Attitudes toward Zionism and Israel." *Journal of Israeli History* 25 (2006): 203–22.

———. *Jewish Claims against East Germany: Moral Obligations and Pragmatic Policy.* Budapest: Central European University Press, 1997.

Tirosh-Samuelson, Hava, and Edward Dąbrowa, eds. *The Enduring Legacy of Salo W. Baron.* Kraków: Jagiellonian University Press, 2017.

Tobias, Jim G. "Die 'Stürmer-Bibliothek': Ein historischer Exkurs." In *Jüdischer Buchbesitz als Raubgut: Zweites Hannoversches Symposium*, 73–84. Frankfurt am Main: Klostermann, 2006.

Tompkins, David G. "Israel as Friend and Foe: Shaping East German Society through Freund- und Feinbilder." In *Becoming East Germans: Socialist Structures and Sensibilities after Hitler*, edited by Mary Fulbrook and Andrew I. Port, 219–36. New York: Berghahn Books, 2013.

Torpey, John, ed. "Making Whole What Has Been Smashed: Reflections on Reparations." *Journal of Modern History* 73, no. 2 (2001): 333–58.

———. *Politics and the Past: On Repairing Historical Injustices.* Oxford: Rowman and Littlefield, 2003.

Traverso, Enzo. "'Das Bild der Hölle': Hannah Arendt." In *Auschwitz denken: Die Intellektuellen und die Shoah*, 103–49. Hamburg: Hamburger Ed., 2000.

———. *The End of Jewish Modernity.* Translated by David Fernbach. London: Pluto, 2016.

Ujma, Christina. "Nach der Katastrophe: Hannah Arendts Repräsentation der deutsch jüdischen Kultur im Kontext der Nachkriegsdebatten." In *Jews in German Literature since 1945: German-Jewish Literature?*, edited by Pol O'Dochartaigh, 61–75. Amsterdam: Rodopi, 2000.

Vaughn, Chloe Paige Dorris. *The Interim Solution: The Nazification of Hamburg's Germanistik and the Existence of the German University under National Socialism.* 2015. https://ly.smith.edu.

Villa, Dana. "Genealogies of Total Domination: Arendt, Adorno and Auschwitz." *New German Critique* 100, no. 34 (2007): 1–45.

Volkert, Natalia. "Der Kulturgutraub durch deutsche Behörden in den während des Zweiten Weltkrieges besetzten Gebieten." In *Kulturgüter im Zweiten Weltkrieg: Verlagerung—Auffindung—Rückführung*, edited by Uwe Hartmann and the Koordinierungsstelle Magdeburg, 21–48. Magdeburg: Koordinierungsstelle für Kulturgutverluste, 2007.

———. *Kunst- und Kulturraub im Zweiten Weltkrieg: Versuch eines Vergleichs zwischen den Zielsetzungen und Praktiken der deutschen und der sowjetischen Beuteorganisationen unter Berücksichtigung der Restitutionsfragen.* Frankfurt am Main: Lang, 2002.

Vowinckel, Annette. *Geschichtsbegriff und Historisches Denken bei Hannah Arendt.* Cologne: Böhlau, 2001.

——. *Hannah Arendt: Zwischen deutscher Philosophie und jüdischer Politik.* Berlin: Lukas-Verlag, 2004.

Wachsmann, Nikolaus. *KL: A History of the Nazi Concentration Camps.* London: Little Brown, 2015.

Waite, Robert G. "Returning Jewish Cultural Property: The Handling of Books Looted by the Nazis in the American Zone of Occupation, 1945 to 1952." *Libraries and Culture* 37, no. 3 (2002): 213–28.

Wasserstein, Bernard. "The Myth of 'Jewish Silence.'" *Midstream*, August–September 1980, 10–16.

Weidner, Daniel. *Gershom Scholem: Politisches, esoterisches und historiographisches Schreiben.* Munich: Fink, 2003.

Weigel, Sigrid. "Entgeltung durch Geld: Zum Nachleben vormoderner Tauschbegriffe in der Entschädigungspolitik." In *Nachleben der Religionen: Kulturwissenschaftliche Untersuchungen zur Dialektik der Säkularisierung*, edited by Martin Treml and Daniel Weidner, 237–53. Paderborn: Fink, 2007.

——. "Shylocks Wiederkehr: Die Verwandlung von Schuld in Schulden oder: Zum symbolischen Tausch der Wiedergutmachung." In *Fünfzig Jahre danach: Zur Nachgeschichte des Nationalsozialismus*, edited by Sigrid Weigel and Birgit Erdle, 165–92. Zurich: vdf, Hochschulverl. an der ETH Zürich, 1996.

Weiser, Kalman. "Coming to America: Max Weinreich and the Emergence of YIVO's American Center." In *Choosing Yiddish: New Frontiers of Language and Culture*, edited by Lara Rabinovitch, Shiri Goren, and Hannah S. Pressman, 233–52. Detroit: Wayne State University Press, 2013.

——. "Saving Yiddish, Saving American Jewry: Max Weinreich in 1940s New York City." In *Languages of Modern Jewish Cultures: Comparative Perspectives*, edited by Joshua L. Miller and Anita Norich, 204–23. Ann Arbor: University of Michigan Press, 2016.

Weiss, Yfaat. "'Nicht durch Macht und nicht durch Kraft, sondern durch meinen Geist': Die Hebräische Universität in der Skopus-Enklave." *Simon Dubnow Institute Yearbook* 14 (2015): 59–90.

——. "The Tricks of Memory: Salo Baron, Cecil Roth and the Salvage of Jewish Cultural Property in Europe." In *Contested Heritage: Jewish Cultural Property after 1945*, edited by Elisabeth Gallas, Anna Holzer-Kawałko, Caroline Jessen, and Yfaat Weiss. Göttingen: Vandenhoeck and Ruprecht, 2019 (forthcoming).

——. "Von Prag nach Jerusalem: Jüdische Kulturgüter und Israelische Staatsgründung." *Vierteljahrshefte für Zeitgeschichte* 63, no. 4 (2015): 513–38.

Weldler, Norbert. *Die Jüdische National- und Universitätsbibliothek in Jerusalem: Ihr Werden und Wirken*, edited by the Swiss Friends of the Hebrew University. Zurich: Verlag "Der Scheideweg," 1957.

Wenger, Beth S. "Salo Baron and the Vitality of American Jewish Life." In *The Enduring Legacy of Salo W. Baron*, edited by Hava Tirosh-Samuelson and Edward Dąbrowa, 259–71. Kraków: Jagiellonian University Press, 2017.

Wiese, Christian. "The Janus Face of Nationalism: Zionist Identity in the Correspondence between Robert Weltsch and Hans Kohn." *Leo Baeck Institute Year Book* 51 (2006): 103–30.

Wilke, Carsten L. "Von Breslau nach Mexiko: Die Zerstreuung der Bibliothek des Jüdisch-Theologischen Seminars." In *Memoria: Wege jüdischen Erinnerns*, edited by Birgit E. Klein and Christiane E. Müller, 315–38. Berlin: Metropol, 2005.

Wojak, Irmtrud, and Peter Hayes, eds. *"Arisierung" im Nationalsozialismus: Volksgemeinschaft, Raub und Gedächtnis*. Frankfurt am Main: Campus-Verlag, 2000.

Wyman, David S. *The Abandonment of the Jews: America and the Holocaust, 1941–1945*. New York: Pantheon, 1984.

Yablonka, Hanna. *Survivors of the Holocaust: Israel after the War*. New York: New York University Press, 1999.

Yavnai, Elisabeth M. "Jewish Cultural Property and Its Postwar Recovery." In *Proceedings of the USHMM Symposium "Confiscation of Jewish Property in Europe, 1933–1945: New Sources and Perspectives,"* 127–43. Washington, DC: Center for Advanced Holocaust Studies, United States Holocaust Memorial Museum, 2003.

Yerushalmi, Yosef Hayim. *Zakhor: Jewish History and Jewish Memory*. Seattle: University of Washington Press, 1996.

Yoel, Yonatan. "The Jewish National and University Library, Jerusalem." *Alexandria* 12, no. 2 (2000): 99–112.

Young-Bruehl, Elisabeth. *Hannah Arendt: For Love of the World*. 2nd ed. New Haven, CT: Yale University Press, 2004.

Zadoff, Noam. *Gershom Scholem: From Berlin to Jerusalem and Back: An Intellectual Biography*. Waltham, MA: Brandeis University Press, 2018.

Zertal, Idith. *Israel's Holocaust and the Politics of Nationhood*. Cambridge, UK: Cambridge University Press, 2004.

Zimmermann, Moshe, and Yotam Hotam, eds. *Zweimal Heimat: Die Jeckes zwischen Mitteleuropa und Nahost*. Frankfurt am Main: Beerenverlag, 2005.

Zweig, Ronald. *German Reparations and the Jewish World: A History of the Claims Conference*. 2nd ed. London: Cass, 2001.

———. "Restitution, Reparations and Indemnification: Germany and the Jewish World." *Journal of Israeli History* 18, no. 2/3 (1997): 129–37.

INDEX

ABOUT THE AUTHOR

Elisabeth Gallas is research associate at the Leibniz Institute for Jewish History and Culture—Simon Dubnow in Leipzig, Germany. After earning her PhD in history from Leipzig University, she conducted postdoctoral research at the Vienna Wiesentahl Institute for Holocaust Studies and the Hebrew University of Jerusalem.

ABOUT THE TRANSLATOR

Alex Skinner holds a first-class MA in Scandinavian studies and German from the University of Edinburgh and an MSc in social anthropology from the London School of Economics. He has translated more than twenty books from German to English in the humanities and social sciences.